BRIDGES TO KNOWLEDGE

BRIDGES TO KNOWLEDGE
Foreign Students in Comparative Perspective

Edited by Elinor G. Barber, Philip G. Altbach, and Robert G. Myers

The University of Chicago Press
Chicago and London

Most of the articles in this volume originally appeared in the
May 1984 issue of *Comparative Education Review*. © 1984 by the
Comparative and International Education Society.

The University of Chicago Press, Chicago 60637
The University of Chicago Press, Ltd., London

Library of Congress Cataloging in Publication Data
Main entry under title:

Bridges to knowledge.

       "Most of the articles ... originally appeared in the
May 1984 issue of Comparative education review"—T.p.
verso.
       Bibliography: p.
       1. Educational exchanges—Addresses, essays, lectures.
2. Foreign study—Addresses, essays, lectures.   3. Com-
parative education—Addresses, essays, lectures.
I. Barber, Elinor G.   II. Altbach, Philip G.   III. Myers,
Robert G.   IV. Comparative education review.
LB2375.B75   1984   370.19′62   84-16374
ISBN 0-226-03708-8
ISBN 0-226-03709-6 (pbk.)

Contents

Preface

This volume has its origins in the special issue of *Comparative Education Review* published in May 1984 as volume 28, number 2. All the articles from that issue are included here. Our effort there was to bring together research-based studies and to assist in providing insights for policymakers and others involved in international education affairs. Our publisher, the University of Chicago Press, felt that interest in this field justified a book-length volume. We have added additional articles to those that appeared in the May 1984 issue. Those by John N. Hawkins, Robert B. Kaplan, Norman Goodman, David Lansdale, and Alan Smith appear here for the first time. In addition we are printing in revised form an article by Robert G. Myers that first appeared in *Prospects* (vol. 13, no. 4; © Unesco 1983).

We are indebted to Unesco for permission and to the authors of the new articles for their willingness to adhere to very short deadlines. We appreciate the suggestions and comments of John Reichard and Robert Mashburn of the National Association for Foreign Student Affairs and Manfred Stassen of the Deutscher Akademischer Austauschdienst. All royalties from this book will be used to assist the work of the Comparative and International Education Society.

ELINOR G. BARBER
PHILIP G. ALTBACH
ROBERT G. MYERS

Introduction: Comparative Perspectives

Foreign study provides an important educational option for individuals and nations. The usefulness of this option has been most obvious where national systems of higher education are limited in size and quality. But even in relatively rich educational environments, foreign study satisfies the desire for cross-cultural learning experiences and provides ways of dealing with overflows in educational demand, as in the case of American medical students abroad. The growing importance of the foreign study option is evident in the approximately eightfold increase that has occurred worldwide in the last 30 years.

While the option to study abroad solves certain problems, it also raises difficult educational issues. A few examples may suffice. Thus, in Malaysia, where at the present time more students are abroad than at home, debate rages over the national implications of foreign education that many consider to be largely irrelevant. In the United Kingdom, where some 10 percent of all university students are foreign, heated discussions have arisen about the justification of subsidizing the education of foreigners. In the United States, a not entirely welcome reverse dependency has developed in some institutions and departments, where foreign students compensate for the dearth of U.S. students and help permit the institution or department to survive.[1] More generally, the seemingly inevitable flow of students from developing countries to industrialized nations is now very much part of the North-South debate and the quest for a new educational order.

Efforts to conceptualize and examine the process of foreign study or overseas training have shifted in focus over the last 30 years. Prior to 1965, psychological and cultural approaches characterized the foreign student literature, reflecting a post–World War II view of foreign study as an individual cross-cultural experience.[2] That strain of research has continued to the present, often focusing on students from particular countries, in particular fields, or at particular universities. Margaret Cormack and Barbara Walton have provided excellent reviews of the early literature.[3] More recently, a review by Lee et al. has summarized studies about foreign students in the United States, relating their experience to such independent variables as age, sex, marital status, English language proficiency, academic

---

[1] Craufurd D. Goodwin and Michael Nacht, *Absence of Decision: Foreign Students in American Colleges and Universities* (New York: Institute of International Education, 1983), p. 14.

[2] Otto Klineberg, *International Exchanges in Education, Science and Culture: Suggestions for Research* (Paris: Mouton, 1966); also, Claire Selltiz et al., *Attitudes and Social Relations of Foreign Students in the United States* (Minneapolis: University of Minnesota Press, 1963).

[3] Margaret Cormack, *An Evaluation of Research on Educational Exchange* (Washington, D.C.: Department of State, Bureau of Educational and Cultural Affairs, 1962); Barbara Walton, *Foreign Students Exchange in Perspective*, Publication 8373 (Washington, D.C.: Department of State, Office of External Research, 1967).

1

level, and sponsorship.[4] Except for English language proficiency, which is unambiguously related to satisfactory educational experiences, studies of the other variables have produced no consistent results.

Beginning in the mid-1960s, as the goals of foreign study became more closely tied to economic development, numerous studies appeared on the impact of foreign study on home-country institutions and on national development. A partial summary of this literature is provided in Spaulding and Flack.[5] Foreign study was assessed in terms of its effect on the development of human resources and human capital in developing countries, and since many foreign students failed to return to those countries, there were also efforts to assess the significance of the brain drain.[6] An overview of relevant work was also provided by Diether Breitenbach,[7] and the bibliography included in this book provides an updating of the existing literature.

Until rather recently, policies underlying foreign study have been based on the implicit assumption that both those who study abroad and the sending countries can and should benefit if carefully selected students are provided with well-designed overseas educational experiences. Personal and cultural dislocation, academic problems, and, to a certain extent, brain drain could be mitigated or prevented. Lately, however, policymakers and practitioners, as well as scholars, have come to realize not only that it is very difficult to get things right but also that there are structural conflicts and dilemmas that make it possible, at best, only to balance benefits and costs rather than to eliminate negative outcomes.

The emerging view of foreign study as something other than an appropriate educational fix for the human capital needs of developing countries is only in part a reflection of diminished confidence in the benefits of education per se. It is also a reaction against technocratic approaches to development, and it is related to a new emphasis in many developing countries on their need and growing capacity to solve their own educational problems. Indeed, postsecondary education has grown rapidly in recent years, making it less necessary than in the past to look abroad. There is, as well, a keener awareness that the interests of individuals studying abroad are not necessarily congruent with national interests and that it is hard to force congruence. Foreign study is seen increasingly in all its

[4] Motoko Y. Lee, Mokhtar Abd-Ella, and Linda A. Burks, *Needs of Foreign Students from Developing Countries at U.S. Colleges and Universities* (Washington, D.C.: National Association for Foreign Student Affairs, 1981).

[5] Seth Spaulding and Michael Flack, *The World's Students in the United States* (New York: Praeger, 1976).

[6] Robert G. Myers, *Education and Emigration: Study Abroad and the Migration of Human Resources* (New York: McKay, 1972); William Glaser, *The Brain Drain: Emigration and Return* (New York: Pergamon, 1978).

[7] Diether Breitenbach, "The Evaluation of Study Abroad," in *Students as Links between Cultures: A Cross-cultural Survey Based on Unesco Studies,* ed. Ingrid Eide (Oslo: Universitets Forlaget, 1970).

complexity—sometimes an unalloyed blessing but more often the result of difficult choices and leading to both satisfaction and frustration. This new view of foreign study is reflected in many of the articles in this book.

The book is an effort to examine foreign study from different perspectives, especially comparative ones. Foreign study has significance for the countries from which students go abroad for study and for their host countries, for the quality of education in institutions in both the home country and the host country, and for the participating students. This significance is reflected in national policies on the conditions of admission of foreign students or the financial support of foreign students. A variant of these national foreign student policies are those development policies of both poor countries and those providing development assistance that grapple with the pros and cons of training in the West. The significance of foreign study is reflected also, but to a lesser degree, in the actions and policies of institutions of higher education that "send" and "receive" foreign students.

Contributions to this volume have been grouped under four substantive headings. Under the first heading, "Influences and Impact," there are four articles that examine in various ways the significance of foreign study for developing countries. The article by Norman Goodman analyzes the roles foreign study plays in what he calls the "international institution-alization of education," more particularly, how the continuing high prestige of education obtained in Western countries, especially in the United States and Britain, shapes basic economic and social concepts and theories in developing countries and defines who are considered to be experts. Goodman's empirical data are drawn from Malaysia. John Hawkins, in his examination of the effects of study by Chinese scholars in the United States, identifies a related phenomenon, that is, the efforts of returned Chinese to modify higher educational institutions in their country in ways that show American influences. As he puts it, "Returned scholars have brought home with them not only knowledge of computers and plasma physics but also a whole range of administrative, management, and institutional forms that in their minds are closely associated with the knowledge thus obtained" (p. 30). While Hawkins is analyzing an ongoing process, James Coleman is looking back on the role of foreign study in university development in Thailand and Zaire. His analysis shows dramatically how political circumstances within these countries worked for and against institution-building efforts, reinforcing in the Thai case and attenuating in the Zairian case the influence of foreign study. The last article in this set, by Gerald Fry, attempts a broader assessment of the economic and political outcomes of foreign study for developing countries. His principal indicator of outcome is growth in real GNP, but he also presents instances of positive outcomes for Thailand (the country he knows best) and Costa Rica in the form of case studies.

The second grouping of articles is headed "National and Regional Policies and Trends." The particular "nations" and "regions" involved are Britain, Australia, the countries of Western Europe, and Asia. Peter Williams reports on the establishment of the full-cost fees policy in Britain, the efforts of institutions of higher education to deal with the effects of this policy, and the compromises the government eventually made to mitigate those effects. Stewart Fraser's article charts the changes in government policy in Australia over the last twenty years. With regard to Western Europe, Alan Smith describes, on the one hand, the increasing efforts by individual countries to restrict access by foreign students to their educational institutions and, on the other hand, the measures to stimulate "organized mobility" that have been taken. Organized mobility, he concludes, is second best to free movement of students since it involves only a limited number of institutions and students. William Cummings examines national policies from the "other" end: not the policies of receiving countries but the policies of those that send students abroad. He analyzes the determinants of sending levels for a number of Asian countries (Burma, Malaysia, Iran, and Korea), identifying such positive forces as a country's degree of interdependence with other countries, the number of young people who have completed secondary education, and GNP per capita and such negative forces as domestic opportunities for higher education and the lack of availability of information about foreign study.

The third and fourth sections of the book are briefer than the first two. The third one is titled "Development Strategies." It contains an article by Robert Myers, in which he lays out two main strategies that have been adopted by external funders of development with regard to postgraduate study abroad: institution building and knowledge generation. He then examines the relative effectiveness of each of these strategies as implemented by the Ford Foundation in Peru and concludes that the knowledge-generation strategy was superior. Joyce Moock explores the pros and cons of foreign study in the context of African development, comparing training at home and abroad. She concludes that the optimal course is the integration of the advantages of African-based education with those of foreign study. Foreign study is most effective when it is closely related to national development objectives, when it produces "more *educated* and *not merely trained* people to cope with the complexities and social instabilities of transitional economies" (p. 182).

In the fourth section, "Political and Institutional Dilemmas," the article by Hans Weiler echoes some of Moock's concerns, though from a somewhat different perspective. He points out the extent to which it is, at least in part, in the nature of Western universities generally, and American universities in particular, to provide the very kind of overseas education that is not readily compatible with patterns of national development, especially in Africa. The training foreign students receive in the United States consists too often of equipping them with oversimple technological solutions and monoparadigmatic conceptual systems. The second article in this section, by David Lansdale et al., is entitled "Institutional Culture and Third World Student Needs at American Universities." Lansdale and his collaborators have obtained empirical data to test Weiler's hypotheses, and they conclude that there are, indeed, tensions between the culture of faculty members in an engineering school and the expectations of Third World students and that, by modifying these expectations, the students may be handicapped when they return home to apply what they have learned.

The last section of the book, as is indicated by its heading, "Literature Surveys," is of a different nature from the foregoing ones. It contains a select bibliography on many aspects of foreign study, prepared by Y. G-M. Lulat, and a review article by Robert B. Kaplan on the teaching of English as a second language. Kaplan deals with both theory and practice, with special application to foreign students.

As many of the articles in this book show, there is among those making policy with regard to foreign study a certain reluctance to perceive its determinants and consequences in all their complexity. Policymakers, in this field and others, though in principle committed to spelling out the pros and cons of viable alternatives, in fact often take on the role of advocates or opponents, stressing too strongly either the benefits or the costs. The articles indicate how subtly benefits and costs tend to be balanced when it comes to foreign study. The task for policymakers is, therefore, much more difficult, and at the present stage, social scientists are not able to offer very much help. Almost all the articles suggest, directly or indirectly, the need for a considerable amount of further research, not in the conventional sense that all studies invariably point the way to further problems but, rather, because there is a genuine lack of good data and good studies on which to build. Several of the authors clearly realized that they were taking a first cut at a problem, often asking questions rather than providing answers, and providing answers that would surely need to be refined as the questions become more precise.

In the future, foreign study will continue, but its rationales and functions are likely to change as relationships among the countries of the world change. As these political and economic relationships change and, along with them, the distribution of human resources, patterns of foreign study will be altered. Better understanding of the dynamics of foreign study would permit more effective adaptation to the forces that lie behind it and the shaping of realistic policies in this field.

It is our conviction that insufficient scholarly attention has been devoted to foreign study and its ramifications. The topic permits scholarly concerns and policy-related research to intermingle constructively. In a call that is not new, we urge practitioners, policymakers, and academic researchers involved in the field of international exchange to combine forces. We hope this book will help provide a basis for such collaborative effort, focusing attention on the topic, providing some new information, and encouraging a continuation of the strain of sophisticated policy-oriented research that has begun to emerge.

ELINOR G. BARBER*
PHILIP G. ALTBACH†
ROBERT G. MYERS‡

* Research director at the Institute of International Education, New York.

† Professor in the Faculty of Educational Studies, and director of the Comparative Education Center, State University of New York at Buffalo.

‡ On the staff of the High Scope Foundation.

The Institutionalization of Overseas Education

NORMAN GOODMAN*

Introduction

Just as societies are affected by the complex set of relationships among nations, so too are national education systems conditioned by the larger international environment in which they exist. In this article, I concentrate on education as a structure that is internationally institutionalized in that its values appear largely to be defined by Western educational models and more generally by Western society. More specifically, I explore how this institutionalization of education relates to overseas education.[1] An analysis of the international institutionalization of education adds a new dimension to the more common interpretation of overseas education provided by development and dependency theorists.

"Institutionalization" refers to the acceptance in societies of certain ideas that come to define the proper conduct of daily life. As these ideas become relatively fixed and presupposed within societies, they become the social construction of reality.[2] In this sense, education as a structure may have an effect on society that goes far beyond the interactions that occur in a classroom. To support this approach to the analysis of education, I will present and discuss empirical results from research done in Malaysia on the perceived relative value of higher education abroad and at home.[3]

Education as Defining Knowledge and Expertise

Education institutionalizes and legitimates particular theories of knowledge and expertise for societies, apart from the direct socializing effects of schools on students. Thus, traditional, sometimes sacred, approaches to establishing the validity of knowledge and expertise have been replaced by education systems. For example, medical science is defined

* On the staff of the Institute of International Education based in Jakarta.

[1] In this article, "overseas education" will be used to refer to the flow of students from developing countries to Western countries. This flow represents the bulk of study abroad in the world, amounting to approximately 80 percent of all overseas study. See Norman Goodman, "The Institutionalization of Foreign Education and the Effects of the Charter: A Study of Malaysian Student Attitudes and Adjustment to Overseas Education Opportunity" (Ph.D. diss., Stanford University, 1981).

[2] Peter L. Berger and Thomas Luckman, *The Social Construction of Reality* (New York: Doubleday, 1975).

[3] This article was presented in an earlier form to the annual conference of the comparative and international Education Society, Atlanta, March 16–19, 1983. It is based on my dissertation research (see Goodman).

by and gains legitimacy from medical schools and, correspondingly, shamanism loses its authority and legitimacy. Educational systems also define and legitimate those who are experts, that is, those who are to be treated as commanding certain bodies of knowledge and the authority that derives from those bodies. Continuing the medical example, education establishes the criteria for deciding who possesses medical knowledge and is, therefore, a doctor or medical expert. A number of scholars have affirmed the status-allocation authority of education.[4] Empirical research by Blau and Duncan; Duncan, Featherman, and Duncan; and Sewell and Hauser confirms that years of education, regardless of what is learned in those years, is an important indicator of status attainment.[5]

What is true of education in general takes on even greater significance when considering elite education, which establishes the "authority of specialized competency." Specialized bodies of knowledge (e.g., economics, business administration, medicine, or engineering) are defined and created by education and, in turn, authoritatively describe and explain social life. If social actors are not to be considered ignorant or irrational, they must take these bodies of knowledge into account. At the same time, these actors must acknowledge the authority of economists, management experts, doctors, engineers, scientists, or whomever.

This conception of education, which may be attributed principally to Meyer, greatly expands the role of education in society and its contribution to social change.[6] Imposed on a traditional society, a modern educational system redefines much of social reality. Meyer and Rubinson have identified several ways in which the introduction of modern education might influence a traditional society:

1. Schools define the nation's language, history, and culture.

2. Schools establish the universalistic criteria according to which positions in the modern institutional order are allocated.

3. Professionalism is based on educational credentials (however meaningless these may be) and becomes the basis for new positions in society with new purposes.

4. Mass education provides a moral basis for the shift of authority and participation to the citizenry.[7]

[4] For example, Samuel Bowles and Herbert Gintis, *Schooling in Capitalist America* (New York: Basic, 1976); and Martin Carnoy, *Education as Cultural Imperialism* (New York: David McKay, 1975).

[5] P. M. Blau and O. D. Duncan, *The American Occupational Structure* (New York: Wiley, 1967); O. D. Duncan, D. L. Featherman, and B. Duncan, *Socioeconomic Background and Achievement* (New York: Seminar Press, 1972); William H. Sewell and Robert M. Hauser, *Education, Occupation and Earnings* (New York: Academic Press, 1975).

[6] John W. Meyer, "The Effects of Education as an Institution," *American Journal of Sociology* 83 (1977): 55–77.

[7] John W. Meyer and Richard Rubinson, "Education and Political Development" (Sociology Department, Stanford University, 1975, typescript).

As these examples suggest, the institutionalization of modern education in society can have a significant effect on the way people view their society and their roles in it.

Adding an International Dimension

Now consider the implications of the international institutionalization of education. If modern education is viewed as a network of structures operating throughout the world, it is easy to see that it plays much the same role internationally as it does within one society. Specifically, I would argue, modern education in the world system institutionalizes Western science and technology as the authoritative form of knowledge for development. Further, it defines and allocates typically modern categories of work and legitimates elite status claims not merely to the Western-educated but to those actually educated in the West.

The dominance of Western educational models stems largely from the historical relationship in which Western systems of education were imposed on colonial societies.[8] This has had the effect of institutionalizing modern (Western) theories of knowledge and expertise in the developing countries of the world. As Kumar explains: "The reason is simple. The lifestyles, beliefs, value systems and world views of the metropolis are generally presented as the main cause of the economic and political superiority of these [Western] nations. Thus, the masses and elite of the [developing countries] come to idealize them; they begin to accept them uncritically and develop a feeling of inferiority about their cultural systems. In fact, their own self images are shaped by the images held by people in the metropolis."[9]

The establishment of institutions of higher education in developing countries was merely an extension of the acceptance of "center" thinking by the colonies. Local universities were very closely modeled after and linked to the metropolitan "parent" university. Mazrui likened African universities to subsidiaries of cultural multinational corporations head-quartered in the metropolitan center.[10] Fuenzalida puts it as follows: "The 'cultural superstructure' is shaped and guided by the philosophical and epistemological tenets of North American and European universities, and

---

[8] Carnoy.

[9] Krishna Kumar, ed., *Bonds without Bondage* (Honolulu: University Press of Hawaii, 1979) p. 12.

[10] Ali A. Mazrui, "The African University as a Multinational Corporation: Problems of Penetration and Dependency," *Harvard Education Review* 45, no. 2 (1975): 191–210. See also Edmundo F. Fuenzalida, "Incorporation in the Contemporary Stage of the Modern World System: Conditions, Processes, and Mechanisms" (paper presented to the Conference on Constancy and Change: The Political Economy of Global Differentiation, University of Southern California, Ojai, California, November 14–17, 1979), and (paper presented for the 4th Agency for International Development/National Association for Foreign Student Affairs Workshop, Washington, D.C., March 1980).

the incorporation of universities from underdeveloped countries has the dual effect of assimilating their institutional culture to these tenets while at the same time dissociating institutions of higher education from the national context in which they were established."[11]

Western educational systems and structures continue to define education for the rest of the world, and, by extension, they define what is knowledge and who may claim competence in it.

Education and Development

The education established in the West represents, as Kumar has suggested, the knowledge supposedly necessary to achieve standards of living comparable to those in Western countries. Given the authority of Western knowledge for development, there is a ready explanation for the "underdevelopment" of the Third World, namely, that it does not possess the requisite knowledge; Third World countries must acquire this knowledge before they can move up the development ladder.

The knowledge that is considered appropriate emphasizes scientific and technological approaches to questions. Moreover, specialized fields of development knowledge have been created in Western universities, including such subjects as development economics, international development education, rural sociology, development communications, and, most recently, farming-systems research. These and other academic fields constantly produce new "truths" about the processes of development and new strategies to speed the process of modernization. "Knowledge" about development has changed over time; current and past theories have not always been consistent, as in the instances of the "trickle-down" and "bottom-up" approaches. Yet, as these theories gain currency in Western academic circles, they gain authority and legitimacy throughout the world, and they become the bases of policies for development in the Third World. The influence of Western education in defining the problems and their solutions in the developing world is extraordinary, almost regardless of the validity of the knowledge that is being promulgated.

Expertise and Development

Definitions of expertise are also internationally institutionalized by education. As explained earlier, education establishes categories of expertise and certification procedures to identify individuals who can claim competence in specialized and typically Western bodies of knowledge. These definitions of expertise inform and explain to the home society who should

[11] Edmundo F. Fuenzalida, "The Contribution of Higher Education to a New International Order" (Stanford University, School of Education, 1979, typescript).

be allocated elite (expert) status. Very commonly throughout the developing world, expertise is equated with higher degrees from Western-style universities. As R. P. Dore has illustrated in *The Diploma Disease*, degree certification may play an even greater part in the definition and allocation of elite-status roles in developing societies than it does in the West, and this explains the great demand for higher education in developing societies.[12]

If degrees from Western-style institutions at home are highly valued, then degrees earned overseas take on an even greater significance. Education in the West establishes another category of expert in developing societies because the overseas educated are presumed to have had more direct access and exposure to the dominant and authoritative knowledge of the West. As Eide has observed: "One remarkable fact is that a student who has been trained abroad enjoys a certain prestige and even a privileged status in his home country. This is due not only to such objective factors as his training and actual ability but also to additional subjective factors, the good reputation of the host country being transferred in some curious way to his own person."[13]

Indeed, numerous studies of foreign graduates in developing countries confirm that Western educational certification has become an important factor in gaining access to modern elite status at home.[14] Writing specifically about Africa, Ekeh notes that foreign education, particularly from a former colonial power, is a valuable key to social mobility. As he puts it, it has "become part of the anti-colonial African bourgeois ideology" to show that they are as good as the colonists because they have the same qualifications.[15] Thus, regardless of the quality or relevance of the education received overseas, overseas Western education has legitimation and certification functions in the world system of education.

Comparison with Other Theories of Education

This interpretation of the flow of foreign students from developing countries to the West and of the influence overseas education has on developing societies differs considerably from the interpretations offered by both development theorists and dependency theorists.

[12] R. P. Dore, *The Diploma Disease* (Berkeley: University of California Press, 1976).

[13] Ingrid Eide, "Students as Bridges between Cultures," *Kultura* 17 (1972): 98.

[14] John Useem and Ruth Hill Useem, *The Western Educated Man in India* (East Lansing, Mich.: Institute of International Studies in Education, 1955); John A. Gardner, *A Beacon of Hope: The Exchange of Persons Program* (Washington, D.C.: Government Printing Office, 1963); James F. Davis, "Cultural Perspectives of Middle Eastern Students in America," *Middle East Journal* 14 (1970): 250–64; Ingrid Eide, *Students as Links between Cultures* (Oslo: Universitetforlaget, 1970); Mary C. Hodgkin, *The Innovators: The Role of the Foreign Trained in S.E. Asia* (Sydney: University Press, 1972).

[15] Peter P. Ekeh, "Colonialism and the Two Publics in Africa: A Theoretical Statement," *Comparative Studies in Society and History* 17, no. 1 (1975): 112.

Most development theorists view overseas education as a means of transferring critical development knowledge and technology from the West to the developing world. Foreign education is a process of developing essential human capital.[16] In the development paradigm, the direct socialization and education of the foreign student is the operating mechanism for this process. It is easy to see that the development paradigm is the dominant theory operating throughout the world as an explanation for overseas education regardless of the validity behind the assumptions it makes about such things as the relevance of overseas education, the quality of overseas education, or the effectiveness of overseas education in actually imparting the targeted information.

Dependency theorists are more sensitive to the problems of the cultural incorporation of Third World countries by the dominant Western developed countries. They view the development paradigm as a Western ideological construct imposed on the rest of the world to rationalize the world economic system and to define the role of the Third World in it. Overseas education is ostensibly explained as required for human capital acquisition and the transfer of technology, but most dependency theorists argue that the real, underlying agenda in overseas education is the socialization of Third World students to Western ideas, values, tastes, et cetera. When these people return to their countries, dependency theorists argue, they identify more with the West than with their own cultures, and they tend to work toward the reorganization of their societies around Western ideas.[17] Alatas describes individuals in developing countries whose thinking has been shaped by higher education abroad (or by Western dominated institutions at home) as having "captive minds": "A captive mind is the product of higher institutions of learning, either at home or abroad, whose way of thinking is dominated by Western thought in an imitative and uncritical manner. . . . It is alienated from its own national tradition, if it exists, in the field of its intellectual pursuit. It is unconscious of its own captivity and the conditioning factors making it what it is. . . . It is a result of the Western dominance over the rest of the world."[18] As in the development paradigm, the operation of overseas education lies in its direct socialization and education of the overseas student. While it does not make the same assumptions about the relevance or quality of overseas education, de-

---

[16] Stephen Bochner, "Cultural Diversity: Implications for Modernization and International Education," in Kumar, ed., pp. 231–56. See also F. H. Harbison and C. A. Myers, *Education Manpower and Economic Growth* (New York: McGraw-Hill, 1964).

[17] Syed Hussein Alatas, "The Captive Mind and Creative Development," *International Social Science Journal* 27 (1975): 691–700. Karl P. Sauvant, "Socio-cultural Decolonization" (Center on Transnational Corporations, United Nations, New York, 1976, typescript); Fuenzalida, "Incorporation in the Contemporary Stage of the Modern World System."

[18] Alatas, p. 691.

pendency theory does assume that Western education is particularly effective in inculcating Western ideas, values, and so on.

In fact, there is probably some validity to both points of view. I am not interested in disputing these perspectives. However, the institution-alization of education adds a whole new dimension to the discussion. The operational element in my conception of overseas education is not the socialization or education of the individual student studying abroad but rather the institutionalization of modern education in society as a whole, shaping the way people at home view the development of their society, the way education should be organized and articulated to other institutions, and the way returning foreign graduates are to be understood and treated. I do not assume the quality or relevance of overseas education for de-velopment. It is only important that the home society believes that overseas education is relevant and good. I also do not assume that the student necessarily either learns new knowledge and skills or is socialized to Western values while abroad. The important thing is that the student can claim to be certified in a specialized field by Western education. The home society will allocate high-status roles to Western graduates if it accepts the legitimacy and authority of modern education to define what is knowledge and who is qualified to understand and apply that knowledge.

Further Empirical Support

In order to generate empirical support for my contentions regarding the worldwide institutionalization of education, I conducted research in Malaysia on the perceptions of Malaysian students considering study abroad.[19] Specifically, I wanted to investigate how Malaysian students perceived the status-allocation authority of higher education imparted in five countries: the United States, the United Kingdom, India, the Phil-ippines, and Malaysia. By extension, the results of such an inquiry indicate the way in which higher education is viewed throughout Malaysian society.

The five countries selected possess several characteristics that make them valuable cases for comparison. First, Great Britain and India are

[19] The results reported here are a small part of a much larger study of Malaysian students and overseas higher education conducted in 1978–79. For a more thorough discussion of this topic and the methodology involved in the research, see Goodman (n. 1 above). There has been a dramatic change in the patterns of Malaysian overseas higher education since this research. The major flow of students has shifted from Britain to the United States, where there are now over 20,000 Malaysian students. This change, however, does not alter the arguments presented here. In fact, it tends to confirm my claims. Students surveyed were selected from among those who visited the Malaysian-American Commission for Educational Exchange and expressed an interest in studying in the United States. This suggests a possible bias in favor of overseas education and specifically American education among the students surveyed. However, my research revealed that many students eventually did not apply anywhere overseas. When their opinions were analyzed separately, the results were almost identical to the entire group. Nevertheless, the group surveyed was not a representative sample of all Malaysian students, and some caution should be exercised in interpreting the results.

major centers for Malaysian overseas study. Second, both India and Malaysia follow the British model of education, while higher education in the Philippines is modeled after the American system. All four receiving countries use English as the medium of instruction, so language was controlled for as an explanatory variable. While both the United States and Great Britain are considered developed countries, India and the Philippines also have extensive systems of higher education with potential at least for absorbing large numbers of Malaysian students. Both India and the Philippines are neighbors of Malaysia and often have comparable problems in national development; the Philippines also shares membership in the Association of Southeast Asian Nations (ASEAN) region with Malaysia.

Given the proximity, lower cost of living, and lower tuition fees, both India and the Philippines represent bargains in higher education for Malaysians. Malaysia has close ties to Great Britain that result from its colonial heritage, and many Malaysians of Indian descent have ties to India. On the other hand, there are few Malaysians with personal ties to the Philippines or the United States. Finally, the Malaysian government recognizes nearly all degrees from the United Kingdom and the United States but only some from India. It handles Philippine degrees largely on a case-by-case basis because there are very few Malaysians currently studying in the Philippines. Government recognition of degrees is important for employment in the public sector but is not essential for private-sector employment.

The students were asked five questions concerning the status-allocation authority of higher education from the two "developed" and three "developing" countries:

1. What is your general opinion of the universities in the following countries?

2. How successful do you think Malaysian graduates from universities in these countries have been in achieving highly valued positions in Malaysian society?

3. When a student has a Bachelor's degree from universities in one of these countries, how confident can he or she be that he/she will become a leading member of Malaysian society?

4. How much do Malaysia's leading businesses and government institutions rely on the expertise, research, and technological advances produced in universities in the following countries?

5. It has been said that in some countries a student can pursue almost any field of study and his degree will help him get a highly valued position in Malaysia. There are other countries, however, from which only a few degrees are helpful in getting a highly valued position. For each of the following countries, please indicate how many different fields of study a person could choose from and expect to get a highly valued position in Malaysia when he or she finishes.[20]

[20] These items were based on theoretical indicators of the charter, discussed by John W. Meyer, "The Charter: Conditions of Diffuse Socialization in Schools," in *Social Processes and Social Structures*, ed. W. R. Scott (New York: Holt Rinehart & Winston, 1970). Justification for the operationalizations of these items are given in Goodman.

The students rated these items on a five-point scale with a sixth "I don't know" option. Their answers were summed and averaged to create a rating score for the status-allocation authority of higher education from each of the five countries.

Results

Table 1 presents the mean rating of status allocation authority for the five countries. The results in table 1 show the average status-allocation ratings for each of the countries, including Malaysia. Interestingly, higher education in both the United Kingdom and the United States is highly rated; in fact, the two countries are rated almost equally. This is somewhat surprising given the substantial historical ties between the United Kingdom and Malaysia and the fact that the majority of the Malaysians studying overseas at the time the research was conducted were in the United Kingdom.

The second interesting observation is that Malaysian higher education was rated only third and markedly lower than either British or American higher education. Moreover, there was somewhat less consensus on the status-allocation authority of Malaysian higher education (the standard deviation was .644).[21] Students, in this study at least, think that Malaysian higher education has less status-allocation authority than higher education obtained in either the United States or the United Kingdom.

The third observation that can be made about the results in table 1 is that the United States and the United Kingdom, the two developed countries, rate more highly than India, the Philippines, and Malaysia, the three developing countries. Moreover, many more students decline even to express an opinion about the status-allocation authority of higher education from India or the Philippines. In fact, less than half the students gave ratings for Philippine higher education. Those who did opt to express opinions on Philippine education rated it as very low. Furthermore, though India hosts approximately 6,000 Malaysian students, it was rated as low among those who rated both countries.

Interpretations

These results lend support to my thesis of an international institutionalization of education. First, they indicate that Western education is highly valued (at least in one developing society) because higher education in both the United States and the United Kingdom was rated very highly.

---

[21] Given the ethnic politics of Malaysian education and society, one might expect variations in the evaluation of the status-allocation authority of Malaysian higher education. In fact, when I analyzed these results by race, there were some differences. Malays rated Malaysian higher education somewhat higher than the Chinese or Indians did. However, all three races rated American and British education higher in status-allocation authority than they did Malaysian higher education.

TABLE 1
MEAN STATUS-ALLOCATION RATING FOR HIGHER EDUCATION FROM FIVE COUNTRIES

Country	Mean	SD	N
United States	4.15	.473	477
Malaysia	3.52	.644	487
Great Britain	4.19	.487	487
India	2.52	.555	348
Philippines	2.52	.650	153

One might have expected British higher education to do well given the large number of Malaysian students in the United Kingdom at the time the research was conducted (approximately 16,000), but American higher education fared almost equally well. At the time the research was conducted American higher education was not well known in Malaysia, and there were just 3,000 students in the U.S. By contrast, there were about 6,000 Malaysians in India. Education in the United States appears to be rated highly not so much because Malaysia had great experience with American education as because it is identified as Western and highly developed.

The results also indicate that the status-allocation authority of Western education is ranked more highly than education from developing countries including Malaysia. This lends credence to the contention made earlier that Western education is perceived as dominant and that home-country education in developing societies is considered to be second best. Despite the facts that the educational systems of India and Malaysia are modeled after the British system and that Philippine education is patterned on an American model, the education received in these three developing countries cannot compete with that obtained in the West in terms of its perceived ability to allocate high-status positions. The international institutionalization of modern education apparently establishes certification rules that hold that elite status is attached to those who study in the West.

If we remind ourselves that the students who rated these items were primarily form 5 and form 6 students, it is not difficult to generalize their beliefs to the rest of Malaysian society. In fact, their beliefs about the value of Western education are based on the impressions they have received from parents, teachers, friends, the media, et cetera. They do not yet have any direct experience with seeking employment, nor have they been abroad to study. They are reflecting the generally held beliefs about the relationship between Western education and Malaysian society. In other words, they are reflecting the international institutionalization of modern education and its theories of knowledge and expertise.

Summary, Conclusions, and Implications

In this article I have attempted to describe the international institutionalization of education and to provide a small piece of evidence to support my contentions. I have taken Meyer's ideas of the institutionalization of education in one society and tried to show how they apply in the emerging world system. According to Meyer, education institutionalizes theories of knowledge and theories of expertise in society. I have argued that modern education is a worldwide phenomenon and that it institutionalizes theories of knowledge and expertise on an international level. For primarily historical reasons, modern education is dominated by Western higher education. Consequently, the institutionalized theories of knowledge and expertise are predominantly Western. With the international institutionalization of modern (and Western) education, developing societies tend to accept Western knowledge as the most authoritative. Western definitions, concepts, and formulations of the way society should be organized and developed are attributed the highest legitimacy. Moreover, the theories of expertise institutionalized by the world education system establish rules and certification procedures that legitimize claims to elite status and accord the authority of specialized competence not only to those educated in Western-style universities in the developing countries but also, to an even greater extent, to those actually educated in the West.

The results of the research conducted in Malaysia tend to support the assertions made in this article. The Malaysian students surveyed attributed the highest status-allocation authority to Western higher education. Higher education from Malaysia was rated below both American and British higher education. Higher education from India and the Philippines was rated even lower. This tends to confirm the idea that developing-country education is viewed as second best relative to Western education. It also supports the contention of an international institutionalization of education.

As I have attempted to point out, this conceptualization of education does not assume the actual validity, accuracy, or relevance of the theories of knowledge or expertise that are institutionalized. Nor do I assume, as most development and dependency theorists do, that the most important effects of education occur through direct socialization of students. Perhaps the greatest effects of the world education system are in the theories of knowledge and expertise that it establishes for societies around the world.

Assuming the validity of the arguments presented here, there are several further implications that I will only mention. Given the dominance of Western knowledge in the international institutionalization of education, there will be a continuing reliance by developing countries on both Western-style training at home and Western education abroad. Moreover, developing countries will continue to seek Western expertise to validate and legitimize their development strategies. The current international institutionalization of education contributes to a dependence and lack of self-confidence in the developing world, and this will tend to inhibit the development of local theories of society and homegrown strategies for change.

Educational Exchanges and the Transformation of Higher Education in the People's Republic of China

JOHN N. HAWKINS*

Introduction

It is virtually impossible to identify a nation whose educational system and technical expertise have not been influenced somewhat by the ideas, practices, techniques, and technologies of other nations. This is particularly true of China, despite its historical background of insularity. My focus here is on changes in Chinese higher education that are currently being proposed by some of the scholars that have recently returned from study periods in the United States. China has a long history of educational change and development. Clearly, in the case of higher education, China's current institutions reflect influences from various periods of international exchanges (from early relations with neighbors to more recent influences from the West and the Soviet Union) on an indigenous pattern of higher education.[1]

China's current quest for education and training has resulted in thousands of students, scholars, and practitioners being sent abroad for advanced education and training to achieve, in their terms, the Four Modernizations plan, by once again "making foreign things serve China." The rationale for such programs is often pragmatic and focuses on the technical aspects of whatever skill is being pursued. However, there are often a variety of unintended outcomes of such scholarly exchange programs. China may send scholars to the Massachusetts Institutes of Technology to study plasma physics, but they may return demanding radical changes in laboratory procedures, departmental organization, and peer relations. The result is

I would like to express gratitude to the Council on International and Comparative Studies at the University of California, Los Angeles, particularly James S. Coleman, director, and to Open Grants at the East West Center in Honolulu, especially Douglas Murray, vice-president of the center, and Dean Sumi Mackey and Glenn Shive of Open Grants for generous financial assistance that made this preliminary study possible.

* Professor and chairman of the Department of Education, University of California, Los Angeles, and current president of the Comparative and International Education Society.

[1] I am currently preparing a monograph on the history of Chinese higher education and the nature of international influences. The literature on this topic includes Sally Borthwick, *Education and Social Change in China* (Stanford, Calif.: Hoover Institution, 1983); Y. C. Wang, *Chinese Intellectuals and the West: 1872–1949* (Taipei: Hung-Ch'iao Su-tien, 1971); Huang Fu Ch'ing, *Chinese Students in Japan in the Late Ch'ing Period* (Tokyo: Centre for East Asian Cultural Studies, 1982); John N. Hawkins, *Mao Tse-Tung and Education* (Hamden, Conn.: Shoe String Press, 1973); and the more current developments are covered in John N. Hawkins, *Education and Social Change in the People's Republic of China* (New York: Praeger, 1983).

what Burton Clark has called the "migration of academic forms among nations."[2]

Clark notes two forms that such interactions might take: external imposition and voluntary importation. The British and French colonial legacies, for example, left their imprint in the forms of classical curricula, university autonomy in staffing, and selection of students (by the British in India, Jamaica, and Canada) and centralization and nationalization of higher education (by the French in their colonies). Of the latter mode of voluntary importation, Japan is a good example. In the words of one Japanese specialist on higher education, "One must start from the fact that Japan created its higher educational system by using Western universities as models."[3] Significantly, the four nations that served historically as models for the borrowers (the United States, Britain, Germany, and France) are precisely those nations chosen by the Chinese for their expanding visiting-scholar program. The study reported here focuses on the perceptions that returned Chinese scholars have of higher education as a result of their study period in the United States and on their suggestions for higher educational reform in China. Before reporting this information it will be useful to provide a brief background to this most recent exchange program.

Background to the Exchange Program

Delegations of scholars from the People's Republic of China (PRC) first began to visit the United States in 1976, but it was not until 1979 that larger numbers of scholars came from China for advanced study and training. Although these visits were originally a centralized activity under the Academy of Sciences and the Ministry of Education, the Chinese government soon decided to allow each university and research institute the opportunity to pursue within a set of broad guidelines relationships with American academic establishments.

The current high numbers of scholarly exchanges are the result of a general agreement signed in 1978 entitled "Understanding on Student and Scholarly Exchanges." When the former presidential science adviser Frank Press signed the agreement in Beijing, this ended almost 30 years of scholarly isolation between the United States and China. Later in 1978, a Chinese delegation led by Zhou Peiyuan visited selected higher educational institutions in the United States to begin the implementation process. Those meetings resulted in additional formal and informal agreements

---

[2] Burton Clark, *The Higher Education System: Academic Organization in Cross-national Perspective* (Berkeley and Los Angeles: University of California Press, 1983), p. 227.
[3] Ikuo Amano, quoted in Clark, p. 229.

to pursue exchanges of students and scholars between the two countries.[4] By 1979 the PRC announced that over 2,000 government-sponsored students and scholars had been sent to over 33 nations. The bulk of scholars were sent to the United States, the Federal Republic of Germany, Great Britain, France, and Japan. The Chinese projected that by 1985 approximately 20,000 students and scholars would be studying abroad. The overall goal was to provide China with a corps of highly trained students and scholars to direct research and development activities and to administer a variety of educational and research institutions.[5]

China's leaders have recently been reassessing the scope of this exchange program, and it appears there has been a curtailment in the numbers of scholars projected to be sent abroad. Nonetheless, although precise figures are not available, it was thought that within the United States alone there were in 1981 over 6,000 students and scholars attending over 300 colleges and universities.[6] A recent survey revealed the following profile of the U.S./China exchange program. About one-third of the 6,000 are undergraduate and graduate students. About two-thirds are in the visiting scholar category. These visiting scholars are generally midcareer academics and professionals, carefully selected to upgrade their subject area before returning to assume responsible positions in their home institutions. The bulk of the visiting scholars are attending colleges and universities on the East and West coasts; 42 percent are in 10 major universities. The vast majority are studying in the fields of mathematics, physical sciences, and engineering. A smaller number are in the life sciences, and the smallest group is studying in the social sciences and in various professional schools. Sixty-five percent are PRC-government funded, although there is now encouragement to seek financial support from host institutions. The trend is turning toward decreasing the number of visiting scholars and increasing the number of degree students; the pattern clearly has been one of first training midcareer and senior personnel to restructure educational and research programs in China and then shifting the emphasis toward student exchanges.[7]

Sending Chinese scholars to the advanced industrial nations of Japan, Western Europe, and the United States can be viewed as a means of achieving two goals: building and renewing an intellectual resource base and providing a catalyst for institutional higher education reform. It is

---

[4] *An Introduction to Education in the PRC and U.S. China Educational Exchanges* (Washington, D.C.: Committee on Scholarly Communication with The People's Republic of China [CSCPRC], 1980), pp. 22–33.

[5] Ibid., pp. 24–27.

[6] Thomas Finger and Linda A. Reed, *Survey Summary: Students and Scholars from the People's Republic of China Currently in the United States* (Washington, D.C.: CSCPRC, 1981), pp. 1–8.

[7] Ibid.

the latter goal that is my focus here. My own experience, and conversations with Chinese educators, has convinced me that the current exchange program between China and the United States would involve a complex array of institutional change issues falling into at least four major clusters. In preparing for the interview sessions with the returned scholars, I generated a series of questions for each of the four clusters. The actual responses fell into seven areas, as can be seen in the next section. However, the following clusters and questions guided my thinking and my discussions with the scholars in China.[8]

1. *The role of the professional educator.*—What will the exchange program mean for the future roles of research, teaching, and professional service? Will the definition of an "intellectual" change?

2. *Curricular change.*—The literature written on other nations indicates that, following a significant exchange program, the curriculum of the sending institutions is likely to be affected in at least four areas: (*a*) structure (role of faculties, schools, departments, and programs), (*b*) administration (central presidents, chancellors, provosts, local deans, chairs, directors, etc.), (*c*) courses and degree programs (degree differentiation, credit system transfers, etc.), and (*d*) facilities (support services, communications processing, laboratory needs, library, etc.).

3. *Personnel.*—Change in policy of academic personnel is another area often influenced by cross-national experiences: (*a*) use of titles (professional series, research series, administrator series, etc.), (*b*) reform of the reward structure (salary mechanism, stipend, research grants, travel funds, etc.), and (*c*) promotional criteria (concepts such as tenure, merit review, etc. are now being discussed in China as a direct result of recent U.S. contacts).

4. *Administration.*—What changes are likely to occur with respect to the relative role of central (ministry-level) and decentralized (university-level) authorities in planning, policy formulation, and implementation as related to higher education, in general, and individual universities, in particular?

Preliminary Results

In December 1982 groups of returned scholars were interviewed in

[8] These questions were enjoined by a variety of reports and studies, such as Otto Clineberg, *International Educational Exchange* (The Hague: International Social Science Council, 1976); H. M. Phillips, "The Redeployment of Educational Aid," in *Education and Development Reconsidered*, ed. F. Champion Ward (New York: Praeger, 1974), pp. 266–68; Nancy Parkinson, *Educational Aid and National Development* (London: MacMillan, 1976); D. Goulet, *The Uncertain Promise* (New York: IDOC, 1977); Edward H. Berman, "Foundations, United States Foreign Policy, and African Education, 1945–1975," *Harvard Educational Review* 49, no. 2 (1979): 145–79; Martin Carnoy, *Education as Cultural Imperialism* (New York: McKay, 1976); I. Tuqan, *Education, Society and Development in Underdeveloped Societies* (The Hague: Centre for the Study of Education in Changing Societies, 1976).

Beijing.[9] Questions were formulated around the four clusters referred to above; however, when the responses were sorted out, they fell under seven main headings: (1) faculty development—teaching, (2) learning, (3) curriculum, (4) lifelong education, (5) student affairs, (6) administration and management, and (7) intra- and interuniversity organization and cooperation. It should be noted that their responses reflect only their *perceptions* of potential higher educational change issues. Some changes were viewed as more feasible than others, but all were identified as being critical to the future of higher education in China. A summary of their comments in each of these areas follows.

Faculty Development—Teaching

Scholars expressed interest in instructional development strategies they witnessed while in the United States. Particularly interesting to them were courses on how to teach effectively. The whole area of faculty relations was of special interest, including faculty incentives, promotion methods, faculty governance models, use of tenure and merit-review systems, and faculty recruitment. The role of faculty unions and associations was also an area identified as important in future higher education reform efforts in China. Here, comments by the scholars reflected somewhat the dilemma many American faculty express: are university faculty primarily professionals or part of organized labor? The Chinese scholars noted that while in the United States they witnessed some campuses undergoing collective bargaining negotiations and that as a result of that bargaining the American faculty had received resources in the way of additional salary and fringe benefits, on the one hand, but had created a more conflict-ridden relationship with the university administration, on the other. What emerged from this discussion was a consensus that university faculty in China needed more autonomy, more self-governance if creativity and a "more lively" atmosphere were to flourish. It was recognized, however, that it

---

[9] The returned scholars were identified throught the UCLA Exchange Program network and through personal contacts. Coordination was located at Beijing Normal University through the offices of the vice-president. Initially, one large group was assembled (42 students and scholars) and a round-table discussion was held. Out of this discussion there emerged the categories of change areas discussed here. I then met with smaller groups of three of four at their homes or in my room at the Beijing Hotel. In the small groups, 11 individuals were interviewed, bringing the total to 53. The comments of the small groups did not differ substantially from those of the initial large group, but the atmosphere was more relaxed. In both cases, the interviews were highly unstructured, resembling brainstorming sessions, and were designed to elicit the widest range of responses possible. It was not feasible at this stage to administer a written questionnaire, although it was proposed to officials in the Ministry of Education that a more formal survey be taken in the future, and this was agreed to "in principle." The scholars had widely varied backgrounds, but they were primarily science and technology personnel and were from three universities in the Beijing area: Beijing Normal, Beijing University, and Qinghua University. Their responses were frank and coincided with private conversations I have had with individual scholars both in China and in the United States.

would be many years before this desired degree of autonomy would be realized. Additional specific comments were to the effect that faculty mobility was too difficult, the salary too fixed, and the use of seniority applied too mechanically with respect to the mobility and salary issue. The relationship between faculty work load and their salaries was also noted, as was the area of university-provided research opportunities, that is, academic-senate research grants, et cetera. The most popular topic, however, focused on faculty recruitment, promotion, and dismissal. There was clear agreement on the need to end China's current "iron rice bowl" system, whereby "once hired never fired" prevails, and to replace it with a system similar to peer-review systems many scholars witnessed in the United States. One scholar opened this discussion by making the comment, "One of our biggest problems is, to be quite frank, how do we 'get rid of' some of the dead weight in our departments?" Others then commented on the value of implementing a merit-review system, complete with tenure requirements for new entering professors and a more rigorous retirement criteria, including some form of phased retirement for China's aging professional population. Throughout this discussion, the returned scholars continued to focus their comments on the apparent rigidity of the Chinese faculty personnel process and the diversity and perceived flexibility of those institutions in which they had studied in the United States. Given China's history of higher educational development and the tradition of scholars serving the state, it is not likely that the faculty personnel process will be dramatically decentralized in the near future despite pressure from the returned scholars.

Learning

Particularly significant for those Chinese scholars interviewed were learning methods centered on either individualized or experiential learning. Notions such as independent study, on-campus experiential learning, peer teaching, and so on were all areas thought to be important to the future reorganization of higher education in China.

The notion of experiential learning, as practiced in the United States, was especially intriguing. Both off and on campus, experiential learning programs that allow students to engage in activities that partially fulfill requirements for certificates and degrees were viewed from the Chinese perspective as being feasible. Cooperative education programs that allow students to integrate academic study with work experience, internships, and practicums were indentified as desirable additions to China's higher educational structure. Although this slogan is not currently popular, some scholars referred to the concept of combining "theory with practice" to justify how China might adopt experiential learning into its higher educational structure. One scholar remarked that it was ironic that the integration of academic study with work experience (a fundamental Marxist pedagogical principle) was much more developed and accepted in the capitalist United States than in socialist China. However, despite fascination with this concept, most of those interviewed recognized severe implementation difficulties.

Concerns focused on methods of assessment of such experiential learning—in short, how to measure educational outcomes. There was great interest in learning more about U.S. practices and methods used to figure experiential credits into the degree requirements. The scholars demonstrated some knowledge of the parallel, the additive, and the no-credit systems but acknowledged difficulty in implementing such programs, given China's current higher educational structure.

Some of those interviewed commented that Chinese culture is unique and returned scholars have reentry problems because they forgot that fact while abroad. Related to this concern was one that was referred to as the "appropriateness of training received while abroad." One scholar commented that "in American higher education there is too much emphasis placed on individual study and not enough on guided training. This creates difficulty for the Chinese scholar while he is in the United States and again after he returns and meets the relative rigidity of the Chinese system." This scholar and others went on, however, to note that this problem may be more a weakness of the American system than of the Chinese and that American scholars and professors should spend more time training students and junior scholars than they do currently under the "sink or swim" approach. This view was reinforced by another scholar who related how he was given little guidance by his sponsor while in the United States and was simply left to conduct his own research, albeit with excellent laboratory facilities and other material resources. This experience was contrasted with the Chinese treatment of foreign scholars, which is characterized by project teamwork and a full schedule of lectures and other activities (indeed, many American scholars in China complain of the time-consuming full schedules imposed on them by their Chinese hosts). The individualization of much American research was not a comfortable concept to most of the scholars interviewed.

Finally, those interviewed stressed the need better to understand the process of foreign-language instruction, the development of study skills (note taking, organization of research, research methods, etc.), and student grading policies (evaluation and student assessment procedures). Specifically on the language issue there was some criticism that foreign-language instruction in China was divorced from context and only concentrated on the mechanics of the language being learned. Thus Chinese students of English and other foreign languages learned little of the culture and history of the region where the language was dominant. In general, those scholars interviewed were interested in but not totally accepting of learning styles that focused on individually determined goals and objectives.

Curriculum

Closely related to the area of learning were interests in curricular reform in higher education as expressed by the scholars. This was one area where it was felt institutional change could occur more readily, as returned scholars were often looked to for advice in restructuring courses of study in their particular discipline. The procedure for making such changes, however, operated from the bottom up. One scholar related his own experience whereby in redesigning courses and adding new courses in his field he was able to effect curricular change throughout his college. Had he attempted first to approach the central administration with a curricular package, the answer would probably have been negative. In his own words, "One must first build a consensus among colleagues in the department and then approach the vice-president for academic affairs; then change key courses and in an evolutionary manner bring about more general reforms."

Other scholars expressed the desire to increase individually designed programs. There was also a desire that international and interdisciplinary studies in Chinese colleges and universities be increased in line with this emphasis shown in the United States. At the undergraduate level, it was felt that greater emphasis should be placed on curriculum and general educational needs, as opposed to early specialization, and on improving the quality of teacher education (referring to senior middle-school teachers preparing entry-level undergraduates). The present emphasis on early specialization was viewed as part of the Soviet legacy and something that should be reformed. One scholar remarked, "The Soviet Union attempted to impose on us a higher educational system mirroring theirs; there was no effort to adapt it to the special situation in China. The American undergraduate model of a general education is one that better addresses our need to produce a corps of broadly educated citizens as we expand higher educational opportunities."

There appeared to be general fascination with ideas such as competency-based programs and use of media and instructional technology, particularly computer-based instruction in mathematics and science at the under-graduate level. The incorporation of modern library techniques and learning centers were also of interest and something visiting scholars indicated would be of value to higher-learning institutions in China.

Finally, and somewhat surprisingly, scholars noted what they considered to be more advanced and sophisticated use of values or political education. The general perception was that American college and university students were more effectively trained morally and politically than were Chinese youth. There was an interest in replicating this experience in Chinese institutions of higher learning, or at an earlier point if that was where it had occurred, through curricular reform. It was noted that "political education in China still followed too mechanically, the emphasis on ideology imported from the Soviet Union; we must break with this pattern." In general, political education was though to have been carried out in the United States more effectively than in China.

Lifelong Learning

Although many scholars referred to items under this cluster as "adult education," it was clear that a more expanded view of this educational practice was intended. There was interest in developing innovative post-secondary programs that could be alternatives to the current structure of higher education in China. The notion of external degrees emerged several times, as did the idea of developing specific new programs on campus for adults. Acknowledging that problems still exist among the adult population in China's struggle to overcome illiteracy and to maintain literacy, it was suggested that, to reach the adult population, China adopt the university-extension model incorporating special literacy programs. Similar suggestions were made for the vocational-technical area. Since the Cultural Revolution, there has been a less than enthusiastic attempt to continue the education of China's millions of industrial and rural workers. There was knowledge of the effect the Vocational Education Act and the Manpower Development and Training Act had in the United States. Some scholars suggested that the Chinese government play a more active role in incorporating special educational and retraining programs for the work force and not concentrate so heavily on higher educational resources for a few "key" academic universities. Some recommendations made during the interviews described a system, since partially dismantled, strikingly similar to the vast informal and nonformal educational network constructed during the Cultural Revolution.

Suggestions for new lifelong learning programs ranged from giving college credit for life's experiences to allowing radio and television courses college credit. Given China's large college-age population, a small percentage of whom can enter the regular university system, it is understandable that the area of lifelong learning would be of great interest. Yet, a few of the scholars interviewed felt that a major obstacle to developing and implementing "education and work" programs was a culturally imbedded aversion to manual labor. Given a choice, it was suggested, parents of college-age children would prefer to enroll their children in one of the standard universities rather than in a vocational and technical education program, regardless of the student's abilities. An interesting comment from one scholar suggested, "While in the United States I observed that even college professors and other professionals pride themselves on having a history of manual labor in their family. Either their parents rose from the working class or they themselves worked part-time in a factory or other productive enterprise. Furthermore, they continue to value their ability to 'fix things' around the house, and indeed some of their garages were virtual workshops. This positive attitude toward manual labor is virtually absent among China's educated classes. It is no wonder the American professional parents are more positively disposed to sending their children to a vocational educational program if that is what they are best suited for." This particular respondent proposed that these antilabor attitudes would have to be reformed through more effective political-moral education.

Student Affairs

Since many of the visiting scholars attended classes and, in general, were engaged in student activities, they were aware particularly of differences between student life in the United States and in China. Of particular interest was the idea of building into the structure of individual departments and schools a special office of student affairs, with administrative support, staff, and a budget. The perception of student life in the United States was that relations with faculty were informal and friendly, that students received both personal and career counseling at the department level, that financial support of various kinds (work study, merit, need, etc.) was available, and that students were involved not only in student governmental efforts but also on many campuses as part of the university administration. In short, there was general amazement that students in the United States were not solely engaged in academic pursuits but also involved in a variety of extramural activities. Some scholars noted that this range of student involvement in clubs, fraternities and sororities, and student government and university administration provided a very effective form of political socialization and contributed to the relative stability of American college campuses. By contrast, some scholars described the post–Cultural Revolution period as being almost devoid of any student-organized activities. Despite some new encouragement from educational officials for university students to take a more active interest in politics and society, students themselves viewed this as a dead end. One faculty member confided that, if a student approach him with an interest in participating in social and political activities organized by the Communist Youth League, he advised against it and instead urged the student "to continue his studies because you don't know when the next political campaign will come along and you will be on the wrong side."

Other areas of interest related to the American university were student housing practices, health programs, and academic-policy formation processes. There was general agreement that China's higher educational system, with respect to the whole area of student affairs, would need to undergo significant reform if changes based on the U.S. model were to be made.

Administration and Management

The general area of university administration and management also aroused the interests of most scholars interviewed. Before getting into this discussion, however, several scholars reminded me of the inherent historical legacy of the Soviet Union in Chinese higher education, which resulted in an unwieldy, overly specialized, too compartmentalized university administrative pattern. Their own experiences while in the United States introduced them to two major models of university administration, which can be called "faculty governance" and "administrator's schools." The decentralized and committee-based system, such as that which prevails in the University of California, intrigued several of the scholars. Despite the fact that the University of California system is large and, on the individual campuses, bureaucratic, faculty committees wield a great deal of power when compared to universities where deans and other high-level administrators are primary decision makers.

Of interest, as well, was the variety of financing schemes utilized by American colleges and universities and the relative roles of state funding as opposed to extramural funds. The notions of private universities and various private-public configurations were viewed as possible directions for higher education in China. It was suggested that higher education, like industry, might experiment with the concept of "joint enterprises," attracting capital and resources from abroad (Hong Kong was mentioned specifically) and integrating this with existing universities and colleges in China. Utilizing grants for research purposes was also of interest to those interviewed, whether such funds were generated within China or attracted from outside. What most of the scholars were rejecting was the concept of a centrally administered and funded system of higher education. A host of other issues emerged as well, in such areas as admissions practices, organization of the school calendar, use of computer technology in general administration, various methods employed for record keeping, funding and construction of new facilities, and differing methods of long-range planning. Generally impressive to the Chinese scholars was the diversity that characterized American higher education. When asked about the feasibility of implementing administrative changes, it was made clear that the central authorities are getting ideas from the returned scholars and are beginning slowly to make administrative and management reforms. The reforms envisioned thus far are to increase university autonomy generally and, specifically, to extend autonomy for individual and group research projects.

Intra- and Interuniversity Organizations and Cooperation

A final cluster of interest developed around the idea of university consortia and exchange programs. Some scholars participated in various programs, such as in the "college within a college" present on some American campuses and in different university-to-university exchange programs. These unique efforts to expand the horizons of higher education were seen as feasible within the Chinese context. It was generally thought that, while in the near future overall reform (of higher educational administration) was unlikely, individual universities and programs within universities could, under the leadership of interested faculty, develop alternative higher educational experiences through the mechanism of consortia and exchange programs. One such effort has already begun in the Beijing area, pulling together the resources of several area university faculty and some government offices. This organization is called the Social University (*Shehui Daxue*) and is being tested as a model for possible nationwide adoption.

Conclusion

In the flurry of activity surrounding the current U.S.-PRC exchange program it is at least clear that the Chinese have entered a new phase in their centuries-old history of scholarly exchanges with other nations. This time the commitment appears strong, the pace is intensive, and the focus is narrow yet potent—science and technology. Despite what appears to be an embracing of Western techniques and technologies, there is still a concerted effort to "make foreign things serve China" and to avoid dragging along the baggage of Western political-economic structures and the accompanying value system with the hardware. The hope, at least among official spokesmen, is that China can find its own modernization route while not abandoning the "Chinese road to socialism" and can develop in a specifically Chinese way.

However, initial evidence suggests that among the returned scholars there is an overt desire not only to transfer the techniques and technologies learned in the West but also to transform institutions and interpersonal relations in line with practices in the West and Japan. With respect to the United States, a desire to reform higher educational institutional relations can be seen, ranging from those involving student and faculty concerns, to administration and management, and finally to wholesale curriculum reform. Returned scholars have brought home with them not only knowledge of computers and plasma physics but also a whole range of administrative, management, and institutional forms that in their minds are closely associated with the knowledge thus obtained.

The cautiousness and initial reluctance demonstrated by the returned scholars interviewed suggests that forces of reaction may be present and building. At Beijing Normal University particularly, some returned scholars indicated that faculty associated with the now-discredited Cultural Revolution are still active members of various departments and that the two factions do not speak to each other. There is evidence that China's policy toward the West is beginning to undergo stress and strain over Taiwan and a variety of other issues. Recent reports indicate a possible rapprochement with the Soviet Union, beginning with improved relations with Eastern Europe and leading to a possible realignment of Chinese-Russian relations. American-Chinese relations are precarious at best, and several scholars openly expressed fears that the day may come when their experience abroad and their suggestions for institutional reform at home may be a stigma resulting in ruined careers or worse. For now, however, the "modernizers" are hopeful that the current trend toward pragmatism—Deng Xiaoping's "whatever works" philosophy—will continue to prevail and that China's future will be one of successfully mixing Chinese socialism with Western technology and techniques.

Professorial Training and Institution Building in the Third World: Two Rockefeller Foundation Experiences

JAMES S. COLEMAN*

This essay compares efforts undertaken by the Rockefeller Foundation to further the advanced professional education of prospective members of the professoriate located in the highly contrasting national settings of two very different developing countries. It seeks to identify the various factors associated with the success or failure of those efforts and the lessons learned about the opportunities for and the limits to external assistance in the formative phase of the creation of the indigenous professoriate and their institutions. Broader issues raised and illuminated by the study include the effects of the sociopolitical-cultural environment and the professional infrastructure in home countries on the reception, retention, and professional performance of the first generation of those members of the professoriate educated abroad; the alternatives to the full-term Ph.D. program of study in a foreign university as a mode of university academic staff development; and the effects of employing meritocratic criteria for the recruitment of candidates for overseas training on the societies concerned.

In its 70-year history as the oldest of America's private foundations continuously engaged in international programs, the Rockefeller Foundation developed and utilized a variety of strategies for the global advancement and diffusion of knowledge—the liberation of the creative and gifted individual, the development of a discipline, the amelioration of a critical problem in the human condition, and the building and development of academic scientific institutions. In all four strategies the core ingredient—the centerpiece—has been the priority of training individual intellectual and scientific leaders. Institution building, the fourth strategy, has been a part of the foundation's repertoire since the 1920s, symbolized most notably by the Peking Union Medical College (PUMC) in China.[1] In the mid-1950s it launched an "Expanded Program" explicitly

Grateful acknowledgment is due to the following colleagues who read and offered valuable comments on an earlier version of this paper: Joseph E. Black, Ralph K. Davidson, James S. Dinning, Howard Elliott, Willoughby Lathem, and M. Crawford Young.

* Professor of political science and director of the Council on International and Comparative Studies at the University of California, Los Angeles.

[1] Mary Brown Bullock, *An American Transplant: The Rockefeller Foundation and Peking Union Medical College* (Berkeley and Los Angeles: University of California Press, 1980); Alan Gregg, "Report of the Commission Sent by the Rockefeller Foundation to China to Study the Problem of the Development

directed toward university institution building in less developed countries (LDCs). By 1960 it had active programs with 35 LDC universities and research institutes. To counter a drift toward scatteration and to impose a sharper focus, the trustees of the foundation in 1961 formally approved the University Development Program (UDP), which envisaged a 10–15-year commitment at an estimated cost of over $100 million. Under this new mandate, the officers in the ensuing decade (the "first phase") initiated UDP activities in 10 LDC universities while at the same time phasing out programs in others. In 1972–73 the name of the program was changed to Education for Development (EFD), and three additional "second-phase" universities were added to the program. Finally, in 1977 the trustees decided on orderly termination of the UD/EFD program at all centers by the end of 1983.[2] This essay reviews two of these experiences.

The central declared objective of the foundation's UDP was the creation of a critical mass of well-trained, indigenous scholars who could assume the intellectual and scientific leadership in building strong, high-quality LDC universities. Two key mechanisms were employed, both aimed at indigenous staff development. One was the foundation's fellowship for advanced, usually full-term Ph.D., education anywhere outside the students' own countries, but mainly in the United States or other Northern countries; these fellowships were awarded to meritorious indigenous candidates in a selection process in which foundation officers participated and had the final word. The other was the foundation-recruited and -financed interim expatriate professors who would initiate the institution-building process and "hold the fort" pending the return of their professionally qualified indigenous successors. The latter mechanism, involving direct foundation participation through their own personnel, can be characterized as an "operating" as opposed to a "dispensing" mode; it had been used extensively

---

of Medicine and Public Health," November 15, 1946, Rockefeller Foundation Archives, New York. For a critical analysis, see E. Richard Brown, "Rockefeller Medicine in China: Professionalism and Imperialism," in *Philanthropy and Cultural Imperialism,* ed. Robert F. Arnove (Boston: G. K. Hall, 1980), pp. 123–46.

[2] The original universities selected after a global canvass included the Universidad del Valle, Cali, Colombia; the University of Khartoum, Sudan; the University of Ibadan, Nigeria; the University of East Africa; Thammasat, Kasetsart, and Mahidol universities in Bangkok, Thailand; and the University of the Philippines at Diliman, Los Baños, and Manila. During the 1960s, UDP activities were also initiated at the University of Chile at Santiago and the Federal University of Minas Gerais, Brazil, but these, together with the program at the University of Khartoum, were terminated early. In 1970 the University of East Africa ceased to exist, and its three constituent colleges emerged as separate universities (the University of Nairobi, Kenya; Makerere University, Kampala, Uganda; and the University of Dar es Salaam, Tanzania) at each of which UDP activities continued. In 1973 activities were launched at the three second-phase universities: the National University of Zaire at Kinshasa, Lubumbashi, and Kizangaui; Gadjah Mada University, Yogyakarta, Indonesia; and the Federal University of Bahia, Salvador, Brazil. See Laurence D. Stifel, Ralph K. Davidson, and James S. Coleman, eds., *Social Sciences and Public Policy in the Developing World* (Lexington, Mass.: D. C. Heath, 1982), pp. 57–82; Rockefeller Foundation, *The President's Review and Annual Report, 1977* (New York: Rockefeller Foundation, n.d.), pp. 41–43.

over the years in the foundation's highly successful health and agricultural programs in LDCs.

In the LDC operating mode, projects and programs in their early stages would be conceived and directed, and frequently even administered, by the foundation's own professional field staff, with due deference to local input, leadership, and the ultimate goal of full indigenization. This was believed to set standards and to enhance professionalism, to ensure fiscal probity in the use of funds, and to accelerate achievement of goals with minimal encumbrance by the obstacles and constraints of the local environment. The dispensing mode was typically used in making grants to educational and research institutions in the United States and Europe. Recipient institutions were responsible not only for administering and accounting for the funds but also for seeing that projects were executed by their own personnel. The operating mode was particularly favored by agriculturalist J. George Harrar, who in 1960 assumed the presidency of the foundation and fathered the UDP.[3]

As the UDP got under way it became increasingly apparent that regular field staff had to be supplemented by nonfield staff "visiting professors"; by the end of the program, of the more than $43 million expended on expatriate staffing, 64 percent went to support field staff and 36 percent to cover visiting professors under a variety of funding arrangements.[4] Even among those holding the status of field staff, a significant number were visiting professors on maximum 2-year leaves from their home universities and not career professional employees of the foundation self-consciously engaged in any direct sense in the "foundation program." They were given no instructions by and were not expected to report to the foundation. Foundation policy emphasized that their identity should be with the department in which they were serving. This had the advantage of maximizing the image of the foundation as a source of neutral, non-interventionist assistance. Nor did more than a small minority hold authority (line) positions as deans or department heads in the UDP universities in which they served, contrary to the expectations of some. The net result was that the expatriate staff who served in the UDP was remarkably heterogeneous and the legacy of its members extraordinarily heterodox as regards ideology and theoretical orientation in the different disciplines.

Whatever its makeup, the expatriate professoriate was ideally expected to perform several key functions in the institution-building and staff-

[3] J. George Harrar, "A Proposed RF Operating Program in Foreign Universities," March 11, 1960, Rockefeller Foundation Archives, New York, pp. 1–3.

[4] One major constraint in the expansion of field staff to meet the expanding commitments of the UDP was not only their escalating cost but also Harrar's desire to avoid a repetition of the painful experience of dismantling a massive corps of career field staff on the foundation's books, as had to be done in the early 1950s when it was decided to phase out the International Health Division, the first major overseas operating program of the foundation.

development process, including (1) service in interim leadership roles in the university where this was desired and politically tolerable, (2) assistance in the identification of the most outstanding candidates for foundation fellowships, (3) provision of leadership and senior counsel in the development of the curriculum and degree structure and in launching new specializations and research programs, and (4) furthering where appropriate the development of new postgraduate degree programs designed to accelerate the indigenization process. Above all, Harrar repeatedly insisted, they were not to be "mere teachers," carrying heavy teaching loads in basic courses and thereby contributing to the socialization of newly arrived indigenous colleagues into role expectations of light teaching loads and opportunities for moonlighting and second jobs.

The quality of the performance of the expatriate professors was relative to time and place and to personal disposition and competence. A few were maximally self-serving, while many others were highly motivated and dedicated and left a deep imprint on the institution they served. Moreover, the roles and the functions they could acceptably and effectively perform evolved over time. In the early 1960s in Africa, as in Mahidol University, expatriate leadership was required provisionally in line (i.e., departmental chair) positions; as indigenization of staff progressed, only senior staff with special expertise in graduate guidance were still needed. The original UDP conception of a clearly identifiable "team" of field staff functioning in an operating mode with high visibility at the commanding heights of the university was only fleetingly possible during a particular phase, and then only at particular centers; it was counterproductive in others, and it was unacceptable in all centers at later stages.

It was not the magnitude of its commitment that was distinctive about the Rockefeller Foundation's experience in university staff development and institution building during the decades of the 1960s and 1970s. During that period the foundation expended over $135 million, but for the same purpose and starting early in the 1950s, the U.S. Agency for International Development spent more than $1 billion—indeed, at one point it was assisting 75 universities;[5] the Ford Foundation spent more than $250 million;[6] the British government through the Inter-University Council for Higher Education Overseas was a vital source of support for an array of new universities in former British colonies;[7] and as part of its billion-dollar-a-year aid program, the French government was providing virtually

[5] John J. Hilliard, "A Report on the Agency for International Development Assistance to Developing Country Universities, 1960–1980" (Rockefeller Foundation, New York [1981?], photocopy).

[6] Joyce L. Moock, "Ford Foundation Assistance to University-Level Education in Developing Countries" (Rockefeller Foundation, New York, 1980, photocopy).

[7] Richard C. Griffiths, "Review of British Assistance to University Development in the Third World" (Rockefeller Foundation, New York, 1980, mimeographed).

all support for new universities in francophone Africa. Nor was there anything particularly unique about the inputs provided by these various agencies—the standard fare consisted of visiting professors, scholarships, equipment, library support, and teaching materials. Rather, the foundation's distinctiveness was the combination of its explicit long-term commitment to specific universities; its field-staff operating mode, however incompletely applied; its breadth of disciplinary engagement and the concomitant concern, however insubstantially fulfilled, for the development of the institution as a whole; and the close integration of its fellowship program into a particular institution-building commitment.

Here we will focus on the "academic staff development" dimension of two of the foundation's UDP experiences: Mahidol University in Bangkok, Thailand (a first-phase, 1963–75 UDP center) and the National University of Zaire (a second-phase, 1973–80 case). Juxtaposition of these two extremely contrasting cases strikingly underscores the enormous diversity among LDCs and the distortions and misconceptions engendered by regarding them as homogeneous and belonging to a common typological category.

An ancient independent kingdom with a very highly developed civilization that escaped a colonial experience, Thailand possesses a relatively homogeneous and assimilative (as regards its Chinese minority) culture with a strong sense of national unity. It has been able to maintain a balance, admittedly precarious at times, between the preservation of its own very unique culture and both the self-generating pressures for modernization from the royalty and the technocratic class and the intermittent, but cumulative, pressures for greater democracy from newly mobilized elements. A constitutional monarchy since 1932, real political power, with a few exceptions, has been in the hands of a military oligarchy, whose rule has been marked by factional infighting, with a measure of stability being provided by the king, the powerful university-educated technocratic class, and a consistently successful pattern of economic performance.[8] By the early 1960s Thailand had a comparatively well-developed university system with higher educational planning and rationalization of university control replacing an earlier tradition in which the universities were "monocollegiate" professional training schools for particular government ministries.[9]

By sharp contrast, Zaire is a country of extreme cultural heterogeneity whose peoples suffered not only harsh precolonial exploitation but also a 50-year colonial experience that was among the most paternalistic, au-

---

[8] Laurence D. Stifel, "Technocrats and Modernization in Thailand," *Asian Survey* 16, no. 12 (December 1976): 1184–96.

[9] Keith Watson, *Education Development in Thailand* (Hong Kong: Heinemann Asia, 1980), pp. 193–210.

thoritarian, and penetrative in history. The colonial educational system virtually excluded the Zairian youth from secondary and higher educational opportunities, a fact starkly demonstrated by the existence of only 16 Zairian university graduates at independence in 1960. Since then the country has witnessed 5 years of anarchy and civil war followed by consolidation of monolithic personalistic power over all sectors of activity by one of Africa's most corrupt and corrupting, and seemingly irremovable, presidential monarchs.[10]

In contemplating the initiation of a program in Zaire, there were sufficient reservations harbored by some officers that, despite the signing of a formal agreement with the goverment of Zaire in 1973, the foundation continued to regard at least the agricultural and medical aspects of the venture as mere "explorations."[11] In contrast to this lingering hesitation, at Mahidol there was high expectation of success from the start. This difference in psychological climate at the commencement of the two programs probably had some effect on the final outcomes.

The Mahidol Technical Success

The core of the foundation effort at Mahidol University was the development, virtually from scratch, of six life science departments in the Faculty of Science. Employing the fellowship and field-staff mechanisms in tandem, 30 highly promising young Thai scholars were identified by the Thai dean and awarded foundation fellowships for Ph.D. programs in the United States in relevant disciplines. Although the recommendation of the foundation's field-staff representative was essential, and the final decision of the fellowship committee in New York was decisive, the nominations of fellowship candidates by the indigenous dean were almost always respected, within the obvious limits of the fellowship budget.

During the trainees' study abroad, a total of 22 Rockefeller Foundation field-staff members were phased in and out of service at Mahidol, spending varying periods (the average being 4 years) in the faculty. Five of them served as acting department heads for 6–9 years until the return of their trained Thai successors. During their service they set the pattern for teaching courses and organizing the curriculum; when the new Thai Ph.D.'s returned, their field-staff counterparts remained for an overlap period to induct them into departmental processes and the teaching and research program. By 1975 the faculty was entirely Thai.

The Mahidol program was clearly an outstanding technical success, fulfilling the model Harrar had in mind in advocating the operating

---

[10] James S. Coleman and Ngokwey Ndolamb, "Zaire: The State and the University," in *Politics and Education*, ed. R. Murray Thomas (Oxford: Pergamon Press, 1983), pp. 55–56.

[11] Edouard Bustin, "Education for Development: National University of Zaire, a Review" (Rockefeller Foundation, New York, August 1979, photocopy), pp. 1–6.

program mode. Three of the indicators of that success are the return rate, the professional performance of the returnees, and the institutional performance of the faculty. First, there was a remarkably high return and retention rate (80 percent) of the Thais who completed their Ph.D.'s and returned home to take up the positions for which they had been trained. Moreover, in 1983, 8 years after the exercise had been completed, all returned Thai scholars were still serving in their departments, 3 of them as chairmen. Second, these new Thai staff returnees have established and maintained an impressive record of productivity in research and publication, reflected in the more than 200 articles in international professional journals they have authored during a recent 5-year period and in the accelerating numbers participating in international professional meetings.[12] Third, the Mahidol faculty through 1978 had produced 34 Ph.D.'s and 270 master's in the life sciences. Recipients of those degrees now constitute a substantial majority of the teaching staff in the preclinical departments at the newly established medical schools in the provincial universities of Thailand. The Mahidol Faculty of Science thus served in important respects as a national center for graduate studies and cadre formation in the life sciences.

Several critical factors help to account for the successful outcome of the Mahidol program. One was the scrupulous Thai fulfillment of all of its undertakings: the presence and cooperative leadership of two successive Thai rectors spanned a 15-year period (1964–79), assuring continuity and sustained institutional commitment; promised new buildings and physical plant were provided; appropriations for the recurrent budget of the faculty remained stable; and the university library budget was significantly augmented, pari passu with the phaseout of foundation support. A second factor was the collaborative development of and agreement on a concrete detailed plan covering the entire exercise before it was launched, a plan that identified specific measurable objectives and a schedule that was adhered to at every step until completion. A third factor was provision by the foundation of the requisite funding in terms of magnitude, duration, flexibility, and immediate availability. This included coverage of the full costs of the 30 fellowships, the 22 expatriate field staff, scientific equipment and library materials, and support services as well as a senior scientist who served as the Rockefeller Foundation representative in Bangkok for 13 years, first to plan and then to monitor the progressive fulfillment of the plan. Mahidol was a comparatively costly project (approximately $11 million, a bit less than 10 percent of the total global UDP/EFD expenditures), but at no point did finance appear to constitute a constraint.

Another crucial ingredient was the cooperative assurance by the university and by the foundation of attractive and competitive conditions for

---

[12] J. Wayne Reitz, "Education for Development: Mahidol University, Bangkok, 1963–78, a Review" (Rockefeller Foundation, New York, February 1979, photocopy), pp. 72–79.

the reception and retention of the newly trained returning Thai scientists. These conditions included an assurance of an established position in the faculty, a salary supplement for meritorious teaching and research intended to ensure that emoluments of Thai staff were competitive with alternative opportunities in government or the private sector,[13] and the creation of a mature research environment endowed with the requisite scientific equipment, library resources, and other support services that made meaningful pursuit of a professional scientific career both possible and rewarding. Indeed, in the Faculty of Science staff members spend on average approximately half their time on research.

A reward structure very favorable to a Ph.D. returnee from abroad was also deeply rooted in Thai culture. In Thailand, as elsewhere in mainland Asia, a special legitimacy has long been accorded the learned official. The Thai bureaucracy has been a powerful force favoring higher education, which serves as a device for elite reproduction; bureaucratic families are enabled through the higher-education system to preserve their social position over several generations and to maintain a "calibrated correspondence between university attainments and official position and salary."[14] In his study on the rate of return to education in Thailand, Blaug concludes that "education alone contributes more to the explanation of age-specific earnings than any other variable," that the reward structure ensures that M.A.'s earn more than B.A.'s and Ph.D.'s earn more than M.A.'s, and that a Thai with a Ph.D. from a foreign university had a significant income-earning advantage over a colleague with a Thai Ph.D.[15] This helps further to explain the favorable Thai return and retention rate.

Even though the UD/EFD program at Mahidol was officially phased out in the mid-1970s, foundation support for research continued to flow uninterruptedly to the university under other programs (mainly the "Great Neglected Diseases" program). Between 1979 and 1982 the total granted

[13] The Thai university professoriate is part of the public service and as such is disadvantaged by the rigidities of that service. The devastating effects this would have had on the retention of Thai scientists inspired a successful demarche, before the program got under way, to the Thai prime minister and the director of the Bureau of the Budget by the foundation representative and the dean of the Faculty of Sciences. The proposal made by the latter two was approved, namely, that a special $1-million endowment for salary supplementation be created, the income from which would be for grants for meritorious teaching and research to professorial staff in the Mahidol Faculty of Sciences. Emphasis is on "retention" as the indicator of successful institutionalization. Under Thai law scholarship recipients are effectively bonded to "return" to the positions for which advanced training has prepared them; otherwise the value of their fellowships must be repaid.

[14] Richard C. Kraus, William E. Maxwell, and Reeve D. Vanneman, "The Interests of Bureaucrats: Implications of the Asian Experience for Recent Theories of Development," *American Journal of Sociology* 85 (July 1979): 135–55.

[15] Mark Blaug, "An Economic Analysis of Personal Earnings in Thailand," *Economic Development and Cultural Change* 23, no. 1 (October 1974): 24, 31. I am indebted to Howard Elliott for drawing my attention to this point.

was $325,400, an average of more than $80,000 per year.[16] Because of the faculty's reputation for maintaining international standards of excellence, it has attracted and continues to receive substantial research grants from a variety of international funding agencies.

Other factors also contributed to the Mahidol success. The program began in a situation of maximum plasticity, permitting the foundation to get in on the ground floor unencumbered by constraining traditions, by the rigidities of established structures, by the resistance of threatened incumbents, or by obstructive penetrations—political, ideological, or otherwise—from the university's external environment. The foundation's representative to the universities in Bangkok observed, "We were not faced with the problem of upgrading the faculty; we were faced with the problem of creating one, because in 1963 there were no modern life scientists in Thailand, not a single, solitary one."[17] Linked to this was the singularity of the opportunity to create the vital core of what could become the nation's—indeed, the region's—leading Faculty of Science. This made achievements more easily measurable and unambiguously creditable.[18] Also, the ambience of the early 1960s was maximally receptive, hospitable, and cooperative. It was the halcyon period of uncritical acceptance of human capital theory, of the acknowledged desirability of foreign aid, and even of tolerance of expatriates holding authority positions temporarily in the LDC institutions they were trying to build.

One major objective of the Mahidol institution-building program was not achieved. This was the expectation that it would become a regional exemplar, a center of excellence for the life sciences that would be a pole of gravitation for graduate training and advanced degrees for the Southeast Asian region as a whole. The high promise that it could and would perform this role was one reason for trustee approval as well as for the heavy investment made in Mahidol. Powerful arguments supported the pre-

[16] Rockefeller Foundation, *The President's Review and Annual Report, 1979* (New York: Rockefeller Foundation, n.d.); Rockefeller Foundation, *The President's Review and Annual Report, 1980* (New York: Rockefeller Foundation, n.d.); Rockefeller Foundation, *The President's Review and Annual Report, 1981* (New York: Rockefeller Foundation, n.d.); Rockefeller Foundation, *The President's Review and Annual Report, 1982* (New York: Rockefeller Foundation, n.d.). Mahidol is the front-runner among those very few ex-UDP/EFD institutions that could claim to benefit from the 1977 declaration of intent by the foundation when it terminated the EFD program, namely, that a special effort would be made to continue foundation interest in EFD universities in LDCs under its other ongoing programs. See Rockefeller Foundation, *The President's Review and Annual Report, 1977* (n. 2 above), p. 43. Thus, both in its birth and in its maturity Mahidol has served as a model.

[17] "Proceedings of a Meeting for UDP Review of the Rockefeller Foundation," November 20, 1972, Rockefeller Foundation Archives (typescript), p. 70.

[18] "By 1975, eight years after the program started, the faculty was completely staffed by Thais. . . . Each department which enjoyed substantial Foundation support now has a solid core of faculty holding the Ph.D. None existed in 1965" (Reitz, p. 64). By January 1979 the faculty had 102 members of teaching staff, 50 of whom held a Ph.D.; thus other sources of staffing assistance had been active as well. However, it was the foundation's assistance that produced the core and helped to create the genetic imprint of professional standards through the field-staff members who served as founding heads of departments.

sumption of such a regional role. The basic life sciences are not culture bound; hence, there would be no deterrence to study abroad on the grounds of cultural nationalism. The language of instruction was to be universal scientific English. The cost savings per student from the region would be enormous: a 4-year Ph.D. program at Mahidol would cost a little over $5,000, whereas the same program in the United States would be $20,000 and, later, double that. Donor agencies would find the cost-effectiveness arguments for their support of a facilitating scholarship program irresistible. Moreover, the Los Baños campus of the University of the Philippines had already convincingly demonstrated the feasibility of the regional center of excellence idea for agriculture. In fact, during the period 1969–74, 20 candidates enrolled in Mahidol from Indonesia, Malaysia, and the Philippines, and six of these completed the Ph.D. and 12 the master's degree. Commencing in 1975, however, the number of candidates enrolled from other Southeast Asian countries dropped to zero, and in 1978 there were no applicants at all from elsewhere in the region. Why? World Health Organization scholarship funds had ended, and, more decisively, with the departure of the last English-speaking expatriate professor, Thai became the language of instruction.[19]

Despite its technical perfection in both design and execution, nagging doubts about the appropriateness of the massive investment in Mahidol were recurrently raised. In a retrospective review of the program, one senior officer remarked, "We wouldn't do it again, but since it was done, we're glad that it was done well."[20] At the core of the doubts was a concern that the investment in Mahidol produced a research orientation in science that was not explicitly committed to an understanding and amelioration of the immediate problems of development in Thailand, that the preclinical sciences being taught to future medical students were designed to serve a Western system of medical education that was not appropriate for a developing country like Thailand, and that such a system was inherently both self-perpetuating and unadaptable to the health care needs of the mass of the population.

[19] Reitz, p. 83.

[20] "Transcription of Conference on the Review of the Review of the UD/EFD Program," September 25–29, 1979 (discussion of Thailand, author's files, typescript), p. 12. At the same conference a distinguished medical educator and former foundation trustee questioned whether the American model of medical research tied to medical schools is the best for LDCs and stated that he was "not sure that the mission at Mahidol was the most appropriate one." Midway in the Mahidol project the same sort of doubt was expressed by the late John Knowles, also a distinguished medical educator, shortly after assuming the presidency of the foundation in 1972: "Forty-five percent of the research is not in areas of any prime concern . . . , has no immediate implications for the developing countries other than taking the long-range view of developing fine scientists and their universality. . . . It still sticks in my craw that no matter what we say, we still have a [large] body of advanced western science going on in the universities of developing countries" ("Proceedings of a Meeting for UDP Review of the Rockefeller Foundation," pp. 79–80). See also Peter J. Donaldson, "Foreign Intervention in Medical Education: A Case Study of the Rockefeller Foundation's Involvement in a Thai Medical School," *International Journal of Health Services* 6, no. 2 (1976): 265–66.

This concern was related to the "Great Debate" among health scientists over the content and orientation of medical education in LDCs: Should it aim at inculcating the highest standards and the creation of a specialized, professional medical elite working in hospitals and providing acute medical care mainly for the upper classes and urban populations? Or should it concentrate primarily on a more practical and mass-oriented training of large numbers of paramedical personnel serving the overwhelming majority of the population in the rural areas? Positions in the debate tended to become polarized and ideologized, posing the issue in either/or terms.

Both orientations had been present in foundation doctrine and practice since the early 1920s. During the epoch of building the Peking Union Medical College in the early 1920s, the doctrine of elitism and adherence to the highest standards was clearly ascendant.[21] Nevertheless, serving as a foundation field-staff member in the same institution at the same time was "Medical Bolshevik" Dr. John Grant, who helped pioneer the development of community medicine and delivery of mass health care in China, presaging in many ways the "barefoot doctor" model.[22] Fifty years later, during the epoch of the UDP, the community medicine doctrine was ascendant. In Ramathibodi Medical Faculty and Hospital, next door to the Mahidol Faculty of Science, four members of the foundation field staff of community medicine persuasion and fame assisted in the development of a community health program and a rural health station.[23]

Like all dichotomies, it would seem that the elite-mass dichotomy in medical education tends to distort, if not falsify, reality. Both approaches have a degree of validity and necessity; indeed, they are mutually complementary and reinforcing. The subsequent role of more than 300 PUMC graduates in China is illuminating in this regard. Peking Union Medical College itself never really became institutionalized because of prolonged foundation overprotectiveness followed by the cataclysmic succession of events in China. Nevertheless, despite their elitist education, PUMC graduates not only provided leadership in public health during the war years but also since the 1950s have emerged as the new China's medical elite. In recent years there has been concern, as Bullock observes, "over the need to replenish the aging corps of highly trained biomedical scientists and professors. As China enters a post-Mao, post–Cultural Revolution

---

[21] Bullock (n. 1 above), pp. 44–45.

[22] Ibid., pp. 158–61. Dr. C. C. Ch'en, the father of China's rural health care delivery system, was a 1929 PUMC graduate. See Conrad Seipp, ed., *Health Care for the Community: Selected Papers of Dr. John B. Grant* (Baltimore: Johns Hopkins University Press, 1963); and esp. Willoughby Lathem, ed., *The Future of Academic Community Medicine in Developing Countries* (New York: Rockefeller Foundation, 1979), pp. 161–68.

[23] John Bryant, *Health and the Developing World* (Ithaca, N.Y.: Cornell University Press, 1969); Willoughby Lathem and Anne Newberry, eds., *Community Medicine* (New York: Appleton-Century-Crofts, 1970).

era, it is becoming clear that there will be a new emphasis upon quality training in all scientific fields. And an aging, dwindling group of PUMC graduates is again being called into service."[24] It is in this context that the senior medical educator who had questioned the appropriateness of the Mahidol project observed: "The irony is that China today badly needs an elite medical school because it already has developed a pretty effective system of medical care . . . ; the Peking Union Medical College graduates are still clearly going to have a profound effect on medicine in China, and maybe that is the most important thing that comes out of these programs—the training of people who can recreate something even though it may have been destroyed."[25]

The Explorations in Zaire

If the program in Mahidol was a virtually flawless exemplar of the application of the UDP institution-building model, the program in Zaire was an exemplar of everything that can go wrong.[26] The undertaking proved to be a far higher risk than originally thought possible. The program was initiated in mid-1972 at a fleeting conjuncture of two circumstances— the existence of strong pressures within the foundation to select a new second-phase UDP institution, preferably in francophone Africa, and Mobutu's Zaire being at its one momentary zenith of promise and credibility. One year later, as Crawford Young notes, "things fell apart, internally and externally."[27] The fate of the program was inevitably affected by Zaire's successive economic catastrophes, regime excesses and misman-agement, and the resultant progressive degradation of conditions in both the university and the society at large. Launched in an atmosphere of cautious exploration, each new unexpected obstacle reinforced a growing skepticism among foundation officers. This led to a forgoing of new initiatives, a progressive narrowing of focus to minimal nurturing of a few residual activities to which commitments had originally been made, and a final decision in 1978 for early but orderly termination.

---

[24] Bullock, p. 229. In 1980 the preclinical (basic life science) part of the Chinese medical curriculum was increased two-and-a-half times.

[25] "Transcription of Conference on the Review of the Review of the UD/EFD Program," p. 10.

[26] A colleague has pointed out that the rhetorical purposes served by the juxtaposed illustrations lead to some possible overstatement—shining success vs. appalling disaster—and that there is some tendency in this analytical mood to exhibit all the dreariest facts and not to search hard for mitigating evidence.

[27] Crawford Young, "Zaire: The Unending Crisis," *Foreign Affairs* 57, no. 1 (Fall 1978): 171. Young recalls the brief halcyon moment before things fell apart: "[In 1972] Zaire would have belonged on the list of secure and stable African countries . . . ; it had real domestic strength and a generally positive external image. . . . Mobutu appeared to have created a new and broadly legitimate political order. . . . Inflation had been halted; there was by 1970 a stable, convertible currency, negligible debt, and ample foreign exchange reserves. Real wages went up. . . . GNP surged well beyond the pre-independence level . . . ; and even agricultural production seemed on the way up" (p. 170).

The expectation that the institutionalization of any innovation or structure would be possible in Mobutu's Zaire proved to be unrealistic. His calculated and adroit use of mechanisms of anti- or deinstitutionalization of any potentially autonomous structure, be it the Zairian public service, the army, or the national university, has been and remains part of his strategy for the survival of his personalistic authoritarian rule. Annual rotations of all personnel in public office (*remaniement*), co-optation and permissiveness regarding corruption while fleetingly in office, strategic insertion into authority roles of confreres from his region (Equator), and, if necessary, punition have been among the mechanisms employed by Mobutu to manipulate and to neutralize the university professoriate and administration, like all other sectors of society.[28]

Quite apart from the difficulties of developing a university under such conditions there were additional disabilities from which the National University of Zaire (UNAZA) and other second-phase UDP/EFD universities of the 1970s suffered. Unlike the close attachment and understanding many New York foundation officers had formed for most first-phase universities and their cultural settings, their feelings about Zaire lacked any close personal or experiential basis. Nor did the new incoming foundation president in 1972 identify with or develop a strong commitment to the decade-old UD/EFD program he inherited from the previous administration; on the contrary, he regretted the fact that he was confronted with three new UDP university commitments made as faits accomplis on the eve of his arrival, thereby reducing for a decade that measure of budgetary flexibility for new programs (which would have amounted to roughly $26 million by 1982) his own administration would like to have initiated. Moreover, these new long-range commitments had been made at the very time the Rockefeller and Ford foundations and other major donors were engaged in a critical reexamination of the relationship between education and development provoked by the growing evidence of donor overinvestment in higher education.[29] At the time, a massive retreat from universities was in progress by virtually all donors except the Rockefeller Foundation. The whole international environment was radically changing—the bullish and buoyant 1960s were becoming the bearish and pessimistic 1970s. Also, a subtle but fundamental metamorphosis was far advanced in LDC attitudes toward foreign aid and in the psychology of the North-South relationship. The fierce determination of developing countries to assert and to preserve their independence, and to be seen by other new

---

[28] Coleman and Ngokwey (n. 10 above), pp. 59 ff. See Robert H. Jackson and Carl G. Rosberg, *Personal Rule in Black Africa: Prince, Autocrat, Prophet, Tyrant* (Berkeley and Los Angeles: University of California Press, 1982), pp. 167–81.

[29] F. Champion Ward, ed., *Education and Development Reconsidered* (New York: Praeger, 1974); Hans N. Weiler, "Education and Development: From the Age of Innocence to the Age of Scepticism," *Comparative Education* 14, no. 3 (October 1978): 179–98.

states as doing so, no longer permitted a highly visible expatriate-professoriate presence, particularly in *postes des commandes*, such as departmental heads or faculty deans. In terms of this environmental change alone, it was inconceivable for the stunning Mahidol success of the late 1960s to be replicated in Zaire in the late 1970s. The second-phase universities in general did not present the single-actor ground-floor opportunities in situations of seemingly unbounded plasticity. All of these major contextual, psychological, and structural differences between the two decades produced a very different ambience for whatever was undertaken in Zaire.

The principal mechanism for staff development, as previously noted, has been the official foundation fellowship awarded for advanced Ph.D. study abroad and administered from the foundation's New York office.[30] By long-standing policy no fellowship could be awarded for a degree program in a candidate's home country. As table 1 shows, the fellowship was almost the exclusive mechanism used at Mahidol, which was appropriate, given the carefully planned and tightly synchronized nature of the foundation's staff-development strategy and the imperative of creating as quickly as possible a critical mass core group that had completed full-term Ph.D.'s in closely related disciplines. At UNAZA, with the social, agricultural, and health sciences spread across three campuses each over 1,000 miles from the other, the program clearly required a different formula. For any staff-development effort to have had a significant impact in any one field the number of fellowships required would have been financially prohibitive for the foundation to undertake. Although the annual appropriation for fellowships remained constant worldwide, maintenance of those already in the graduate pipeline from all ongoing UD/EFD programs devoured most of the funds; there was increasingly little margin for new fellowship awards. Moreover, the cost of an individual full-term Ph.D. fellowship had escalated from around $20,000 in the early 1960s to around $50,000 in the mid-1970s. In addition, the Zairian government and university authorities increasingly encouraged or pressured Zairians to pursue UNAZA doctorates.[31] The combination of these considerations led the foundation, in cooperation with UNAZA, to concentrate staff-development support on individually tailored grants (*stages*) providing partial facilitating support

---

[30] Central administration from New York has served various functions (quality and program control, protection of local foundation representatives and local academic leaders, opportunity for foundation officer guidance on study post and program of study, and adherence to common standards). Flexibly adapted to a variety of categories of recipients, the fellowships range from full-term 5-year Ph.D. fellowships to 1-year (or less) postdoctoral study programs.

[31] The reasons were several: to obviate disaffection or expatriation, which extended residence overseas tended to generate; to affirm cultural independence (*authenticité*) and to counter cultural dependence, particularly in the social sciences and humanities; and to make a virtue out of necessity (i.e., available funding for overseas training should concentrate on the sciences). See Bustin (n. 11 above), pp. 11–12.

TABLE 1
DISTRIBUTION OF UDP/EFD EXPENDITURES: MAHIDOL UNIVERSITY
AND THE NATIONAL UNIVERSITY OF ZAIRE (%)

Category of Expenditure	Distribution of Funding within the Category		Total Foundation Funding of the University	
	Mahidol University	National University of Zaire	Mahidol University	National University of Zaire
Visiting professors:			45	40
Foundation field staff	96	87		
Nonfield staff	4	13		
Total	100	100		
Staff development:			16	29
Foundation fellowships/ scholarships	96	55		
Local staff-development grants (*stages*)	4	45		
Total	100	100		
Foundation-supported fellowships for region	. . .	. . .	1	. . .
Research training support	. . .	. . .	5	5
Equipment	. . .	. . .	15	5
Library/teaching equipment	. . .	. . .	10	2
Operating budget and construction	. . .	. . .	8*	19
Total			100	100
Total in dollars			$10,963,736†	$6,629,743

SOURCE.—Rockefeller Foundation, "Education for Development Centers: Expenditures, Allocations and Appropriations, 1963–1982," Rockefeller Foundation, New York, n.d., photocopy.
   * Mahidol University's proportionate share of total operating costs of universities in Bangkok.
   † Figure for only Faculty of Sciences, Mahidol University.

to doctoral candidates to enable them to complete their dissertations and obtain their degrees largely from a UNAZA base.[32]

The *stage* mechanism had the advantage of being far less costly, thereby making it possible to spread available funding far more broadly. Thus, as table 1 shows, of available staff-development funding in Zaire, 45 percent facilitated in varying ways (some only marginally, others substantially) the professional advancement of 91 doctoral candidates, and 55 percent covered the full (usually 5 years) overseas doctoral programs of 27 Zairian doctorates.[33] *Stages* also seemed to ensure smoother reintegration and

[32] These grants were administered by the local foundation office and included overseas *stages* of up to 6 months to fill critical lacunae (i.e., to enable recipients to pursue an individually tailored program of graduate study and library research [mostly] at a European university or to complete their dissertations in close contact with an expatriate supervisor) as well as to support doctoral field research, usually in Zaire.

[33] Bustin (p. 12) correctly notes that the fellowship formula represented the most cohesive and concentrated form of training as well as intensive exposure to international norms and methods of scholarship and that it can also be the quickest way of completing a doctoral program.

TABLE 2
POSTTRAINING ORIENTATIONS OF FORMER ZAIRIAN FELLOWS AND *Stagiaires* (%)

Orientations	Foundation Fellows (N = 27)	Recipients of Foundation *Stages* (N = 91)	Total (N = 118)
Returned to position intended or another in higher education	41	60	56
Government or private sector	15	23	21
Remained abroad	26	7	11
Completing studies	18	3	7
Deceased/unknown	. . .	7	5
Total	100	100	100

SOURCE.—Author's tracer study of former UDP/EFD fellows and *stagiaires*.

more certain retention of positions on the UNAZA staff. This is shown by the figures in tables 2 and 3, the most revealing of which concern the case of the Department of History (see table 3). Its retention rate is 84 percent (i.e., more than Mahidol's 80 percent), compared to only 41 percent for Zairians who received foundation fellowships for full-term Ph.D. degrees abroad. The vast majority of Zairian members of the professoriate in history in UNAZA obtained their doctorates as foundation *stagiaires;* the only one who received a foundation fellowship is entering his seventh year abroad with return to Zaire still problematic.[34]

From the perspective of the internationality of science and scholarship, however, the short-term *stage* is no substitute for the full-term Ph.D. study program abroad. A brief 6-month period of library research and consultations with one's specialist external adviser in Brussels, Paris, or Quebec does not provide that sustained and total immersion in the culture of an international class university in which one absorbs in depth a broader comparative perspective and understanding.[35] The enormous strains toward a deadening intellectual isolation are omnipresent in most Third World university settings in any event; not to have had a sustained exposure to an intellectually more interactive environment during one's professional formation could only accentuate one's vulnerability to parochialism.

[34] There are other factors that explain the remarkable retention rate in history—the unusual excellence, dedication, and continuity of engagement of several expatriate professors in the department both before and after their departure; an ethos of professional collegiality and of commitment to research and publication that evolved very early in the department's development; the relatively greater commitment to "history" as a felt vocation than to other social sciences, and therefore a greater willingness to tolerate frustration and penury; the lesser marketability of historians in the private sector and for high posts in government (compare in table 3 the career paths of economists); and, for the conduct of local history, the nonessentiality of an expensive infrastructure.

[35] An intermediate formula advocated by some is completion of a 2-year M.A./M.Sc. degree abroad followed by a doctoral degree program in the home country. Where this requires the heavy investment in mastering a new language, not proceeding to the Ph.D. level is seldom considered acceptable. Moreover, in most LDC universities a terminal M.A./M.Sc. has little value in terms of income or career.

TABLE 3

POSTTRAINING CAREER PATHS OF FOUNDATION-SUPPORTED ZAIRIANS AND THAIS (%)

Area of Career Activity	National University of Zaire							Foundation Fellows Only (N = 27)	Foundation Fellows, Faculty of Science, Mahidol University, (N = 30)
	Social Science Lubumbashi Campus (N = 34)	History, Lubumbashi Campus (N = 19)	Economics, Kinshasa Campus (N = 24)	CRIDE* Kisangani (N = 17)	Total Social Science (N = 94)	Other (N = 24)	Total All Fields (N = 118)		
Returned to position intended or another in higher education	53	84	33.3	58	55	58	56	41	80
Government or private sector	18	…	50.0	18	22	17	21	15	4
Abroad (brain drain)	15	11	8.3	…	10	17	11	26	13
Completing studies	12	5	8.3	6	9	…	7	18	…
Deceased/unknown	2	…	…	18	4	8	5	…	3
Total	100	100	99.9	100	100	100	100	100	100

SOURCE.—Author's tracer study of former UDP/EFD fellows and *stagiaires*.
* Centre de recherches interdisciplinaires pour le développement de l'éducation.

A major explanation for the low retention rate of full-term Ph.D. foundation fellows has been the inhospitable reception and the daunting and dispiriting conditions they have confronted on their return to Zaire. Problems with reentry readjustment to local living conditions are predictably common, but usually transient. The alienating and demoralizing circumstances typically encountered were not just the lack of housing or transport but also the discovery that one had no assured position at the university (i.e., all of the assigned courses had been allocated); that one had to wait endlessly before getting on the computer payroll (*mécanisation*);[36] that because of one's specialization one was assigned to a campus 1,000 miles from Kinshasa, the national center of power and of all rewards and opportunities for those who had benefited from foreign training; that there was total absence of even the barest essentials of an infrastructure or support services for a productive academic career; and/or that for survival of one's family a second job and moonlighting, or even retreat to one's home village, were necessary. Added to all this was the veiled, sometimes overt, resentment established faculty members often felt toward new arrivals who had had the advantage of a long American Ph.D. program. Such hostility was evident among two elements in the professoriate already there—*les vieux professeurs,* who had long since abandoned serious scholarship, and the Zairian *assistants,* who had remained behind, quickly completed their UNAZA theses, and now jointly with *les vieux* shared power positions in the university academic hierarchy. As one despairing Ph.D. returnee put it: "Newcomers are always losers in matters of power relationships."[37] The stark contrast between this array of demoralizing conditions of reception confronted by the 27 Zairian returnees and the carefully prearranged reception of the 23 life scientists who returned to Mahidol largely explains the 41 versus 80 percent difference in retention shown in table 3.

In sharp contrast to Thailand, the reward structure in Zaire did not unambiguously and assuredly mean high status and relatively high income for a returning Zairian with a foreign Ph.D. Education in general continued to be highly valued and perceived as the main source of upward mobility, yet almost everyone knows someone who has reached a high position with only limited education. As one observer noted, "Many people returned from five difficult years abroad to find their former classmates in positions as Commissaire or Directeur saying condescendingly, 'Well, my boy, what can I do for you?' "[38] The president himself (who has no degrees) has

[36] A returning fellow "may not get the salary to which he is entitled until a year or more after he has assumed his new professorial duties . . . ; [or] returnees may discover upon assuming their professorial duties that their names have been deleted from the payroll in their absence, in which case they will get no salary at all" (Bustin, p. 21). Theoretically, all Zairian fellowship recipients were guaranteed a university position on return; in fact, in volatile Zaire, whether this was honored depended on whether in the meantime the post had been filled by someone else or no longer existed or on whom one might know close to power at the time.

[37] Private communication.

[38] Private communication.

TABLE 4
BACKGROUND OF FORMER THAI FOUNDATION
FELLOWS: MAHIDOL UNIVERSITY ($N=23$) (%)

Prior education of fellow:	
B.A./B.S.—Australia, U.K., or USA	30.4
Mahidol University	39.2
Other main Thai universities	30.4
Total	100.0
Father's occupation:	
Businessman	43.5
Civil servant	17.4
Professional (physician, teacher)	17.4
Deceased/unstated	21.7
Total	100.0
Ethnic origin:	
Chinese or Chinese descent	100.0

SOURCE.—Author's tracer study of former UDP/ EFD fellows.

stated that a degree is not enough, and his own case certainly proves it. Indeed, a Ph.D. from a prestigious foreign university could not only carry no advantage but also be useless or even a liability. The more ordered wage structure in the Thai case, of course, reflects a more ordered society. In Zaire the elite is less well established, has less of a sense of corporate identity, and is not defined by higher-education credentials. And given the overriding personalism and caprice of Mobutu's system of governance, nothing is stable, including particularly the reward structure for academics.

In one respect the staff-development programs both at Mahidol and in Zaire had very similar effects: both operated unintentionally—in a limited way—to reproduce existing differences in the Thai and Zairian societies.[39] In the UD/EFD program as a whole, operating in LDCs where 80 percent or more of the population are rural peasants, among the fathers of former fellows, 55 percent had completed secondary education and 51 percent were in professional, managerial, or administrative occupations. As the data on Mahidol in table 4 show, nearly 80 percent of the fathers of former fellows either were in the professions or were businessmen or civil servants, and reportedly all were of Chinese descent, although the Chinese constitute a minority of only 10 percent of the Thai population.[40] And the data on Zaire in table 5 confirm the startling ed-

[39] This is a generic and historic phenomenon and is not unique to higher education in LDCs. Hoselitz made the point: "A program designed to enhance high-level manpower training in developing countries is likely to perpetuate and possibly even strengthen, the social inequalities . . . which exist today" (Bert F. Hoselitz, "Investment in Education and Its Political Impact," in *Education and Political Development*, ed. James S. Coleman [Princeton, N.J.: Princeton University Press, 1965], p. 559).

[40] There is an extensive literature on the remarkable degree of assimilation of Chinese into Thai culture and society. Fry has noted that in recruitment to public service discrimination against Thais of Chinese descent does not seem to exist, reflecting a Thai opportunity complex that is impressively open (Gerald W. Fry, "Education and Success: A Case Study of the Thai Public Service," *Comparative*

TABLE 5
REGIONAL (ETHNIC) IMBALANCES IN THE PROFESSORIATE IN ZAIRE (%)

Region	Portion of Total Population (1975)*	Portion of Total Enrolled for Primary-Teacher Training (1973)†	Portion of Total Enrolled for State Examination (July 1981)‡	Portion of Total Social Science Professoriate Faculty, National University of Zaire (1977–78)§	Portion of Total Foundation Staff-Development Recipients, National University of Zaire (N = 118)‖
Kasai—East and West#	15	27	31	39	31
Lower Zaire	7	12	7	10	12
Bandundu	14	11	14	13	10
Shaba	13	12	10	14	8
Kivu	17	8	11	16	19
Upper Zaire	15	13	4	3	4
Equator	12	7	6	5	8
Kinshasa	7	10	17**	. . .	. . .
Unknown	. . .	. . .	. . .	. . .	8
Totals	100	100	100	100	100

SOURCE.—This table is an adaptation of table 3.2 of James S. Coleman and Ndolamb Ngokwey, "Zaire: The State and the University," in *Politics and Education*, ed. R. Murray Thomas (Oxford: Pergamon, 1983), p. 67; it is used with permission.

* J. Boute, "La Population du Zaire d'ici à 1985," *Zaire-Afrique*, no. 133 (Mars 1979), p. 131.

† Department de l'éducation nationale, Direction de la planification, *L'Enseignement au Zaire à la veille du plan national de développement* (Kinshasa: Department de l'éducation nationale, 1977).

‡ *Zaire-Afrique*, no. 153 (Mars 1981) p. 156. Those enrolled for state examination indicate the number who are in their terminal year of secondary education.

§ Bustin (n. 11 above).

‖ Tracer conducted by author among Zairian recipients of fellowships or support for *stages* from the Rockefeller Foundation.

East and West Kasai regions are combined because of the difficulty of distinguishing regional origin of names of the Luba inhabiting both regions.

** A majority of those enrolled during the period 1973–81 in Kinshasa probably came from Kasai, Lower Zaire, and Bandundu regions.

51

ucational advantage of the peoples of Kasai (mainly the Baluba) over the peoples of other regions.[41] In comparing this with the region of origin of recipients of foundation support (fellows and *stagiaires*), shown in the right-hand column of table 5, it is clear that the effect of the foundation program, operating essentially according to meritocratic criteria, was to reproduce the preexisting regional differences. This occurred despite the official Zairian policy since 1971 of imposing regional quotas for admission to the university; had these quotas been respected, there would have been 50 percent fewer Kasaians and far more Equatorians (i.e., those from the president's region). Furthermore, none of the 30 Thai or the 27 Zairian fellows were female; only two women were among the 91 Zairian *stagiaires*, one of whom was the first female *assistant* to have been appointed to the Faculty of Social Sciences of UNAZA.

These imbalances in socioeconomic status, ethnic or regional origin, and sex had their roots deep in the cultural fabric and history of the two societies concerned. They seldom were raised as considerations either by the foundation or by the universities being assisted in the selection of fellowship or grant recipients. Such selection was governed by meritocratic criteria applied nondiscriminatorily to those eligible individuals immediately on the scene, irrespective of ascriptive considerations. The UD/EFD program was not, nor did it essay to be, an affirmative action program, even though, paradoxically, it was a vehicle for upward mobility for well-qualified individuals from minorities in their own setting. Under the changed ethos of our current epoch it can, of course, be argued that interventions to liberate talent have no more compelling justification than interventions to further equality.[42]

A second feature common to the two programs was the disproportionately heavy expenditure on expatriate visiting professors (45 percent of the total budget at Mahidol and 40 percent in Zaire [see table 1] as against an average of 35 percent for the UD/EFD program as a whole) compared to the amount expended on indigenous staff development (16 percent at Mahidol and 29 percent in Zaire). A significant dimension of the role of the visiting professors (both field staff and nonfield staff) was,

---

Education Review 24, no. 1 [February 1980]: 21–34). Stifel ([n. 2 above], p. 189) shows that fathers of three of the five most prominent junior technocrats in the Thai government service are Chinese. See William Edgar Maxwell, "The Ethnic Identity of Male Chinese Students in Thai Universities," *Comparative Education Review* 18, no. 1 (February 1974): 55–69. The statement that the foundation fellows from Mahidol were all of Chinese descent is based on the fact that they considered themselves to be ethnically Chinese. However, many came from families that had resided in Thailand for several generations and spoke Thai at home, and considerable intermarriage had taken place.

[41] The background to these Zairian ethnic and regional imbalances in education is detailed in Coleman and Ngokwey (n. 10 above), pp. 66–71.

[42] One disadvantage of the institution-building focus as compared to the individual scholar focus in staff development is the forced recruitment of candidates from a much smaller pool. Some officers with comparative experience argued that there was a discernible decline in the overall quality of candidates after the foundation's shift to institution building under the UD/EFD program. The disadvantage of the individual approach is the production of a group of stranded individuals without institutional affiliation, which then makes it difficult to assess the impact of the program.

of course, furthering staff development. Ideally this included assisting in the selection of qualified candidates, organizing and teaching courses while prospective indigenous staff members were completing their advanced degrees, supervising research and dissertations, launching and conducting local graduate degree programs designed to produce new staff members for the institutions of the country for generations into the future, and in general preparing the groundwork so that when their successors returned with their Ph.D.'s everything would be ready for them to land running with maximum impact on their profession and the country. In retrospect, however, the issue of proportionality and relative cost effectiveness is unavoidable when it is noted that the total cost of the 22 expatriate staff members at the Mahidol Faculty of Science was just short of $5 million. This could have covered 250 doctoral fellowships in the early 1960s or at least 100 such fellowships in the mid-1970s. Still, had there been no expatriate presence on the return of the Thai Ph.D.'s—that is, in the case of Mahidol, no high-quality ongoing research program or concern with established standards and mechanisms for quality control and a capacity for self-reproduction—would the institution, by the international standards to which the Thais themselves aspire, be as strong as it has turned out to be and have the nationwide impact it has had?[43]

Conclusions

No assessment of the value, impact, and significance of foreign advanced degree programs for Third World scholars aspiring to careers in the professoriate of their home universities can be confined to the quality and relevance of those programs or to the legacy of their overall experience while abroad. These will obviously affect their professional performance. However, of equal or possibly greater importance is the situation that they confront on their return and with which they must work and live during their professional lives, namely, the constraints and opportunities in their university and national environments, the quality and supportiveness of the professional infrastructure, and the prevailing structure of rewards in their society. The contrasting cases of Thailand and Zaire examined here have illuminated the importance of these variables in determining the effectiveness of returning foreign degree holders. The externally assisted effort in Thailand was technically an outstanding success but not a widely replicable model because of the disproportionately heavy financing required for expatriate faculty, a salary supplementation arrangement ensuring retention of indigenous faculty that is inherently ungeneralizable,

---

[43] The issue of relative cost effectiveness as between expatriate staff and indigenous staff development is even more compelling in the Zaire case, where it proved impossible to persist in any institution-building effort. If available, the roughly $2,800,000 expended on visiting expatriate staff for the Zaire program during the period 1972–82 would have made possible nearly 60 additional 5-year Ph.D. fellowships or, alternatively, would have made possible four times the amount actually expended on staff-development grants for Zairian *stages*.

and a radical negative change in the 1970s in the climate of receptivity in LDCs for such large-scale, externally directed interventions. The contrasting abortive experience in Zaire underscores the negative consequences of unsupportive university, societal, and international environments.[44]

The application of meritocratic criteria in the recruitment of candidates for advanced overseas education inherently skews the selection in favor of those groups in the society already advantaged by education, and their return to their home countries after training can further reinforce the preexisting imbalances and elite structure that led to their selection in the first place. Not all imbalances, of course, are equally sensed or resented. But even if they were, this would not constitute an argument either for or against the rigorous application of such criteria. The point is that a program that does not have a specified affirmative action goal is not likely to alter preexisting socioeconomic stratification; and if greater equality of opportunity for various subgroups of a society—whether economic, social, gender, or ethnic—is a desideratum, identification and cultivation of the meritorious among the disadvantaged must be deliberately pursued.

Finally, a notable characteristic of all major investments in development, particularly in the face of unending miscalculations, disappointments, and failures, is the rush to assessment. The fallacy of prematurity in assessment is particularly manifest in human resource investment. Yet past experience strongly suggests that only a decade or two hence can any firm judgments be made regarding outcomes. It was from the foundation fellows of the 1920s and 1930s spread throughout Europe and the United States that many of the Nobel laureates of the 1940s and 1950s appeared, just as it has been from among the remaining Peking Union Medical College graduates of the late 1920s and early 1930s that the new Chinese medical elite has emerged in the 1980s, phoenixlike, to try once again to build institutions, this time more genuinely Chinese in character. The Chinese experience suggests that, while the early signs of achievement may be highly promising, the full weight of the impact of the Rockefeller Foundation fellowship and *stage* programs will not be manifest for another decade or so. Only then will it be possible to make firmer judgments about the performance and achievements of the many exceptional individual scholars who are products of the seemingly faultless investment in Mahidol and the seemingly vain effort in Zaire.

---

[44] The mitigating evidence in the Zairian case is that a high percentage of the candidates— much higher than most American doctoral cohorts—did complete their doctoral programs and a large majority returned to Zaire. Some are heroically exerting a significantly positive role despite the caprices and enormous discouragements and frustrations of the system. Moreover, as a group they constitute a potential nucleus of human resources that might form the basis for a resurrected higher educational system if overall circumstances change.

The Economic and Political Impact
of Study Abroad

GERALD W. FRY*

Study abroad and the related migration of scholars and professionals is a pervasive phenomenon dating back as early as 500–300 B.C., when intellectuals migrated to Athens. In subsequent centuries there were similar migrations to major intellectual centers such as Alexandria, Rome, and Gundi Sapur in East Persia.[1] In the Thai language there is a concept and term, *chup dua*, which connotes acquiring significant prestige by study and/or travel abroad. Study abroad, with its associated cultural dilemmas, is also a major theme in Thai literature.[2]

The migration of scholars seems to be a nearly universal phenomenon, characteristic of most societies with the possible exception of nations with highly isolationist policies, such as Burma and Albania. Americans and Europeans tend, however, to associate the phenomenon of study abroad to enhance prestige as primarily pertaining to Third World societies. Actually the phenomenon is much more pervasive, and in industrial societies such as the United States and Germany study abroad also carries high social prestige. The intense competition for the Marshall, Rhodes, and Fulbright overseas fellowships reflects the importance of study abroad in the United States. Though the study-abroad phenomenon is important in nearly all societies, the focus in this article is on the impact of study abroad in the developing nations.

Related Literature and Research Objectives

Most literature on study abroad has focused on only two principal issues: the problem of cultural adjustment for students from developing nations who go to study in industrial countries such as the United States or the United Kingdom, and the so-called brain drain.[3] In this research, much of which appeared in the 1960s or early 1970s, there is relatively

---

* Assistant professor of political science at the University of Oregon; he has worked for the Ford Foundation in Thailand.

[1] G. Lakshmana Rao, *Brain Drain and Foreign Students: A Study of the Attitudes and Intentions of Foreign Students in Australia, the U.S.A., Canada, and France* (New York: St. Martin's, 1979), p. 161.

[2] See Wibha Senanan, *The Genesis of the Novel in Thailand* (Bangkok: Thai Watanapanich, 1975).

[3] See, e.g., Walter Adams, ed., *The Brain Drain* (New York: Macmillan, 1968); Tai K. Oh, *The Asian Brain Drain: A Factual and Causal Analysis* (San Francisco: R & E Research Associates, 1977); France J. Pruitt, "The Adaptation of African Students to American Society," *International Journal of Intercultural Relations* 2 (Spring 1978): 90–118; and S. J. Jean Barry, *Thai Students in the United States: A Study in Attitude Change*, Southeast Asia Program, Data Paper no. 66 (Ithaca, N.Y.: Cornell University, Department of Asian Studies, 1967).

little, if any, analytical empirical work at the macro, national level to assess the economic and political impact of study abroad.[4] The primary purpose of this article is to attempt a preliminary assessment of the long-run impact of study abroad for a large group of diverse developing nations by presenting an analytical model (quasi-longitudinal) which incorporates a variety of ideological and disciplinary perspectives. I begin with a review of various possible positive and negative effects of study abroad, primarily synthesizing the existing literature on the topic.

Supplementing the global model analysis is a series of case studies on study abroad in Thailand, drawing on both empirical and qualitative data related to the actual activities of Thai students who returned from abroad.

Data Sources

Multiple sources provide the basic empirical data used in the analyses of this article. For the global model testing the long-run impact of study abroad, data are used from 84 developing countries, representing nearly all major Third World nations. The data are from various international agencies, such as Unesco and the World Bank.[5] For the Thai case study data were derived from several sources: (1) a major study of education and occupational attainment in Thailand;[6] (2) an ongoing study of the origins of the Thai elite;[7] (3) a study of the social and educational backgrounds of Thailand's highest-ranking civil servants;[8] (4) impressionistic qualitative data based on approximately 10 years of practical experience in working with many Thais who were former foreign students abroad.

Possible Positive Effects of Study Abroad

Political Development

Homer Barnett, in his important book on innovation, suggests that overseas experience can be a major stimulant fostering social change.[9] Experience in another political, cultural, social, and economic environment can be a powerful motivating force. In Thailand, for example, the major momentum for a shift from absolute to constitutional monarchy came from a group of younger intellectuals and military officers sent to France

---

[4] Michael J. Flack, "Results and Effects of Study Abroad," *Annals of the American Academy of Political and Social Sciences* 424 (March 1976): 116–17.

[5] *Statistics of Students Abroad, 1962–1968: Where They Go, Where They Come from, What They Study* (Paris: Unesco, 1971); and *World Development Report 1982* (New York: Oxford University Press, 1982), pp. 112–13.

[6] Gerald W. Fry, "The Educational Correlates of Occupational Attainment: A Bangkok Case Study of Large-Scale Organizations" (Ph.D. diss., Stanford University, 1977).

[7] Gerald W. Fry, "The Origins of the Thai Elite" (in preparation).

[8] Likhit Dhiravegin, *The Bureaucratic Elite of Thailand: A Study of Their Sociological Attributes, Educational Backgrounds, and Career Advancement Pattern* (Bangkok: Wacharin, 1978).

[9] Homer G. Barnett, *Innovation* (New York: McGraw-Hill, 1953), p. 39.

to continue their studies. Living in France's political milieu, they quickly became frustrated with the nature of Thailand's traditional absolute monarchy.[10] Though no hard evidence is available, it would appear that Thailand's surprising student revolution of October 1973 was at least partially stimulated by the students of progressive, democratically oriented faculty members who had recently returned from study abroad during a major period of student activism.[11] The memoirs of African early nationalist leaders such as Nkrumah and Azikiwe indicate that it was while abroad that they developed their strong determination to work for the independence of their countries and the common interests of their regions.[12] Similarly, key Asian leaders such as Ho Chi Minh, Chou En-lai, and Chen Yi developed revolutionary consciousness while studying in France.[13]

Development of Technical Skills

One of the most common arguments for study abroad is that it is a mechanism for acquiring important technical skills relevant to development. This has been a major motivation for fellowship programs sponsored by agencies such as the Rockefeller Foundation, the Ford Foundation, the United Nations Development Programme, and the Population Council. During the early phase of Japanese development, there was a strong emphasis on sending Japanese technicians and students abroad to acquire new technical skills in a wide variety of fields relevant to national development.[14] Even today, Japan continues to send thousands of students abroad, particularly in fields related to science and technology.

Development of Foreign Language Competencies

Study abroad provides one of the most effective means to acquire skills in a foreign language. Competency in a foreign language is particularly important for professionals in countries where the national language is not one used internationally. For example, professionals in countries like Japan, Indonesia, Thailand, and Nepal greatly need knowledge of an international language such as English to be able to interrelate with professionals in other parts of the world as well as in their own regions. Knowledge of an international language also opens up access to a wide range of scholarly materials of a diverse ideological nature. In a number of rather repressive political regimes, virtually no Marxist or radical literature is available in the local language. Through knowledge of English or French,

---

[10] See Pridi Banomyong, *Ma vie mouvementée et mes 21 ans d'exil en Chine populaire* (Paris: VARAP, 1974), pp. 27–35.

[11] Ross Prizzia and Narong Sinsawasdi, *Thailand: Student Activism and Political Change* (Bangkok: Allied Printers, 1974), pp. 6, 72.

[12] Flack, p. 116.

[13] Banomyong, p. 32.

[14] Endymion Wilkinson, *Japan versus Europe: A History of Misunderstanding* (Harmondsworth: Penguin, 1983), p. 252.

the individual can gain access to a wide diversity of ideological perspectives on major issues. Finally, foreign language competency is often highly related to career success in both the private and public sectors in societies where the national language is not an international one.

Development of Regional Consciousness and Greater Sensitivity to the Need for Cultural Democracy

While abroad, students often become much more familiar with various cultures from their own region and become more conscious of an "African identity" or a "Southeast Asian identity" while experiencing a variety of "cultural collisions" during their stays in industrialized countries. They may make considerable progress in overcoming what Jean Monnet terms the "curse of nationalism,"[15] developing multicultural, regional, and international identities. Numerous foreign students also encounter some type or form of racism while abroad; Gandhi's experiences in South Africa are perhaps the most dramatic example of this phenomenon. Affected individuals may develop more sensitivity to cultural democracy and the need to be fairer to cultural minorities in their own societies.

International Economic Effects and Foreign Exchange Remittances

Approximately one-third of the foreign students coming to the United States do not return to their countries of origin.[16] This phenomenon is normally referred to negatively as the "brain drain." But it can also be viewed positively from an international economic perspective. For certain highly skilled professionals with specialized training, it may well be that their economic contribution is significantly higher in a foreign country such as the United States or the United Kingdom. In their own country, they might not find a suitable position to utilize their technical skills and become engaged in primarily "nonproductive" bureaucratic tasks. Those trained as scientists and researchers may lack adequate facilities and laboratories to pursue their professional work optimally.[17] In Thailand, for example, there is a marked trend for those with Ph.D. research training to move eventually into administrative positions. As a result of study abroad, brains may be funneled into milieus where their marginal productivity is greatly enhanced. Such migration of high-level talent, then, raises world productivity, though it may have negative distributional effects, which are, however, quite complex.

Given the strong extended family ties in the typical Third World setting, children with high ability who have migrated abroad will commonly return remittances to their families at home. Rao strongly emphasized

---

[15] Jean Monnet, *Memoirs* (Garden City, N.Y.: Doubleday, 1978).

[16] William S. Greer, "Foreign Students: Boon or a Threat?" *New York Times* (March 27, 1983), sec. 12.

[17] Marion H. Groves, "Contributions to Development by Asians Who Have Studied Abroad," *Exchange* (Summer 1967), pp. 14–15.

this phenomenon in his empirical research on foreign students in Australia, the United States, Canada, and France.[18] Illustrative of the dramatic potential of migrants is the case of one Korean who has established a successful electronics company in Silicon Valley, south of San Francisco. Though there are no exact data on this, it is extremely likely that this entrepreneur has shared some of his profits with relatives in Korea. I personally have been involved in carrying funds from a Thai who migrated to the United States approximately 15 years ago to a remote village in Northern Thailand. Empirical data on foreign exchange remittances to Pakistan, a country which has had a serious brain drain problem for years, may provide a sense of how economically significant such transfers may be. According to a recent World Bank survey, in 1978 the remittances from Pakistani expatriates were higher than the country's total net receipts from foreign aid; currently such remittances account for 43.6 percent of Pakistan's foreign exchange earnings and total US$7 billion for the past 5 years.[19]

With respect to the distributional question, there are other potential positive effects of what Rao terms "brain overflow."[20] Being from the Third World itself, such individuals may do important research work having implications for the developing nations. An interesting example is the Jamaican, Sir Arthur Lewis, a Princeton professor who recently received the Nobel Prize for his research on development economics. By migrating, Lewis has contributed not only to Jamaica but also to the development process globally. A number of talented professionals who have migrated from the Third World have become prominent and influential in key international organizations, such as the World Bank and other specialized agencies of the United Nations. Their presence in such organizations provides a greater opportunity for viewpoints and perspectives from the Third World to be heard. Given the types of effects just discussed, brain overflow may also have significant positive distributional effects.

Enhancement of Mobility Opportunities through Study Abroad

Like schooling in general, overseas study can be an important factor in upward social mobility. The prestige of overseas study can in some cases compensate for "deficiencies" in socioeconomic background. Later in this article, empirical data from Thailand are examined to see to what extent those of lower socioeconomic background have access to overseas study opportunities. Unfortunately, in most Third World societies women who study abroad are more likely to be of higher socioeconomic background than men studying abroad; therefore, this avenue of mobility seems much less open to women. In societies where both educational and occupational

---

[18] Rao (n. 1 above), p. 150.
[19] Minhaj Barna, Kuldip Nayar, and K. Nadarajah, "Waiting for the Fall-Out," *South: The Third World Magazine* 34 (August 1983): 69–70.
[20] Rao, p. 150.

opportunities may be limited for certain cultural minorities, overseas study can be an important alternative source of mobility.

Cross-cultural Enrichment Effects

Though study abroad by Third World nationals is primarily oriented toward the acquisition of technical skills and personal career advancement, it can also be an intensive cross-cultural experience that has deep and fundamental meaning for many sojourners.[21] Given the extensive research on attitude changes associated with foreign study, this is certainly an area of considerable impact. Such attitude changes may have many positive intangible benefits related to the building of a peaceful cooperative global community.[22]

Possible Negative Effects of Study Abroad

Foreign Exchange Costs

In most Third World societies, lack of foreign exchange is a considerable development constraint. As foreign study has become increasingly expensive, it definitely represents a serious loss of foreign currency. For example, 6,550 Thais are currently studying in the United States.[23] Assuming a stay of approximately 2 years on the average, this would represent a total expenditure of roughly $130 million, a considerable sum of foreign exchange.[24] In considering the foreign exchange costs of overseas study, it is important to look carefully at the opportunity uses of the foreign exchange.

Individual Opportunity Costs

Study abroad, particularly at the doctoral level, may involve considerable opportunity costs. Key professionals of high talent may be lost to a nation for periods of between 3 and 10 years. In countries such as the Philippines and Egypt, with large pools of educated manpower available, such opportunity costs may not be serious. But for many smaller countries with less educated talent to draw on, particularly some of the poorer African countries, the opportunity costs associated with study abroad can be considerable.

Socialization into a Consumer Culture

As a by-product of study abroad, foreign students living in industrial societies may become part of consumer-oriented cultures stressing the

[21] Richard W. Brislin, *Cross-cultural Encounters* (New York: Pergamon, 1981).

[22] Congressman Paul Simon, "Commencement Address" at the University of Oregon, June 12, 1983.

[23] *Open Doors: 1980/81 Report on International Educational Exchange* (New York: Institute of International Education, 1981), p. 11.

[24] Actually, this amount overestimates the foreign exchange costs to Thailand since some students work or receive fellowship assistance from U.S. or other external sources. This figure, however, underestimates the total costs of study abroad since Thai government staff on official leave continue to receive their local salaries while studying abroad.

purchase of luxury goods, such as videotape recorders, home computers, washing machines, and the private automobile. In fact, consumerism is a distinct and explicit element in Inkeles's modernity syndrome.[25] In countries trying to increase their rate of savings to foster development, the presence of former foreign students with a luxury consumption orientation can be a serious problem, inhibiting necessary tax or distributional reforms.

Incorporation into the Structure of the Dominating Center

In his book, *Dependent Development,* Peter Evans discusses the close alliance between Brazil's national bourgeoisie, its government, and transnational corporations.[26] Through study abroad, with its associated value changes and language skill development, individuals can be easily incorporated into the global system of transnational corporations. Through such employment, the loyalties of individuals may shift to the transnational institution, and they may develop a strong vested interest in preserving existing socioeconomic structures which provide them with significant personal financial benefits. Some scholars such as Arnove argue that study-abroad programs for key elites are part of a subtle system of political control, domination, and dependence.[27] The influential role played after the 1965 coup in Indonesia by key economists educated at Berkeley under Ford Foundation support is frequently cited as an example.

The Problem of Cultural Marginality

Given the rather significant attitude and cultural changes associated with study abroad, individuals face the problem of "cultural collisions" when they return home. Some are able to integrate their new cultural values with the old and become what Brislin calls multicultural or what Lifton calls Protean individuals.[28] But for many the process of readapting is complex. In his autobiography, Nehru eloquently presents the ambivalent feelings often held after socialization to Western culture while studying abroad: "I have become a queer mixture of the East and West, out of place everywhere, at home nowhere. . . . I cannot get rid of either that past inheritance or my recent acquisitions. They are both part of me, and though they help me in both the East and the West, they also create in me a feeling of spiritual loneliness not only in public activities but in life itself. I am a stranger and alien in the West, I cannot be of it. But in my own country also sometimes, I have an exile's feelings."[29] During my own fieldwork in Southeast Asia, I have noticed a tendency among some Western-

---

[25] Alex Inkeles and David Smith, *Becoming Modern* (Cambridge, Mass.: Harvard University Press, 1974), pp. 30–31.

[26] Peter Evans, *Dependent Development* (Princeton, N.J.: Princeton University Press, 1979).

[27] Robert F. Arnove, ed., *Philanthropy and Cultural Imperialism: The Foundations at Home and Abroad* (Bloomington: Indiana University Press, 1982).

[28] Brislin, pp. 297–99; and Robert J. Lifton, *Boundaries: Psychological Man in Revolution* (New York: Random House, 1969).

[29] J. L. Nehru, *An Autobiography* (London: Bodley Head, 1955), p. 596.

educated Asians to show Western cultural traits in doing development work with peasants or rural dwellers. An example is the introduction of abstract English terms into the indigenous language, which creates considerable distance between the Western-educated professionals and the peasants with whom they are trying to communicate. An Indian villager, in providing advice to a grandchild about to study abroad, echoes a similar sentiment: "People go to England and forget about their religion and culture. They come back and smoke in the presence of their elders and even shamelessly offer them cigarettes. They are ashamed of their poor farmer fathers whom they introduce to their officer friends in town as servants from their village home."[30] The problem of cultural marginality is also vividly present in Micronesia. Nevin emphasizes the major contradictions between Western education and Micronesian cultural and economic realities. His informants talk of university graduates returning to Micronesia and just hanging around drinking.[31]

Operationalization

In the general discussion above, many positive and negative effects of study abroad were considered. Unfortunately, global data on these many aspects of study abroad are not readily available. For example, data on the quality of technical skills of former foreign students are rarely attainable; similarly there are few macro data available on the language skills of those having studied abroad. Even more intangible are the hypothesized enhanced motivation and drive of former foreign students. Such outcomes are not ends in themselves but intermediate means related to the ultimate goal of development. These factors are considered to be unmeasured variables mediating the influence of study abroad on national development; therefore, each of the aspects considered in the general discussion is not necessarily operationalized separately.

The focus is on the use of macro indicators reflecting the total overall impact of these various factors in the aggregate. For example, it is assumed that improved technical skills and stronger motivation for change among returned graduates contribute to national development. Similarly there is the assumption that foreign exchange remittances received from those abroad will contribute to improved economic performance in the recipient country. Thus, the major outcomes of special interest here are long-run economic and political performance. The relationship between study abroad and these outcomes has been rarely examined. Though there are several possible indicators to measure economic performance, the measure used here is the conventional one of growth in real GNP during the 1970s.

[30] Amar Kumar Singh, *Indian Students in Britain* (New York: Asia Publishing, 1963).
[31] David Nevin, *The American Touch in Micronesia* (New York: Norton, 1977), p. 154.

With regard to political performance, three empirical indicators are used: (1) degree of political repression, (2) number of political coups, and (3) number of deaths from political violence. Poor political performance is assumed to be reflected in repression, coups, and violence.

A Global Model to Assess the Long-Term Impact of Study Abroad

The general discussion above is ambiguous in that it suggests that study abroad may quite reasonably have either positive or negative effects on national development. The empirical model presented here is designed to provide a preliminary assessment of the long-run impact of study abroad. The basic strategy is to relate prior data on study abroad in the mid-1960s with economic and political performance in the 1970s. A number of diverse ideological perspectives are also incorporated in the model tested. The variables selected represent both dependency theory and the conventional human capital approach. The data also allow some assessment of Simon's extreme position that population is the ultimate resource and not the obstacle to development commonly assumed.[32] The sample comprises 84 developing nations, selected according to the availability of data.

The Hypothesized Model—Specification of Variables

The basic variables (all aggregated at the national level) used in the model are classified as follows:

Background control variables:
X_1: income per capita in 1966;
X_2: population in 1966;
X_3: whether nation exports oil (dummy variable).
Major explanatory variables:
X_4: extent of concentration of exports, 1965;
X_5: number of political coups (in 1960s and 1970s);
X_6: percentage of population studying abroad, 1966;
X_7: percentage of students studying abroad in Germany or Japan, 1966;
X_8: percentage of population enrolled in higher education nationally, 1966;
X_9: percentage of females in higher education system nationally, 1966.
Outcome variable:
X_{10}: growth in real GNP during the 1970s.

The hypothesized direction of the relationship of each of the background and explanatory variables is indicated in table 1. Prior to presenting the empirical results, I discuss briefly the rationale for the inclusion of each of the variables.

---

[32] Julian L. Simon, *The Ultimate Resource* (Princeton, N.J.: Princeton University Press, 1981).

TABLE 1

A Regression Model for Assessing the Possible Long-Term Economic Impact
of Study Abroad

Explanatory Variable	Hypothesized Sign	b	β	t	r
Income per capita, 1966	+	−.00	−.01	.12	−.09
Population in 1966	−	−.00	−.11	1.0	.06
Oil exporter	+	2.41	.34	3.2**	.34
Extent of export concentration, 1965	−	−.06	−.49	4.4**	−.48
Number of coups	−	−.49	−.25	2.3*	−.14
Percentage of population studying abroad	+	.96	.24	2.1*	.17
Percentage of students in Germany or Japan	+	.06	.23	2.1*	.26
Percentage of population in higher education, 1966	−	−.22	−.22	1.4	.27
Percentage of females in higher education system nationally, 1966	+	7.71	.35	2.4*	.22
Constant	. . .	5.47	. . .	. . .	. . .

NOTE.—The dependent variable is economic performance in the 1970s. Multiple regression statistics: $F(9,50) = 5.54$; $N = 84$; $R^2 = .50$**; $|R| = .24$. Notation: b = unstandardized regression coefficient; β = standardized regression coefficient; t = t value for the regression coefficient; r = simple bivariate correlation; $|R|$ = the determinate of the correlation matrix of independent variables, a measure of multicollinearity. Plots of regression residuals indicated almost perfect randomness.

* $P < .05$.
** $P < .01$.

Income per Capita

This variable is included primarily as a control variable. Without inclusion of this variable, any relationship found between study abroad and economic performance in a subsequent decade might be considered spurious since there is obviously a positive correlation between income per capita and the financial capability of a country to send its students abroad for further study. Inclusion of this variable is also interesting to test the hypothesis that the gap between the richer and poorer developing countries is widening. A positive correlation between income per capita in the mid-1960s and subsequent economic performance in the 1970s would be supportive of the increasing-gap hypothesis.

Population

Julian Simon has become rather unpopular, particularly among environmentalists, for arguing that population is the ultimate resource and that its negative economic effects, particularly in the long run, may be overstated. A major part of Simon's argument is that larger populations make possible important economies of scale in the education area. Although it is still too early to provide a final test for the Simon hypothesis, the population variable is included as a major control variable with some theoretical interest as well.

Whether Nation Exports Oil

Given the rapid increases in the prices of crude oil after the 1973–74 oil crisis, the presence of oil as a resource must be considered as a factor affecting economic performance. The variable is included as a control variable. Without its inclusion, the model would certainly have specification error.

Extent of Concentration of Exports

This variable is operationalized as the percentage of export earnings generated by the primary export commodity.[33] The greater the percentage, the more the reliance on a single export. It is included to reflect the dependency perspective. Excessive reliance on a single export epitomizes the dependency syndrome. Also, an assessment of the impact of this variable may provide useful insight into the potential economic effectiveness of export-diversification programs to reduce dependency.

Number of Political Coups

This variable is included because it is commonly argued that unstable political environments inhibit successful economic performance. With frequent coups, it may be difficult to have continuity of economic policies. Thus, this variable is hypothesized to have a negative relationship with economic performance.

Percentage of Population Studying Abroad

This is the major explanatory variable of interest in this study. The key question is whether it is possible to note in the 1970s any impact of prior study-abroad phenomena in the mid-1960s. Ideally, it would also be useful to look at economic performance data in the 1980s since students returning from abroad may be utilizing and applying their new talents for many years.

Percentage of Students Studying Abroad in Germany or Japan

During the 1960s, both West Germany and Japan were considered "economic miracles." Both nations have had a long history of emphasizing effective and practical training related to development. Thus, the basic assumption is that study abroad in Germany or Japan during the 1960s would have been highly inspiring and motivating. Individuals so motivated, and having acquired important technical skills, could contribute significantly to future economic performance. Thus, the hypothesis is that this variable is positively related to economic performance.

---

[33] Charles L. Taylor and Michael C. Hudson, *World Handbook of Political and Social Indicators* (New Haven, Conn.: Yale University Press, 1972), pp. 366–68.

Percentage of Population Enrolled in Higher Education Nationally

The inclusion of this variable is motivated by Ronald Dore's extensive research on the "diploma disease."[34] My own research in this area has also led me to considerable skepticism about the desirability of "overinvesting" in local higher education, as would seem to be the case in countries like Egypt or the Philippines.[35] Thus, it is hypothesized that this variable will have a negative relationship with future economic performance since overinvestment in higher education can divert funds away from secondary and primary schools serving the majority of a developing country's population.

Percentage of Females in Higher Education System Nationally

Developing countries vary rather markedly with respect to the opportunity provided to females in higher education. The basic assumption here is that countries which fail to provide adequate opportunities for females in higher education will suffer in the long run economically as the result of the serious underutilization of female talent.

Empirical Results

The empirical results of testing this global model are summarized in table 1. The explanatory power (roughly 50 percent of the variance) is rather high, considering that the model is a new one including several variables not conventionally used in predicting economic performance. Except for the control variables, income per capita and size of population, nearly all the other explanatory variables are significantly related to the outcome variable, economic performance in the 1970s. As hypothesized, study abroad does have a positive and significant relationship with economic performance (β = .24). The dependency variable, extent of export concentration, is found to have the highest explanatory power of all variables considered (β = −.49). As suggested by dependency theory, it has a strong negative relationship with long-term economic performance. Findings with respect to both the study abroad and dependency variables reflect the importance of external factors on development. The only variable for which the direction of the relationship is opposite to that hypothesized is income per capita. The size of the relationship is, however, extremely small and the overall result suggests that there has been no major change in the gap between the richer and the poorer developing countries during the past decade. For those concerned with improving opportunities for women, it is encouraging to note that those countries providing females

---

[34] Ronald P. Dore, *The Diploma Disease* (Berkeley: University of California Press, 1976).

[35] Gerald W. Fry, "Degreeism: Disease or Cure?" *Higher Education* 10 (1981): 517–27, and "Schooling, Development, and Inequality," *Harvard Educational Review* 51 (February 1981): 107–16.

greater access to higher education have shown significantly stronger long-term economic performance.

The impact of other variables is as hypothesized. For example, number of coups has a negative impact on long-run economic performance ($\beta = -.25$). Frequent coups imply a lack of continuity in public policy and also may be reflective of unsatisfactory government performance. The variable with the next greatest statistical influence ($\beta = .23$) is that related to study in Germany or Japan. As hypothesized, countries which have emphasized sending their students abroad to these two countries have shown superior long-term economic performance. There are several possible explanations for this finding. Perhaps most significant is the emphasis in both Japan and Germany on technology development.[36] Japan's rapid transformation from a feudal state to a technological society is unparalleled in the history of technology.[37]

Two other variables considered in the global model are total population and percentage of the population in higher education. The population variable has the expected negative effect ($\beta = -.11$), though the small size of the relationship provides some support for Simon's argument that the adverse effect of population size on economic performance has been exaggerated. With respect to percentage of the population in higher education (locally within the nation), this variable is found to have a rather sizable negative relationship ($\beta = -.22$) with economic performance. A major explanation for this finding would be the production of "surplus" graduates relative to the capacity of the labor market to absorb more highly educated graduates.[38] This finding is highly consistent with the research of both Blaug and Dore.[39]

Since this sample includes nearly the entire population of major developing countries, the values in table 1 basically reflect true population values and the question of statistical inference from a sample to a population is not directly relevant. Nevertheless, statistical tests of significance are indicated to provide a basis for considering inferences related to the consistency of the hypothesized model with the empirical data.

The relationship between study abroad and certain political outcome variables is also considered. For this analysis, simple bivariate correlations are used, and results for this population of developing nations are reported in table 2. Given that the time ordering of the political outcome variables is not completely subsequent to the study-abroad data, unambiguous causal

---

[36] See Masanori Moritani, *Japanese Technology: Getting the Best for the Least* (Tokyo: Simul, 1982).

[37] Ralph E. Gomory, "Technology Development," *Science* 220 (May 1983): 579.

[38] Henry M. Levin and Russell W. Rumberger, "The Low Skill Future in High Tech," *Stanford Educator* (Summer 1983), pp. 2–3.

[39] Mark Blaug, "An Economic Analysis of Personal Earnings in Thailand," *Economic Development and Cultural Change* 23 (October 1974): 1–31.

TABLE 2
RELATIONSHIP OF STUDY ABROAD AND KEY POLITICAL OUTCOME VARIABLES

Relationship	Bivariate Correlation Coefficient
Study abroad and degree of political repression	−.11
Study abroad and number of political coups	−.13
Study abroad and deaths from political violence	−.07

inferences are impossible. Nevertheless, it is encouraging to see the consistency in negative signs, suggesting that investing in foreign study does seem to be associated with a greater degree of political openness.

Case Studies

A major weakness of the global model tested above is its reliance on growth in real GNP during the 1970s as the only economic outcome variable. Although many governments and international agencies have stressed this economic performance measure, there has also been increasing concern in the 1970s and 1980s with broader outcomes of development such as equity, attainment of basic needs, and ecological balance. The qualitative case studies presented here have been chosen to demonstrate how study abroad may also have a significant impact on these other important dimensions of development. The case studies may help as well to illuminate the processes underlying the significant economic and political effects of study abroad. An important qualification concerning the qualitative case studies is that they have been selected purposely and are not necessarily representative.

Prior to presenting the qualitative case studies, I will briefly summarize important empirical findings from several extensive quantitative surveys in Thailand. These studies show the individual benefits of study abroad and may help provide insight into explaining the anomaly of accelerating global demand for study abroad, despite the rapid expansion of indigenous systems of higher education in many countries of the Third World.

Quantitative Results from Various Thai National Studies

Previously I conducted field research on the occupational attainment process in Thailand.[40] Study abroad was considered a key explanatory variable. This research involved a sample of approximately 600 employees from large-scale private and public organizations in Bangkok. In this study, study abroad was found to have a simple correlation of .43 with occupational attainment, broadly defined to include earnings, wealth,

[40] Gerald W. Fry, "Education and Success: A Case Study of the Thai Public Service," *Comparative Education Review* 24 (February 1980): 21–34.

Comparative Education Review

Comparative and International Education Society

Devoted to expanding a cross-cultural perspective of education: Comparative and International Education Society and **Comparative Education Review**

COMPARATIVE EDUCATION REVIEW
published quarterly

COMPARATIVE EDUCATION REVIEW ORDER FORM

YES! A cross-cultural perspective is important to me: enter my 1-year subscription at the following 15% discount rate: ☐ Individuals $23.80 ☐ Institutions $45.05

☐ Students (attach copy of ID) $14.45 *Membership in CIES concurrent with all subscriptions.* **OUTSIDE USA?** Add $3.00 for postage.

(J)

Name _____

Address _____

City _____ State/Country _____ ZIP _____

☐ **Payment enclosed** Charge my ☐ **Visa** ☐ **MasterCard** Exp. date _____

Acct. # _____ Signature _____

Please mail to The University of Chicago Press, P.O. Box 37005, Chicago, Illinois 60637.

BtK 10/84
MOOAB

The University of Chicago Press

5801 S. Ellis Avenue, Chicago, Illinois 60637

👉 YOUR BOOKMARK

Comparative Education Review

Edited by Philip G. Altbach

Reading *Bridges to Knowledge* may have aroused your interest in **Comparative Education Review**, the journal in which these essays originally appeared. **Comparative Education Review** investigates education throughout the world and the social, economic, and political forces that shape it. Founded in 1956 to advance knowledge and teaching in comparative education studies, the **Review** has since established itself as the most reliable source for the analysis of the place of education in countries other than the United States.

Bridges to Knowledge is representative of the **Comparative Education Review's** international quality and diverse methodological perspectives.

COMPARATIVE
EDUCATION
REVIEW

administrative power, and occupational prestige. Given a rather sizable correlation between socioeconomic status (SES) and study abroad (.32 for the whole sample), the relationship between study abroad and occupational attainment dropped to a β of .12 when SES was included in the model. This suggests that many of the individual benefits associated with study abroad are primarily reflecting the higher socioeconomic background of the individuals having access to such opportunities. In this study it was also found that there was a statistically significant correlation of .20 between study abroad and individual attitudinal modernity, confirming the value changes suggested in the literature on study abroad and cultural change.

Currently, I am engaged in a study of the origins of Thailand's elite. Utilizing data from the complete files of contemporary *Who's Who in Thailand* ($N = 1,210$), I am statistically analyzing the backgrounds of the Thai elite. Formal study or prior training experience abroad is quite common in this elite population. For example, 70.3 percent of the elite have had some type of overseas training or study experience: 24.1 percent completed bachelor's degrees abroad, and 35.8 percent completed graduate degrees abroad. Given such data, it is easy to understand the great demand among Thai students for overseas study opportunities. Among the Thai elite studying abroad, 60.7 percent studied in the United States, while 17 percent went to the United Kingdom. Table 3 indicates the American universities that produced the greatest number of Thai elite; it is interesting to note that only six American universities account for 26.5 percent of the Thai elite who studied in the United States.

Likhit's impressive study of the bureaucratic elite of Thailand also provides detailed data on the relationship between foreign study and access to and promotion to top-level civil service positions. Using the records of the Thai Civil Service Commission, Likhit obtained a complete sample ($N = 2,160$) of the highest-ranking special grade civil servants and a 20 percent sample of first-grade officials ($N = 2,394$). Likhit found that, in seven of the 13 Thai ministries, more than half of the special grade officers were foreign trained. In the Ministry of Education, for

TABLE 3
U.S. UNIVERSITIES MOST COMMONLY ATTENDED BY MEMBERS OF THE THAI ELITE

University	Thai Elite Produced (N)	% of All Thai Elite Having Studied Abroad
Indiana University	28	6.7
University of Pennsylvania	20	4.8
Harvard-Radcliffe	20	4.8
University of Michigan	16	3.9
University of Illinois	14	3.4
Cornell University	12	2.9

example, 77.6 percent of the special grade officers were foreign trained. In only three of Thailand's 13 ministries were less than 40 percent of the top officials foreign trained. Likhit also found that those with foreign training achieve promotion within the public bureaucracy considerably faster than those without such training.[41]

Qualitative Case Studies

A Costa Rican Case of Institution Building for Ecology

Mario Boza and Alvaro Ugalde were two young Costa Rican men trained in national park management in the United States. On their return to Costa Rica, they dedicated themselves to the development of a national park system for Costa Rica. After 5 years of serious effort, they were able to convince the government of Costa Rica to set aside 400,000 acres for the park system and to provide a healthy budget to maintain the system. The Costa Rican government also agreed to pay $1.2 million to relocate squatters living in the park. Boza and Ugalde served as the park system's first and second directors, respectively. Costa Rica is now considered perhaps the most ecotopian of the developing nations, and its park system has helped to preserve a remarkably rich area of rain forests with marvelous biological diversity.[42]

Educational Reform in Thailand

Dr. Sippanondha Ketudat, currently a senator in the Thai Parliament, has been a key figure in Thailand's educational reform movement. Sippanondha obtained his undergraduate degree from the University of California, Los Angeles, and a doctorate in nuclear physics from Harvard University. After becoming a professor of physics at a Thai university, Sippanondha became involved in educational administration, initially promoting the development of the sciences in Thai universities. Eventually, he emerged as the chairman of Thailand's educational reform committee. Later, as secretary-general of Thailand's National Education Commission and as minister of education, he was able to implement a number of the reform recommendations, including a major change in the control of rural primary education, which many observers felt was politically impossible. Sippanondha's leadership has been characterized as dynamic and idealistic with a strong commitment to social justice. Of course it is not legitimate to attribute Sippanondha's achievements solely to his overseas educational experiences; nevertheless, it seems reasonable to suppose that these experiences played an important role.

[41] Dhiravegin (n. 8 above), pp. 128–29, 177.
[42] Jacques-Yves Cousteau et al., *The Cousteau Almanac* (New York: Doubleday, 1981), p. 70.

Thailand's University Entrance Examination and the New Open University

Dr. Wichit Sri-saan, deputy undersecretary of the Ministry of University Affairs, provides another example of a former foreign student (Ph.D. in education from the University of Minnesota) who has made a dramatic impact on Thailand's system of higher education. Most notable is his strict administration of Thailand's Joint Higher Education Entrance Examination, which determines admissions to Thailand's highly selective universities. It is not uncommon for children of Cabinet ministers to fail to gain admission to one of Thailand's selective universities. It is well known that Wichit will not break the rules for anyone and would resign rather than do so.[43] Wichit's commitment to administer this examination with no favoritism in a bureaucratic polity and a highly affiliative society is a remarkable accomplishment. Wichit has also been the moving force behind the establishment of Thailand's new long-distance open university, which appears to offer a feasible solution to Thailand's political "time bomb" of having excess social demand for higher education. Wichit is noted for attracting dynamic young scholars to his staff, many of whom were educated abroad in Europe or the United States.

Educational Budget Reform in Thailand

In 1979, Thailand undertook a major reform of the way it allocated funds for rural education. A new computerized system, based on detailed subnational indicators, was introduced to shift greater allocations to the poorer, more remote provinces. This reform involved complex interactions among a number of different Thai agencies and ministries. Two of the key actors in different ministries had become close friends while doing doctoral work at the same university in the United States. This greatly facilitated informal relationships between the two ministries, central and crucial to the reform. The chair of the special committee appointed to develop the reform procedures was a Ph.D. graduate in political science from the University of Oregon. The basic idea for the reform was developed by Dr. Rung Kaewdang while doing his doctoral work in the United States at the State University of New York at Buffalo.[44]

Institutionalization of Graduate Studies—the NIDA Case

The National Institute of Development Administration (NIDA) is a Thai university offering graduate training in public administration, development economics, applied statistics, and business management. The

---

[43] Great credit for maintaining this system should also go to Dr. Kasem Suvannakul (Ph.D., New York University), a career civil servant who served as minister of university affairs for many years under a number of different governments. Currently, however, for the first time since 1976, a politician has been appointed minister of university affairs. The new minister may receive considerable political pressure to provide more "flexibility" in admissions to selective universities.

[44] See Gerald W. Fry and Rung Kaewdang, "Budgeting for Greater Equity: A Normative Regression Analysis," *International Journal of Policy Analysis and Information Systems* 6 (1982): 115–31.

institute was established in 1966 and received during the 1960s and early 1970s considerable support from the Ford Foundation primarily for staff development through overseas training.

Currently NIDA is totally self-sufficient with no expatriate staff other than an occasional foreign language teacher or visiting scholar. Many of its faculty members are foreign trained. During the 1970s a policy was established whereby a certain percentage of research and consulting grants received by staff members was donated to a special fund to support staff development. With this fund, NIDA continues to be able to send many staff members abroad without external assistance. Also, NIDA now offers doctoral study. Thus, NIDA represents an ideal example of how study abroad has contributed to the institutionalization of a now self-reliant quality graduate school. Its strong research capacity, largely deriving from the overseas training of its staff, has brought considerable financial resources to NIDA and produced some excellent research studies related to Thailand's development.[45]

Conclusion

During the past several decades, private individuals, numerous governments, and major international agencies have invested heavily in supporting study abroad for individuals from developing nations. Unfortunately, there has been little systematic or concrete evidence related to the long-term impact of such investments. The empirical results presented here, both at the global level and at the national level (for Thailand and Costa Rica), strongly suggest that such investments have been well justified. This should be heartening to the dedicated staff members of institutions such as the major foundations, the Institute of International Education, Unesco, and other agencies committed to building human capacity through cross-cultural exchanges and training. Given the findings of this research, it is discouraging that funding for cross-cultural study abroad is becoming more and more difficult, while global spending on military armaments continues to spiral. The global empirical data analyzed here indicate positive economic and political effects of study abroad over the long term. But, even more important, study abroad is a basic building block in the development of a peaceful cooperative global community.

---

[45] Choop Karnjanaprakorn, Lawrence McKibben, and William Thompson, *NIDA: A Case Study in Institution Development* (Bloomington, Ind.: International Development Research Center, 1974).

Britain's Full-Cost Policy for Overseas Students

PETER WILLIAMS*

In the autumn of 1980 Mrs. Thatcher's Conservative government in Britain imposed tuition fees on overseas students reckoned on a "full-cost" basis and removed a substantial slice of public financial support from British postsecondary education institutions. The main casualty of this move was perhaps in the diplomatic and trade spheres in the form of lost reputation and goodwill, and the pressure of foreign governments was largely responsible for the review and mitigation that was announced in 1983. But the full-cost fees policy originated in the search for domestic economies by the Treasury and the Department of Education and Science, and the impact of the policy on tertiary education institutions in Britain has been important. They always had a far higher proportion of overseas students in their overall student clientele than was the case in the United States, for example, and a sizable part of their funding was paid to them in respect of their overseas enrollments.

The ensuing difficulties for British higher education institutions have stemmed less from an actual heavy loss of overseas student numbers— for, at levels other than "nonadvanced further education" (explained below), recruitment surprisingly has been comparatively buoyant—than from making good the cash removed by the government cuts. Income could only be sustained by fully maintaining student numbers and at an average-cost fee, and this was deemed a virtual impossibility for the typical university or college. The financial implications of overseas student policy have been the dominant ones from the institutional point of view and, as will be discussed, have had their impact in terms both of weakening the overall viability of institutions in the medium term and also of simultaneously presenting fundamentally different alternative models of how tertiary education in Britain might be financed to an increasing extent in the future. There has been much less debate about the academic implications of the policy change than might have been expected.

One can distinguish three levels of discussion about international student exchange. The first is that of international student flows and the factors which promote or impede them at both individual and state policy levels. The second concerns institutional policy and provision for students from abroad on the part of the host education system. The third level focuses on the academic and social interactions and experiences of such students both on and off the campus.

* Professor in the Department of Education in Developing Countries, Institute of Education, University of London, and soon to be education director at the Commonwealth Secretariat, London.

This review of British experience in the light of the United Kingdom's new policy of charging overseas[1] students full-cost tuition fees stays at the second of these levels and concerns itself with the response of academic institutions to the British government's newly introduced regime for the admission and financing of students from abroad. Students are both an end in themselves for universities and colleges, which exist largely in order to educate them (as well as to pursue knowledge), and also means for the continuation of institutional existence and the basis for the provision of the resources which enable the institution to carry out its functions. Accordingly, there will be a strong interest on the part of academics and the college community in arrangements made for students from abroad but motivated by national considerations of overseas policy or of domestic finance. The mechanisms adopted for implementation of "first-level" foreign student policy, particularly insofar as they affect the regulation of student numbers, the composition of the foreign student body, and the distribution of foreign students in the receiving system, can have a profound effect on the academic and financial health of the receiving education system. In turn they may significantly affect foreign student experience at the third of our levels.

This account of recent British experience with its full-cost fees policy will stay largely on the plane of description and reporting of a momentous change for the British public system of postsecondary education, in which overseas students have regularly accounted for around 10 percent of student enrollments (a much higher proportion of student enrollments than in the United States, though bearing approximately the same relationship to the total tertiary education age group). I shall, however, inevitably be drawn into discussion of the issues raised by the full-cost fees policy: issues of cost calculation in higher education, of dual pricing policies, of the place of a private enclave in a public system, of accountability and shifts in accountability when the price to the consumer of a service is steeply raised.

British Higher and Further Education

The British differentiate in their postsecondary education system between higher education and nonadvanced further education. Higher education consists of university education and of those courses in the maintained (i.e., funded by a local education authority) sector of public institutions (e.g., polytechnics, colleges and institutions of higher education) which are designated as "advanced" by virtue of the fact that their level of entry

---

[1] The British debate uses the term "overseas" students to describe students from abroad, reflecting British reluctance to refer to Commonwealth citizens as foreigners. I have generally adhered to the term "overseas" when discussing the British experience and to "foreign students" or "students from abroad" when the context is international.

is roughly equivalent to completion of a full secondary education and possession of advanced-level passes on the General Certificate of Education. Nonadvanced further education courses have a lower level of entry: they are sometimes provided in institutions specializing in courses at this level; but they may also take place, side by side with advanced courses, in the same public sector institutions. In the United Kingdom in 1982–83 there were roughly 550,000 full-time higher education students (just over half in the 45 universities and two business schools and the remainder in 300 maintained public establishments), 300,000 part-time students (a tenth in universities), and about 375,000 students at nonadvanced level in maintained further education establishments.

Basically, the British system of higher and further education is publicly financed.[2] Universities are autonomous and receive the greater part of their budget (about 70 percent) from the centrally funded University Grants Committee (UGC), a smaller part (roughly 20 percent) from tuition fees, and the remainder from research grants and private benefactors. Where students are in receipt of awards, the fees are paid by the award-making body, and for home students this is in most cases the local education authority. Public sector institutions such as polytechnics and colleges of higher education fall under local education authorities, but the major part of the cost is met indirectly via the rate-support grant from the central government, which finances over half of all local authority expenditures (the remainder being mainly met by local property taxes known as "rates"). Public sector institutions also levy fees, and, as with the universities, most home students receive a local education authority award to pay them. There are means-tested maintenance grants for living expenses and for ancillary expenditure on books, travel, et cetera payable to home students; in the bulk of cases it is mandatory for local authorities to pay these.

Since 1967–68 Britain has operated a system of differential fees for students from abroad in its public system of higher and further education. The differentiation has now reached a somewhat extreme level, largely because of the introduction of full-cost fees for students from abroad from autumn 1980, but also because the fees for home students at the undergraduate level have been reduced. Thus a home undergraduate university student in 1983–84 pays tuition fees of £480 per annum (approximately US $720 at October 1983 exchange rates), whereas the equivalent student from abroad typically pays a minimum of £2,900 ($4,350) for an arts or social science course, £3,800 ($5,700) for a science or engineering course, and £7,000 ($10,500) for the clinical stage of a medical or veterinary science course. (In the maintained sector the equivalent

---

[2] A useful recent series of papers on British higher education organization and financing is contained in House of Commons, *The Funding and Organization of Courses in Higher Education: Interim Report on Overseas Student Fees* (London: HMSO, 1980).

minimum is £3,180, irrespective of discipline.) At the extreme, therefore, the ratio of home to overseas tuition fees is 1:15. The cost to a student from abroad of studying in Britain is of course further raised by nontuition expenses, including accommodation, ranging from £3,000 to £4,000 for a full year; so that the total cost, including tuition, maintenance, and travel from and to the home country, of a full academic year's program for an overseas arts or science student in Britain would now (1983–84) average about £8,000.

Dramatic as the 1979 announcement that full-cost fees would be charged to overseas students from autumn 1980 was, it in fact represented only the culmination of a process which had been under way since 1967.[3] Prior to that, students from abroad had been treated on a par with British students, paying the same fees as Britons, but in December 1966 the Labour administration announced a differential fee for overseas students of £250 per annum compared with a fee for home students of £70. Many British academics protested against the introduction of discrimination, on the grounds of principle. Curiously, their institutions would actually gain revenue from the change since, at least in the case of universities, overall fee receipts do not appear to have been at all closely taken into account when fixing the subventions they received from the University Grants Committee: overseas students counted alongside home students in earning them resources from the UGC.

Here indeed one notes a curious anomaly which had particular effect until the late 1970s. On the one hand, the government was worried about the proportion of overseas nationals in the overall student body because of the large hidden subsidy (the difference between average costs and fees paid) involved, and so it charged higher fees to choke off overseas demand; but, on the other hand, it does not appear to have altered the incentive system operating on the institutional decision makers. From their point of view the policy had effects directly contrary to those intended by the government: they collected more revenue in total if the government raised fees to foreigners, without at the same time reducing institutional grants by a corresponding amount. This perhaps helps to explain why it was possible for some institutions, notably the University of Bradford, to stand out against the government policy of discriminatory fees for some considerable time and to refuse to introduce them.[4]

---

[3] For a brief account of the development of British government policy on funding and fees for overseas students, see Overseas Students Trust, *Overseas Students and Government Policy* (London: Overseas Students Trust, 1979); Peter Williams, ed., *The Overseas Student Question* (London: Heinemann, 1981), pp. 35–40.

[4] Government fee fixing for universities is only by recommendation, which the universities, as autonomous bodies, are not obliged to follow. Without in any way decrying the University of Bradford's principled stand, it should be pointed out that it was not in fact at the period in question one of the institutions with the highest proportion of overseas students.

The furor that greeted the introduction of differential fees in 1966–67 must have been largely responsible, in the period between 1967 and 1974, for the government's decision not to widen the differential any further even though the depressed state of the British economy made it anxious about the rising public expenditure and prompted a search for means to contain it. Since inflation was gathering pace, the freezing of the overseas fee at an absolute level of £250 over this period meant that in real terms fees fell by about one-third. Demand from abroad for higher education opportunities was steadily intensifying, and as a result the numbers of overseas students in British further and higher education rose strongly, virtually doubling over the period of stable fees from 1967–68 to 1974–75. After a period of rather rapid growth in the post-Robbins era of the 1960s the size of the British higher education system was growing slowly in the 1970s and indeed stabilized in the later 1970s, reflecting a conjunction of slackening domestic demand for demographic and other reasons and, on the supply side, public expenditure constraints. The net effect was that overseas students began to take an increasing proportion of places in the British higher and further education system, a trend which the government could not willingly contemplate at a time when it was urgently seeking scope for public savings.

In 1974 the Heath administration fell and Labour was returned to power. In the ensuing period of the Labour government, fees were raised every year from 1975, when they were increased to £320 in higher education, to 1979 when they reached £940 at the undergraduate level and £1,230 for postgraduates (differentiation by levels dated from 1977–78). The fee increases did not appear to stem the rise in numbers of students from overseas, and early in 1977 the secretary of state for education and science, Mr. Mulley, announced new curbs to restrain the growth of numbers. Government, he said, "cannot accept the continued rapid growth in the number of overseas students coming to our institutions. . . . I am therefore proposing to ask universities and local education authorities to aim at overseas student intakes in 1977/78 and subsequent years which will stabilise total numbers at recent levels,"[5] these being defined in terms of a 1975–76 baseline. In effect what was proposed was quantitative restrictions to back up the effects of rising fees.

There then followed a curious interlude of about 2 academic years during which higher education institutions started to grapple with the problem of self-regulation through quotas on the overseas side; this at a time when, on the home-student front, the Robbins principle that higher education should be available to all qualified students who sought it still

[5] United Kingdom, *Department of Education Circular*, DES 1/77 (January 14, 1977).

reigned supreme.[6] The irony lies in the fact that this was the exact reverse of the present situation in which the overseas-student segment of the market is quota-free, while target numbers have been fixed for home students. Somewhat belatedly, then, in 1977 and 1978 institutions started to set about the task of ensuring that their overseas numbers would fall within the prescribed limits, and in several cases courses with a large intake of overseas students were sacrificed in order to keep within the quota. The public sector institutions moved further and sooner than did universities, but the latter also found themselves having to respond. At the institution to which I belong, the University of London Institute of Education, I vividly remember a diploma in audio-visual aids catering mainly to students from abroad being allowed to wither for just this reason. Ironically, only a few months later we were wishing we had not made such a decision, since the government reversed its signals and sent institutions the implicit message that they should recruit every overseas student they could attract.

Retrospectively, one can see that Mr. Mulley's directive did begin to bite, for the combination of response to this and of mounting fee levels reduced levels of entry to higher education from 29,200 in 1977, the year of Mr. Mulley's statement, to 26,900 in 1979. But, as with the modern supertanker, it takes time to turn education trends right around, and furthermore the data base available to policymakers is often out of date. How far these slippages did actually affect policymaking is not known, but it seems probable that when the full-cost fees decisions were made in 1979 the visible trends of overseas student enrollment would still seem to have been upward. Ministers and civil servants could well have concluded either that their wishes had been deliberately flouted by institutions or that the potential for steerage of the system through advice was very limited, particularly when, as was observed above, the institutions were apparently being asked to move in directions contrary to their own financial self-interest.

By 1978 it was already becoming clear that the government, beset by economic difficulties, felt increasing impatience with developments and intended to overhaul radically the national policies on overseas students. Whether Labour or Conservatives would be returned to power in the general election that had to take place no later than spring 1979, there was bound to be some sort of a New Deal.[7] Haunted by this specter, the Overseas Students Trust (OST) decided late in 1978 to try to fill the

---

[6] The reference is to Committee on Higher Education, *Higher Education: Report of the Committee Appointed by the Prime Minister under the Chairmanship of Lord Robbins* (London: HMSO, 1963).

[7] For example, the address by the Labour Secretary of State for Education and Science, Mrs. Shirley Williams, MP, to the World University Service annual conference in December 1978, in which she enunciated the "Robin Hood principle" of making rich overseas students subsidize poor ones, was regarded as one of the many straws in the wind.

vacuum by commissioning its own studies on the dimensions of the overseas student problem in the expectation that these might contribute to formulation of policy under the next government. Although this (OST) project was indeed carried through,[8] it was completely overtaken by events and the published results only appeared 18 months after a completely new policy—that of full-cost fees—had already been promulgated by the new Thatcher administration.

How had it come about that there had been a vacuum in institutional thinking about overseas student policy? Mrs. Williams had been at the Department of Education and Science 10 years earlier, in 1969, and had then thrown down the challenge to the universities to come up with suggestions on containing the growing overseas student subsidy; as one of 13 points for discussion put to vice-chancellors at that time. Yet university policymakers and administrators appear to have ignored the issue completely in their deliberations in the 1970s, and were it not for the grave repercussions of the full-cost fees policies on higher education as a whole, one would be tempted to experience a malicious glee that the universities and colleges got what they deserved when millions of pounds were struck off their grant with the full-cost fees policy. In 1978 Mrs. Williams gave her own interpretation of the institutions' abysmal failure to contribute constructively to the debate:

> One of the great problems is the profound wish of all of us not to have to make changes at all. In the world of higher education, and I include students as well as the institutions in this, there is a profound desire to see the whole problem go away and not make any systematic or fundamental changes. Frankly I don't believe we can. I think in trying to do so we will simply get ourselves deeper into difficulties. . . . [We must] try to think through the nature of a more satisfactory system. Let me say that it will not be easy. Whatever you try to do there will be colossal resistance to it, because it either involves administrative change or it involves changes in the admissions habits of our great institutions, or it involves changes in realising that a curious mixture of quotas and fees is not going to work in any socially just way over the next ten or fifteen years. If you are willing to face this, and I hope you are, then I will give you a promise that, when the Government's document comes out, I will listen most carefully to any representation that you want to make to me. But I will take no notice of representations that simply pretend the problems will go away—because they won't.[9]

All this was less than 6 months before the first rumors that a victorious Tory government under Mrs. Thatcher would introduce full-cost fees. Although the document referred to by Mrs. Williams never appeared, it is quite clear that the system would have been overhauled had Labour

[8] The results were published in Williams, ed.

[9] United Kingdom, Department of Education and Science, *WUS News Spring Term, 1979*, no. 1, p. 7.

been reelected. But it is not clear how much input would have been made to the document by institutional leaders. In passing one may observe that the advance thinking being undertaken by the American Council for Education and the Institute of International Education in the United States, and by the Bureau for International Education in Canada, provides some hope that this dismal British experience will not be repeated elsewhere.[10]

Very soon after the May 1979 British general election, which the Conservative Party won, the first reports circulated that overseas students were to be charged full-cost fees as part of a program of government expenditure cuts, and despite vigorous protests this was confirmed in October of that year when the government announced that full-cost fees would be introduced for new overseas students as from October 1980, with minimum charges for university courses of £2,000 for arts and social science courses, £3,000 for science and applied science courses, and £5,000 for clinical studies in medicine and veterinary science. Currently enrolled students would avoid the full force of the new fee rises; there would be concessions for hard-hit specialist institutions; European Community students might be exempted (they subsequently were given home-student status for fees purposes); and a new scheme of special awards for overseas research students was inaugurated.

The mechanism for making the change was the drastic one of withdrawing a grant from educational institutions in respect of their overseas student enrollment and inviting them to make this good by levying fees at the full-cost level. The grant was withdrawn over 3 years on a 40 percent, 40 percent, 20 percent phasing basis to reflect the fact that the average length of an overseas student course was 2–3 years. The amount removed from the grant was estimated at £100 million in April 1979 prices, this figure being the amount by which average costs of overseas students in U.K. institutions were reckoned to exceed the level of fees they were being charged. There was an outcry from individual institutions over the government computation of the sum that should be withdrawn, though the University Grants Committee has acknowledged that it found the figure about right for universities, and it seems possible that the UGC itself helped the government to arrive at its calculations.[11] The main criticisms leveled against the calculations were (i) that overseas students were marginal to a system created to serve British students and that therefore marginal rather than average costs should have been used. In

---

[10] I refer particularly to such reports as *Foreign Students and Institutional Policy* (Washington, D.C: American Council on Education, 1982); *The Right Mix: The Report of the Commission on Foreign Student Policy* (Ottawa: Canadian Bureau for International Education, 1981).

[11] See the evidence of Dr. E. Parkes on this point to the Education, Science and Arts Committee of the House of Commons in House of Commons (n. 2 above), p. 70.

any case notional average expenditure was not the same as potential savings to be realized if the enrollments contracted through the withdrawal of overseas students. (ii) At least in universities, a sizable proportion (perhaps a third?) of the most expensive resource, the time of academic staff, was supposed to be devoted not to teaching students but to research. Therefore it was argued that the cost of overseas students should have been based on a figure for teaching expenditures only. The government's retort to these criticisms was that per contra the calculation may well have been too low because average cost figures had been taken for overseas students as a whole, whereas in practice these students were concentrated in the most expensive engineering and technology subjects and at the most expensive postgraduate levels. Moreover the government estimates of cost per student omitted any element for the use of capital locked up in college premises and equipment.

Whatever the rights and wrongs of these arguments, and we must return briefly to them later in discussing current controversies over "flexible fees," it seems clear that institutions did suffer severe financial loss as a result of the policy. Total revenue would only have been maintained if numbers of overseas students had held up in face of the price (fee) rise and if fees had been charged on the basis of true average costs instead of—as was actually the case—the level of average expenditures at the cheapest institutions. Overseas student numbers did in fact diminish, as will be seen, and colleges did not feel able to recoup as much as they might have wished because they were afraid that competitors would scoop the overseas student pool if they raised fees above the minimum and that in any case overseas students were ill prepared to afford more than the minimum permissible fee rise. So the implication is that a rather considerable loss of resources was suffered by institutions, and this may have affected adversely their overall viability and the quality of their teaching and re-search.[12]

Developments since Full-Cost Fees Were Introduced

Political Developments and Modifications to the Policy

The government policy was widely criticized, especially by the academic community with its concern for the internationalism of the academic enterprise and for its own resource base. Particularly vocal were student organizations. They were joined in their protests by sections of British industry and commerce who feared the repercussions on their trade and investment from hostile overseas reaction, notably in countries like Malaysia and Nigeria, and there was also widespread dismay among members of

---

[12] For further discussion of this, see Overseas Students Trust, *A Policy for Overseas Students: Analysis, Options, Proposals* (London: Overseas Students Trust, 1982).

Parliament. The effort to secure reconsideration of the policy was orchestrated within the government by the Foreign and Commonwealth Office, which had to bear the brunt of the heavy criticism from other countries, and outside the government principally by a small voluntary organization, the Overseas Students Trust. The Overseas Students Trust, working partly independently and partly in collaboration with other bodies like the U.K. Council on Overseas Student Affairs (UKCOSA), succeeded in winning the confidence of Whitehall by the reasonableness of its approach in contrast to what the government regarded as unduly shrill and uninformed comment coming from elsewhere. Two major pieces of work issued by the Overseas Students Trust were its commissioned analytical studies collected together in *The Overseas Student Question,* published in 1981, and its policy recommendations under the title *A Policy for Overseas Students: Analysis, Options, Proposals,* published in June 1982.[13] These two publications, and more particularly the second, were informed by a close continuing dialogue between ministers and officials on the one hand and the Trust on the other.

Important as the work of the Overseas Students Trust may have been in providing a means for the government to escape from the corner into which it had driven itself, it was the weight of overseas opinion and pressure which was probably crucial. The evidence that Britain had sacrificed goodwill and done her own long-term diplomatic and commercial interests tangible harm was plain for all to see; and the point was endlessly rammed home on official journeys by British ministers abroad, on visits to Britain by foreign dignitaries, and in Commonwealth and other international fora. The full-cost fees decision looked more and more like a colossal mistake both from the point of view of what was done and for the way it was done with a lack of consultation. On the other hand, the British government was totally unrepentant about its need to secure cuts in expenditure and to find some way of regulating the flow of students from abroad, which had escalated so alarmingly under the regime of subsidized study.

The partial way out of the impasse was to maintain the full-cost fees policy but to pump back some public expenditure into the system via scholarship awards. Britain already had a rather sizable program of awards, predominantly under its Technical Cooperation Training Programme on the aid budget of the Overseas Development Administration, but also through the Commonwealth Scholarships and Fellowships Scheme and through the British Council. The Overseas Students Trust had suggested that the government provide an additional £34 million per year from

---

[13] Williams, ed.; Overseas Students Trust, *A Policy for Overseas Students.*

public funds for awards to assist overseas students, some but not all of which was "new money," the remainder being transfers.

In the end the government moved significantly, but not all of the way demanded by the Overseas Students Trust report. It announced a program on February 8, 1983, generally referred to as the "Pym Package" named after the foreign secretary who issued the statement. This provided £46 million extra assistance for awards programs over 3 years, of which £21 million was for transfers within the aid program to Technical Co-operation Training and Commonwealth Scholarships, and the remainder was "new money" mainly for concessionary help to Malaysia, Hong Kong, and Cyprus and for a new scheme of awards on the Foreign and Commonwealth Office vote. It was less than half in total of what the OST had asked for but more than some lobbyists had dared to hope.

Trends in Charging for Tuition

What the Pym Package did not do was to repudiate in any way the policy of full-cost tuition fees for overseas students. Indeed, the government ignored the recommendation of the Overseas Students Trust that nationals of some overseas countries and territories should be given a concessionary status, entitling them to reduced fees (in the same way as other members of the European Community are entitled to home-student fees for their citizens). Instead the British government chose to give all its concessions via awards schemes for selected scholarship holders. The government could thus claim that its full-cost fee policy was intact and that the only modification was that some students from abroad were being helped by the British authorities to pay these fees. Ostensibly, apart from the special case of the European Community, there was no dent in the full-cost fees system of charging.

The way tuition fees have moved since full-cost fees were first introduced in 1980 is shown in table 1. For comparison, the movement in the British retail price index (RPI) over the same period was 25 percent; and, because of wage restraint and higher pupil-teacher ratios in higher education, the index of higher education costs has risen less rapidly than has the RPI.

Trends in Demand for Places in the Face of Full-Cost Fees

The basic trends are as shown in table 2, which shows that total enrollments of overseas students in British higher and further education have declined since 1979–80 (the year before full-cost fees) from 82,400 to 55,800,[14] or by 32 percent in a 3-year period. The number of first-year enrollments has fallen over the same period from 45,400 to 29,900 or by 34 percent. The somewhat steeper percentage fall in entrants suggests

---

[14] These data are in fact for Great Britain (i.e., excluding Northern Ireland) and not for the United Kingdom as a whole. A recurring problem with British data on overseas students is to bind a constant data base.

TABLE 1

FEE LEVELS FOR OVERSEAS STUDENTS IN BRITISH FURTHER AND HIGHER EDUCATION,
1979, 1980, 1983

Institution and Course Type	September 1979 (£)	September 1980 (£)	September 1983 (£)	% Change 1980–83
Universities:				
Art, etc.	940	2,000	2,900	+45
Science, etc. (undergrad)	...	3,000	3,800	+27
Clinical medicine, etc. (postgrad)	1,230	5,000	7,000	+40
Advanced further education (maintained sector):				
Laboratory based	(940)	3,300	3,180	−4
Classroom based	...	2,400		+33
Nonadvanced further education:				
Laboratory based subjects	(520)	1,890	1,750	−8
Classroom based subjects	...	1,380		+27

SOURCE.—Compiled from information supplied by the U.K. Department of Education and Science, London.

that in the face of higher fees the average length of stay of overseas students is declining. The most rapid falls in intake have been in non-advanced further education, a sector whose experience has been markedly at odds with that of higher education.

In interpreting these trends, one should be aware of a number of factors serving to reduce the actual and observed impact of rising tuition fees on overseas student numbers. In the first place it has to be remembered

TABLE 2

OVERSEAS STUDENTS ENTRANTS AND ENROLLMENTS IN BRITISH HIGHER AND FURTHER EDUCATION,
1979–80 to 1982–83 (Thousands)

Level	First-Year Enrollments (Entrants)				All Enrollments			
	1979–80	1980–81	1981–82	1982–83*	1979–80	1980–81	1981–82	1982–83*
Universities	17.1	15.3	16.3	16.5	34.9	33.2	31.8	30.0
Advanced further	9.8	8.9	8.5	7.0	20.9	19.7	18.5	16.0
Total higher	26.9	24.2	24.8	23.5	55.8	52.9	50.3	46.0
Nonadvanced further	18.5	11.7	6.1	6.4	26.6	19.5	11.1	9.8
Total	45.4	35.9	31.0	29.9	82.4	72.4	61.4	55.8

SOURCE.—United Kingdom, Department of Education and Science, *Statistical Bulletin 9/83* (London, June 1983), tables 1, 4, 5.
    * Provisional.

that overseas students would be affected by total costs rather than simply by tuition fees alone. Rises in tuition fees from £940 per annum (undergraduates) or £1,230 (postgraduates) to £2,000 or £3,000 were certainly steep, but it should be noted that this rise of around £800 to £2,000 should be seen in the context of total costs of £3,000 to £5,000. Put another way, the fee rise generally applied to students and to their sponsors, who were already wealthy enough to invest £3,000 or so in their education in Britain. If this served to mitigate the initial impact of higher fees, then the changing external value of sterling, particularly in relation to the dollar, was a second factor of longer-term importance. Full-cost fees were introduced when the sterling/dollar parity was £1 = $2.4 as against the October 1983 rate of £1 = $1.5: when coverted to U.S. dollars, tuition fees in Britain are actually lower in 1983 than in 1980. This depreciation of sterling against the dollar has certainly helped to halt the swing of students away from the United Kingdom to the United States and may even have reversed it, for rather sharp tuition fee rises have occurred in the United States in the last year or so, making Britain much more competitive than formerly. Third, many students have been shielded from the impact of the awards by expanded British scholarship programs. A fourth factor is more cosmetic and has to do with statistical definitions. It seems possible that there has been some element in the overseas student figures of reclassification from home status, producing some inflationary tendency in recorded trends of overseas numbers.

What table 2 suggests is that, in the face of rapidly rising fees, the university part of the market in particular has remained remarkably buoyant, offering as it does qualifications with a ready market value in the countries from which students come. It is also the case that universities, being able to retain the fees they collect from overseas students, have an incentive for overseas recruitment that is denied to the public sector institutions, who return income earned to the authorities controlling them. The non-advanced sector of further education has fared worst. In the past it has been largely used by overseas students to collect the qualifications for entry to higher courses, and one may surmise that this has now become too expensive and risky. There may possibly be a consequent future decline in higher-level intake as this source of entrants dries up. Within higher education the proportions of first degrees have been steadily increasing, so that they composed 46 percent in 1977–78. There has not been that shift, predicted in the past, to postgraduate studies as overseas education provision developed. Among the subjects of study, there was a variable trend pattern. In universities in the latest year (1981–82) for which enrollment data by subject are available at the time of writing, the trends were for the most expensive subjects (medicine and agriculture) to exhibit a relatively steady state, science and engineering to show a decline, and the arts and social science subjects to show a mixed pattern of increases and decreases.

In terms of countries of origin, developing countries suffered more from the tuition fee changes than did developed countries. In the first 2 years of full-cost fees new entrants from developing countries dropped by 36 percent (13,600) to 24,300; while those from developed countries dropped by only 10 percent (700) to 6,100. Naturally enough the European Community, whose students were granted home-student status, fared best of all. Outside the Community the countries for which higher education enrollments were most buoyant were Hong Kong, Iran, and Nigeria, all of which experienced an increase in first-year enrollments in universities and other advanced courses between 1979 and 1981. But these same countries experienced steep falls in entrants to nonadvanced further education, as did Malaysia, too (table 3).

The Response at the Institutional Level

This has of course varied enormously from institution to institution, reflecting both the history of individual universities and colleges and their traditional commitment to overseas students, on the one hand, and, on the other hand, the perceptions of their management about the importance for the institutions' resource base and the need to protect it by raising revenue from overseas student fees. Many institutions have been very responsive to the changed circumstances and their reactions have been manifested in three main ways.

Redesign of academic offerings.—For almost the first time British public education institutions have been aware of being in a market in which the customer calls the tune. Instead of a selective supply-oriented system in which institutions would choose from a queue of applicants, the course designers have had to look hard at what students want. For overseas

TABLE 3
OVERSEAS ENTRANTS TO COURSES OF HIGHER AND FURTHER EDUCATION IN GREAT BRITAIN, 1979–80, 1981–82

Country	Higher Education			Nonadvanced Further Education		
	1979–80	1981–82	% Change	1979–80	1981–82	% Change
Hong Kong	1,452	1,750	+21	2,546	1,087	−57
Iran	1,297	1,498	+15	3,315	700	−79
Malaysia	3,747	2,859	−24	2,929	550	−81
Nigeria	2,028	2,696	+33	762	518	−32
All countries (including those above)	29,643	24,844	−16	18,493	6,131	−67

SOURCE.—United Kingdom, Department of Education and Science, *Statistical Bulletin 9/83* (London, June 1983), table 9.

students it is clear that their needs are predominantly for courses giving degrees and diplomas that will bring enhanced remuneration on their return home; courses which provided rich experience but no tangible recognition have lost in popularity. And the degree is more favored than the diploma or certificate; so there has been some tendency to restructure courses and redesignate them. Short course offerings have also, however, proliferated, geared to the purses of would-be students. In some cases the offering is a short enrichment course as part of an overseas degree for, say, undergraduates from the United States who may be encouraged to take a semester away from home. In another case it may be that students from overseas have their stay in the United Kingdom shortened, with leave to spend longer periods for data collection and fieldwork studies in their country of origin. All kinds of experiments are being considered for dual-location courses providing a spell of study in Britain but avoiding a financially ruinous 3 or 4 years at full-cost fees. Simultaneously schools and faculties are reexamining their entry requirements to make them more flexible. There seems little doubt that in some instances "more flexible" means "lower" or "easier" and that at some universities and colleges entry standards for students from abroad have dropped. Elsewhere it is rather a case of a more liberal attitude (and sometimes a more informed judgment) toward the equivalence of overseas school or college qualifications and a greater value put on relevant work experience. Whereas in the past a registrar might have rejected an overseas application out of hand through ignorance of how to evaluate the qualifications offered, now there is a tendency to follow up with requests for transcripts, scrutiny of dissertations presented for an earlier qualification, and a request for academic references.

Energetic recruitment.—Tied in with the foregoing is more market research and more energetic marketing. British academics are much more likely to be found these days visiting Kuala Lumpur or Lagos, discussing development plans, seeking out government personnel officers responsible for staff training, and inquiring about the training components of international assistance loans. In inverse proportion to the drop in student inquiries at British Council offices through the capital cities of Asia and Africa are the rise in calls by vice-chancellors, registrars, and professors seeking student business. Private entrepreneurial firms like Gabbitas Thring are offering their services (for a commission) to help bring in the students from abroad, and the British Council is for the first time engaging in market research on behalf of the public education system. Prospectuses and course brochures are proliferating, and advertisements for courses of study in Britain appear in the *South China Morning Post,* the *Standard,* and the *Daily Nation.* Alumni associations are encouraged, and links with overseas universities and colleges developed and fostered. A transatlantic observer, used to American approaches to student recruitment, would marvel that such absolutely commonplace activities could possibly be thought novel; but they are a radical departure for British institutions, which have traditionally enjoyed the luxury of waiting for students to queue up with applications at their gates.

Better student facilities.—A third reaction has been to improve the responsiveness to student social and academic needs. A traditional argument for the private financing of education through fees has been that it makes the education system both more efficient in terms of the need to match the attractiveness of competitors' course offerings and more accountable to students. Lecturing staff are undoubtedly more conscious of the notion of a client-centered approach[15] and of the need to give value for money in terms of better courses and more materials and facilities as fees rise. Student complaints are listened to more readily, hospitality and welfare services are being improved, and courses in study skills and language tuition are being provided more often. The fear that moving higher and further education for overseas students into the marketplace would produce a worse deal for the students appears not to have been borne out, as prior study of the professionalism of many North American institutions in caring for foreign students would possibly have indicated all along.

Strains in a Dual-pricing System

Such are the obvious reactions of British institutions to the new situation in which the recruitment of overseas students is important for the maintenance of the institution and for the preservation of jobs. But may there also be less obvious longer-term consequences for the system of tertiary education in the United Kingdom as a whole? Could it lose some of its traditional international character? Will the disappearance of many overseas students redirect attention to the problems of lack of demand by home students for educational opportunity? Or will the attractiveness of overseas students in financial terms encourage institutions to cut corners in their admission standards and in conferring academic awards? Can a dual-pricing system be long maintained in the same institution and at what cost? Or will the system of a private market for overseas students lead logically and inevitably to other forms of privatization of higher and further education in the United Kingdom? In an essentially competitive situation, can competition be confined and differential costs and quality be glossed over by maintaining the present regime of minimum recommended fees? Or are we about to see a disintegration of the long-proclaimed uniformity of quality and standards in the U.K. higher education system?

---

[15] For a useful discussion of this issue in relation to overseas students in Britain, see Ruth Reed, Jran Hutton, and John Bazalgette, *Freedom to Study: A Report Prepared by the Grubb Institute for the Overseas Students Trust* (London: Overseas Students Trust, 1978).

The fact that all of these questions are increasingly being asked underlines the point that overseas student policy, while ostensibly primarily a dimension of overseas relations, has profound implications for the operation of the domestic education system, particularly where—as in the British case—an attempt is made to run a dual regime, with all its inherent contradictions.

Parts of the British tertiary system have undoubtedly lost something of their international character as a result of the introduction of full-cost fees. Nonadvanced further education colleges have lost two-thirds of their overseas clientele in a very short spell of time. But the universities have been far less affected than other institutions and still retain an astonishingly high proportion of students of non-U.K. nationality. A recent analysis by the Department of Education and Science showed that as many as 14.4 percent of full-time students in the United Kingdom were of overseas nationality, one in seven.[16] Even though the figure has been as much as 16 percent in the recent past, it is still high; and both the number and proportion of overseas students in the United Kingdom remains considerably above what it was 10 or 15 years ago. Any impression that British higher education has somehow opted out of providing for students from abroad is a travesty of the real facts: there are twice as many overseas students now as in 1969–70.

It is hard to know whether there is or could be a "right" proportion of overseas students in an education system. The traditional view in Britain has been that, at the university level at least, 10 percent of the student body from overseas was about right, a view reiterated in the recent past by the chairman of the University Grants Committee.[17] The difficulty obviously arises that, if 10 percent is about right overall, then most of the parts of the system that contribute to such an average have got it quite seriously wrong. As pointed out in the *Overseas Student Question* an average of 11 percent for overseas students (just those paying overseas fees) in 1979–80 was compounded of 7 percent at the undergraduate level and 36 percent at the postgraduate level; 34 percent at the University of Manchester Institute of Science and Technology, but only 4 percent at neighboring Keele; at the undergraduate level 4 percent of students in the humanities but 22 percent of those in engineering and technology; and at the postgraduate level an overseas proportion of 57 percent in engineering and technology, 56 percent in agriculture and forestry, and 44 percent in medicine.[18] It is clear from the above figures that, on the one hand, some universities and courses may have had such a thin sprinkling

---

[16] Department of Education and Science, *Overseas Students in Great Britain in 1981–1982 and Provisional Information for 1982–1983* (London: Department of Education and Science, 1983).

[17] See the evidence of Dr. E. Parkes to the Education, Science and Arts Committee of the House of Commons in January 1980 in House of Commons (n. 2 above), p. 71.

[18] Williams, ed. (n. 3 above), pp. 27–29.

of overseas students that their claim to have been international in character may have been seriously in doubt; whereas in other cases a facility was being maintained for, and catered predominantly to, an overseas clientele at great expense to the British taxpayer. Yet it is not apparent whether or not British students were actually being displaced, even in cases of heavy concentration of overseas students.

Students from abroad have in the past generally had to meet the same admissions standards and have in the majority of cases been enrolled in subject areas where U.K. demand (admittedly as defined in terms of qualified applicants) has been broadly satisfied. During the great overseas student debate of recent years the universities and polytechnics have hotly maintained that the great proportion of overseas students in postgraduate courses, far from displacing or dispossessing the British, is in fact an instrument for ensuring that essential research is undertaken and vital facilities and posts kept in being against the day when British demand picks up. It would have been interesting to test the hypothesis that overseas students were displacing home students by empirical observation of what happened to vacated overseas places as soon as overseas demand fell away. Unfortunately, however, the possibilities for home students to take up any slack caused by a fall in overseas numbers have been limited by public expenditure cuts in the area of financial support for British postgraduate students. So it is hard to make the charge stick that a ready overseas student availability for research projects diverted attention from ways to attract homegrown brains into this enterprise.

Some of the most interesting aspects of the current overseas student policy in Britain concern its attempt to maintain a dual-pricing system, with two very distinct policies toward home and overseas students, and it may be useful to consider this by way of illustration in the context of universities. The education of home university students is funded by the University Grants Committee: their numbers are currently restricted in an attempt to contain public expenditure, and effectively they are on quota with a threat of sanctions should institutions seek to admit more students in ways which would increase their demand on resources. Increases in admissions of home students will not attract any extra resources to an institution and may in fact bring financial penalties: it is important nevertheless to ensure that one recruits up to the target figures provided by the UGC.

Overseas students, on the other hand, are quota free. They earn the institution a sum equivalent to the difference between marginal revenue and marginal cost. This will vary from department to department, course to course, and year to year; one cannot speak of a single marginal cost. Since many university costs are virtually fixed costs, however, because buildings cannot be released for other purposes and staff may be tenured, it will often be the case that extra overseas students do yield a worthwhile surplus of revenue at current fee levels. There is in fact a profit in many instances for institutions at levels well below even the £2,000–£3,000 minimum recommended fees for an arts course. This became only too clear in 1982–83 when the government found it necessary to reduce the tuition fees to home students from £900 to £480 so as to discourage institutions from recruiting more of them to obtain the fee of £900 per head (even though marginal revenue from such activities could by no means cover average expenditure per place).

The realization that in many instances marginal revenues might yield a handsome profit over marginal costs has led to pressure from some within the system to adopt the recommendation of the Overseas Students Trust report that flexible pricing should be followed and the system of recommended minimum fees for institutions should be abandoned. This would enable colleges and universities to lower their fees, thus possibly attracting more overseas students and benefiting the overseas customer, while at the same time possibly enhancing the institution's resources if demand for places was sufficiently elastic. It now seems likely that the system will gradually move in this direction—provided that institutions can satisfy the authorities that there is no subsidization involved—and that there will be an element of genuine competition in the pricing of courses for overseas students. Indeed, by the Education (Fees and Awards) Act of 1983, the government has now withdrawn from the business of recommending minimum fees for overseas students, leaving it to universities and local education authorities to decide whether to secure the same effect through a form of cartel or whether to accept differential charges. This will exacerbate the trend for the equalization of resources in the higher education system to disappear and for more attractive and better-managed institutions to gain custom and revenue at the expense of others. Particularly sought-after universities like Oxford and Cambridge could then command the highest prices if they were so minded; and more generally the most prestigious institutions might attract the wealthiest students or—by virtue of their greater ability to raise scholarship money privately—skim off the best brains.

Competition between institutions in a less orderly system is certainly one of the strains that may appear in British higher education. Another possibility of friction is that between British and overseas students. When British students are on quota, but foreign students are not, resentments may easily build and an often mistaken impression arise that foreigners are depriving Britons of higher education places. Cases are already reported of overseas students being offered a place "off quota" for an overseas fee, but being told that they cannot have the place if they wish to claim entitlement to pay a home fee. In other celebrated cases the impression has gained ground that overseas students may in a sense be able to "buy" places at a time when this is not permitted to home students.

Another area of tension is the situation of overseas students themselves. A dual-pricing system gives rise to enormous strains. A high fence divides the paradise of tuition at £480 for designated home students from the harsh climes where £3,000 or more is charged to overseas students. The result is that it is a matter of no small moment how a student is classified. There are the overt anomalies like the fact that a Commonwealth Cypriot pays the overseas fees while a non-Commonwealth Greek pays the home level of fee because his country is in the European Community. But beyond these lie a myriad of official decisions that result in the extraordinary situation that, out of 43,300 students of overseas nationality in the universities in 1981–82, only two-thirds were classified as overseas students and probably only about 25,000 actually paid the full-cost overseas fees. The question of classification becomes crucial for a person's economic survival, and it affects such categories as refugees, newly arrived immigrants, British nationals living abroad, et cetera in acute form. The manifest arbitrary unfairness of the present system is its most obnoxious characteristic.

Further challenges lie ahead. The scramble for overseas students could well intensify as demographic decline hits U.K. institutions. The overseas market may then become steadily more important to those who have learned to tap it. Indeed, it is not beyond the bounds of possibility that the overseas student policy of the government may come to develop in new directions, recognizing new opportunities in the overseas student presence that are currently obscured by peak domestic demand. But with the crisis of international indebtedness, will foreign countries have the wherewithal to pay, and what kind of tensions of international competitiveness will arise as other countries, faced with the same domestic demographic problems, seek to secure their own share of the overseas student market? Will the privatization of overseas students be followed by other privatization initiatives? There are signs in the United Kingdom that it may, and that institutions in a strong market position may begin to turn their advantage of reputation into a major advantage of resources. The overseas student question has given rise to thoughts and speculations which may cause the landscape of British higher education to change out of all recognition by the end of the century.

In conclusion, then, we find that the effects of the full-cost fees policy in Britain have been less clear-cut and dramatic than many of us anticipated. Other trends and subsequent events have blurred the sharply defined blacks and whites into fuzzy grays. The diplomatic provocations have been glossed over and the political scars partially healed by Mr. Pym's package of concessions. The sharpness of the fee rises has been partly blunted by the falling value of the pound and rapid fee hikes in other

English-speaking countries. The damage to college and university physical and financial viability has been half obscured by attacks on the financial base of postsecondary education on a broader front than overseas students and by the crisis of domestic provision as home numbers reach their peak.

But the longer-term issues will not go away and the overseas student question is likely to remain as important domestically as it is internationally. When the next strong challenge comes to the philosophical and organizational dualism represented by the present over discrimination against overseas students, the direction of change is most unlikely to be a reversion to the status quo ante. Much more probably it will be toward some form of economic charging to home students and economic entrepreneurship domestically on the part of institutions. The present overseas student policy regime is probably a harbinger of rather fundamental shifts in British postsecondary education management. Still, within the domestic context, overseas students will be important for reasons beyond this, most notably insofar as the domestic demographic slump is coming and has been ill prepared for. Those British institutions which have learned to respond most flexibly to the overseas student crisis of the last 3 years may weather the approaching storms best of all.

Overseas Students in Australia: Governmental Policies and Institutional Programs

STEWART E. FRASER*

It has been 80 years since the first private overseas students are recorded (1904) as coming for tertiary studies to the Commonwealth of Australia, which had just been established in 1901. The history of international educational exchanges from the point of view of Australia has been dominated by an outflow, or by a desire to study predominantly in the United Kingdom and, to a lesser degree, in Europe and North America, at least up to the beginning of the Second World War in 1939. After the war, and especially with the advent of the Colombo Plan in 1950, encouragement of students particularly from the new Commonwealth countries started to change the international exchange balance, with more overseas students coming to Australia than the number of Australians going abroad for postgraduate education and professional training. Various Australian governments since 1949 have emphasized, with differing priorities, a variety of objectives for encouraging overseas student programs. Foreign policy considerations as well as those of defense, trade, and commerce have also been noted. Development and training assistance to "emerging societies," promotion of "cultural exchanges," and the fostering of "international goodwill" have always been part of the rhetoric in explaining Australia's position in both government and nongovernment schemes to broaden the institutional and educational bases for overseas students coming to Australia.

A 20-Year Summary

In 1962 there were 12,049 overseas students and trainees (both secondary and tertiary) in Australia, of whom 10,903 or 90.5 percent were privately or home-government sponsored, while 1,146 or 9.5 percent

Acknowledgment is made to the generous provision of statistical data and relevant official ministerial policy statements by various colleagues of the Department of Foreign Affairs, Australian Development Assistance Bureau (Development Training Branch), the Department of Education (International Education Branch), the Department of Immigration and Ethnic Affairs (Student Section, International Division), the Australian Vice Chancellor's Committee (AVCC), and the Australian Committee of Directors and Principals of Advanced Education (ACDPAE), all located in Canberra, Australian Capital Territory (ACT). Their generous cooperation and sharing of preliminary results from ongoing research is acknowledged, especially the interim results of surveys conducted by AVCC, *Overseas Students Enrolled at Australian Universities* (July 1983), the ACDPAE report *Overseas Students in Colleges of Advanced Education* (August 1983), and the report *Overseas Students of the University of New South Wales* (May 1983), provided by the registrar of the University.

* Professor of education in the Center for Comparative and International Studies in Education, La Trobe University, Australia.

came under various Australian development-aid schemes such as the Colombo Plan.[1] Two decades later, in 1982, there were approximately 20,000 overseas students and industrial/occupational trainees, of whom 18,000 or 90 percent were privately or home-government sponsored. The overall ratio between private and home-government-sponsored students, and those Australian-government-sponsored students, has shown a moderate movement away from private sponsorships to Australian government assistance over this 20-year period. In the tertiary sector private students in 1962 amounted to 3,613 or 33.1 percent of the total, while in 1982 there were 9,492 or 74.1 percent. During the past 2 decades tertiary education in Australia has seen an expansion of universities and a considerable upgrading of colleges of advanced education which, with universities, now take three-quarters of all private overseas students coming to Australia. In spite of a gradual increase and upgrading in tertiary facilities in many of the sending countries, growing population, increasing aspirations, and pressures from an expansion of secondary education are contributory factors affecting the domestic supply and quality of educational services. From being principally a provider, in 1962, of secondary specialized and technical education to approximately 67 percent of private overseas students, Australia had changed by 1982 to become a predominant supplier of tertiary education to nearly three-quarters of all private overseas students. Within Australian universities the proportion of overseas students has gradually dropped from just over 11 percent in 1962 to approximately 7 percent in 1982.[2]

With respect to country of origin, in 1962 Malaya, Singapore, and Borneo accounted for 49.1 percent of all private students in Australia, while in 1982 Malaysia and Singapore accounted for 59.1 percent. In terms of tertiary private students, in 1962 the three above-mentioned countries accounted for 58.1 percent, and in 1982 Singapore and Malaysia accounted for 62.5 percent (see table 1). The attraction of Australia for tertiary-level students from these countries has not diminished; in fact it has increased, and in 1982 some 48.1 percent of all secondary students from overseas were from Malaysia, the majority of whom are expected to go on to tertiary education in Australia after completing the Higher School Certificate (i.e., year 12 or matriculation certificate).

---

[1] Note that the basis for classification has changed between 1962 and 1982 and also that there has been an upgrading of training facilities during this period, raising fields such as nursing-accountancy to a tertiary level. For 1962 statistics, see Mary C. Hodgkin, *Australian Training and Asian Living* (Nedlands: University of Western Australia Press, 1966), p. 221.

[2] Statistics on 1982 data are derived from incomplete tabulation sheets from the International Education Branch, Department of Education, Canberra. These figures are based on the student census conducted annually in June. See also Tertiary Education Commission, *Report for the 1982–84 Triennium: Advice of the Universities Council*, October 1980 (Canberra: Australian Government Publishing Service, 1981), vol. 1, pt. 2; table 3.16 on p. 32 provides statistics on overseas students at Australian universities, 1959–80.

TABLE 1
PRIVATE OVERSEAS TERTIARY AND NONSECONDARY STUDENTS IN AUSTRALIA
BY REGION/COUNTRY, JUNE 30, 1982

Country/Region	N	Percentage of All Asia	Percentage of All Overseas Students
Asia:	**8,536**	· · ·	**89.9**
Malaysia	5,426	63.6	57.2
Hong Kong	1,172	13.7	12.3
Singapore	502	5.9	5.3
Indonesia	442	5.2	4.6
Japan	248	2.9	2.6
Thailand	190	2.2	2.0
India	157	1.8	· · ·
Sri Lanka	122	1.4	· · ·
Other Asia	80	.9	· · ·
Philippines	70	.8	· · ·
Korea	42	.5	· · ·
Pakistan	38	.4	· · ·
China	33	.2	· · ·
Taiwan	14	.2	· · ·
Oceania:	**469**	· · ·	**4.9**
Fiji	332	70.0*	3.5
Tonga	44	· · ·	· · ·
Papua New Guinea	33	· · ·	· · ·
Solomon Islands	15	· · ·	· · ·
New Caledonia	14	· · ·	· · ·
Other Oceania	14	· · ·	· · ·
Nauru	11	· · ·	· · ·
Vanuatu	6	· · ·	· · ·
Other:	**487**	· · ·	**5.1**
Europe	148	· · ·	1.6
Africa	135	· · ·	1.4
North America	117	· · ·	1.2
South America	24	· · ·	· · ·
Middle East	52	· · ·	· · ·
Not specified	11	· · ·	· · ·
Total	**9,492**		**100****

NOTE.—Boldface subtotals add up to boldface totals.
* Percentage of all Oceania.
** Total percent is rounded off.

Both the geographical and the student classification bases for the year 1962 differ slightly from those employed in 1982; accordingly the figures noted above can provide only a general indication of developments at the beginning and at the end of a 20-year period rather than detailed trend analysis.

The responsibility for determining policy in regard to private overseas students is shared somewhat unequally between three Australian Federal Government departments—the Department of Immigration and Ethnic Affairs (DIEA), the Australian Development Assistance Bureau of the Department of Foreign Affairs (ADAB/DFA), and the Department of

Education and Youth Affairs (DEYA), with the first coordinating policy in consultation with the latter two. In administering programs and proctoring academic progress, the Department of Education has primary responsibility with the Australian Development Assistance Bureau (ADAB) supervising Australian-government-sponsored students from abroad and assisting with welfare needs of both private and sponsored students.

Students and Trainees Sponsored by the Australian Government

In 1982 the countries with the largest number of sponsored students and trainees were Indonesia, 404; Papua New Guinea, 175; Thailand, 170; Malaysia, 85; the Philippines, 80; Sri Lanka, 57; and Bangladesh, 51, with a somewhat similar rank order in 1981 and 1980. Of the sponsored students and trainees during 1979–80, 2,357 were male (80.4 percent) and 373 were female (19.6 percent), while the corresponding figures for 1981–82 were 2,895 male (79.5 percent) and 747 female (20.5).

Those students sponsored by the Australian government include higher degree and undergraduate students at universities or colleges of advanced education (CAE), technical and further education (TAFE) colleges, and industrial trainees. The total time spent in Australia, as well as the type of training and qualifications received on completion of the program, needs to be considered apart from the percentage gross figures reported. During 1980–81 the total number of persons financed by Australia numbered 3,283, and the "man months" were estimated to be 18,877 or barely less than an average of 6 months per person; however, some trainees come for 2 weeks and some stay for 2 years or longer.[3]

Financing Tertiary Education

As a generalization it perhaps should be noted that tertiary education in Australia is virtually free (tuition charges were abolished in 1973) and that, with the exception of some religious and some commercial colleges, there are no private tertiary institutions in Australia. The Commonwealth and, to a much lesser extent, the states bear the main costs of funding higher or postsecondary education. The tertiary education sector is funded on a triennial forward-planning basis, and monies paid to colleges and universities are generally a direct reflection of the number of students currently enrolled and, indirectly, of the numbers permitted for future enrollment by the Commonwealth Tertiary Education Committee (CTEC). Accordingly, while there are provisions overall for increases and decreases in general student numbers (both undergraduate and postgraduate) these are made without specific reference to overseas students. Generally, grants

[3] Statistics on 1981–82 data are derived from incomplete but current tabulation sheets from the Development Training Branch, Australian Development Assistance Bureau, Canberra.

are not provided for the expansion or development of a specific course, program, or faculty to cater either specifically or generally to the needs of overseas students, the only possible exception being with regard to the development and maintenance of language centers, linguistics departments, or programs catering to the teaching of English as a second language (TESL). In these cases cost-benefit considerations, special funding procedures, and fee collections may be involved to make them financially viable. Apart from these specific language or cultural programs for overseas students, the CTEC financial guidelines and funding allocations do not generally take into direct account changes in student numbers influenced by the demand or supply of overseas students wishing to study in Australia.

Overseas Students, 1982–83

There were approximately 22,000 students and trainees, both private and Australian government sponsored, in 1982. Private overseas students enrolled in formal studies in Australia numbered 12,814, of whom 9,492 or 74 percent were enrolled in tertiary institutions and 3,322 or 26 percent in secondary schools (including a few in primary grades). To this number should be added a further 4,500 private overseas students enrolled in nonformal studies such as English language classes, industrial-occupational trainees attending various short-term courses, and some 3,500 Australian-government-sponsored (ADAB) students enrolled in both formal studies and short courses. The private overseas students represent over 90 percent of all overseas students and industrial trainees. On the basis of still incomplete figures, the overseas student population in mid-1983 is approximately 25,000 persons, including 11,000 at the tertiary and 5,500 at the secondary level, 5,000 other short-course students or occupational trainees, and 3,500 ADAB-sponsored students and trainees.

The tertiary sector accounts for over 74 percent of all private overseas students in formal education; the universities enroll 76 percent of all tertiary students, with only 17 percent in colleges of advanced education (see table 2). Overseas students in Australian universities represent just over 60 percent of all categories of foreign students studying formally in Australia, whether at the secondary level, at the technical and further education college level, or at colleges of further education.

For the tertiary sector there has been a slight growth in the enrollment in CAEs compared with that in universities between 1980 and 1982. This may be a reflection either of the relatively easier entry to some CAE institutions or of overseas students' deliberate choices and/or their own, or the Australian, governments' decisions to encourage placements and thus enable more students to enroll in the nonuniversity sector.

The increasing imposition of quotas at universities, particularly at the undergraduate level in certain "popular" or "oversubscribed" faculties,

TABLE 2

PRIVATE OVERSEAS TERTIARY AND NONSECONDARY STUDENTS IN AUSTRALIA:
SUMMARY TOTAL POPULATION, JUNE 30, 1982

	Enrollment	%
Institutional affiliation and type of program:		
University, bachelor's degree	5,987	63.1
College of advanced education, bachelor's degree	1,395	14.7
University, higher degree	1,128	11.9
English language course program	343	3.6
Technical and further education certificate	250	2.6
University, graduate diploma	110	1.1
CAE, undergraduate diploma	92	1.0
CAE, graduate diploma	66	. . .
Trade—miscellaneous	42	. . .
Professional qualification	27	. . .
Commercial-secretarial	24	. . .
CAE, master's degree	21	. . .
TAFE—CAE equivalent	7	. . .
Total	9,492	100*
Enrollment by type of institution:		
University:	**7,225**	76.1
Bachelor's degree	5,987	. . .
Higher degree	1,128	. . .
Graduate diploma	110	. . .
College of advanced education (CAE):	**1,574**	16.6
Bachelor's degree	1,395	. . .
University graduate diploma	92	. . .
Graduate diploma	66	. . .
Master's degree	21	. . .
Technical and further education (TAFE):	**257**	2.7
Certificate	250	. . .
CAE equivalent	7	. . .
Other	**436**	4.6
Total	**9,492**	100
Enrollment by type of degree or qualification:		
Bachelor's degree:	**7,382**	77.8
CAE	1,395	. . .
University	5,987	. . . .
Higher degrees:	**1,149**	12.0
CAE	21	. . .
University	1,128	. . .
Other certificates, diplomas, etc.	**961**	10.2
Total	**9,492**	100

NOTE.—Statistics on population include only tertiary and nonsecondary students as at the time of annual student census but do not include occupational training or short-term exchange students who will normally not exceed a 12-month stay in Australia. Boldface subtotals add up to boldface totals.

* Total percent is rounded off.

may eventually contribute to an increase in enrollment for overseas students at CAEs, especially if CAEs have more flexible entrance standards and course requirements, providing a greater range of undergraduate programs more suitable for overseas students, particularly those from Pacific and regional developing countries.

In 1981, 6.2 percent and, in 1982, 6.8 percent of all students at the 19 Australian universities came from overseas.[4] However, the increase was more marked for undergraduate students; higher-degree students increased as a percentage from 8.98 percent in 1981 to 9.14 percent in 1982, while undergraduates increased from 5.81 percent to 6.38 percent. Rather than focus on the overall percentage of overseas students in Australian universities, it may be of greater importance to look at individual institutions and particular faculties or disciplines.

In regard to higher-degree, that is, postgraduate, students, the rank order of institutions enrolling overseas students shows: Australian National University (ANU), 36.2 percent (1981), 36.0 percent (1982); University of New England, 12.4 percent (1981), 12.9 percent (1982); Newcastle University, 11.0 percent (1981), 12.7 percent (1982); and James Cook University, 12.2 percent (1981), 12.7 percent (1982). In explanation of the apparently inordinately high percentage of higher-degree students at ANU, it should be remembered that this institution was established originally as an advanced or research university (in 1946). However, in terms of undergraduate enrollments, especially in professional fields such as medicine, dentistry, engineering, and architecture, which are all first-degree fields, this picture changes somewhat: Monash University, 9.9 percent (1981), 11.7 percent (1982); University of New England, 10.4 percent (1981), 12.1 percent (1982); University of New South Wales, 9.9 percent (1981), 11.7 percent (1982).

Faculties and Disciplines

Table 3 reflects the particular areas of studies currently attracting overseas students and the universities' response of imposing quotas because of limited places overall. Australian universities have imposed various quotas on overseas students for undergraduate programs, more generally stated as "other than higher degrees" (OTHD) in the nomenclature.

The autonomy of each institution is reflected in the somewhat varying standards for initial entry set by, say, medical faculties of different universities as well as by different faculties or disciplines within a university.

For example, in the state of Victoria there are two medical schools, both located in Melbourne. Private overseas students are not eligible for

---

[4] Statistics on 1981–82 data are derived from the Australian Vice Chancellor's Committee, "Overseas Students Enrolled at Australian Universities," Interim Report Working Paper (Canberra, July 18, 1983, mimeographed), with 38 tables providing data on individual universities and faculties.

TABLE 3

AUSTRALIAN UNIVERSITIES: FACULTY QUOTAS OTHER THAN HIGHER DEGREES (OTHD), 1983

Discipline	Adelaide	Flinders	Melbourne	Monash	Murdoch	New South Wales	Queensland	Sydney	Tasmania	Western Australia
Agricultural science	5	…	4	…	…	…	1	4	…	…
Architecture	…	…	18	…	…	…	10	5	…	1
Arts	…	…	17	…	…	…	64	20	…	…
Arts/law	…	…	…	…	…	…	1	…	…	30
Commerce	3	…	2	…	…	…	36	4	…	…
Dental science	…	…	…	…	…	…	22	…	…	…
Design studies	…	…	…	…	…	…	7	…	…	…
Economics	…	…	46	…	…	…	4	10	…	…
Education	…	…	…	…	…	…	21	1	…	…
Engineering	9	…	44	80	…	…	33	10	…	40
Human movement studies	…	…	…	…	…	…	1	…	…	…
Laws	…	…	5	…	…	…	11	5	…	…
Medicine/surgery	5	4	12	8	…	20	58	6	4	…
Music	…	…	…	…	…	…	1	1	…	…
Occupational therapy	…	…	…	…	…	…	4	…	…	…
Pharmacy	…	…	…	…	…	…	12	4	…	…
Physiotherapy	…	…	…	…	…	…	2	…	…	…
Regional and town planning	…	…	…	…	…	…	3	…	…	…
Science	30	…	29	…	…	…	27	12	…	…
Social work	…	…	…	…	…	…	2	4	…	…
Surveying	…	…	…	…	…	…	16	…	…	…
Veterinary science	…	…	2	…	4	…	11	4	…	…

NOTE.—The following universities impose no quotas: Australian National University, La Trobe, Macquarie, Newcastle, New England, Wollongong; for Deakin, a maximum of 30 percent of new student places in the Bachelor of Architecture program and a maximum of 10 percent for the Bachelor of Commerce is to be taken up by overseas applicants; for James Cook, the number of first-year overseas students must not exceed 25 percent of the total intake in a particular faculty; for Griffith, the number of undergraduate places to be filled each year by students with overseas qualifications should not exceed 8 percent of the full-time places available throughout the university. For Western Australia, an overall quota of 125 was imposed in 1981, 1982, and 1983 on new overseas students entering the first year of bachelor's degree courses.

101

entrance to the undergraduate medical program at Monash University. The exceptions are Commonwealth-sponsored students, financed by the Australian government; up to eight places each year are set aside for this group. In 1983, some six Malaysian students (all Malay and all of whom had completed their last year of secondary studies including the Higher School Certificate [HSC] in Victoria) were admitted. At Melbourne University the faculty of medicine permits annually between 12 and 15 private overseas students to enroll, but they must have a substantially higher HSC result. The normal Australian first-year student entry is 334 points on the so-called Anderson (composite examination) Rating Scale, while overseas students require 365 points. In 1983, 12 overseas students were admitted to study undergraduate medicine at Melbourne out of some 200 first-year students.

In noting the quota figures regarding the admission of overseas students in certain faculties, two immediate practical problems are presented or policy questions raised: what does the presence of a "large percentage" of overseas students in a particular discipline or course of studies mean for the direction, quality, and level of instruction; and second, what effect does it have in terms of excluding Australian students? These kinds of basic questions can only be seen as part of the overall policy considerations which a university must make in relation to the role it wishes to play generally in international educational exchange and its reception, sustenance, and training of overseas students. These must be matched if not at least considered in terms of the obligations it must maintain to Australian matriculants who might otherwise be excluded because of limited faculty quotas in a particular university.

The University of New South Wales Study

Perhaps some brief extracts from a recent case study of what has happened to one Australian university may illustrate some of the problems, dilemmas, and difficulties in approaching the phenomenon of "too many overseas applicants and potentially too few places for Australian students."[5] These concerns are thoughtfully reflected in a position paper recently released by the University of New South Wales. The university, located in Kensington (Sydney), places no restriction on the entry of overseas students to any course, the only exception being medicine (for the M.B. and B.S. degree), where a quota of 20 is in effect. However, the steady rise of overseas students from 7 percent in 1978 to 12 percent in 1982 has caused some unease and prompted a review of the situation and consideration of the imposition of quotas in other faculties. Extracts from this report (May 1983) are as follows:

[5] Registrar's Office, "Overseas Students" (University of New South Wales, Kensington, May 1983, mimeographed), p. 5; with appendix, eight pages of tables.

Concern is being expressed in some quarters about the current capacity of Australian universities in regard to the present levels of admission of overseas students. This concern is generally expressed in the light of the Government's policy to facilitate the entry of private overseas students for long term study on the understanding that the capacity of educational institutions should be fully utilised without significant displacement of Australian students. [P. 1]

In particular, in 1982 overseas undergraduate students in Architecture represent 18.3% of total enrolments and in Engineering the percentage is 19.9%. The percentages in 1980 were 9.2% and 11.5% respectively. [P. 3]

Some courses within these faculties have a higher proportion of overseas students. Those courses with the largest number of overseas students are:

Architecture	35.9%
Building	22.2%
Accounting, Finance and Systems	18.6%
Civil Engineering	25.9%
Electrical Engineering	25.6%

The trend towards an increasing proportion of overseas students in these courses becomes more prominent when new full-time enrolments in 1982 are considered. The figures are:

Architecture	43.9% (51.1)
Building	38.6% (54.5)
Accounting, Finance and Systems	23.7% (32.3)
Civil Engineering	39.2% (34.3)
Electrical Engineering	35.0% (43.8)

The recently completed figures for 1983 (given in brackets above) show that the trends are even more prominent this year, with the overall percentage of overseas students in all courses at Kensington being 13.5%. [P. 3]

In conclusion the University of New South Wales' report on overseas students noted:

Because of the economic climate in which the University finds itself we are faced with the necessity of decreasing our student load by some three percent over the next triennium [1985–87] if we are to achieve a reasonable match between our resources and enrolments. To do this effectively and fairly, consideration will need to be given to exercising some control over the proportion of some permanent and temporary resident students who are admitted to some courses. The present proportion of 13.5 percent of overseas students is the highest of any University in Australia, is especially high in some undergraduate areas, e.g., Architecture and Electrical Engineering and is increasing each year. These proportions will need to be regulated if an increasing number of good quality Australian students are not to be displaced by the unrestricted entry of overseas students. The Government's intention of liberalising the entry of overseas students was to fully utilise educational capacity without significant displacement of Australian students. Some overseas applicants not gaining places at this University should be able to take up places in other tertiary institutions where they could be enrolled without displacing local applicants, in most courses.

Faculty Quotas on Student Composition: Options

If universities and colleges of advanced education wished to allocate a specific number or percentage of places overall in an institution or a specific faculty or department for overseas students, this would be an institutional decision. The supervising body in Canberra, the Commonwealth Tertiary Education Commission, is more concerned with the overall numbers and general program direction of students irrespective of their specific national origin or immigration status. This situation may allow one institution to impose strict quotas on overseas students, particularly in certain faculties, while another institution may attempt to build up its student numbers to the permissible ceilings imposed by the CTEC in Canberra by deliberately encouraging overseas students to take up these places.

On June 30 each year a student census is conducted by the Department of Education, and these statistics, as well as those provided directly by tertiary institutions to CTEC, may be used for monitoring ongoing funding arrangements. This leaves open the possibility that some institutions and even specific departments may recruit, encourage, and enroll overseas students who make up numbers, occupying the places not taken up by Australians, and form the basis for an application for additional funds. While this situation may be masked temporarily because CTEC does not necessarily require detailed information on the national origin and immigration status of students in particular faculties, the problem would be highlighted eventually by a major imbalance and evidence of too high a proportion of overseas students to Australian students in certain courses.

If particular programs and courses are undersubscribed by Australians, it is not necessarily the case that overseas students will automatically drift or move to these faculties to gain a place. On the other hand, a popular faculty may have a much greater number of qualified overseas students seeking to gain entrance. If they are better qualified academically than the average Australian student seeking entrance, then an internal institutional policy decision needs to be made: (1) to impose a quota on the overseas student applicants; (2) to allow the best entrants on qualifications, irrespective of student origins; or (3) to seek an expansion of programs and adequate funding from CTEC to cater to a larger student intake. The last option takes time and needs careful planning and justification, especially as there is generally considerable competition for funds and for determining funding priorities within a university or college.

The second option could, in theory, lead to a very much increased intellectual level in the student body; however, with the whole Asian and Pacific region supplying its best students from a potential supply of several million high school leavers competing with a few thousand Australian high school leavers, a course could quickly be dominated by a student body of overseas applicants!

The first option of imposing a quota on overseas applicants is the easiest to effect and can be adjusted upward or downward without repercussions beyond the institutions' control. This flexibility allows for both teaching and administrative staff to make adjustments in the short run without drawing adverse comments or criticism from CTEC. However, the application of quotas may be somewhat ambiguous to applicants from abroad who may not have informed themselves clearly about the exact nature and operation of the quota schemes. Universities in correspondence with overseas students, as well as Australian diplomatic posts abroad, endeavor to communicate this information clearly to overseas applicants.

Postgraduate/Higher Degree Scholarship Awards

Among the 19 Australian universities, only one, the University of Western Australia, imposed a quota on the number of university scholarships awarded to overseas students, namely, that no more than 25 percent of all awards could be so allocated. All other Australian universities (with the exception of Macquarie where it was not applicable) did not set quotas on scholarship awards to overseas students undertaking higher degrees.[6]

In 1982, 245 or 42 percent of all postgraduate awards went to overseas students and in 1983 (data complete to mid-1983) 219 or 41 percent went to applicants from overseas. The current situation indicates a high percentage of university awards given to overseas students and reflects as much the overall quality of overseas applicants as a selective policy of positive discrimination. However, it should be noted that Commonwealth Post Graduate Awards (CPGA) are awarded only to Australians and differ somewhat from awards made by individual universities from their own scholarship provisions. It is apparent that Australia is currently awarding a high percentage of postgraduate awards to higher-degree applicants from overseas, which should be seen perhaps in context of the ratio of similar awards made by other countries such as Britain, the United States, West Germany, and France. The principal universities in Australia that have provided the bulk or a substantial number of postgraduate awards to overseas students are the following: ANU (66 percent in 1982, 73 percent in 1983), New South Wales (48 percent in 1982, 50 percent in 1983), Sydney (53 percent in 1982, 72 percent in 1983), Monash (42 percent in 1982, 58 percent in 1983), Melbourne (34 percent in 1982, 37 percent in 1983); figures for 1983 are current to mid-year.

[6] See Australian Vice Chancellor's Committee.

Government Policy

During the 1960s the government's overseas student program could best be characterized as threefold, being a decade of, first, indirect "aid abroad" through training and second, the fostering of direct technical assistance to regional countries with, third, the strict requirement that students would return home after studies were completed. The advent of the Whitlam (Labour) government in 1973 changed somewhat this last objective of aid, allowing overseas students to remain in Australia after training if they adhered to immigration procedures. The private overseas student programs still focused "generally" on "aid and development" as principal objectives, but greater emphasis was placed on developing or extending specific cultural and educational agreements on a bilateral basis. Aid, development, cultural exchanges, and modified immigration were all characteristic of the new programs starting in 1973. Not unexpectedly, considerable numbers of Chinese students from Hong Kong, Singapore, but predominantly from Malaysia, as well as students from the Indian subcontinent, made use of the newfound opportunity to apply for permanent residence after their tertiary program of studies was completed. This was characterized and criticized as a deliberate policy of brain drain by many of the countries in the Asian region.

With respect to international educational exchange programs, many other developed countries in the mid-1970s showed a general tendency toward the gradual tightening of regulations for initial entry to study and certainly for permanent residence after completion of studies. A new Liberal–National Country Party Coalition government took office in 1975 and continued with only modest variation the programs of the previous Labour government until 1978. In mid-July 1978 the Liberal-NCP Coalition government undertook a partial review of the overseas student policy to which the Australian Vice-Chancellor's Committee (AVCC), representing the university sector, among other interested parties, was asked to provide statistical information and make policy recommendations.

When the review was completed a year later, the Minister for Immigration and Ethnic Affairs M. J. R. MacKellar issued a new government policy statement that briefly reviewed the findings and plans for updated program initiatives, including the introduction of an annual "visa" charge of between $1,500 and $2,500 (August 22, 1979) (all amounts are given in Australian dollars). He also noted that, in the immediately preceding years, three-quarters of the overseas students who finished their courses stayed in Australia instead of returning home. The previous Labour government's policy was criticized as "having not worked" and "the criteria for entry having been based mainly on the inability of students to obtain enrolment in courses in home countries. This has sometimes led to students proposing to undertake courses of little value to the home country but thereby gaining preference over other students of higher academic ability and other students seeking to undertake courses which would be useful to the home country."[7] Unfortunately, there was no specific evidence to support this somewhat convoluted statement concerning the "value" of certain programs of studies. However, the minister was probably on sounder ground when he also noted that "almost 75 percent of students completing formal studies in recent years have applied successfully for resident status." This statement could be certainly verified from Department of Immigration and Ethnic Affairs statistics and research and undoubtedly was again an indirect criticism of the previous Labour government's policy. As MacKellar noted of "the non-returning student," "this development has negated the main objectives of the program," which of course were to "contribute to extending cultural exchange and goodwill" and to provide "benefits to developing countries, especially those in areas close to Australia, through additional educational opportunities, and skilled manpower training for their people" (p. 1).

The policy review also noted that new criteria would be developed for accepting students to Australia, with priority being accorded to (1) students who were sponsored by their home governments, (2) those granted scholarship assistance for studies abroad, and (3) those intending to undertake postgraduate research and qualify for higher degrees in Australian universities. It was estimated that the average annual costs of educating a full-time student at an Australian university amounted to $5,500 in 1979, while costs at other tertiary institutions such as colleges of advanced education were in the vicinity of $4,100 per annum. No precise details were provided about how these estimates were derived, or whether they were based on total (including capital) costs for tertiary education or only on recurrent costs.

The rationale for the introduction of a charge to overseas students was based on the fact that in Australia specific tuition fees were not normally charged for public tertiary education. Advanced studies or specialized training was financed from consolidated revenue, in other words, indirectly from the Australian taxpayer at large. Parents of overseas students accordingly were seen as having their children educated in Australia free of tuition charges that they or their own government would have had to pay if the students had remained at home for their postsecondary studies. The charges imposed, commencing with the academic year 1980, ranged between $1,500 and $2,500, which was said to be approximately 30–50 percent of the "real" tuition cost, that is, charges normally borne by the Australian taxpayer for the tertiary education sector.

[7] M. J. R. MacKellar, Minister for Immigration and Ethnic Affairs, "Budget Statement: Entry of Overseas Students—Review of Policy . . . ," News Release (Canberra, August 22, 1979, mimeographed), p. 1.

Curiously, but without providing specific details, in introducing the new overseas student charges, the government linked the likely income to be received from the new visa charges directly to a roughly equal expenditure to increase deliberately the number of overseas students coming to Australia in 1982 and subsequent years. The cost of such an exercise has never been made public; in fact, a full and comprehensive cost-benefit analysis of the entire overseas student program has never been undertaken to analyze the expenditures and returns to (1) the Australian government, (2) home governments, (3) individual overseas students and their families, (4) Australian educational institutions, and (5) the Australian community, especially the banking, business, trading, and cultural sectors.

The government's official justification for introducing the charges was presented without any attempt at detailed analysis, stating only: "The new policies have been designed with a view to an increase in the number of students who will be admitted for study at Australian universities and colleges of advanced education. The revenue from the new charges will facilitate this and offset the additional public cost of the increase in overseas students studying in Australia."[8] Exemptions from the charges would be made to overseas students who, if coming to Australia under bilateral education-training and development arrangements, would have their fees (visa charges, etc.) paid under the appropriate bilateral aid agreement.

Because a "high proportion" of overseas students had taken up permanent residence when their studies were completed, the government also decided to close this so-called back-door immigration loophole, noting: "The Government has decided that, in future, overseas students will be required to leave Australia on the conclusion of their studies. Applications to return to Australia for residence will not normally be received or considered within two years. This requirement has received general support from overseas governments consulted."[9]

Australia has indicated from time to time that countries in close geographical proximity would be considered on a priority basis for educational aid and training facilities. To justify as well as to explain the imposition of student fees, the government policy statement of August 22, 1979, reiterated the specific regional bias of Australia's overseas student development program: "The new policies will make the private overseas student program more effective and facilitate opportunities for an increased number of people to study in Australia within the limits of Australia's educational and training capacity. It is envisaged that most of the increased numbers

[8] Ibid., p. 4.
[9] Ibid., p. 5.

will be drawn from students such as the ASEAN countries, Papua New Guinea and the South Pacific."[10]

Details of Charges

Full-time students commencing in 1980 were to be liable for tuition charges at the following rates: (1) $2,500 a year for higher-degree studies for master's or Ph.D. qualifications; (2) $2,000 a year for medicine, veterinary science, and dentistry courses; (3) $1,500 a year for all other students at universities and colleges of advanced education enrolled in award courses; (4) half the annual rate charges for part-time or semester program if not involving more than the equivalent of half a year's course of study.

The government also estimated on previous experience that "about three-quarters of all overseas students would be paying the minimal fee of $1500 p.a." Two years later all fees had been raised except master's and doctoral programs, which remained at $2,500. Students already enrolled in secondary or tertiary programs were exempted. In August 1981 students from Papua New Guinea and the South Pacific region were also exempted from visa fees.

A new minister for immigration and ethnic affairs, John Hodges, indicated on August 17, 1982, that charges for medicine, veterinary science, and dentistry would be raised to $2,350, while students in all other courses would be charged $1,850.[11] These new changes would apply to the academic year starting in February 1983. Based on 1982–83 figures of minimally 10,000 tertiary students (with 7,500 paying $1,850, 1,000 paying $2,350, and about 1,000 paying $2,500) the figure of approximately $18 million would be received in annual visa charge fees by 1985. In explanation the minister stated:

> The increases since the charge was introduced [in 1980] were significantly less than the education cost increases and now represented only around 33 percent of the average per student cost for higher education . . . ; the government believes it is reasonable to ask overseas students to continue to make a contribution toward the cost of their education in Australia.
>
> It is intended to review the charge on an annual basis, taking account of cost increases over the previous year.
>
> The overseas student charge is not intended to reduce the overall number of students coming to study in Australia.
>
> By requiring some contribution from overseas students Australia can assist additional students to study in Australia without substantially increasing the cost to the Australian taxpayer.[12]

[10] Ibid.

[11] John Hodges, Minister for Immigration and Ethnic Affairs, "Overseas Students Charges," News Release (Canberra, August 17, 1982, mimeographed), p. 1.

[12] Ibid.

Exceptions were made for (1) students already in tertiary programs and those who were already in Australia completing secondary schooling as a preliminary to entering an approved tertiary course of study; (2) students who came to Australia for the specific purpose of entering an English-language course as a preliminary to tertiary study; (3) those overseas students holding university or college of advanced education scholarships with a stipend of at least $3,500.

Apart from the visa fees, which currently could be bringing in approximately $12 million annually, a minimal estimate would suggest that the nearly 13,000 overseas private students in Australia in 1983 would require between $4,000 and $5,000 annually for basic individual support. This would represent an inflow of funds in the vicinity of at least $50 million annually, which would be expended in Australia on goods and services generated for the Australian economy or as an invisible export, of which perhaps 20–25 percent could be attributed as profit accruing directly to the Australian private and commercial sector. Counterbalancing these credits would be the $75 million annual expenses to Australia for subsidizing the higher education of this particular group of students.

A full review of the Private Overseas Student Program was jointly announced on July 5, 1983, by the minister for immigration and ethnic affairs, Stewart West, and the minister for education and youth affairs, Senator Susan Ryan. Irrespective of the review findings, new quotas would be set on the intake of private overseas students who would be admitted to formal studies commencing with the academic year starting in February 1984. The joint ministerial statement issued by West and Ryan noted:

> The number of new students entering Australia next year will be limited to 3,500. This number will comprise 2,000 secondary students and 1,500 tertiary students. In addition, 2,500 overseas secondary students currently in Australia are expected to enter tertiary institutions next year, allowing a total of 4,000 private overseas students to commence tertiary studies here. This represents an increase of 400 over the number of places available in 1983.
>
> Ministers said that these numbers reflected a balance between Australia's desire to assist other countries, and the demands of local students for tertiary places. These and other issues require further examination before decisions are made for future years.
>
> The Government has therefore agreed to a major review of the overseas student program. Details of this review will be announced in the near future by the Minister for Immigration and Ethnic Affairs, the Minister for Education and Youth Affairs, and the Minister for Foreign Affairs.[13]

---

[13] Stewart West, Minister for Immigration and Ethnic Affairs, and Susan Ryan, Minister for Education and Youth Affairs, "82/83 Private Overseas Student Program," News Release (Canberra, July 5, 1983, mimeographed), p. 1.

Restrictions on Overseas Student Entry, 1984

The July 6, 1983, announcement by the government included the commencement of a long-term review of the overseas program and also indicated a cutting back, for the short term, of the number of students who would be permitted to begin studies in the new academic year beginning in February or March 1984. Some 4,000 new overseas students were admitted in 1983, but the intake for 1984 will be only 3,500, comprising some 2,000 new secondary students and 1,500 new tertiary education students coming directly to Australia from overseas. To this latter figure should be added almost 2,500 secondary students who are already studying in Australian high schools and who will be sitting for higher school certificates in December 1983. In all a total of 4,000 overseas students will be entering tertiary education for the first time in 1984. Over the past 3 years there has been a gradual buildup of overseas students entering high school for studies at years 10 and 11 as well as year 12, preparing themselves for university or college entry. In previous years, certainly from 1975 to 1980, overseas students at the secondary level generally came to Australia for a single or final graduating year of studies, but increasingly the tendency has been to come for at least 2 or more years of senior high school study to ensure a better chance of achieving success at the increasingly competitive high school certificate examinations conducted in each of the various Australian states. In 1983 the government planned a balance between new secondary and new tertiary students: 2,500 to 2,000. In 1984 the ratio is to be 2,000 to 1,500.

Government Policy Review of Private Overseas Student Programs

The Labour government in September 1983 announced details and terms of reference for a committee to review the various programs involving private students from overseas. The committee was asked to examine whether the program currently served Australia's best international interests, to recommend appropriate policy changes which would ensure development of the program without incurring additional public costs, and to examine critically student admission policies and procedures. The review committee was specifically cautioned to "assess the extent of hidden aid subsidy in the present program"[14] and what effects, if any, modification to the program would have on relations with countries sending students to Australia.

In consideration of Australia's special regional interests it was expected that the committee would make appropriate recommendations "regarding the form of the program over the next 5 to 10 years."[15] It was charged

[14] Stewart West, Minister for Immigration and Ethnic Affairs, Susan Ryan, Minister for Education and Youth Affairs, and Bill Hayden, Minister for Foreign Affairs, "Review of Private Overseas Student Policy," News Release (Canberra, September 8, 1983, mimeographed), p. 1.
[15] Ibid.

with inquiring into some nine specific areas of concern, the answers to which would form the criteria needed for determining governmental policy and administrative procedures and ensure effective program implementation:

1. The proportion of the cost of training to be borne by the student (including the possibility of full cost recovery);
2. Whether priority should be given to students from particular countries;
3. The basis upon which selection should be made bearing in mind inter alia matters of distributional equity and ways of encouraging overseas students with limited economic means;
4. What criteria can be adopted for measuring and evaluating the benefits to Australia of the activity;
5. The role of non-formal studies and courses outside the normal educational provision;
6. The role of secondary school studies;
7. The need for advisory or co-ordinating bodies;
8. The sharing of administrative responsibility among government authorities and between them and other agencies;
9. The need for administrative simplicity.[16]

The Private Overseas Student Policy Review Committee was also required to "consult with the Committee reviewing Australia's development assistance on relevant issues."[17] This was in reference to the Jackson committee, which is presently inquiring into the performance of Australia's overseas aid program and, in particular, into the working of the Australian Development Assistance Bureau of the Foreign Affairs Department.

It is now becoming more evident that the three major government departments concerned with overseas students have somewhat different perceptions of their role in policy decisions and program implementation with regard to initiating and maintaining the flow of foreign students into Australia. These differences are being highlighted by the increasing financial restrictions now placed on tertiary education expansion and criticisms of the value of heavily subsidizing a significant proportion of the overseas students, perhaps at the critical expense of Australian students, without a concomitant increase in international goodwill or at least some evidence that the program has some tangible foreign policy returns.

In a carefully worded submission by the DIEA to the Jackson committee, the private overseas student program is described as having dismally failed to meet its basic objectives because of the enormous financial subsidies involved, which have done little to advance "Australia's interests in countries of particular importance to Australia by improving communication, un-

[16] Ibid.
[17] Ibid.

derstanding of and sympathy for, Australian policies and to promote cultural exchange."[18] Furthermore, the DIEA submission recommends that private students should pay their own way (or have it paid for them by employers, home governments, institutional awards, etc.). Its conclusion is devastatingly critical and is summed up in the sentence, "We consider that the mixture of aid, foreign policy, and general response to demand motives operating within the Private Overseas Student Policy have produced a confused and ineffective policy."[19] If this kind of interdepartmental washing of dirty linen in public is typical of the kind of submissions now being presented to the Jackson Committee of Review on Foreign Development Assistance, then some of the papers that are expected to be presented to the newly formed Review Committee on Private Overseas Students should in all likelihood be both illuminating and acrimonious. The committee is expected to have its final report completed in less than 6 months, that is, by February 1984.

Conclusion

The committee gave interested parties barely 6 weeks to prepare their submissions (from September 8 to October 31, 1983) and itself has been asked by the government to respond by the end of February 1984, only some 4 months later. One wonders whether a 4-month review is sufficient to provide enough material for Australian foreign policy initiatives in developing international educational exchanges for "the next five to ten years" as the government expects. For those who have spent some time working in the field of international educational and cultural exchanges it is obvious that governments generally have only a limited capacity to purchase, ensure, or maintain the goodwill of any country simply through manipulating the quantity or quality in the flow of foreign students. There are a host of significant intervening variables between an entry visa obtained or an initial scholarship awarded and a satisfied, properly trained student returning home to satisfactory employment.

The review is being conducted at a sensitive moment, demographically and educationally. Australian governments, both federal and state, are in the process of increasing the student participation retention rate in high schools and encouraging graduates to proceed to some form of further or higher education. Throughout Australia, but particularly in populous states such as New South Wales and Victoria, an increasing number of students will in any case be graduating from secondary school—the product of the baby boom which occurred some 17 or 18 years ago. In Victoria

---

[18] Department of Immigration and Ethnic Affairs, "Submission to the Committee to Review the Australian Overseas Aid Program: Overview on Private Overseas Student Programs" (Canberra, August 5, 1983, mimeographed), p. i.
[19] Ibid.

the projections for 17-year-olds from 1983 to 1986 suggest an annual increase of 2.6 percent, rising to a 6 percent increase by 1986. Accordingly the pressure for tertiary places by Australians is about to rise considerably, due to both demographic reasons and deliberate educational policy decisions. In the tertiary sector, unless Australian universities can expand sufficiently in the next 3 years, some 10,000 students annually could be denied entrance. It is most unlikely that overseas applicants will be granted preference over Australian students in the contemporary political and educational climate. On the contrary, there is every likelihood that increasing quota restrictions will be imposed and that the participation rate of overseas students will be lowered as a consequence.

There are obvious and serious ramifications for foreign policy in the Asean and Pacific region countries implied in the likelihood of a progressive reduction in the number of overseas students allowed into Australia, hence the need for considerable care and sensitivity regarding the present policy review. Unfortunately, government policy in regard to foreign student admissions may have little direct influence on the independent deliberations of universities which value to a high degree their autonomy. Unless specific and selective funding is provided for the tertiary sector to cater to an increasing demand by both Australian and overseas students, these institutions will be forced on a priority basis to cater predominantly to the former to the obvious detriment of the latter.

Foreign Study in Western Europe:
Policy Trends and Issues

ALAN SMITH*

International education—or at least the aspect of it that has come to be known as the "Overseas Student Question"[1]—has recently become a topic of increasing public debate in a number of Western European countries.[2] For the most part, this has been due to the introduction of various measures designed to restrict the inflow of students. Whether it be the introduction of "full-cost" tuition fees in the United Kingdom and Ireland, similar fee differentials in Belgium, attempts to curb the influx of students from various countries in the Federal Republic of Germany, the total exclusion of new foreign entrants from several medical courses in Austria and Switzerland, or the temporary introduction of more centralized admission procedures in France, the trend has been clearly one of limitation rather than of expansion, toward "closing doors" rather than opening them.

The haste with which many of the measures were introduced, and in many cases subsequently modified or indeed rescinded altogether, suggests a lack of coherent policy with regard to foreign students in the countries concerned, with governments frequently acting in a situation of perceived emergency and in response to a specific set of circumstances rather than reflecting on the long-term aims and outcomes of the steps taken. What is more, each country initially tended to act on an individual basis, with little or no regard for the effects that its policies might have on its neighbors and similarly minimal consultation with the states involved.

Naturally, given the diversity of higher education systems in Europe, the precise configuration of reasons for the introduction of measures varied from country to country. Viewed in a broader perspective, however, they may be attributed for the most part to an interplay of two main factors, namely, statistics and economics. First, the 1970s had witnessed a marked tendency toward a concentration in the numbers of foreign students enrolling in certain receiver countries. Thus by 1976, more than 60 percent of the world's total foreign student population was studying in just five countries, namely France, the United Kingdom, the Federal Republic of Germany, the United States, and Canada. Within Europe,

---

* Director of the Brussels Office for Cooperation in Education of the European Institute of Education and Social Policy.

[1] Peter Williams, ed., *The Overseas Student Question* (London: Heinemann, 1981).

[2] "Europe" may be defined in many different ways. The present paper will be exclusively concerned with developments in Western Europe, with an emphasis in the seond part on the ten member states of the European Economic Community.

the situation was exacerbated by local factors: for example, the introduction of a stringent *numerus clausus* (system of restricted admissions) in an increasing number of academic disciplines in the Federal Republic of Germany and the growing difficulty in keeping pace with rising demand for higher education in Greece led to a substantial exodus of rejected candidates from those countries to seek admission in neighboring countries, such as Belgium and Italy, where access was less limited. Thus the phenomenon of "mobilité sauvage" (wildcat mobility) was born, proving, it is true, that students are demonstrably willing to be mobile when to opt for immobility would be to abandon ambitions of access to higher education, but causing unadvoidable friction between the "emitting" and "receiving" countries. What has served to move authorities to legislative action has been the combination of sharply rising numbers of foreign students on the one hand with the markedly worsening economic situation on the other. What is more, these statistical and economic changes in themselves might not have sufficed to produce reexamination of policies had they not emerged at a time of heightened concern about immigration issues and about the shrinking graduate labor market. In these circumstances, the cost of providing study opportunities to students from other countries[3] has come under increasingly close scrutiny: the politicians discovered foreign study.

Patterns in National Policies

Just as it is possible to pinpoint the main underlying factors that have given rise to foreign student policy changes in Western Europe generally, so it is possible to identify certain broad characteristics of the type of measures introduced.[4] Common to most is a trend away from more open, indiscriminate policies toward more "regulatory" and "differentiated" approaches. The several West European countries—for example, Austria, Switzerland, Denmark, the Netherlands and the Federal Republic of Germany—now operate a foreign student quota or numerical limitation system of one kind or another though various safeguards for foreign student access are sometimes built in (the Federal Republic of Germany, for example, reserves 6–8 percent of university places for beginning foreign students in various disciplines, such as medicine, pharmacy, psychology, architecture, and chemistry, and this in the face of a dearth of university places to satisfy the demand from German students.) In the United Kingdom, the

---

[3] Compare Mark Blaug, "The Economic Costs and Benefits of Overseas Students," in Williams, ed., pp. 47–90.
[4] For a more detailed examination of these characteristics, see J.-P. Jarousse, A. Smith, and C. Woesler, *Les Etudiants étrangers: Comparaison internationale des flux et des politiques, 1960–1980* (Paris: Institut européen d'Education et de Politique Sociale, 1982), a modified version of which appeared under the title "Foreign Student Flows and Policies in an International Perspective," in Williams, ed., pp. 165–222.

imposition of tuition fee differentials for foreign students may be seen as constituting a modification or adaptation of the existing system rather than a rupture with it, given that tuition fees form a traditionally strong element in the funding of British higher education. This is less true of a country like Belgium that, for reasons however comprehensible in view of its geographical position, introduced in the 1970s a system whereby most students from industrialized countries (a particularly high proportion of foreign students in Belgium fall into this category, due not least to the "knock-on" effects of *numerus clausus,* mentioned above) are required to pay a notional 50 percent of the calculated cost of providing them with the course in question. In high-cost subjects such as medicine or engineering, the fees involved can thus be very considerable indeed. The methods typically used to regulate the influx of foreign students in Europe may therefore be said to be twofold: regulation by number or regulation by the purse. For a while, with the government seeking to introduce a quota via voluntary action on the part of the universities, the system in the United Kingdom may be said to have constituted a mixture of the two approaches.

No less accentuated than the trend toward greater "regulation" has been that toward a more "differentiated" approach to foreign student admissions. Instead of regarding them as a homogeneous mass, many European countries now distinguish with increasing exactitude between foreign students according to such factors as geographical origin, the level and duration of the educational course to be followed, and the students' chosen fields of study. In so doing, they identify the groups with which they associate a particular commitment and orient their admission policies (and government-funded scholarship schemes) accordingly. As regards students' geographical origin, political refugees and students from the developing world are often given particular preference, as are students from countries lacking a fully developed higher education system of their own (Luxemburg's arrangements with Austria, Belgium, France, and Germany are a case in point). A Nordic Council agreement provides for preferential treatment to ensure enhanced student flows among Scandinavian countries, and the particular arrangements between the ten member states of the European Economic Community will be mentioned in more detail below. Increasing emphasis is often placed also on the need to facilitate access for graduates seeking admission to higher-degree courses rather than for those wishing to pursue an entire undergraduate education in the host country. This is particularly the case with students from developing countries. Finally, positive discrimination is also exercised (or at least advocated) by a growing number of countries with respect to students wishing only to spend a part of their undergraduate studies abroad, in the context of a degree program to be both commenced and completed in the students' country of origin. This latter trend constitutes a rallying point for government policymakers in various inter- and supragovernmental settings within Western Europe.[5]

Restrictiveness and Differentiation in Policies at the European Level

The process of European-level consultation and coordination with regard to foreign student policies was slower to establish itself than might have been expected. What is more, for those who cherish a mentality of "open doors," the moves toward greater attention to and coordination of foreign policies came, unhappily, at a time when circumstances favored a disposition to cautious policies, this tendency toward caution and restrictiveness was not entirely avoided when the matter was eventually taken up within the framework of the Council of Europe. The "Conference on the Situation of Foreign Students in Member States of the Council for Cultural Cooperation (CDCC),"[6] in Strasbourg in March 1981, had first and foremost a safety-valve function, as the final report points out: "Since its foundation, the Council of Europe has always regarded the encouragement of student mobility both in Europe and outside as one of its priorities. . . . However, in the second decade, the influx of foreign students to European universities has made reception problems—on both the teaching and the material levels—increasingly acute. It is because of this new situation, which affects some European countries more than others, that the CC-PU [Council for Cultural Cooperation] decided to consider all aspects of the problem at the present conference."[7]

Many of the individual policy measures proposed, and later adopted by the Council of Europe, bear indelible traces of the negative or defensive undertones of the debate. To cite four of the most important: (1) Students should not be encouraged to complete a full study course in a foreign country (a measure aimed at students from developing countries but on which certain Mediterranean European states, notably Turkey, expressed reservations); it is strongly recommended that studies be begun in the country of origin. (2) Students from developing countries should first complete university studies in their own country before embarking on professional specialization by means of complementary intensification and research studies in foreign countries, provided that such further education is needed and recognized in their own coutries. (3) "Foreign students shall be informed that they should not anticipate paid employment to meet

[5] A critical assessment of the role played by the various organizations concerned (European Communities, Council of Europe, Unesco, etc.) has recently been made by John Banks, "European Co-operation in Education," *European Journal of Education* 17 (April 1982): 9–16.

[6] That is, almost all Western European countries.

[7] *Proceedings of the Conference on the Situation of Foreign Students in Member States of the Council for Cultural Cooperation (CDCC)* (Vienna: Council of Europe, 1981), p. 5. The CC-UP is the official abbreviation for the Standing Conference on University Problems, a subsidiary body of the CDCC.

their living costs. . . . Before their arrival, they shall make provision for the financial means needed to complete their studies. They are expected to furnish proof of their ability to do so."[8] And (4) "The academic standards set for the admission of foreign students may not be more favourable than those governing access to the same disciplines in their countries of origin. In principle the host country may not accept a candidate who would not be entitled to go on to higher education in his own country in the case that there were no admission limitations."[9] This measure is significant in that it encapsulates the success of the smaller receiver countries, such as Belgium, Austria, and Switzerland, in pressing for recognition of the need to ban *numerus clausus* mobility or wildcat mobility as far as possible.

Such a measure would, of course, impose an unusual degree of limitation on national government and individual institutions in the education sector by means of international agreement. It is therefore mitigated by a clause giving each member state the right to adopt a more liberal approach if it wishes, and a number of other policy proposals put forward would, if implemented, "soften the blow" at the fringes. These proposals include quotas for foreign students in *numerus clausus* subjects, financial aid for certain foreign students, more favorable terms of access for foreign students from developing countries and countries with limited higher education resources, orientation and guidance facilities, and provisions for refugees and certain types of immigrants and refugees. Despite these palliatives, however, the tone of caution and restriction underlying the document remains clear.

The measures decided on as common guidelines for the admission of foreign students by the Council of Europe countries are not legally binding on member states. Nor are the positive measures decided on backed up by a budget that would enable them to be centrally supported to a meaningful extent by the Council of Europe itself. They are, however, highly significant as a barometer of government thinking on this matter in member states, and in this context it is particularly worth recording that the "Synthesis Report" closes with a call for institutionalizing the principle of consultation that had earlier been lacking: "While respecting the responsibility of individual member states to fix their own policies on the admission of foreign students, the CC-PU calls on member states to monitor the effects of their own policies on student mobility and to be willing to undertake regular reviews of their own policies both by themselves and in consultation

---

[8] Ibid., p. 6.

[9] *Foreign Students in Member States of the Council for Cultural Co-operation (CDCC): Synthesis Report,* Doc. DECS/ESR (81) 55 final (Strasbourg: Council of Europe, March 31, 1982, mimeographed), p. 5.

with other states. In particular where too many students from one country apply to university establishments[10] in another, the problems presented by such a flow will need to be discussed by the host country and those students' country of origin; such consultation shall take place at governmental or any other appropriate level[11] and should result in bilateral measures."[12]

But if the Council of Europe deliberations have been characterized by a generally restrictive tone, they have been no less significant in their orientation toward a greater "differentiation" between categories of foreign students and an emphasis on the need to give preferential treatment to certain of these categories. Among these, the most clearly stressed is that of students moving among European countries, in particular for part of their course of study and as this has been a significant common factor of policy discussion at both European and national levels, and indeed among higher education institutions themselves, in recent years. The remaining sections of this article will seek to identify and comment on the salient aspects of that policy debate.

Organized Mobility

It will be recalled that "freedom of movement for persons" is one of the basic principles on which the European Community is based.[13] "Education" as such, it is true, is scarcely mentioned in the Treaty of Rome, figuring notably in the provision for a "common vocational training policy" (art. 128) and for the "mutual recognition of diplomas, certificates and other evidence of formal qualifications" in order to "make it easier for persons to take up and pursue activities as self-employed persons" throughout the community (art. 57). Considerable political debate has surrounded the question as to whether or not the treaty provides a mandate for community action in educational matters. To analyze that debate would go far beyond the scope of this article. Suffice it to say therefore that it has been increasingly recognized that there is an educational dimension to the realization of the underlying objectives that led to the

---

[10] Explicit reference is made in the document to the fact that the term "university" is taken to refer to all types of higher education establishments.

[11] The aside is clearly designed to take account of the institutional autonomy enjoyed in very many instances by higher education institutions in Europe in respect of foreign student admission policies.

[12] *Proceedings of the Conference on the Situation of Foreign Students,* p. 7. It is worth recording that European level deliberations on this matter among representatives of the universities themselves (as opposed to those also involving governments) have given rise to a generally less restrictive position (cf. "Foreign Students in Europe," *CRE-information,* no. 57 [1st Quarter 1981], which contains the main papers and proceedings from a conference held by the European Rectors Conference [CRE] in September 1981).

[13] "Treaty Establishing the European Community, March 25, 1957, art. 3(c).

establishment of the community, notably as regards the free movement of persons, and that recognition of this has given rise to a number of actions over the past decade, some introduced by individual member states, others agreed on an intergovernmental basis, and others again taking the form of concerted measures at community level.

Yet it is necessary to note here that freedom of movement for students within the European Community, even if it were realized to the maximum extent intended, could never approximate the kind of mobility that is possible in the United States. There is, to be sure, a certain amount of control exercised over mobility among states by individual state governments—principally through the imposition of higher tuition and fees for out-of-state students, as also on foreign students (for the most part at the same level)—but the dominant sources of control over student mobility are the individual institutions of higher education. A concerted foreign student policy is possible only at the federal level and is virtually nonexistent. This perspective on the nature and level of student flows to the countries of Europe and among the countries of Europe is useful.

The extent to which students actually flow among the countries of the community was, however, and indeed still remains extremely modest. When the ministers of education of the then nine member states[14] met for the first time in the early 1970s, less than one student in 200 of those enrolled in the community's three thousand plus higher education institutions came from another community country, and as the debate developed, it soon became almost axiomatic to recall with nostalgia the lost millennium of the Middle Ages when students and scholars had supposedly moved with self-evident ease across the many borders that otherwise divided the continent. Leaving aside the question as to the reality behind such assertions, and the equally legitimate and perhaps even more challenging one as to whether the comparison is in any way valid given the fundamental changes that the character, extent, and social function of higher education have undergone during the intervening centuries, the problem nevertheless remains, Why are the students of Europe's twentieth-century nation-states apparently reluctant to move—be it to another European country or anywhere else, even the United States?[15]

There are no easy explanations, but the case of the extent of study abroad of German students may be instructive. Sparked by the publication of Unesco figures that suggested that the percentage of German students

[14] Belgium, Denmark, France, the Federal Republic of Germany, Ireland, Italy, Luxemburg, the Netherlands, and the United Kingdom. Greece joined the community with effect from 1981.

[15] In a press communiqué (no. 68/1978) issued by the German Federal Ministry of Education, August 31, 1978, it is noted that only 1 percent of all German students receiving a student-support grant in 1977 used the grant for the purpose of studying abroad.

studying abroad had fallen from 3.1 percent in 1962 to 1.2 percent in 1975, [16] with the absolute number remaining virtually constant at 10,000, public debate of this matter has been particularly intense in the Federal Republic. It may not be plausible to expect study abroad to grow proportionately to the total number of persons attending universities: that total now reflects a far more diversified student body than hitherto, including many students attending universities close to home and therefore not involved in travel to a German university, let alone a foreign one. Furthermore, the processes of growth and diversification of the past twenty years have brought higher education to very many students from social backgrounds lacking a tradition of mobility. Finally, scholarship support for study abroad is still quite limited, and the reception of foreign students in other countries has, as noted above, tended to become less rather than more hospitable. Be that as it may, the German debate of the subject soon transcended party political lines, and a consensus emerged that, for reasons both of foreign cultural policy and—perhaps more significantly— of economic and employment policy, urgent measures were required. As the government replied to one of the many parliamentary questions posed on this topic since the late 1970s: "Study abroad also has an increasingly important dimension from the point of view of the economy and employment. The Federal Republic of Germany is involved in a continuing process of world-wide interlinkages, growing dependence on international economic developments and in particular the increasing division of labour. The more our economy has become oriented towards exports, the greater our need has become for highly qualified experts and managers with sound knowledge of other countries and first-hand experience of those countries in the fields of business, administration and research." [17]

I have dwelt at some length on the case of the Federal Republic of Germany not just because the call for an increase in study abroad has been particularly marked there but also because in a sense the arguments put forward in the German debate may be seen as reflecting the position of the European Community as a whole in its efforts to promote growth in intracommunity student flows. For just as Germany, a country relatively poor in raw materials and thus with particularly high dependence on high-quality technology and exports, sees the need for providing more young people with foreign experience, so the community as a whole has come to regard the development of a "Community scientific area" as a

---

[16] The figures are—correctly—relativized by the government in its reply to a parliamentary question shortly afterward (Drucksache 8/2519, 26.1.1979), p. 3.

[17] Ibid., p. 1. The philosophy expounded here is clearly very much akin to that expressed in the title of the report submitted to the president of the United States by the President's Commission on Foreign Languages and International Studies, *Strength through Wisdom* (Washington, D.C.: Government Printing Office, 1979).

possible means of meeting "the challenge of American and Japanese competition."[18]

Essentially, however, the arguments advanced for the development of community action to enhance higher education cooperation in general and student exchange in particular, are community oriented and emanate from the statement of the community's basic aim as expressed in the very first substantive article of the Rome Treaty (art. 2), namely: "The Community shall have as its task . . . to promote throughout the Community a harmonious development of economic activities, a continuous and balanced expansion, an increase in stability, an accelerated raising of the standard of living and closer relations between the States belonging to it." Since the early 1970s, there has been increasing recognition of the need to take greater account of the "human" or "social" dimension of these essentially economic goals, and education, including higher education, has formed part of this enhanced social dimension in community policy. As the above-mentioned resolution passed by the European Parliament puts it, the "initial work of European integration has tended to be directed at economic objectives, but such objectives, the achievement of which is in any case still a long way away, seem too limited and do not answer the legitimate aspirations of the peoples of the Community."[19] As far as higher education is concerned, the same document suggests that the "ultimate objective of successful cooperation at Community level is to improve the quality of higher education and research by promoting the exchange of experience between higher education establishments, which implies much greater mobility of teaching staff, research workers and students within the Community," and the potential labor-market impact is stressed: "Possibilities for studies, teaching staff and research workers to pursue their studies or careers wholly or partly in another Member State would in the long term make it easier for them to find openings on the job market in view of their larger fund of scientific experience, better knowledge of foreign languages and contact with different modes of living and thinking."[20]

Two approaches, not mutually exclusive, have been developed to promote student mobility within the European Community. The first is based on the assumption that students have on the whole a very positive attitude toward study abroad, and that the fact that only relatively few of them

[18] European Parliament, "Resolution on Higher Education and the Development of Cooperation between Higher Education Establishments," *Official Journal of the European Communities*, no. C 104/50ff. of 16.4.1984, art. 29 (March 13, 1984).
[19] *Report on Higher Education and the Development of Cooperation between Higher Education Establishments* drawn up on behalf of the Committee on Youth, Culture, Education, Information and Sport of the European Parliament (Rapporteur: N. Péry), European Parliament Working Document 1-1351/83 (February 13, 1984), p. 28. The report formed the basis for the resolution referred to in n. 18 above.
[20] Ibid., p. 29.

eventually take the plunge must therefore be attributed to obstacles that deter them from availing themselves of study abroad opportunities.[21] If such obstacles are removed therefore, students will, according to this theory, become more mobile of their own volition, and in particular if they are better and more comprehensively informed. There are, clearly, some real obstacles, like the absence of adequate financial support and the problem of receiving academic credit for work done in foreign institutions, as well as more elusive risks, like the difficulty of obtaining employment in a shrinking graduate employment market after prolonged absence in a foreign country. Policymakers have come to accept the existence of these obstacles and the need for measures to overcome them.

The second approach is based on the assumption that the decision to study abroad will be positively influenced (a) by making the advantages of such study more apparent and (b) by creating structures whereby much of the academic and organizational burden of arranging it is assumed by the higher education institution(s) concerned and whereby many of the obstacles facing the individual student are obviated from the start. It is the premise that has given rise to the growth of various forms of what has come to be termed "organized mobility"[22]—probably the main single talking point with regard to student mobility and exchanges in Western Europe over the past 4 or 5 years.

For certain specific groups of persons, notably the children of migrant workers, wide-ranging and far-reaching provisions have long since been introduced, the effect of which is to place such persons on a par with host-country nationals. No such provisions exist with respect to students whose parents were not, and have never been, employed in the host country. Consequently, the section of the "Action Program in the Field of Education" decided by the education ministers of the community in 1976 and that is still the main basis for community action in the educational field stressed the need "to promote the free movement and mobility of teaching staff, students and researchers"[23] and included measures designed to improve the situation with regard to the availability of financial support, the academic recognition (in American terms, "credit") of studies carried out abroad and the adoption of common principles for the admission of community country students. At the same time, steps were agreed on to

[21] For a discussion of this debate, see Alan Smith, "From 'Europhoria' to Pragmatism: Towards a New Start for Higher Education Co-operation in Europe?" *European Journal of Education* 15 (Spring 1980): 77–95.

[22] Compare J.-C. Masclet, *The Intra-European Mobility of Undergraduate Students* (Paris: Institute of Education of the European Cultural Foundation, 1975). The concept is further differentiated by Smith, pp. 81ff.

[23] "Resolution of the Council and of the Ministers of Education Meeting within the Council of 9 February 1976 Comprising an Action Programme in the Field of Education," *Official Journal of the European Communities,* no. C 38/1 of 19.2.1976, art. IV.14.

improve the information available to students on opportunities for study in other member states.[24]

By 1980, agreement had been reached with regard to the common principles for admission, and though (for reasons too complicated to be dealt with here) never formally adopted by ministers, they are highly significant in incorporating the principle that students from other community countries should be treated not less favorably than those from the host country admitting them.[25] Inevitably with such agreements reached at international level, clauses were agreed that safeguarded the perceived particular interests of certain member states, but even with regard to the thorny question of differentials in tuition fees, some progress was made: with effect from the 1980/81 academic year, the British government modified its policy by stipulating that students from other community countries would henceforth not be obliged to pay higher fees than their British counterparts. With regard to the availability of financial support for foreign study in another community country, EEC policy has been mainly directed toward ensuring that, in cases where students receive support for study in their home countries, such support should also be tenable for study abroad. In addition, a new budget line has been created with effect from 1984 for the purpose of providing direct community support for some of the students participating in EEC-supported exchange programs. Clearly, however, the time is hardly favorable for actions requiring substantial additional expenditures at member state or indeed at community level.

Rather more progress has, at least potentially, been made with regard to the other main obstacle to free movement referred to above, namely, the difficulties surrounding the award of academic credit for study abroad on a student's return. A number of surveys have identified students' uncertainty in this regard as being a significant deterrent to study abroad, and while both member states and community institutions alike are agreed that the wide diversity of education systems and programs throughout the community should be regarded as potentially a major source of strength for the community as a whole, it is equally clear that it also gives rise to problems when it comes to recognition of courses pursued and qualifications obtained in other community countries. While preserving the autonomy of each national system, and the institutions within it, there is therefore a growing feeling that present arrangements for recognition should be

[24] The main follow-up to the information-oriented parts of the resolution takes the form of the publication entitled *Student Handbook: Higher Education in the European Community*, 3d ed. (Luxemburg: Office for Official Publications of the European Communities, 1981) (the 4th ed. will appear in late 1984). See also *Directory of Higher Education Institutions: Higher Education in the European Community*, ed. Edward Prosser (Luxembourg: Office for Official Publications of the European Communities, 1984).

[25] "General Report of the Education Committee Agreed to in Substance by the Council and the Ministers of Education Meeting within the Council at Their Session of 27 June 1980," in *European*

improved, and this has been accentuated since agreement was reached at community level on the mutual recognition of terminal qualifications for entry to various liberal professions in the mid- to late 1970s. Certainly considerable frustration has been voiced by politicians, both in national parliaments[26] and in the now directly elected European Parliament, which in March 1984 adopted a 25-point resolution calling for urgent action to improve the present situation.[27] Furthermore, the "Conclusions of the Council and the Ministers of Education Meeting within the Council of 2 June 1983 concerning the Promotion of Mobility in Higher Education,"[28] which constitutes the main policy thrust toward European cooperation in higher education since the promulgation of the Education Action Programme in 1976, includes a whole range of measures designed to meet this policy objective. With respect to academic recognition, the document calls for member states to "be guided by the principle of greatest possible generosity and flexibility" (art. 1), attaches considerable importance to bilateral agreements at national level or among individual higher education institutions, and provides for the establishment of recognition information centers in all member states.

Given the complexity of the situation caused by the divergence of higher education systems and programs as described above, given the many ways in which administrative practice can weaken or even counteract policy objectives in this sector, and given the high degree of autonomy exercised by higher education institutions in recognition matters, it remains to be seen to what extent the new agreement will lead to noticeable improvements, and such caution appears equally if not more appropriate still with respect to the sections of the ministers' "Conclusions" relating to an improvement of the funding arrangements for study abroad. Here, the only commitment is to "examine the feasibility of adopting measures" (art. 6), though the measures enumerated, notably the transferability of national student support for study abroad and nondiscrimination against community students as regards tuition fees, are potentially far-reaching.

Educational Policy Statements, 1974–1983 (Luxemburg: Office for Official Publications of the European Communities, 1983), pp. 59–84.

[26] As Secretary of State H. Hamm-Brücher bitterly exclaimed in the Bundestag in late 1979, "If there is one place in the world where flies' legs are counted (or should I say 'peas are counted', to avoid complaints from societies for the prevention of cruelty to animals) it is in the field of equivalences" ("Protocol of the 180th. Plenary Session," *Deutscher Bundestag—8. Wahlperiode*, Bonn, 18.10. 1979, p. 14165). The frustration extends to many senior officials also; cf. Eberhard Böning, "Thoughts on the Further Development of European Co-operation in Higher Education," *European Journal of Education* 17 (April 1982): 17–22.

[27] In April 1984, the European Parliament, on the basis of a report prepared on behalf of its Committee on Youth, Culture, Education, Information and Sport by European parliamentarian O. Schwencke, adopted a "Resolution on the Academic Recognition of Diplomas and of Periods of Study."

[28] In European Educational Policy Statements, pp. 41–46.

Conclusions

In at least two respects, however, the community level ministerial agreement of June 1983 appears of direct and immediate significance. First, it comes out very strongly in favor of "special efforts to promote study periods abroad of limited duration which as a rule should be relevant to the home qualifications sought by the student" (art. 3). While the same article makes it clear that this accentuation does not actually "preclude the possibility of undertaking a complete course of study in another Member State," ministers are agreed in contending that part-course study abroad "enables more foreign students to be admitted with the same number of study and residential places than would be the case with students undertaking an entire course of study abroad; avoids certain problems regarding professional recognition, because the final examinations only take place after the return to the country of origin; makes it easier for the admitting institution to handle admissions, recognition, and fees regulations (where these apply) as flexibly as possible" (art. 3). This line of policy may be said to have been the key "philosophy" characterizing governments' attitudes toward the promotion of intracommunity student flows in recent years, and it is fully echoed in the wider Council of Europe forum in respect to most of the Western European states.[29]

Operationally, the concept of part-course study abroad is based on the development of interinstitutional (or interdepartmental) arrangements ensuring that students' educational experience abroad forms an academically meaningful and in many cases highly "integrated" component of their overall degree program. In the present generally unfavorable "environment" the advantages of such organized structures are immediately evident: for governments and funding agencies they appear as "good investments" since they involve a high level of commitment on the part of the participating institutions and precise definition of the activities to be supported; for the institutions they present means of putting the meager resources available for international activities to best use; students going abroad in the framework of such programs have a prior guarantee of credit; and employers know that their graduate employees have had firsthand foreign country experience directly related to their subject fields.

Both at the European level and in certain individual member states, recent years have witnessed the creation of support schemes for the purpose of developing "organized mobility" programs of this kind. Significantly,

---

[29] In the Council of Europe context, a succession of conferences devoted to the theme of academic mobility (Luxemburg 1981, Stockholm 1982, and Madrid 1983) has stressed the need for intensifying this type of mobility, and a special report has been written to bring out the policy requirements: Ulrike Dolezal and Ludwig Gieseke, *Measures and Models for the Implementation of Part-course Study Abroad at the Undergraduate and Postgraduate Level* Doc. DECS/ESR Mob (83) 4 rev. 2, (Strasbourg: Council of Europe, 1984, mimeographed).

the echo that they have encountered from the higher education institutions of the European Community countries has been exceptionally positive. This year, around five hundred applications were submitted for support under the terms of the commission's "Scheme for the Development of Joint Study Programs," and around 330 such programs, over half of them based on student-exchange arrangements, have received commission support since the scheme began in 1976. Significantly, the programs supported often report a markedly above-average level of student demand. At national level, the "integrated study abroad" scheme recently introduced by the German Academic Exchange Service has been described by its secretary-general as the "most strikingly successful program for German undergraduates to study abroad,"[30] and a comparable British scheme has been similarly acclaimed.

The organized programs developed in this framework vary considerably in structure, ranging from comparatively short periods of 3-6 months' fully credited study abroad to arrangements whereby students can spend half of a 4-year degree program in each of two countries and receive fully validated degree awards from both. With programs such as these, "bridges to knowledge" clearly means bridges to academic, subject-oriented knowledge as well as to general knowledge of the host country. This being so, it might be expected that the programs would be restricted to just a few academic disciplines (languages, literature, and the like) for which study abroad has an immediately recognizable content relevance. But on the contrary, "joint study programs" funded by the European Community cover almost the entire spectrum of academic disciplines available, with some of the most highly integrated programs being in the field of business studies—an interesting point of comparison and contrast with the situation in the United States.

In a sense, of course, "organized mobility" is second best to complete "free movement" within the community since by definition it involves specific institutions of higher education and a limited number of students in each case. In the short term, however, it does appear to offer the most promising way forward, and indeed it can itself contribute significantly to the creation of favorable conditions for more generalized mobility.

Viewed in this perspective, therefore, the two approaches to the policy objective of promoting increased mobility among European countries that we have identified, namely, the dismantling of barriers to free movement on the one hand and the stimulation of greater "organized mobility" on

[30] Karl Roeloffs, "International Mobility in Higher Education: The Experiences of an Academic Exchange Agency in the Federal Republic of Germany," *European Journal of Education* 17 (1982): 37–48, 42.

the other, may rather be seen as an integrated dual approach comprising two mutually complementary elements.

With the adoption of the March 1984 Resolutions of the European Parliament, the community-wide ministerial agreement of June 1983, and emerging signs that, from a purely legal point of view, the Treaty of Rome may provide a more solid basis for promoting the free movement of students than had previously been assumed, it is possible that, despite continuing economic stagnation and the current budgetary crisis besetting the European Community as a whole, the period ahead may be one of interesting developments for student interchange in Europe.

Going Overseas for Higher Education:
The Asian Experience

WILLIAM K. CUMMINGS*

Over the quarter century from 1950 to 1978 the number of tertiary-level students studying in foreign countries increased from 107,589 to 842,705—nearly eight times.[1] Between 1968 and 1978, the most recent 10-year period for which data is available, the increase was nearly 250 percent. If a straight-line projection is fitted to past numbers, overseas students will number nearly 2½ million by the year 2000.

From a quantitative standpoint, studying overseas has become important only since World War II. During the early postwar years, the number of overseas students remained constant and was a modest proportion of the total number of students in the world's rapidly expanding higher educational institutions. However, in recent years, while the rate of increase in numbers of overseas students has been high, the rate of increase in numbers of places in the world's higher educational institutions has begun to level off. Thus, since the early 1970s, the number of overseas students as a percentage of all students in the world has increased somewhat: from 2.0 percent in 1968 to 2.3 percent in 1978.

Though many observers have commented on the rapid postwar increase in the number of overseas students, few have tried to explain that increase, and no serious attempts have been made to explain the considerable national differences in the numbers of students from other countries in a given country and the number from a given country in other countries. For example, in 1978 the United States hosted over a quarter million foreign students, while many nations received fewer than 100; 67,900 Iranian nationals were registered in tertiary institutions outside Iran in contrast with 176 overseas students from Burma.

The research reported in this article has been made possible by a grant from the Spencer Foundation for which the author wishes to express his deep gratitude. The paper has immensely benefited from the thoughtful comments of John Dixon, Edward Beauchamp, Salman Kasenda, James Johnstone, Robert Myers, and V. Selvaratnam.

* Senior fellow of the East-West Center, Honolulu.

[1] Unless otherwise noted, the figures on overseas students mentioned here are taken from the annual editions of the *Unesco Statistical Yearbook* (New York: United Nations, 1976, 1981). Unesco reports that their figures, obtained from annual surveys conducted by the countries that receive foreign students, account for at least 90 percent of all overseas students. The major bias in the figures occurs because of weaknesses in the data-collection process of certain of the receiving countries and because of differences in their interpretation of the Unesco definitions. These biases, while potentially serious for a refined comparison of receiving countries, have less bearing on a study of senders.

In this article my primary focus will be on national differences in the numbers of students from selected Asian countries who take up higher educational study abroad. Usually in the case of socialist countries such overseas students are officially selected and "sent" by the government. In contrast, in capitalist countries usually no more than 5–10 percent receive government aid.[2] While the majority of students from capitalist countries who study abroad must finance those studies themselves, I will argue here that they make the decision to study overseas in response to their respective national situations. In some cases the students are pulled abroad by opportunity, but at least in the Asian context the push abroad is more determinate. Thus for simplicity of expression we will think of nations as "sending" students abroad, even though most students go on their own.

Approaches to Understanding the Context of Educational Decisions

Two contrasting approaches have been used in recent years to account for differences in national educational systems. The development approach, which views education as an aspect and function of national development, has the longer history.[3] In contrast, the world-system or interdependence approach views national educational phenomena as reflections of external or international processes, primarily of an economic nature.[4] I will draw on both of these approaches in an attempt to account both for the expansion in the number of overseas students and for differences among nations' tendencies to send students abroad.

The Interdependence Approach

The interdependence approach stresses the growing economic interdependence of nations and that many of today's most attractive jobs are in organizations that promote this interdependence, such as multinational corporations and international agencies. People seeking more attractive jobs consider moving overseas to realize their ambition; often they take up a course of study overseas as a first step in this process.[5] Other important factors contributing to increased study abroad include the wider diffusion of information about higher educational opportunities, decreased cost

---

[2] William Glaser, *The Brain Drain: Immigration and Return* (Oxford: Pergamon, 1978); G. Lakshmana Rao, *Brain Drain and Foreign Students* (New York: St. Martin's, 1978).

[3] F. H. Harbison and C. A. Myers, *Education, Manpower and Economic Growth* (New York: McGraw-Hill, 1964); Alejandro Portes, "On the Sociology of National Development: Theories and Issues," *American Journal of Sociology* 82, no. 1 (1976): 55–85.

[4] Insightful discussions of the pull of foreign jobs can be found in Mark Blaug, *Education and the Employment Problem in Developing Countries* (Geneva: International Labour Office, 1974); and especially in Michael Piore, *Birds of Passage* (London: Cambridge University Press, 1979).

[5] Philip G. Altbach, *Higher Education in the Third World* (Singapore: Maruzen Asia, 1982); Robert F. Arnove, "Comparative Education and World-Systems Analysis," *Comparative Education Review* 24 (February 1980): 48–62; Francisco Ramirez and John W. Merer, "Comparative Education: The Social Construction of the Modern World System," *Annual Review of Sociology* 6 (1980): 369–99.

differentials (e.g., as between American and Japanese colleges), and more efficient visa procedures.

A straightforward version of the interdependence thesis is also helpful in accounting for differences in nations' tendencies to receive students. The United States and other industrial nations, being the central actors in the world system, are most likely to provide attractive opportunities for work and study and hence to receive the largest numbers of foreign students. Indeed, in 1978 over 30 percent of all overseas students were in the United States, and two-thirds were concentrated at the colleges and universities of five Western industrial powers.

The peripheral nations of the world system are more likely to send students than to receive them, and a nation's tendency to send students is, at least in part, determined by the extent of its involvement in the world economy. To the extent that multinational and international corporations have branches in a given country and to the extent that that country's economy is involved in international trade, the citizens of that country become aware of international opportunities and consider going overseas to study. For example, in such cases as Burma and, until recently, mainland China where contemporary states close their doors to the world— as did Tokugawa Japan—the number of students going abroad to study has been relatively small. In contrast, tiny Hong Kong, which is highly dependent on international trade, ranked fifth in 1978 in total number of students sent abroad.

The Development Approach

Distinct from the focus on interdependence is the development approach, which links trends in economic growth and the employment structure to various development phenomena, including education. Thus development studies show clear links between such variables as GNP per capita or numbers enrolled in secondary schools and the overall demand for higher education. The logic of the development approach can be extended to account plausibly for the increasing numbers of students who go overseas as well as overseas sending rates.

For example, the financial ability of individuals to go overseas is constrained by the wealth of their country and by the degree of equality in the distribution of this wealth. Overseas study, in that it is usually self-financed, requires substantial private funds; relatively few people are likely to have such funds in poor countries. Thus more affluent countries are more able to send students abroad, and to the extent that a nation "develops," the likelihood that its citizens can afford to finance their study abroad increases.

Most universities around the world require new entrants to have completed secondary school and, often, to have passed some type of internationally recognized achievement exam such as the American SAT or the English Cambridge A- or O-level exams. The extent of a nation's provision of good-quality secondary education places an outside constraint on the number of individuals who are able to meet these admissions requirements. In most Far Eastern nations today, over 50 percent of the secondary-level age cohort complete a secondary education of reasonable quality, whereas in Africa and several of the Middle Eastern countries fewer than 20 percent complete a secondary education. In terms of basic academic preparation, more students from the Far East are prepared; many, however, are handicapped by their poor command of the languages of instruction used in the higher educational institutions of the major recipient countries.

The development level of a country also is related to the number of places available domestically for higher education. To the extent that there are many domestic places, as in the Philippines or contemporary Japan, students may be less inclined to go overseas. On the other hand, relatively large numbers go overseas from countries such as Malaysia, Hong Kong, and several of the Middle Eastern countries where indigenous higher education is relatively small in scale or qualitatively poor.

Neglected Factors

Both the interdependence and the development approaches suggest a number of essentially complementary factors that are likely to influence the international demand for overseas education as well as national differences in this demand. The interdependence approach highlights the "pull" of the international labor market, and the development approach emphasizes the variables that "push" certain students overseas.

Several factors are neglected by both approaches: the national experience with sending students overseas, political and cultural factors, and cultural ties between nations are the most important. The best predictor of how many students a given nation will send overseas in a given year is the number it sent in the previous year. Students who are overseas report back on their experiences, influence the decisions of their younger peers, and help them to gain overseas admissions. Firms become established to facilitate the overseas placement of fee-paying applicants once it becomes apparent that a sufficient number are interested. And the presence of these contacts and facilitating institutions serves to stimulate the demand further.

Political and cultural factors also affect overseas study. Some Asian students elect to go overseas because they worry about the political future of their nation or their places in that future. For example, students from Hong Kong may choose to study overseas because they fear the consequences of the expiration in 1997 of the British treaty with China concerning the governance of Hong Kong. Should the mainland communist government take over after 1997, existing patterns of business would be threatened, and new criteria for career promotions would certainly be introduced. Ethnic discrimination is also prevalent in many contemporary societies. Malaysia's official policy of Malaysianization has led to quotas being placed on university admissions and civil-service recruitments and promotions for non-Malays; many non-Malays are naturally disposed to seek their fortunes, or at least their higher education, elsewhere.

Finally, cultural ties between nations have an important influence on the tendency to go overseas. In most of the former British empire, the belief remains that the best education is obtained at Oxford, Cambridge, the London School of Economics, or one of the other well-known British universities.[6] The new affluence of the oil-exporting Arab countries and the availability of scholarship funds encourage Arab students to go abroad for advanced study. In many instances the Arab students go to advanced societies to pursue technical and other courses. However, an equally prevalent pattern is to study at one of the well-known Islamic universities such as Al-Azhar in Cairo or its equivalents in Iraq, Syria, and elsewhere. Over half of the overseas students from most of the Arab countries are really "over the desert" studying in a nearby Arab country; the extreme case is Yemen, where 85 percent of the overseas students are in either Saudi Arabia, Egypt, Syria, or Turkey.

Comparing National Patterns of Sending

It should be clear from the above discussion that many of the critical forces affecting the overseas-student phenomenon are located at the national level; while some of these forces are stable concomitants of well-understood development processes, others such as regime changes and revenues from international commodities are not so predictable. To illustrate these instabilities at the national level, I will look in detail at the sending patterns of four countries: Burma, Malaysia, Iran, and Korea.

Burma is extreme in its abstention from the international student market. In 1963, 420 Burmese students, or one per 10,000 population (see definition of sending level, below), were studying overseas. The total number overseas has since slowly declined and was down to 176 by 1978.

In contrast, nearby Malaysia sent a relatively large number of students abroad in 1963—7,081, or over 50 per 10,000 population. This number steadily increased to 22,324 by 1978, or 134 per 10,000 population. A straight-line projection would have correctly predicted the years since 1978 when ever-increasing numbers of Malaysians, especially those with a Chinese ethnic background refused admission to local universities, have headed oerseas. The British Council reported 16,323 Malaysian students in England in 1979, a 6 percent increase over 1978, and the Institute of

---

[6] Martin Carnoy, *Education as Cultural Imperialism* (New York: David McKay, 1974).

International Education reported 3,660 in the United States, a 15 percent increase. In 1980 the number going to the United States rose to 6,010, a 65 percent increase over the previous year; and in 1981 the number was up to 9,410, a further 57 percent increase.[7]

In 1963 Iran sent 9,473 students overseas (25 per 10,000 population); the number accelerated rapidly to 67,900 in 1978. A straight-line projection would have predicted a doubling of this number by the mid-1980s. However, in the years since the Islamic revolution, the number of new students from Iran has decreased considerably, and most of these are children of political refugees. Thus Iran's share is actually declining.

The Republic of Korea provides yet another "irregular" example. By 1963 Korea was already sending 5,797 students overseas. This number had doubled by the late 1960s when the government sought to restrain the flow by such means as restricting the issuance of passports. Through the mid-1970s the volume was halved, but when the restraining policies were relaxed in the late 1970s, the number studying overseas climbed once again, reaching 6,438 by 1978. From 1981 on, the government abandoned all controls and at the same time tripled the number of places for applicants to Korean institutions of higher education. The Korean example illustrates how fluctuations in public policy can affect the volume of students.

Comparing National Levels of Sending

The four national examples illustrate the diversity in recent patterns of growth in overseas study as well as the need to inquire into the forces behind these variations.

One possible model for summarizing these patterns and forces revolves around the S-curve hypothesis that all nations start with a low volume (and rate) of sending students, then go through a transition where the rate accelerates, and finally approach a plateau of moderately high volume and rate. The ideal strategy for testing this model would use a classical longitudinal design or some substitute to relate particular national patterns of growth in study abroad to changes in the relevant characteristics of the nation. Unfortunately for most nations, especially in the developing world, it is impossible to collect the appropriate data.

Moreover, a review of the limited available data creates doubt about the appropriateness of the S-curve model. The exceptions are so glaring. For example, the small oil-rich Arab nations generally have much higher volumes and rates of sending than other small nations even though they lack many of the seemingly necessary capacities. Volumes and rates of sending for nations such as Korea and India, however, have stabilized or

---

[7] Douglas R. Boyan, ed., *Open Doors: 1981–82 Report on International Education* (New York: Institute of International Education, 1983).

declined because of particularistic and unpredictable political decisions. These considerations lead us to an alternate strategy that allows for wide variations in national patterns of growth.

An alternate strategy involves a cross-sectional research design where data for a limited period on selected national characteristics for a large number of nations are used to explain the volume or level of students sent by these nations. The cross-sectional design has the advantage of considering more situations but requires the rather extreme assumptions that the data for the cases under consideration are comparable and that the cases are being affected by essentially similar sociopolitical forces.

It would be impossible to select a number of cases that fully meet these assumptions. But by focusing on a somewhat more limited area than a world sample, we reduce the risk of serious violation.[8] Thus this analysis will concentrate on the number of students from 34 Asian nations (listed in the Appendix) that were overseas in 1978. Other reasons for restricting the study to Asian nations include the facts that (1) data for the Asian nations are relatively complete, (2) Asian countries supply nearly half of the students to the international student market, (3) most of the Asian countries are in the transitional stage from low to high sending rates, (4) I am most familiar with the political factors in Asia.

The Determinants of Sending Levels: A Cross-sectional Model

Many studies of overseas students have pointed out that the vast majority of these students go abroad on their own, without assistance either from their own government or from the country or institution where they take up their studies. I recognize that the final decision to go abroad is made by individuals, but I assume that the probability that individuals in different countries will make such decisions depends on forces affecting the educational, economic, and political situations of these countries. The balance of encouraging and discouraging forces determines how many people actually are sent overseas. Below I review the thinking behind the procedures I have used to measure the sending rate and its determinants.

Sending Level, the Dependent Variable

For a cross-national analysis at a given point in time, the first task was to settle on a meaningful measure of sending level. Since a country's population size sets outer limits on the number of students it can send, and since Asian nations vary widely in their degree of approaching their outer limit, we have defined sending level as a ratio, the number of

---

[8] Some of the measurement problems involved in using cross-national data sets are discussed in E. Sheldon and H. Freeman, "Notes on Social Indicators: Promises and Potential," in *Evaluating Education Programs,* ed. C. Weiss (Boston: Allyn & Bacon, 1972).

students overseas for a given year divided by the country's total population over 100,000. This ratio controls for the influence of the outer limit of population size.[9] By this definition Burma in 1978 has the lowest level, less than one per 10,000 population, while Jordan has the highest, 66.5 per 10,000 population. The actual figures for each nation and the source for these figures are reported in the Appendix.

Positive Force Specified in the Interdependence Approach

A. *Degree of interdependence.*—In the theoretical discussion, we viewed the extent to which a nation was involved in the international economic system as the major force pulling students overseas. The percentage of investment capital that derives from foreign sources was considered to be a possible measure of this force, but it proved difficult to obtain meaningful figures for all 34 countries.[10] A somewhat similar indicator, and one for which 1978 figures or reasonable estimates were available, is the ratio of export value to gross domestic product. Singapore and Hong Kong, Asia's two most renowned entrepot economies, led in terms of this index with values of 130.2 and 84.7, respectively.

Positive Forces Specified in the Development Approach

B. *Basic human resource capacity.*—The nation's basic human resource capacity for sending students abroad consists of the number of young people who have completed secondary education and have the necessary qualifications for further study. A sensitive comparison among nations would have to take into account the quality of the nation's secondary institutions and the proportion of graduates who can speak a language that is a medium of instruction overseas. A rough indicator of basic capacity is the number of students enrolled in the academic track of secondary education divided by the population. As reported in the Appendix, there are few surprises in terms of the countries scoring low on this index: Afghanistan, Oman, and Yemen. However, it is of considerable interest to find that Mongolia has the highest value, exceeding even Japan and Korea.

C. *Financial capacity.*—In view of the high cost of overseas study, the greater the financial capacity of a nation, the more students it can send abroad. The GNP per capita is a useful indicator of financial capacity. Generally the oil-exporting Arab countries score highest, followed by the newly industrialized countries.

---

[9] Qatar in 1978 had a population of 200,000, while India had a population of 663 million or 3000 times as many people. Thus it is not surprising that India sends more students overseas than Qatar does, 13,310 vs. 750. Indeed, for the full Asian sample, population size had a substantial correlation of .80 with total volume.

[10] For a discussion of possible indicators, see V. Bornschier, C. Chase-Dunn, and R. Rubinson, "Cross-national Evidence of the Effects of Foreign Investment and Aid on Economic Growth and Inequality: A Survey of Findings and a Reanalysis," *American Journal of Sociology* 84, no. 3 (1978): 651–83.

D. Facilitating institutions.—Once a nation begins sending large numbers of students overseas, the receiving universities gain familiarity with the nation's young people and establish workable channels of communication with the nation's educational and diplomatic officials. The establishment of these ties makes it easier to receive additional students from the country. Moreover, once students start leaving a country in significant numbers, both public agencies and private firms are founded that seek to inform and place prospective students; and it is in their interest to increase the number of students going abroad. While lacking a direct indicator of the number of facilitating institutions, I have assumed that they are more numerous in countries where a substantial volume of students has left the country in the past. Thus the number of students overseas in 1973 provides a rough indicator of the number of these institutions in 1978. Absolute volume was used here since it more accurately reflects the market size and hence the prevalence of firms; for example, while Japan's sending rate is lower than Singapore's, there are easily five times as many firms in Japan to serve its more sizable market.

Negative Forces Specified by the Development Approach

E. Domestic opportunities for higher education.—To the extent that a nation provides sufficient higher educational opportunities at home, young people have less reason to go overseas and are less likely to do so. One indicator of domestic opportunities is the ratio of university places to the number of students in secondary schools. Israel, Thailand, and the Philippines lead in terms of this indicator, while several of the Arab countries and those countries formerly within the British Empire score low.

F. Information scarcity.—Finally, young people in small countries are more likely to have relatives in nearby countries and to have information about overseas study opportunities, whereas those in large countries and especially those in the rural areas of large countries are less likely to have access to such information. Thus population size can be used as a rough indicator of information scarcity.

Evaluating the Cross-sectional Model

Each of the above indicators was found to be correlated in the expected direction with the 1978 sending level (see table 1). While the distributions of some of the indicators were modestly skewed, I decided against transformations in view of the general robustness of regression analysis.[11] When the five indicators were included in a single linear regression that

---

[11] These issues are discussed in E. Hanushek, *Statistical Methods for Social Scientists* (New York: Academic Press, 1976); for a comparable application of regression analysis, see Gerald W. Fry, "Schooling, Development and Inequality: Old Myths and New Realities," *Harvard Educational Review* 51, no. 1 (February 1981): 107–16.

TABLE 1
MODEL 1: STATISTICS FOR SIX VARIABLES REGRESSED ON 1978 SENDING LEVEL

Variable	r	Beta	B	F Value
Total population for 1978 in hundred thousands	−.277	−.234	−.001	2.02
Basic human resource capacity	.440	.225	1.241	1.82
Financial capacity	.295	.125	.000	.465
Domestic opportunities	−.109	−.046	−.727	.092
Number of students studying overseas in 1973	.218	.304	.010	3.096
Degree of interdependence	.461	.302	.167	2.087
Constant			−2.016	

NOTE.—Multiple R = .641; R^2 = .411; F value = 3.143; P = .018.

I will call model 1 (described in table 1), all five continued to be associated in the expected direction. And all except the measure of domestic opportunities made a substantial contribution to explaining the total variance in sending level.

Based on the results of model 1, the following statements are possible:

1. The extent of the national involvement in the world economy and the extent of development of institutions to facilitate the movement of students overseas have the strongest positive relation with sending level.

2. The relative prevalence or absence of information and the relative production of qualified applicants also have a strong relation with sending level.

3. The GNP per capita and the ratio of domestic places available to qualified applicants do not appear to have an independent effect on sending level.

The total variance explained by model 1 is a respectable 40.5 percent, but in examining the residuals reported in the Appendix, it seems that the equation is weak in accounting for certain countries. We turn now to consider several possible reasons.

While model 1 provides a useful summary of the common forces behind sending levels, inclusion of additional variables reflecting special situations might increase the total explained variance.

1. *Impact of the British tradition.*—Relative to other colonial powers, the British were active in promoting basic education for the common people but made exceptional efforts to preserve standards at the secondary and higher educational levels. Since the colonial era, many of the former British colonies have responded to popular demand by allowing gradual

expansion at the secondary level, while continuing to restrict domestic higher educational opportunities.[12] In terms of model 1, the countries with a British tradition are high in human-resource capacity and low in domestic opportunities and hence should have somewhat high sending levels. Indeed, most of the British countries do have somewhat high sending levels, and model 1 comes close to predicting the actual level of all of them, except Hong Kong. As there are other circumstances that account for Hong Kong's large residual, we can ignore it and conclude that model 1 successfully covers the British tradition.

2. *Impact of the American tradition.*—In contrast, the American tradition encouraged not only universal primary education but also extensive opportunities at the secondary and higher educational levels. Thus the Philippines, Japan, Korea, and Taiwan, which were most heavily influenced by the American tradition, are above average in terms of secondary students to population and, in the case of the Philippines and Japan, well above the average in terms of domestic higher educational opportunities. The model reasonably describes the impact of the American tradition on these countries. In the case of the Philippines, model 1 provides a good estimate of actual level. The estimates for Japan, Korea, and Taiwan are high, but this is because of yet another factor that is external to the basic model, linguistic isolation. Thus rather than make an adjustment for the American tradition, we will incorporate it into an adjustment for linguistic isolation.

3. *Linguistic and/or political isolation.*—The consequences of national language education policies are not considered in the basic model. In the cases of Japan and Korea, young people receive their education in unique national languages that are not used by or similar to the languages of other systems. Students in Taiwan also are educated in a language that is not broadly shared; while Mandarin is also the medium of instruction in mainland China, Taiwan-based Chinese cannot readily go for study on the mainland. The only other place where Chinese is the language of instruction is the Chinese University of Hong Kong, and the local competition for places there is so intense that less than 500 foreign students are admitted. Vietnamese students face a similar problem in that, since liberation, national education has been conducted in the national language; in addition, the government prohibits self-financed overseas study. To accommodate these special conditions of linguistic and/or political isolation, we have created an isolation variable by giving a score of 1 to the above-mentioned countries and a score of 0 to all others, expecting that isolation would be negatively associated with sending level.

4. *Arab community.*—In contrast to the "isolated" countries, the subgroup of Arab countries does share a common language. Model 1 underpredicted

[12] See Ronald Dore, *The Diploma Disease* (Berkeley: University of California Press, 1976).

the 1978 sending level of most of these countries. On the assumption that their high sending level was related to their recent OPEC-related gains in per capita income, I experimented by adding several economic-change variables. To my surprise, these did not significantly reduce the residuals for the Arab countries. As an alternate explanation for the high Arab levels, I reasoned that much of the sending is among Arab countries, and I created an Arab community variable, giving a score of 1 to all Arab countries and a score of 0 to all others.

5. *Political uncertainty.*—Finally, it should be recognized that in 1978 at least two countries were looking to a future of political uncertainty that might have influenced students to pursue overseas opportunities. Young people in Hong Kong were worried because of the ever closer 1997 terminal date of the colony's lease from China. Lebanese young people were worried because the ravages of war were destroying their homeland and the peace between the respective ethnically based political groupings. As the sending rates for these two countries were exceptionally high, it seemed desirable to establish yet another special case variable, this time for countries facing political uncertainty.

With a revised model 2 including these three special variables, I was able to account for 74 percent of the variance (reported in table 2). The addition of the Arab community and political uncertainty variables was an especially important factor in improving the model's ability to explain sending levels.

TABLE 2
MODEL 2: STATISTICS FOR NINE VARIABLES REGRESSED ON 1978 SENDING LEVEL

Variable	r	Beta	B	F Value
Total population for 1978 in hundred thousands	−.277	−.135	−.002	1.276
Basic human resource capacity	.440	.348	1.925	8.05
Financial capacity	.295	−.088	.000	.262
Domestic opportunities	−.109	−.068	−1.084	.381
Number of students studying overseas in 1973	.218	.231	.007	3.197
Degree of interdependence	.461	.105	.058	.058
Arab community*	.456	.613	26.178	19.692
Linguistic and/or political isolation†	−.033	.056	3.003	.181
Politically uncertain countries‡	.477	.202	14.827	2.590
Constant			−5.475	

NOTE.—Multiple R = .858; R^2 = .737; F value = 7.472; P = .001.

* Bahrain, Iraq, Jordan, Kuwait, Lebanon, Oman, Qatar, Saudi Arabia, Syrian Arab Republic, Yemen Arab Republic, and People's Democratic Republic of Yemen.

† Japan, Korea, China (Taiwan), and Vietnam.

‡ Hong Kong and Lebanon.

The addition of the three special variables supports most of the conclusions presented for model 1, with one important exception. As can be seen in table 2, export value as a proportion of GNP, my indicator of the extent of a nation's involvement in the interdependent system, no longer makes a significant contribution. Many of the countries that are relatively interdependent are either Arab nations or, as in the case of Hong Kong, experiencing political uncertainty. Thus the statistical analysis leaves me uncertain concerning the main determinant of these countries' high sending levels. Are the factors normally associated with the interdependence approach most critical? Or have I identified some of the more specific political and cultural conditions that explain away the impact of interdependence?

At the country level I conclude that model 2 quite adequately summarizes the major factors affecting the level of sending students overseas in 1978. In subsequent years, additional special cases have emerged that merit discussion below.

Looking to the Future

The above analysis has helped us to identify several of the key variables affecting nations' propensities to send students overseas. As we look to the future trends in numbers of students going overseas, what can be gleaned from this analysis?

We can certainly anticipate that the degree of interdependence among nations will increase over the next decades. My argument has considered interdependence as the principal pull drawing students to the campuses and jobs of center countries. Another, subtle change we can anticipate, but which is beyond the scope of this paper, is the diversification of educational centers in conjunction with the diversification of world economic activity. Also we can expect the newly industrializing countries to launch special campaigns to recover their drained brains.

We can anticipate a gradual increase in the ratio of secondary-level graduates to the population for nearly all Asian countries.[13] The secondary-level expansion will be especially evident in those countries that are currently not so well provided: notably Afghanistan, Oman, Pakistan, Saudi Arabia, Thailand, and Yemen and probably India and Nepal. This expansion should exert some upward pressure on sending levels.

While most countries will expand their tertiary section at a corresponding rate, those countries with a strong British tradition (Hong Kong, Singapore, Malaysia, and the South Asian countries) are likely to continue their conservatism, resulting in increasing numbers of students from these countries who will seek overseas opportunities. In several Asian societies the tertiary expansion was or will be launched specifically to deter overseas

---

[13] John W. Meyer and Michael T. Hannan, *National Development and the World System* (Chicago: University of Chicago Press, 1980).

study. Since Thailand created its Open University in 1973, the nation's sending rate has declined. Korea's decision to double university admissions and Malaysia's recent decision to create a sixth university were motivated in part by the desire to reduce the foreign-exchange drain relating to overseas study and the "undesirable influences" that often accompany overseas study.

The GNP per capita is likely to rise steadily in Southeast and East Asia, while the prospects are somewhat more problematic in the Middle East. Thus, especially in the case of Southeast and East Asia, increasing numbers of students will be able to obtain the necessary funds for overseas study.

Facilitating institutions are certainly becoming more widespread throughout the world, thus equalizing their independent impact. The net effect will be to make it relatively easier for students from countries that formerly sent low levels of students abroad to go overseas.

Several of the countries that formerly suffered from linguistic isolation have strengthened significantly the place of metropolitan languages in their lower- and upper-secondary-school curriculum. Increasing numbers of Japanese and Koreans, in particular, will have the minimum linguistic ability to compete for overseas study; in both countries there are a number of additional reasons for expecting big increases in the number who will capitalize on their new fluency.

Arab unity has undergone a significant change since 1978. Egypt's willingness to enter into the Camp David talks with Israel significantly eroded Egypt's attractiveness as a place for Arabs to study. The off-and-on state of war in Lebanon has aggravated relations among the Arab states. Moreover, from 1982, Arab countries began to experience large cutbacks in oil revenues, thus decreasing their capacity to finance overseas study. We can therefore expect a leveling off or even a decline in the number of students sent abroad from Arab countries.

Iran, while advancing the Islamic revolution and the war with Iraq, has lost much of her financial capacity to send students overseas and, moreover, has developed an official policy of discouraging young people from such ventures. For these reasons, Iran's sending rate also should decline.

Apart from Iran, a number of other countries have intentionally placed obstacles in the way of students seeking to go overseas for study. These obstacles range from limitations on the acquisition of foreign exchange (typical in South Asia) to requirements for fulfilling military service obligations (Singapore). A careful study of the conditions that lead nations to introduce or recall these "brakes" on the student market is certainly needed. In the absence of such a study, there is no basis for judging the future impact of these brakes, though they seem to be becoming less important at least through the early 1980s.

Finally, political and/or ethnic insecurity, which troubled only Hong Kong and Lebanon in 1978, has spread to several other Asian nations. Malaysia's policy of promoting Malay unity has made the country less attractive for ethnic Chinese, and thus rapidly increasing numbers of students have sought to use overseas study as a means for exploring a permanent change of nationality. Essentially the same pattern is emerging in Indonesia, though relatively fewer Indonesian Chinese have the academic or linguistic preparation necessary for seeking a place in an overseas academic institution. Similarly, Vietnam has pushed out large numbers of ethnic Chinese, and while these people initially have refugee status, many will later seek further study "overseas." Thus we can see how the ethnic tensions, especially in Southeast Asia, will lead large numbers to seek overseas study.

Conclusions and Limitations of the Research

The analysis has involved several simplifications of the complex reality of overseas study. For example, I lumped together all overseas students, whereas separate analyses might be attempted by degree level, by field of study, or by sex. I have treated students as if they are sent from their countries; in doing so I have recognized that many pay their own way but have assumed that their decision parameters were essentially shaped by their respective national contexts. In neither of my models have I included the influence of actions taken by receiving countries, including changes in procedures on admissions, visas, tuition, and recruitment. All of these factors need to be reviewed in future research.

Despite these limitations, the analysis has advanced our understanding of the relative importance of several of the key forces behind the post–World War II expansion in the number of individuals studying overseas. The increasing interdependence of national economies resulting in the weakening of national boundaries on labor markets may play an important role in motivating people to seek overseas study. However, this analysis suggests that indigenous forces have the predominant influence on the demand for overseas study. Several of the key national forces are part and parcel of the normal long-term process of economic development and, thus, provide a basis for tentative predictions of national sending levels. However, I also find that essentially unpredictable economic and political developments have considerable impact on the flow of students overseas. These exceptional developments in some instances stimulate (e.g., through political instability and ethnic discrimination) and in others brake the volume and direction. Therefore in my discussion of the future of the overseas student "boom" I have avoided quantitative statements in favor of a qualitative review of the likely impact of known forces.

APPENDIX
VALUES FOR THE VARIABLES INCLUDED IN MODEL 1 AND MODEL 2

Country	Variables*								Residuals for Model 1	Residuals for Model 2
	1	2	3	4	5	6	7	8		
Afghanistan	153	159	.9	.67	170	1.953	88	2.0	2.81	6.82
Bahrain	205	4	51.2	5.75	5,270	.434	108	86.6	28.49	15.81
Bangladesh	182	877	.2	3.3	90	.532	26	6.3	.29	1.17
Burma	18	353	0	2.5	160	1.372	34	5.1	-.09	2.38
China (Taiwan)	2,103	150	14	8.35	2,000	1.262	1,571	20.0†	-9.37	9.17
Hong Kong	2,214	45	49.2	7.33	1,500	.696	1,750	4.7	11.1	9.35
India	1,331	6,636	.2	3.56	190	1.952	1,468	5.6	7.7	3.58
Indonesia	852	1,519	.5	2.35	370	.779	428	17.6	-1.65	1.38
Iran	6,790	374	18.1	5.89	1,600	.707	1,905	30.7	-9.58	-1.42
Iraq	724	131	5.5	6.45	2,410	1.161	351	50.0†	-12.02	-4.60
Israel	560	39	14.3	4.69	4,150	4.737	529	28.9	2.23	11.71
Japan	1,439	1,168	1.2	7.79	8,810	2.675	741	10.1	-13.26	-9.12
Jordan	2,131	32	66.5	7.21	1,180	.883	1,218	15.8	45.39	23.50
Korea, Republic of	644	382	1.6	9.66	1,480	1.134	445	26.7	-15.62	-13.83
Kuwait	389	13	29.9	11.92	17,100	.748	77	68.3	-2.36	11.34
Laos	207	37	5.5	2.08	86	.103	99	1.0	3.98	6.40
Lebanon	1,428	32	44.6	8.06	1,142	3.046	592	40.0†	26.03	-9.36
Malaysia	2,232	134	16.6	7.46	1,370	.393	1,318	47.1	-11.08	-3.51

APPENDIX (*Continued*)
VALUES FOR THE VARIABLES INCLUDED IN MODEL 1 AND MODEL 2

Country	Variables*								Residuals for Model 1	Residuals for Model 2
	1	2	3	4	5	6	7	8		
Mongolia	533	17	31.3	13.94	780	.497	194	1.0	14.03	9.28
Nepal	43	140	.3	2.64	130	.862	123	5.6	−2.02	.78
Oman	145	9	16.1	1	2,970	.111	12	58.3	5.77	−8.89
Pakistan	446	824	.5	2.51	260	.714	499	8.4	−3.48	−.45
Philippines	305	484	.6	5.82	600	4.003	308	14.1	−5.57	−2.68
Qatar	75	2	37.5	7	16,670	1.428	12	85.0†	9.84	5.31
Saudi Arabia	1,011	84	12	3.52	7,280	1.594	169	57.6	−3.51	−15.78
Singapore	362	24	15	7.83	3,830	1.281	184	130.2	−16.93	−.82
Sri Lanka	277	147	1.8	8.45	230	.14	165	30.9	−12.9	−11.47
Syrian Arab Republic	673	90	7.4	6.44	1,030	1.934	688	12.7	−6.08	−2.68
Thailand	1,024	472	2.1	2.54	590	3.127	794	17.7	−5.96	.40
Turkey	1,189	449	2.6	4.62	1,330	1.54	605	4.3	−5.57	−2.47
United Arab Emirates	109	8	13.6	2.87	15,590	.434	29	58.2	−4.83	−10.62
Vietnam	1,516	523	2.8	6.46	300	.405	1,028	38.8	6.97	−12.33
Yemen Arab Republic	266	59	4.5	.42	420	.96	69	.4	5.97	6.93
Yemen, People's Democratic Republic of	130	20	6.5	3.3	480	.378	59	50.0	−4.36	2.89

* Key to variables (see text for definitions): 1 = number of students studying overseas in 1978; 2 = total population for 1978 in hundred thousands; 3 = sending level; 4 = basic human resource capacity; 5 = financial capacity; 6 = domestic opportunities; 7 = number of students studying overseas in 1973; 8 = degree of interdependence.

† Data are not available for 1978; the estimate is therefore based on trends from earlier years.

Foreign Training and Development Strategies

ROBERT G. MYERS*

External aid for education in developing countries was guided during the 1960s by an unwritten doctrine placing faith in planning, science, and the development of human resources. That doctrine allowed little room for natural emergence of homegrown talents and remedies. Rather, deliberate training for new tasks and ways of behaving was thought necessary to spur modernization and development. One consequence of these beliefs was an increase in national and international support for foreign study.[1] This article will focus on externally financed study abroad at the postgraduate level and on the period from 1960 to the present. Two main strategies guiding that assistance will be compared. Support for foreign study provided by one international organization in one country—the Ford Foundation in Peru—will be examined, with particular attention to effects of a changing economic and political climate on policy and outcomes.

Assistance Strategies

At least two main strategies have been adopted by external funders seeking to strengthen economic and social development through support for postgraduate study abroad. One, an institution-building strategy, stresses the importance of strong institutions that can serve as national resources in the development process. The other, a strategy of knowledge generation and use, stems from the conviction that lack of knowledge and understanding impedes progress.[2]

The phrase "insitution building" describes a process of helping formal organizations to become self-sustaining sources of the technical skills, knowledge, attitudes, and values deemed necessary for "modernization." Typically, the process involved improving leadership, technical expertise, program content, physical facilities, and an organization's financial base,

---

The information in this article has been taken from an evaluation carried out by the author for the Ford Foundation of its support for foreign training between 1960 and 1980. Part of that evaluation consisted of a follow-up study of the approximately 350 Peruvians to whom support was provided between 1963 and 1980. A questionnaire was administered to the entire group. A major portion of this article first appeared in "External Financing of Foreign Study: The Ford Foundation in Peru," *Prospects* 13, no. 4 (1983): 503–13.

* On the staff of the High Scope Foundation.

[1] Since 1960, the number of foreign students in the world has increased more than fivefold, according to Unesco statistics.

[2] Other strategies have framed external support for training abroad, such as a human rights strategy and strategies designed to promote international understanding through cultural contact and exchange. This article focuses on the two that were closely related to social and economic development during the first two "development decades."

administrative structures, and ability to communicate—internally and externally.[3] Staff development, often through training abroad, was a central part of most institution-building packages that usually also included support for resident expatriate "experts," construction and purchase of equipment, information gathering or research, and the modernizing of administrative procedures. An institution-building strategy was prominent in the 1960s, lost ground in the 1970s, but seems to be regaining popularity in the 1980s.

The idea that formal organizations should be "built" to lead the process of modernization has about it an air of social engineering. In their institution building, most external assistance agencies and national governments have emphasized imported forms and values. Accordingly, assistance was heavily oriented toward such institutions as universities (with imported British, American, or French structures and traditions—including a research tradition), hospitals (with their expensive bias toward curative medicine), or planning offices (to help rationalize the planning process). Moreover, most staff development occurred in Western institutions and in the developed world. A prominent feature of many institution-building initiatives, particularly in the 1960s, has been a collaborative arrangement between a Third World institution and an institution abroad.

A strategy of improving knowledge generation and use seems to have gained currency among external funders over the years since 1960. Assistance oriented by that goal has taken several forms. One has been to support talented individuals wherever they are found. A second concentrates on improving particular academic disciplines such as biology, economics, or linguistics. A third approach has been to choose broad problem areas such as education or rural development and to provide concentrated support for training as well as research and communication. Because knowledge is presumed to be a free and unbounded commodity available for use by anyone, knowledge generation has about it less of an air of social engineering than institution building does. But creating and using knowledge is a social process with political and economic consequences—a process that can be guided. And the ways of approaching the process of knowledge generation and use tend also to have a strong bias rooted in the developed world.

In practical application, these two assistance strategies often overlap, but it is useful to distinguish between them. For instance, the selection processes associated with each and the people selected for study abroad are usually very different. If the focus is on institutions, control over selection is more likely to rest with the institutions rather than with the

---

[3] John D. Montgomery, *Foreign Aid in International Politics* (Englewood Cliffs, N.J.: Prentice-Hall, 1967), p. 46.

external funder or with a national committee.[4] An institutional focus also limits the pool of individuals from whom selections can be made. Although some programs have used foreign training as a means of trying to attract new people, that has often been difficult because new recruits have not developed institutional loyalty and have left the institution. Choice is therefore restricted to those already employed by the institution. These practical limits on selection have sometimes led to choosing people under an institution-building strategy who would not have been chosen in an open competition.

When training is linked to knowledge production and use, selection is more likely to be carried out either by the external agency or by a committee whose members are chosen by the external agency. The group of individuals from whom selections might be made opens up because the focus is not on particular institutions. The basis for selection changes also. Sometimes choice is made on merit, simply in terms of the potential contribution of individuals to knowledge, without regard to institution or field. More frequently, however, it is limited by choosing a particular field of study or discipline or by restricting awards to work on a particular problem—to which the training should contribute.

Associated with these two strategies of technical assistance and training are different assumptions about how the training should be used and about what its impact should be. The obvious outcome of an institution-building strategy should be a strong, active, productive institution. That goal requires individuals trained abroad to return to the same place of employment from which they were selected for training abroad. If they do not, a program is considered unsuccessful. In many cases, those receiving financing have been asked to sign an agreement saying they will return to work for the institution for a fixed period of time. Whether the returning individual can be productive in the environment to which he or she returns is not considered. But even the return of individuals does not, of course, guarantee institutional strength or continuity. Indeed, institutions have often been more fragile than anticipated. They may be undercut by the political and economic uncertainties of the times or depend too much on one individual. Under such conditions it is difficult to sustain a judgment that training is wasted if individuals change employment.

A knowledge-generating strategy does not depend on the grouping of people in any one place. It allows for individual contributions to knowledge and for regrouping of individuals according to conditions of the times. To evaluate such a strategy, judgments are required about "additions

---

[4] Sometimes that control has been captured by institutions from abroad that are designated as responsible for providing technical assistance. Sometimes expatriate advisers present as part of a technical assistance contract exert an important influence over selection. Still, the main responsibility lies with the assisted institution.

to the stock of knowledge" and about contributions to the growth and maturity of vaguely defined "national scientific communities" or "disciplines." This strategy is, however, also affected by political and economic uncertainties that can quickly change a favorable climate into an unfavorable one.

In the following section the two strategies will be discussed with reference to changing conditions in Peru. Special attention will be given to questions of return to employment at particular institutions in Peru and to growth of the economics discipline.

Foreign Training of Peruvians, 1963–80

From 1960 to 1980, the Ford Foundation's international programs provided approximately one-quarter billion dollars (at 1983 prices) to assist postgraduate study abroad of about 12,000 individuals from Africa, Asia, Latin America, and the Middle East. Although the Peruvian case deals with only a small part of the larger picture, it illustrates changing strategies and provides some insight into the issues highlighted above. Moreover, Peru is an interesting case because of the marked political changes that occurred during the 20 years, allowing examination of the correspondence between those changes and external support for training abroad.

A field office in Peru was first established by the Ford Foundation in 1963 at a time of optimism and economic growth. Over the next seventeen years, the foundation made available $11,000,000 to strengthen academic, governmental, and private institutions, to bolster capacity for analysis in both the natural and the social sciences, and to help seek solutions to persisting problems within such areas as agriculture, population, management, and education. Support for training of intellectual leaders, often outside the country, was a key element in the foundation's programming. Over the 17 years, $2,900,000 (more than one-fourth of the foundation's total program budget) was devoted to assisting postgraduate training abroad of Peruvians.

During the 1960s and the 1970s, three very different governments held power in Peru. A democratic, reformist, civilian regime, elected in 1963, served until October 1968, when a military coup occurred, leading to a period of major social reorganization between 1969 and 1975. That reorganization was cut short by a shake-up in the military, bringing to power, in 1975, generals with a conservative policy of retrenchment. As will be evident below, these political metamorphoses within Peru paralleled and were affected by international changes—in prevailing economic conditions, in political alliances and relationships, and in the doctrine of development. They overlapped as well with changes in the Ford Foundation, which, in turn, were affected by international currents. These national, international, and institutional changes interacted to affect foundation policy toward study abroad and to influence how those trained abroad would make use of their experience.

The Changing Context

1963–68—development and democracy.—The years of democratic rule under President Fernando Belaunde coincided with an international flowering of faith in the power and potential of education, science, and technological transfer as motors of economic development and with an emerging economic doctrine giving increased prominence to investment in "human capital." The Peruvian government and the Ford Foundation shared these beliefs, and a logical outcome was that most of the foundation's $4,000,000 allocated during the period was used to strengthen Peruvian universities. A former university administrator was chosen by the foundation to head the first office in Peru. General program support and support for training were both concentrated on science, engineering, and economics (together these fields accounted for about 79 percent of the training awards). An institution-building strategy guided grant making. Most of the awardees who studied abroad came from and were expected to return to university positions (69 percent). Most studied in the United States (77 percent) and at the master's level (66 percent). Table 1 presents these distributions and compares them with figures for subsequent political periods.

By 1968, the Peruvian economy had deteriorated and the mood of optimism present in 1963 had changed. Fiscal deficits, fixed exchange rates, and free importation created problems the government was unable to solve. General economic stagnation had set in. Moreover, the moderate reforms introduced by Belaunde had done little to modify the ethnic, class, and urban/rural differences in Peru. Pressure for more basic structural reforms grew. The combination of pressures led to the removal of Belaunde by the military in October 1968.

1969–75—social reorganization and change under military rule.—When Peruvian generals took office in late 1968, they sought a "third path" that was neither capitalist nor communist. The new government placed greater emphasis on social and structural change than on economic growth. General Juan Velasco Alvarado and his colleagues decreed major reforms in agriculture, business, mining, and education. Science and technology were no longer afforded such a high priority. Universities were now seen as elitist institutions to be "democratized" rather than as producers of needed high-level human resources. University budgets were cut, and many professors were attracted into government, both by the social reforms being promulgated and by the higher salaries being offered. The political climate

TABLE 1

PERUVIANS FUNDED FOR STUDY ABROAD BY THE FORD FOUNDATION BY POLITICAL PERIODS, 1963–80

	1963–68, Belaunde Reformist: Civilian		1969–75, Velasco Third Path: Military		1976–80, Morales-B Retrenchment: Military		Totals	
	N	%	N	%	N	%	N	%
Field of study:								
Science/math, engineering	61	63	43	23	12	22	116	36
Economics	16	16	53	31	13	24	82	25
Noneconomic social science	9	9	42	24	23	42	74	23
Humanities	8	8	19	11	6	11	33	10
Law	1	1	13	8	1	2	15	5
Agriculture	2	2	3	2	...	...	5	2
Total	97	99	173	99	55	101	325	101
Level of study:								
Masters	62	66	69	42	14	26	145	47
Doctoral	26	28	51	31	36	68	113	36
Nondegree	6	6	44	27	3	6	53	17
Total	94	100	164	100	53	100	311	100
Place of study:								
United States	75	77	105	62	24	44	204	63
Europe	10	10	42	25	23	42	75	23
Latin America	13	13	23	13	8	14	44	14
Total	98	100	170	100	55	100	323	100
Gender:								
Female	8	8	23	13	12	22	43	13
Male	91	92	150	87	43	78	284	87
Total	99	100	173	100	55	100	327	100
Institution prior to departure:								
University	66	69	98	58	34	67	198	63
State	19	20	55	33	12	24	86	27
Private	10	11	15	9	5	10	30	10
Total	95	100	168	100	51	101	314	100

SOURCE.—A follow-up survey of Ford funded fellowship holders, Lima, May 1983.
NOTE.—Omitted from the calculations are individuals for whom information was missing: field of study: $N = 2$; level of study: $N = 16$; place of study: $N = 4$; gender: $N = 0$; and institution: $N = 13$. Totals may not equal 100 due to rounding.

favored politicization of the universities. With these shifts, the locus of social analysis and action moved into the public sector.

These changes within Peru were accompanied and reinforced by widespread impatience with the human-resource strategies applied earlier in the 1960s. Unrealistically high expectations about what education could accomplish were not being met. Unemployment among university and high school graduates had begun to surface. An ideological shift, slight though it was, began to occur within parts of the international donor community toward a definition of development placing much more emphasis than in the past on overcoming poverty, improving the distribution of wealth, and moderating social inequality. Peru's revolutionary third path struck a responsive chord among those external donors interested in approaches adding a social dimension to earlier economic theories of development. That included the Ford Foundation, whose new staff members were social scientists by trade.

Reflecting these national, international, and institutional changes, the foundation's program shifted. Although a large proportion of grant funds still went to universities, the foundation increased its grant making to organizations and individuals within the government, and the percentage of training awards going to the public sector increased from one-fifth to one-third. Support for science declined, and support for engineering virtually disappeared. Economics continued to command a significant portion of program funds (31 percent), and assistance broadened to include a range of subareas, methodologies, and applications. The noneconomic social sciences took on greater importance (24 percent vs. 9 percent in the previous period). A slightly higher percentage of awardees studied at the Ph.D. level than in the previous period. Institution building began to wane as a strategy, and knowledge generation became more important.

1976–80—retrenchment.—In 1975, an ailing Velasco was replaced by General Morales Bermudez, and a policy of retrenchment was set in motion with the hope of restoring the country to economic health. Most of the reforms promulgated under Velasco were dismanteled. Among other things, that process forced many social scientists to leave their government positions. A significant proportion of these did not want to return to full-time university teaching; instead, they established private centers for research and social action, hoping to continue efforts begun earlier and, not incidentally, to earn more than they could in the now debilitated, low-paying universities.

This was a period of retrenchment for the Ford Foundation as well. The amount of money it had to spend had been cut in half following the oil crisis and the subsequent stock market decline. Reductions in spending were relatively heavier in Latin American than in other areas in which the foundation was working. Hence programming in Peru was drastically reduced. Most of the available funds for Peru were concentrated on general support of the social sciences or on applications of the social sciences to population, education, or rural development.

Training during the period focused heavily on the social sciences (economics and other social science disciplines accounted for two-thirds of all awards) and on study at the Ph.D. level (68 percent). The location of study abroad was diversified so that only 44 percent of the awardees studied in the United States. A strategy of knowledge generation had taken over from the earlier institution-building strategy.

Extracting from the above, the following shifts occurred over the three periods discussed: (1) from support for science and engineering to support for the social sciences, (2) from study abroad in the United States to study in Europe or Latin America, (3) from study at the master's level to study at the Ph.D. level, (4) from support for university-based individuals in the reformist period of Belaunde to somewhat greater support for government-based individuals in the social reorganization under Velasco and a return to university-based support in the retrenchment period, and (5) from an emphasis on institution building in the first period to a strategy of knowledge production and use in the last. In addition, the foundation shifted (6) from support almost exclusively for males to support for a higher percentage of females (from 8 percent female in 1963–68 to 22 percent in 1976–80), (7) from an ancillary to a more direct role in the selection of awardees (direct involvement with 11 percent of the awards in 1963–68 to 52 percent in 1976–80), and (8) from nearly full fellowships to partial fellowships (the average award dropped from $8,000 in 1963–68 to $6,000 in 1976–80).[5]

An Institution-building Strategy

An assumption of an institution-building strategy is that individuals will return to their particular institutions to work following foreign study. Did that actually happen in the Peruvian case? To approach that question we can compare the rate of return for the 1963–68 cohort of awardees, who were funded under an institution-building strategy, with the rate of return of later groups funded under a knowledge-generating strategy. The figures (see table 2) suggest that the earlier institution-building approach was associated with a higher rate of return to institutions immediately following study abroad. Of the 1963–68 group, 82 percent went back to the same institution, as compared with only 71 percent and 62 percent, respectively, of the 1969–75 and 1976–80 groups. But two years after completing study abroad, presence in the institution of origin had already

---

[5] If these figures are adjusted to 1980 prices, the change is much greater—from an equivalent of about $16,000 in 1963–68 to about $6,000 in 1976–80.

TABLE 2
INSTITUTIONAL ATTACHMENT, PERUVIANS FUNDED FOR STUDY ABROAD BY THE FORD FOUNDATION,
1963–80

	1963–68, Belaunde Reformist: Civilian		1969–75, Velasco Third Path: Military		1976–80, Morales-B Retrench-ment: Military		Totals	
	N	%	N	%	N	%	N	%
Returned to same institution after study abroad	46	82	67	71	18	62	131	72
In same institution 2 years after return	33	62	48	53	14	50	95	55
In same institution at time of survey	21	39	34	36	15	52	70	40

SOURCE.—A follow-up survey of Ford-funded fellowship holders, Lima, May 1983.

dropped to 62 percent for the earliest group, to 53 percent for the middle group, and to 50 percent for the most recent one. By 1983, the time of the survey, there had been a further decline; only 39 percent of the 1963–68 group remained in their original institutions.

The interpretation of these percentages is not obvious. Is 62 percent after 2 years a high or a low percentage? Is 39 percent a good rate of retention after 15 years? If one uses these figures for return and retention as a narrow indicator of success, an institution-building approach seems to be only moderately successful at best. For that reason, in part, a relatively severe judgment was passed on the insititution-building approach by foundation staff. As early as 1972, a conclusion began to emerge, not only for Peru but also for the Latin American region as a whole, that the foundation's experience in Latin America with general faculty or university development grants, by and large, had been unsatisfactory. Therefore, policy shifted toward work with a single discipline or with problem-oriented groups. There was a general feeling that the real success of most of the training support, institutional or otherwise, lay in the embodied skills and knowledge of those who returned, regardless of their institutional attachment.

A Discipline-building Strategy

Over the 17 years from 1963 to 1980, the Ford Foundation paid special attention to generating knowledge by helping to develop disciplines or fields as different as physics, linguistics, engineering, law, and anthropology. Economics, however, received the most attention of all: 80 Peruvians were helped to obtain postgraduate training in economics and associated areas.[6] These 80 awardees were predominantly male (97 percent). Two-thirds studied in the United States. Slightly less than one-half studied at the doctoral level. At the time the awards were made, about half were affiliated with universities and half were in the public sector; very few awards were made to private-sector individuals.

Economics is frequently cited as a field in which foundation funding has had an important impact in Peru, making it particularly interesting to examine. That reputation derives in part from the obvious comparison of the economics profession today with the field 25 years ago. In 1960, economics faculties in Peruvian universities produced accountants and business managers. A doctorate in the economic sciences was available but seldom sought and was by no stretch of the imagination a modern economics degree. Most students squeezed courses in at odd hours in order to obtain a proper title while doing their real learning on the job. Courses were taught by moonlighting accountants, businessmen, statisticians, and lawyers. A premium was placed on expediency and practicality. Research was not part of standard training or practice. Within the Peruvian government, economic planning was, in the early 1960s, largely under the control of systems engineers, statisticians, lawyers, or political appointees, who only rarely brought with them a background in economics. There were, in 1963 when Belaunde took charge, no more than five Peruvians with a doctorate in economics.

Over the period, support by the foundation to strengthen economics took several forms. The first grant, in 1963, was to the National Agrarian University (UNA) to strengthen its department of agricultural economics. In 1967, a grant was made to the Central Bank to increase the supply of well-trained economists available to the bank and to stimulate Lima's major universities to improve and modernize teaching and research in economics. From 1969 through 1975, the foundation paid greater attention to public-sector institutions.[7] This attention to the public sector was accompanied by assistance in 1972 to the newly created program of economics and development at the Catholic University.

What has been the result of these efforts to fortify the economics community in Peru? One prominent Peruvian economist indicated when replying to our questionnaire, "I believe that today there exists a 'critical

---

[6] Study awards ranged from $600 to $30,000. An average award was about $10,000. The "investment" totaled approximately $750,000, which, spread over 17 years, amounts to less than $50,000 per year (in 1983 dollars, the amounts would be at least $1,500,000 and $100,000 per year, respectively).

[7] Grants were made for study abroad in economics and related fields by individuals in the National Planning Institute, the Higher School for Public Administration, the National Council of Peruvian Universities, and the National Institute for Educational Research and Development.

mass' of professionals of a certain academic level in economics that did not exist before." The contrast with 1960, when modern economics were virtually absent from Peru, is clear: the country can now point to a solid core of well-trained, extremely capable economists of various persuasions, with competence in a range of subfields, including agricultural economics, public policy, international economics, economic history, transportation economics, the economics of education, labor economics, money and banking, and finance.

Foundation funds have helped to institutionalize research and the teaching of economics in Peru. At least three institutions now exist in Peru that are capable of providing excellent instruction at a master's level: Catholic University, the University of the Pacific, and the National School of Business Administration. In an important degree, these programs are run and staffed by individuals trained abroad with foundation funds. Nevertheless, it was not an institution-building strategy that produced results in Peru. Where the emphasis was on institutions, the policy was only moderately successful, with the possible exception of the Catholic University. The Agrarian University, for instance, did not develop a strong department of agricultural economics despite the $850,000 investment there. Of the 13 fellowship awards made by the foundation to UNA staff, only two recipients are now associated with that university. Within the public sector, grant making designed to strengthen governmental institutions must be classified as a failure. With few exceptions, those selected for training have moved on to other institutions, often outside government, leaving little residue in the public sector and almost none in the specific governmental institutions assisted.

Thus, it was a broad disciplinary strategy rather than a focused institution-building strategy that has made a difference. Institutions gained strength as individuals with strong qualifications assembled themselves in institutional locations providing leadership and favorable conditions. In the fragile and mobile climate of Peru, it was difficult to predict where such grouping would take hold or how long it would be maintained at any one place. Institutional fortunes can still rise and fall quickly because they often depend too much on one key person, because finances are not guaranteed, or because of any one of several other factors. Interestingly, the stronger institutions today are those sitting outside the public sector.

Concentrating on numbers of individuals trained and on institutions begs a central question: Has the quality of economics in Peru improved as a result of training and the institutionalizing of modern economics? Measuring quality is risky at best. However, it is clear that the economic research being carried out in Peru is much more sophisticated today than it was in the early 1960s (or even the early 1970s), both in the problems tackled and in the analyses done. It would be incorrect to say that economic

157

research in Peru is strong. Most research is still carried out by a very few individuals, and incentives are still missing, particularly for reflective or basic research in economics. Still, quality has improved.

To some degree, quality is indexed by international standards. Indicative of Peruvian standing, for instance, is the fact that, in competition for admission to Ph.D. programs in the United States, Peruvian-trained master's students are said to perform well above average on graduate record examinations in economics. And the fact that Peruvians are in demand and have secured positions with international organizations attests to an international standard of training.

Well-trained economists have been in demand in the Peruvian government as well. Several have held key positions with the present government: as the head of the Peruvian Central Bank, as Minister of Trade and Commerce, and as vice-ministers in finance, commerce, and labor. Slowly, economics is being integrated into the planning process.

Another indicator of the strength and maturity of a discipline is the degree of diversity and pluralism it displays. On that score Peru does very well. Economists are not concentrated in any one field or tradition. An explicit assumption of foundation policy has been that diversity and pluralism are desirable because they open options and choices and enhance criticism and dialogue. Diversity among the award recipients is evident in their institutional origins, in the choice of institutions for study (the 80 studied in 37 different institutions with no more than seven at any one institution), and in the spread of subfields and approaches represented.[8]

Diversity does not necessarily indicate pluralism, which is more appropriately judged in terms of schools of thought, ideological persuasions, and methodological preferences. To get at the degree of pluralism among foundation-funded trainees, three Peruvian economists who knew the community well and who represented different ideological positions were asked to locate colleagues on a four-point ideological scale running from extreme right to extreme left.[9] The result was a surprisingly normal distribution, with the median falling just to the left of center. The foundation has, then, helped to foster pluralism in a maturing discipline.

To be able to say more about the effect of a knowledge-generating strategy, more detailed study would be necessary, examining the quantity and quality of writings and attempting to document the use of knowledge

---

[8] The list of thematic concentrations includes such specialities as economic history, income distribution, international economic administration, the economics of education, population economics, international trade, economic development, labor economics, and the economics of public administration.

[9] Of the 80 economists, 12 were not known to any of the raters. Another 18 were known only to one of the three. In none of the remaining 50 cases did raters disagree by more than one category on the four-point scale. Simply adding up the ratings produced the following distribution: far right 22, near right 35, near left 47, and far left 22.

in decision making. For the time being, it is enough to say that, on balance, the profession has "modernized," grown dramatically, and broadened along the way. Generally, the economists trained are in Peru (about 85 percent) and working at their trade. Training and research institutions of relatively high quality are in place.

Foreign Study and the Flight of Talent

Whether an institution-building or knowledge-generating strategy is followed, funders and governments alike express continuing concern about possible out-migration of high-level talent, often referred to as the "brain drain." That concern is, understandably, often very nationalistic, disregarding larger contributions to knowledge and action that can be fostered by migration. Moreover, most analyses are insensitive to the human side of migration—as a solution to individual problems. Nor do they take into account that national contributions can be made even if a person works abroad or that migration is often a temporary phenomenon resulting in experiential learning that can be of benefit later to a country. In addition, most analyses of brain drain fail to separate migration related to externally financed postgraduate training from other training abroad. Were that done, it would be clear that permanent out-migration by those receiving external support is relatively low—usually less than 15 percent.[10]

To what extent has a drain of talent from Peru been associated with Ford Foundation support for study abroad at the postgraduate level? Table 3 presents information about the present location of former awardees and about several variables that might be related to permanent out-migration. From the table we see that 78 percent of the awardees were in Peru at the time of the study. Taking out the 4 percent who were studying or temporarily abroad, we are left with a rough figure of 18 percent representing the brain drain associated with foreign study.

Any estimate of out-migration, including the 18 percent figure, is subject to a fairly large margin of error. For instance, the figure does not capture changes over time. At least 25 percent of the awardees have worked abroad at one time or another, and it is likely that the migration figure would have been closer to 25 percent had the survey been carried out in 1980 rather than in 1983.[11] Undoubtedly some of those currently working abroad and considered as part of the brain drain will return to Peru, as has already happened with the reappearance of Belaunde. A concerted effort is being made presently by the National Science Council

[10] There will, of course, be variations by country and at particular points in time, but the general figure seems to hold up well, despite a widespread belief that "talent loss" is much higher.

[11] Unfortunately, the survey did not ask for a detailed employment history, so the percentage cannot be calculated. The estimate is based on interviews and perusal of the employment questions that were asked in the survey.

TABLE 3

PRESENT LOCATION OF PERUVIANS FUNDED FOR STUDY ABROAD BY THE FORD FOUNDATION BY POLITICAL PERIODS, 1963–80

	1963–68, Belaunde Reformist: Civilian		1969–75, Velasco Path: Military		1976–80, Morales-B Retrenchment: Military		Totals	
	N	%	N	%	N	%	N	%
Location:								
Peru	79	80	139	80	37	67	255	78
United States—study	0		3		8		11	
Europe—study	1	1	0	2	0	15	1	4
Latin America—study	0		0		0		0	
United States—work	10		15		4		29	
Europe—work	0	19	7	18	4	18	11	18
Latin America—work	9		9		2		20	
Total	99	100	173	100	55	100	327	100
Field of study:								
Science, math, English:								
Working abroad	11	20	13	30	5	42	29	25
Total awards	54		43		12		109	
Economics:								
Working abroad	3	20	6	11	...	...	9	11
Total awards	15		53		13		81	
Noneconomics social science:								
Working abroad	3	33	6	14	3	13	12	16
Total awards	9		42		23		74	
Other:								
Working abroad	2	14	5	14	2	28	9	16
Total awards	14		35		7		56	
Total:								
Working abroad	19	21	30	17	10	18	59	18
Total awards	92		173		55		320	
Level of study:								
Master's:								
Working abroad	10	16	10	14	2	14	22	15
Total awards	62		69		14		145	

	Group 1		Group 2		Group 3		Total	
	%	No.	%	No.	%	No.	%	No.
Doctoral:								
Working abroad	31	8	22	17	17	6	22	31
Total awards		26		77		36		139
Other:								
Working abroad	17	1	11	2	67	2	19	5
Total awards		6		18		3		27
Total:								
Working abroad	20	19	18	29	19	10	19	58
Total awards		94		164		53		311
Gender:								
Male:								
Working abroad	19	17	16	24	15	7	17	48
Total awards		91		150		47		288
Female:								
Working abroad	25	2	26	6	38	3	28	11
Total awards		8		23		8		39
Total:								
Working abroad	19	19	17	30	19	10	18	59
Total awards		99		173		55		327
Institution prior to departure:								
University:								
Working abroad	24	16	18	18	24	8	21	42
Total awards		66		101		34		201
State:								
Working abroad	···	···	15	8	17	2	12	10
Total awards		19		55		12		86
Private:								
Working abroad	19	18	17	29	20	10	18	57
Total awards		95		168		51		314

SOURCE.—A follow-up survey of Ford Foundation fellowship holders.

NOTE.—Omitted from the calculations are individuals for whom information was missing. The omitted numbers are: location: $N = 0$; field of study: $N = 2$; level of study: $N = 16$; gender: $N = 0$; institution: $N = 13$.

to attract back to Peru additional scientists presently working abroad. Others will go out for an extended period. Nor does the figure capture the fact that Peruvians are working for international organizations, several with responsibilities for programs dealing with Peru. Were these adjustments to be taken into account, they would probably reduce slightly the percentage that could be considered permanently lost to Peru. The reader must decide whether a "loss" of, say, 15 percent is a tolerable figure for migration associated with externally funded foreign study.

The numbers in table 3 indicate that scientists, engineers, or mathematicians are more likely to migrate than are social scientists. When salaries fell in the universities during the 1970s, natural scientists, in contrast with their social science colleagues, did not have good options for employment within government. In addition, the international culture of the natural sciences makes it easier for scientists than for social scientists to migrate. The higher percentage, then, should not be surprising.

Females have a significantly higher rate of migration than do males. Marriage to foreigners provides only a partial explanantion; Peruvian men also marry while they are abroad but are more likely to bring their foreign wives back to Peru than woman are to bring their husbands. The difference probably begins earlier, however. It is apparent from interviews that larger proportion of women than of men were single when chosen for study abroad. This is because social convention makes it difficult for a married Peruvian woman either to leave her family for a period to study abroad or to convince her husband that he should accompany her abroad (unless he too is studying). The pool of women available for possible fellowships is, therefore, severely reduced, and the risk of permanent migration associated with study abroad for women is increased.

Migration is significantly higher among doctoral level awardees than among those at the master's level. That finding is not surprising, given the more marketable nature of the doctoral degree. Migration is also higher among those who were employed in universities than among those employed by government.

Examining table 3 for differences according to political period does not turn out to be particularly fruitful. The general rate of out-migration seems to be about the same for all periods. A higher rate is evident among scientists sponsored after 1968 than among those assisted before. Apparently, the changing political and economic circumstances in Peru affected awardees in similar ways, whether they studied abroad at an earlier or at a later date.

A Concluding Note

The trends in Ford Foundation support evident in the Peruvian data presented do not necessarily reflect larger trends in international support for study abroad. As an independent philanthropic institution, the foundation is different from bilateral and multilateral international agencies that must work directly with governments and that command larger budgets. The foundation's increasing emphasis on the social sciences during the period and on its pluralistic approach, for instance, differed from that of most other external funders, requiring a degree of independence, flexibility, and program continuity that is easier for private organizations to achieve.

The Peruvian case demonstrates that the foundation responded to changes in international and national contexts but that it was able to do so while maintaining some continuity in its programming. It points to the risk associated with a narrow institution-building strategy as a guide to support for study abroad. It suggests that a relatively small continuing investment in foreign training can have an important impact on the growth of a discipline. And it reinforces the position that brain drain associated with external support for training abroad is not large and is not, per se, a very important issue.

Overseas Training and National Development Objectives in Sub-Saharan Africa

JOYCE LEWINGER MOOCK*

This article focuses on the impact of overseas training on national development objectives in sub-Saharan Africa. That old topic is resurfacing as international assistance agencies once again consider support of higher education as a fundamental, long-range strategy for accelerating growth and improving social equity within low-income countries of the region.

During the past 2 decades, economic development has been slow in most of the countries of sub-Saharan Africa. Sluggish agricultural performance, combined with rapid rates of population growth and a balance-of-payments crisis, have led to pessimistic projections of African development in the 1980s, particularly in the face of continuing global recession. Recent diagnostic reports of Africa's special economic problems by the World Bank and other international agencies point to serious shortcomings in existing policies, particularly those affecting agriculture, and to widespread weaknesses in planning, decision making, and managerial capacities with resulting overextension of the public sector. Underlying these limitations is a still acute scarcity of highly qualified, indigenous professionals with the skills that are critical to devising and carrying out effective strategies for national development.

Foreign study is, of course, but one option for meeting Africa's needs for higher education, and it is the option which received the most severe criticism by the international community during the 1970s when priorities shifted from providing postsecondary education to meeting the basic educational needs of the poor. Under colonial rule and in the years immediately following independence, when local provision of higher education was negligible or nonexistent, foreign study was considered the fastest route to expanding the number of Africans with qualifications that would enable them to replace expatriate manpower in the public and private sectors of the economy. Moreover, development pundits believed that returns to investment in overseas training would inevitably "trickle down" to benefit all levels of society and all sectors of the economy. The guiding principle behind the provision of overseas scholarships was the proper allocation of disciplines and subject matter to fit occupational slots in the developing economy.

As national objectives concerning economic growth became coupled with the equitable distribution of benefits and broad-based participation

---

* Assistant director for social sciences at the Rockefeller Foundation, New York.

in decision making, assistance agencies redirected their attention and resources toward basic education, which offered the best prospects for directly benefiting the poor. At the same time, attention to higher education turned toward the developmental role of home-based universities and educational innovations such as localization of the curriculum, community outreach activities, and policy-oriented research and program evaluation for government. As part of this trend, agency support for overseas training diminished and what remained was directed largely toward either short-term, nondegree study or project-related and highly technical training at the graduate level.

With recent economic events highlighting the shortage of high-level skilled manpower in Africa, and with university expansion at home straining existing resources without producing sufficient graduates to meet demand, questions are being raised once more about the appropriate role of foreign study. As of 1979, there were approximately 100,000 third-level students from sub-Saharan Africa, excluding South Africa, studying abroad; this represents about 30 percent of all African students enrolled at the tertiary level. The value of this education requires reexamination in light of the escalating costs of overseas training and the availability of home facilities. It also needs review in terms of its consistency with the tasks of nationalizing institutions and forwarding local objectives related to cultural autonomy, self-reliance, and social equity.

The following section of this article is divided into three parts. The first briefly reviews the current economic crisis in Africa and the need for high-level manpower possessing particular development-oriented skills. The second examines the pros and cons of foreign study as one alternative for meeting national training requirements for competent indigenous professionals. The third points out areas where more systematic information is needed about the impact associated with training in foreign countries and suggests some conditions related to the effective provision of overseas education.

The Current Need for Professionals with Development Skills

Many of the countries of sub-Saharan Africa are facing severe and complicated problems in their efforts to accelerate national growth and improve the well-being of their people. Despite substantial progress over the last 2 decades in overcoming inherited deficiencies in education, institutions, and physical infrastructure, Africa's economic development lags behind the rest of the Third World, and poverty remains widespread.

The *1981 World Bank Atlas* indicates that the gross national product (GNP) per person either fell or grew less than 1 percent a year in 26 African countries during 1970–79. Moreover, of the 32 countries in the world estimated in 1979 to have a per capita income less than $330, 22 or 69 percent are African. Adult literacy remains below 25 percent in most African countries, indices of poor health and infant mortality are among the highest in the Third World, and the rapid rate of population growth shows no signs of decline.

The most alarming trend for a region in which over 70 percent of the nearly 400 million inhabitants depend on agriculture for their livelihood is Africa's persistent inability to feed itself. After more than 20 years of increasing food imports and of crash agricultural development projects, Africa still suffers from agricultural stagnation and from an economic situation marked by a mounting balance-of-payments deficit and large external public debts. According to a recent report by the U.S. Department of Agriculture, average per capita caloric intake has fallen below minimum nutritional standards in most of the region.[1]

To some extent, Africa's economic woes can be blamed on difficult climatic and geographic factors and on the continent's heavy dependence on the depressed international market. But most students of African development agree that domestic policy and managerial inadequacies have exacerbated enormously the problems flowing from adverse terms of trade and poor ecological conditions. Africa is now living with the cumulative effects of nepotism and political patronage, poor management, overprotection of industry, and strong biases against agriculture in price and tax policies.

Reversing Africa's economic crisis will take more than simply increasing foreign aid and initiating another round of short-term development projects. As Eicher has argued recently in an important article analyzing the region's agricultural difficulties, the constraints on Africa's food production are deep seated in nature and have been exacerbated by imported development strategies ill suited to African circumstances:

> Throughout much of the post-independence period, most states have viewed agriculture as a backward and low-priority sector, have perpetuated colonial policies of pumping the economic surplus out of agriculture, and have failed to give priority to achieving a reliable food surplus as a prerequisite for basic national, social, and economic goals. The failure of most African states to develop an effective set of agricultural policies to deal with the technical, structural, institutional, and human resource constraints is at the heart of the present food crisis. Part of the failure must be attributed to the colonial legacy and part to the hundreds of foreign economic advisors who have imported inappropriate models and theories of development from the United States, Europe, Asia and Latin America.[2]

The long-range solutions to Africa's economic problems will involve re-thinking the critical role of the agrarian sector in the development process,

[1] U.S. Department of Agriculture, *Food Problems and Prospects in Sub-Saharan Africa* (Washington, D.C.: Government Printing Office, 1981).
[2] Carl Eicher, "Facing Up to Africa's Food Crisis," *Foreign Affairs* 61 (Fall 1982): 163.

and it will also take continued investment in building indigenous capacities for research, policy, and management, especially through the provision of higher education.[3]

The scarcity of African high-level manpower has been a major constraint in the region's economic development and in Africa's struggle for cultural autonomy and self-reliance. The meager supply of indigenous professionals is evidenced in every country by the number of unoccupied posts and by the quantity of expatriates employed in government, research centers, and universities. It is widely recognized that the great majority of technical assistance used in the Third World is assigned to Africa, mainly in research or advisory positions. This situation is growing less acceptable as resentment mounts over the high salaries and privileges of expatriate technicians who take their expertise and experience away with them on completion of their contracts.

Another aspect of the scarcity problem is the high rate of turnover among professional staff, particularly in government and universities. Difficult terms of service, including frequent changes in posting for civil servants, often result in an exodus to the private sector or, as sometimes occurs in the case of the best trained, to international agencies or business firms that move them permanently away from their home countries. Some degree of professional mobility of this type should be expected as part of normal marketplace competition for scarce, highly qualified manpower. In Africa, however, the turnover problem is particularly serious since there are few graduates in the pipeline to replenish lost stock.

Numerical shortages, however, are only one aspect of the problem and in some ways not the most important. The design of effective policies and development strategies requires considerable analytic skill, knowledge of local conditions and sensitivities, and personal commitment to the implementation of national goals and cultural ideals. With the cost of higher education at a premium and with university students bearing the cross of being a privileged minority subsidized by the masses, it is essential that training produce skills and attitudes that can contribute toward meeting the goals of social and economic progress in Africa. Trained minds, creative thinking, and dedication are particularly important in four key areas of the development process: research and technology, policy formulation and planning, field-level management, and university teaching.

Long-term solutions to the economic crisis in Africa will depend in large part on the accomplishments of scientific research and on the design of technologies tailored to the peculiar conditions and resources of individual

---

[3] For a more detailed argument on the subject, see Joyce Moock and Peter Moock, *Higher Education and Rural Development in Africa: Toward a Balanced Approach for Donor Assistance* (New York: African American Institute, 1977); Uma Lele, "Rural Africa: Modernization, Equity, and Long-Term Development," *Science* 211 (February 1981): 547–53.

countries and localities. Recently devised farming technologies promise major increments in grain output in areas with natural resources highly conducive to productive farming. Much more work, however, needs to be carried out on arid and semiarid agriculture, livestock, irrigation, and systems of farming involving multiple crops and integrated crop and livestock production. It has become clear with the benefit of hindsight that such research requires intimate knowledge of social and economic factors, as well as knowledge of technical ones. This understanding allows development programs to be built on local conditions and aspirations rather than on externally perceived needs and solutions transposed from one country to another. Thus, we can argue that the primary research challenge in Africa is to mobilize the various academic disciplines for an integrated assault on persistent development problems, while at the same time building a reflective capacity to assess the local relevance of overall development goals.

The need to strengthen capacity in the policy area is also a high priority in all African nations. It is often pointed out that major efforts are required to create a strong agricultural sector supported by trade and exchange rate strategies conducive to local production and by "deregulated" state bureaucracies that provide greater market autonomy for low-income farmers. Pragmatic planning in this area as well as in regard to other sectors is a tricky business which involves the clear definition of development objectives, close integration between planning and budgeting, establishment of a solid policy analysis capability, and linkage of plan-writing activities with the process of actually trying to influence political and bureaucratic decisions. Such sophisticated work calls for well-trained economic and social analysts with a capacity for conceptualizing problems, assessing the effects of alternative policies on different populations, and designing sensible long-range strategies which connect projects to policy reforms. The availability of these individuals is a prerequisite for building stronger decision-making institutions throughout the public sector.

Beyond research and policy reforms, Africa's economic development is contingent on increased managerial capability at the field level so that policies, programs, and projects can function as intended. While the ideals of self-reliance and mass participation espoused by many countries imply that it is the people themselves who must achieve economic goals through diligence and the development of local resources, the government has to provide the administrative vehicle for them to do so. In countries where the ideology of African socialism has led to the development of a widespread system of farming cooperatives, para-statals, and state welfare organizations, skilled management is essential for creating the incentive structures to ensure that these bodies operate properly, but, unfortunately, managerial skills in some areas are notoriously deficient. Part of this problem stems from budgetary constraints and shortages of supplies and materials, but there is little question that a great deal of the blame can be placed on inexperienced staff and the tendency to focus on short-term implementation defects rather than on the deep-seated structural factors that generally underlie sustained operational weaknesses.[4] The need for skilled field-level administrators relates, of course, as much to the emerging urban sector as to Africa's rural areas.

Improvements in research and technology, policymaking and planning, and field-level management require continued investments in human capital formation, including the expansion of professional cadres in Africa's universities. There are currently 56 universities in sub-Saharan Africa, with nearly all African states having at least one. Many, however, are very small, with less than 1,000 students, only 11 have over 10,000 students, and there is no discipline in which African universities have achieved self-sufficiency in staffing.[5] With an annual growth of the student population of 10–15 percent in many countries, governments are hard pressed to find sufficient teaching staff who can convey knowledge in traditional disciplines and in area studies, let alone conduct and supervise research applicable to local needs and problems. Also in demand across the continent are university administrators who are able to design and implement the complex structural reforms necessary for African universities to survive despite stringent government funding and, at the same time, to assist these institutions in becoming more responsive to nation-building needs.

It should be noted, however, that the staff shortages in many African universities reflect, in part, regional politics and the general lack of co-operation among neighboring countries in sharing facilities or building joint tertiary institutions. While there is some cross-national student move-ment to the stronger institutions within the region, African states generally do not take advantage of opportunities to benefit from regional economies of scale in higher education.[6]

Yet, even with this political dilemma in mind, it is difficult to deny that sub-Saharan Africa requires a greater supply of men and women

---

[4] See Jon Moris, "What Do We Know about African Agricultural Development? The Role of Extension Performance Reanalyzed" (paper prepared for USAID, 1983); World Bank, *Accelerated Development in Sub-Saharan Africa: An Agenda for Action* (Washington, D.C.: World Bank, 1981).

[5] Emmanuel Ayandele, "Africa: The Challenge of Higher Education," *Daedalus* 111 (Spring 1982): 167, 175.

[6] The breakup of the University of East Africa and of the University of Botswana, Lesotho, and Swaziland are cases in point, as is Nigeria's response to international political tensions by establishing one university in each of its 19 federal states. There has been some regional cooperation through mechanisms such as the Inter-African Scholarship Program of African Universities, conducted by the Association of African Universities, in which several hundred students have been sent to such countries as the Cameroon, Ivory Coast, Kenya, Nigeria, Senegal, and the Sudan annually. However, efforts to develop viable megauniversities to serve students from whole subregions or cooperative programs in specialized areas which could reduce duplication of facilities in neighboring countries have not been very successful.

with professional skills to operate the government, carry out needed scientific research on complex development problems, and pass on these skills to future generations. According to the *World Development Report, 1980,* "their shortage has been one of the biggest brakes on development projects" in Africa.[7] Ways must be found, however, to train people more economically and more appropriately so they can acquire the regionally specific understanding, technical knowledge, cultural sensitivity, and imaginative thinking critical to the challenging tasks of African economic development.

The Pros and Cons of Foreign Study

There are three principal options for meeting the needs for higher education in Africa: strengthening domestic universities, recruiting expatriate teachers, and providing scholarships for foreign study. All three are costly. How economic each is, however, depends on who is picking up the tab and, in terms of social benefits to African countries, on the short- and long-run impact on national development objectives. Moreover, since none of the universities in sub-Saharan Africa is complete in the sense that it can fulfill all the needs for advanced, specialized training, the key question becomes one of the most effective blend of institutional development, expatriate staffing, and foreign study.

Few critics of African higher education would disagree that university-level training should ideally take place in Africa. However, capacity differs nation to nation as does ability to finance expansion of university systems. African higher education is expensive in that it absorbs a significant share of public sector resources and in terms of average costs per pupil. Relative to per capita income, African governments often spend five to ten times as much per university student as do countries in other developing regions. In addition, building an overall undergraduate capacity in Africa is less expensive than building specialized graduate facilities, especially in science-based fields requiring expensive laboratory equipment and sufficient teaching staff for in-depth course work in highly technical fields. Indeed, it is estimated to cost six times more to provide training for a first-year graduate student than for a first-year undergraduate.[8] With knowledge growing more specialized and beyond the capacity of small national universities to accommodate adequately, it will continue to be necessary for assistance agencies and African governments to send students overseas for highly technical training. This situation is unlikely to change until the numbers of pupils preparing for such fields expand sufficiently to lower teaching and equipment costs per student and until learning benefits

---

[7] World Bank, *World Development Report, 1980* (Washington, D.C.: World Bank, 1980), p. 88.
[8] Charles Lyons, "Africa's Overseas Students," *World Higher Education Communique* 3 (Winter 1980): 8.

increase to match more nearly those achieved at research universities in the industrialized world.

But while foreign study will remain a staple in Africa's consumption of higher education for some time to come, not a great deal is known about its comprehensive impact on changing national development objectives in the subcontinent, or elsewhere in the Third World for that matter. Overseas training has received research attention mainly as a factor in manpower training and international brain drain. Where tracer studies of returned graduates are available, the effectiveness of overseas training has been measured on the basis of such indicators as the number completing the program who have returned home, employment in the field of study, and whether graduates found the substance of training useful in their work. These questions remain important but need to be augmented. Overseas training should be subjected to deeper examination in the context of the changing social and ideological environment in Africa, and outcomes of foreign study need to be compared with the results of university training at home.

The subject is further complicated by the fact that the large numbers of third-level students studying outside sub-Saharan Africa are spread across a great many countries. The Unesco statistics for 1979 show African students studying in at least 37 countries outside the continent. The biggest single contingent was in the United States (29,000), followed by France (24,000), then Britain (10,000), and Belgium, Germany, India, and Canada, with 2,000 each.[9] The Eastern bloc countries hosted an estimated 17,000 African students; however, information on the origin of these students is poor, and some may be from North Africa.

Language and former colonial ties are the main factors which determine the location of study abroad. However, political ideology and sources of financial support also play influential roles. Hence, we find that students from individual African countries are widely dispersed for foreign training. For example, approximately 23,000 Nigerians, the largest population of African students overseas, are spread across 28 countries, although 86 percent are in the United States and Britain. The Cameroon sends 5,000 students, the next largest group, to 17 countries, with France accounting for 75 percent of this contingent. Guinea's 698 students abroad also cover 17 countries, with 50 percent in Cuba, China, and the Eastern bloc countries, and 40 percent in France. Even the 260 students abroad from sparsely populated Lesotho are spread across 10 countries, with the majority in North America and Czechoslovakia.

---

[9] Students from North Africa are not included here. Also the *Unesco Statistical Yearbook, 1982* (Paris: Unesco, 1982), from which these figures are derived, contains data from only 45 countries concerning numbers of foreign students enrolled in their tertiary institutions.

It is not possible to obtain consistent data concerning the field of study or length of training in most nations which host visiting African students. There is also little information about the type of skills and understanding being transferred; and thus, the international equivalency of degrees remains highly speculative. We do, however, have some reasonably good estimates concerning African students studying in the United States. Statistics gathered by the Institute of International Education indicate that around 60 percent of African students are undergraduates, 35 percent graduates, and 5 percent nondegree. Leading fields of study are engineering (20 percent) and business (19 percent), followed by the social sciences (12 percent) and the natural sciences (9 percent). Surprisingly, only 6 percent of students from Africa study agriculture, including agricultural economics, despite the paucity of university training available in this critical field at home.[10]

Perceptions of Relevance

What constitutes relevant education for African professionals is a complex and debatable subject. The actual contribution of different types of training to development is very difficult to assess and involves a clear understanding of development processes and tasks, knowledge of the professional culture which exists in the scholars' home countries, and measurement of job performance over time. So far, few empirical relationships have been firmly established between pedagogical systems and societal or even educational outcomes. Indeed, the full benefits of a given training program may not be evident for years after a student has matriculated, and even then it may be difficult to link the outcome with the educational experience. We can, however, make some general observations about the issue of relevance based on several factors which have received attention in the literature on foreign study.

The most common indictment of overseas training is that its content and methodology are too far removed from the realities of the visiting student's home environment. Course materials are said to be irrelevant and the heavily quantitative methods and highly technical scientific equipment to which students are exposed in industrial countries to be too sophisticated for facilities available at home. University training in Africa, on the other hand, is presumed to be based on local content and geared to suit the administrative and technical realities of the subcontinent.

But while these observations seem reasonable on the surface, the relevancy issue is far too complex to be settled by such generalizations. Training in industrial countries need not necessarily be inappropriate for African circumstances if the staff of the host university is aware of the

---

[10] These figures include students from the entire African continent (Institute of International Education, *Profiles* [New York, 1982]).

special academic needs of foreign students relating to their projected professional work. International studies at leading research universities in the United States and Europe commonly include instruction for Third World students on the historical, social, and economic circumstances of countries in their home regions. Many universities have African studies centers staffed by scholars with significant professional experience in the subcontinent. Moreover, libraries and book shops in London, Paris, New York, Boston, and East Lansing, Michigan, to name but a few, are likely to have fuller collections of scholarly material on Africa than an African student can find practically anywhere in his or her home region.

It is also important to remember that the issue of relevancy relates to more than the substance of study.[11] Relevance also pertains to the development of fruitful approaches to learning and to analytic skills for defining and solving problems. While it is hard to deny that a basic education unattached to its social context is inadequate, it is equally clear that applied studies without solid intellectual underpinnings have little value. Of course, the basic versus applied controversy in education is an old one and goes far beyond the issue of foreign study.

Furthermore, the basic versus applied controversy generally pertains more to the liberal arts than to the scientific and technical fields. In this regard, a recent study by Baron of the perceived relevance of graduate programs for Third World students of 93 universities in the United States found that the attitude of universal application of the curriculum was especially prevalent in business and science faculties. Here, most of the staff members sampled felt that it is the students' responsibility to find ways of applying the principles and techniques of the traditional disciplines studied.[12]

So far, it has been argued that overseas education is not necessarily irrelevant for Africa's high-level manpower needs. It is also clear that university training in Africa is not always appropriate for the social and administrative realities of the local environment. In an excellent overview paper on the challenge of African higher education, Ayandele laments that, "despite the efforts made by African universities to give their curricula an African cast, they remain for the most part centers for the diffusion of Western culture. To use a biblical metaphor, although they have 'left Egypt' in abandoning the cravings for 'Britishness' or 'Frenchness' or 'Americanness,' African universities are still far from Canaan, still far from becoming essentially African. This is why the training of Africans outside

---

[11] For a fuller discussion on the multiple dimensions of the relevancy issue, see Peter Williams, "Training Students at Home or Abroad: The Implications" (paper for seminar on foreign aid for education, Nordic Association for the Study of Education in Developing Countries, Oslo, September 1983).

[12] Marvin Baron, "The Relevance of U.S. Graduate Programs to Foreign Students from Developing Countries" (report for the National Association for Foreign Student Affairs, Washington, D.C., 1979).

the continent has in no visible way made them more Western than their colleagues trained at home."[13] In this respect, critics of the current state of African university education often point to the fact that the intellectual interpretation of Africa's economic development, including neoclassical growth models or political economy paradigms of underdevelopment, have been largely fashioned outside Africa. It is unclear at this stage in the evolution of African higher education whether university training at home has an advantage over foreign training in providing the intellectual impetus to produce fresh perspectives, concepts, and even terminology which evolve out of the region's cultural history and the peculiar dynamics of contemporary African society.

In addition to weaknesses in developing new conceptual approaches and original course content in some fields, many African universities simply do not have enough experienced teachers in specialized disciplines or the necessary facilities or equipment to provide a sufficiently high standard of training at advanced levels for professional work. The point of this discussion is that relevance with regard to overseas study is not as simple an issue as it may appear at first glance. Nevertheless, one must be careful not to push the argument so far that locus of study is an inconsequential matter.

Overseas training offers many pitfalls for the African student. Unless the staff of the host university is familiar with the professional climate and development circumstances of the student's country, major problems can occur in translating the content of study into practical application at home. Unfortunately, financial sources are growing increasingly scarce to support university staff members in industrial countries for teaching and research abroad. This problem is particularly serious for U.S. graduate departments of economics, to take but one example, where only 5 percent of all faculty members have any significant professional experience in Africa. Thus, writes Wyn Owen, "It is not surprising that many of the more gifted foreign students shift their research focus to advanced country problems, ones more compatible with the interest and experience of most available thesis advisors."[14]

Another problem relates to the lack of opportunities which African students find during the course of training abroad to construct a program of study which can accommodate their specific professional needs and interests. Baron's study of programs for foreign students at U.S. universities found that only 40 percent of all faculty respondents had permitted students to conduct doctoral research at home, with fewer natural science faculties

[13] Ayandele, p. 172.

[14] Wyn Owen, "Higher Education in Economics: Major Trends and Dimensions," *Higher Education in Economics: The International Dimensions*, ed. W. Owen et al., Monograph Series, vol. 1 (Boulder, Colo.: Economics Institute, 1981), pp. 17–18.

doing so than those in the social sciences. The major difficulties related to this option were lack of local supervision and of facilities needed to carry out technical research.[15] Universities in other host countries may be far more reluctant to alter their curriculum to suit the particular conditions and resources which students from developing countries will face on their return home.

Higher education in industrial societies can also present particular problems for Third World students because of the tendency for these learning systems to be structured to meet the demands of large corporations for persons with highly specialized knowledge. In Africa, however, as well as in other developing economies, competent people are commonly moved in and out of a variety of institutions and professional roles, and it is difficult to predict where they will be utilized.[16] This mobility of highly qualified individuals and their diverse set of professional responsibilities raise troublesome questions about the value of narrow disciplinary training, even in highly technical fields, and about the attempt to gear education to specific job skills. While the high costs of advanced training necessitate that university education be directed toward the provision of technical skills critical to development, technologies change, and specialized training may need to be supplemented by courses of study which have some administrative content and draw on the humanities or social sciences as ways of understanding the complex processes of human affairs.

In contrast to the problems associated with overseas education, training at home offers definite advantages. In an effort to throw off the intellectual and stylistic baggage of their colonial past, African universities are slowly shaping themselves to their immediate environment. Across the subcontinent, there has been a significant reorientation of programs including increased reliance on locally authored texts, research materials, and practical fieldwork; there are as well efforts to reassert traditional values and create a sense of national identity. African arts and humanities courses are beginning to stress the uses of oral traditions, myths, legends, and sculpture in understanding Africa's history and her political institutions. Even in faculties of science, questions are being raised about the thrust and application of science and technology for alleviating poverty, and interest is growing in the development of technologies which capitalize on the local endowment of resources. Moreover, training based in Africa provides an opportunity for work-study programs or apprenticeships in local institutions for a practical learning experience.

As the first section of the paper argued, the abilities to think creatively, conceptualize issues in broad terms, tap local knowledge, and be versatile

---

[15] Baron.

[16] For further discussion on this issue, see David Court, "Scholarships and University Development in Kenya and Tanzania," *Higher Education* 8 (1979): 549.

may well be the most valued professional qualities for African nations undergoing rapid social change. It is difficult to argue that an education which assists the development of such skills and helps the student learn how to continue to learn in professional life is not a relevant education. Such a learning system might best be achieved by integrating the advantages of African-based education with those of foreign study.

Strengthening National Institutions

The issue of foreign study's compatibility with the goals of strengthening national institutions can be divided into two main categories: complementarity with available university training facilities at home and utilization of skills on return.

The purpose of overseas training ostensibly is to complement local facilities and to diffuse the knowledge obtained, which may be available to a lesser degree in the home country. A serious problem can arise, however, if local training facilities are forced to compete for students and financial support with opportunities for overseas study. Most African universities offer undergraduate training across a wide variety of fields and several now have graduate-level programs, especially in the social sciences and humanities. However, some African governments continue to send outstanding students abroad for training despite the availability of these local facilities. There is evidence, for example, that the government of Kenya has made a practice of sending some of its best economists to North America for master's level training despite the fact that a course-based M.A. program in economics has been available at the University of Nairobi since 1973.[17] Even in Tanzania, with its tightly controlled awards system for overseas scholarships, some students are selected for overseas training before vacancies are filled at local institutions. In recent years, this has been a particularly serious problem in the faculties of agriculture, forestry, and veterinary science.[18]

When African governments prefer overseas training to study at home, local programs undoubtedly suffer in terms of both student recruitment and staff confidence in building a nationally valued, postgraduate program. Yet overseas training when offered to African governments as a gift from a donor agency or foreign university is difficult to resist, especially if the local program requires state support to cover substantial tuition costs and other expenses.

At the individual level, foreign study continues to hold considerable prestige and the prospect of patronage from foreign scholars able to boost

[17] I gathered this information for a Rockefeller Foundation review, "The M.A. Program in Economics at the University of Nairobi" (New York, 1980).

[18] S. A. Sumra and A. G. Ishumi, "Development and Trends in Tanzania's Policies toward Higher Training and Scholarships Overseas," in *Policy Developments in Overseas Training*, ed. T. L. Maliyamkono (Dar es Salaam: Black Star Agencies, 1980), p. 54.

one's career in terms of recommendations for consultancy work, research grants, or employment overseas. In addition, some of the best students seek entry to schools abroad because library resources and the research tradition at home are relatively weak and because political attitudes may pervade the university setting. While it is generally believed that foreign study is a complement to higher education at home rather than a substitute for it, we need more systematic information than we now have about the factors underlying demand for overseas training on the part of governments and individual candidates.

Whether a student is trained overseas or locally, he or she can be expected to have little impact on strengthening national institutions unless provisions are made for effective utilization of acquired skills. It is all too common in Africa that efforts to build capacity focus on the skills of individuals or the development of institutions or departments, while deficiencies in the structure of market opportunity and incentives, and the absence in many cases of a supportive professional environment, are largely overlooked. Since market incentives strongly influence educational preferences, occupational decisions, and job performances after graduation, the neglect of salary structure and professional inducements can sabotage the best-laid manpower-training schemes. In their study of higher education in Zambia, for instance, Sanyal et al. found that 58 percent of the university graduates had changed occupations within 3 years following the completion of training. An above-average proportion of changes were made by graduates in the natural sciences (68 percent), engineering/technology (70 percent), and health/medicine (65 percent). The reasons given for occupational mobility include better use of personal talents and training, more favorable conditions of service, and opportunities for promotion.[19]

When higher education and occupational requirements are mismatched, the problem often can be traced to national incentive structures which are inconsistent with long-range manpower needs. This situation is perhaps best illustrated by the difficulty of attracting educated urbanites to postings in the rural areas of their countries. While the tendency for individuals with university degrees to select urban-based jobs is often attributed to elitism and disdain for the needs of the rural poor, low salaries and tough working conditions with few opportunities for upward mobility continue to keep high-level manpower in the cities. In the long run, however, as the supply of such individuals increases, their price should fall, and if terms of service improve and the cost of living remains low relative to city life, rural based employment should become a more attractive option. The important point here is that systems of education by themselves

[19] Bikas Sanyal et al., *Higher Education and Labor Market Needs in Zambia: Expectations and Performance* (Paris: Unesco, 1976), pp. 190–94.

cannot carry the burden of responsibility for national development. They can, however, help to achieve tangible benefits for their constituent societies when reinforced by national policies in other sectors of the economy.

Within the general context of these issues surrounding manpower utilization, we still have limited understanding of the ways in which overseas training differs from local study regarding institution building or strengthening of the civil service. There are, however, two interesting aspects of the situation which deserve consideration. First, one of the most frustrating features of foreign study for African governments and universities alike is the dispersed patterns of placement overseas and the ensuing difficulty of integrating staff with different training traditions. Moreover, one can assume that it is almost impossible for the home country to maintain quality control with students spread across numerous countries and training institutes. In nations with full employment policies for graduates with overseas degrees, this quality-control problem is compounded. On the other hand, practical on-the-job training and national incentive structures should modify the most extreme dimensions of educational differences among returned graduates. In addition, there may be considerable long-term benefit for countries whose institutions are modeled in form and purpose after those in their colonial metropoles to have students exposed to new ideas, professional styles, and educational traditions.

Second, credentials from a foreign institution may affect mid-career professional migration. Given the great demand for high-level manpower by African nations and the cultural discomfort frequently experienced by expatriate Africans, brain drain immediately following overseas training has not been a serious problem for the continent.[20] However, the history of political confrontations within African governments and the closure of universities due to open differences with the state has resulted in considerable professional emigration during the last decade. Ghana, Ethiopia, Zaire, and Uganda, all at one time relatively well-endowed with indigenous professionals, are cases in point. When the professional climate at home is perceived as being heavily oppressive, those with internationally recognized degrees are likely to have greater motivation and opportunity to reestablish themselves elsewhere than their colleagues whose academic frame of reference has been the local university. The emigration of these mid-career academics and civil servants to international agencies and foreign universities appears to be a growing problem with devastating results for countries in which national capacity depends far too heavily

---

[20] After reviewing the literature on this subject, Maliyamkono and Wells conclude that the high rate of return for African graduates results mainly from employment availability in the region (see T. L. Maliyamkono and Stuart Wells, "Effects of Overseas Training on Economic Development: Impact Surveys on Overseas Training," in Maliyamkono, ed.).

on the professional careers of a few key individuals. This worrisome situation undoubtedly calls for further documentation and analysis.

The Composition of National Elites

Higher education is a monopolizer of status in Africa. Therefore, deciding on criteria for determining which individuals and groups have access to training at the tertiary level is a major political issue, especially in countries espousing an egalitarian ideal. Several states in the region have sought to modify entry patterns for home universities in a way that can provide greater access for those in relatively unrepresented parts of the country. Tanzania, for example, has attempted to broaden the requirements for student selection to take into account such nonacademic criteria as prior employment history and degree of political commitment, while Kenya has expanded the total number of university places in an effort to diversify the composition of the student population.[21] As African secondary schools expand at faster rates than facilities in African universities and technical institutes, competition for admission into tertiary institutions at home is bound to heighten, with a consequent increase in applications for entry into universities overseas. The question then arises how the current availability of opportunities for study abroad affects the composition of the educated elite.

In recent years there have been major changes in methods of financing overseas education. Traditionally most students have been supported for foreign study by bilateral or international aid agencies. In addition, most African countries have had their own scholarship scheme. Reductions in aid flows and the increasing growth of an African middle class have led to a situation in which the majority of African students currently abroad are supported by their own or their families' resources. For example, only one-quarter to one-third of the African students in Western Europe are funded under host country scholarships. In the United States, not more than 5 percent of all African students in the country are supported by federal government agencies. Only in the Eastern bloc countries do most visiting African students receive host government fellowship awards.[22]

While it might be expected that this growing shift in financial responsibility for students' overseas training to the students themselves has affected the composition of the African cohort studying abroad, the data base is too shaky to allow us to understand in precisely what ways this is so. We do know that male children of the wealthy elite in Africa have traditionally taken their university studies abroad. Ideally, the provision of overseas scholarships by assistance agencies and home and host governments has served to broaden the composition of the group studying

---

[21] David Court, "The Development Ideal in Higher Education: The Experience of Kenya and Tanzania," *Higher Education* 9 (1980): 666.

[22] Lyons (n. 8 above), p. 7.

abroad. Yet, higher education in most of Africa has long been the preserve of relatively well-to-do males, and even the most egalitarian-minded assistance agencies have had to face the fact that there often exists only a small cohort of female students and others from relatively disadvantaged backgrounds who have made it up the academic ladder to the university level.[23] Moreover, while donor agencies have commonly relied on candidate nominations by universities or government committees as a strategy of facilitating employment for graduates on return home, the process may not always single out the best applicants, and individuals may be proposed on the basis of traits other than suitability for foreign study. When assistance agency support for foreign study is at its best, however, great care is taken in selecting trainees, ensuring sufficient preparation, placing fellows at universities compatible with their skills and needs, and providing backup support on their return to help launch their professional careers.

In contrast, overseas students who are self-financed may receive little help in adjusting to their new environment, carrying out their program of study, and preparing to return home. Self-financed graduates may have less interest in stressing relevancy to home conditions in their educational programs since commitment to national institution building or even to employment at home is not imposed as part of the financial support system for overseas training. In reviewing the curriculum choices of self-supported students from developing countries who are enrolled in U.S. economics programs, Ranis concludes that "the interest and programs of these graduate students now resemble those of U.S. students more than before. The former are more interested in their union cards as economists than in the relevance of their education to their countries' problems."[24] Indeed, there is evidence that, of all students abroad, those who are self-financed are the ones most unlikely to return home.[25] This trend is particularly strong among students from families not closely connected with the ruling elite back home. While Africa has lost few of its highly trained professionals as a direct result of exposure to overseas education, loose national control over student emigration and the growing tendency for foreign study to be once again exclusively the privilege of

[23] It is interesting to note that, on a country-to-country basis in 1979, the percentage of African female students in the United States was often similar to the proportion of female students enrolled in tertiary institutions at home. For instance, 19 percent at home and 14 percent in the United States, for Senegal; 28 percent at home and 31 percent in the United States, for Liberia; 13 percent at home and 14 percent in the United States, for Ghana; and 17 percent at home and 24 percent in the United States, for Tanzania. See Institute of International Education (n. 10 above); *Unesco Statistical Yearbook, 1982* (n. 9 above).

[24] Gustav Ranis, "Dimensions of Change: Aspects of Postwar Experience with International Economics Education," in *Higher Education in Economics: The International Dimensions* (n. 14 above), p. 36.

[25] William Glaser and G. Christopher Habers, *The Brain Drain: Emigration and Return* (New York: Pergamon, 1978).

the children of the wealthy may alter that situation substantially in the future.

As long as higher education continues to provide ample returns to investment and the demand for university places exceeds local supply, African students and their governments will take advantage of opportunities for training abroad. Given the region's desperate need to expand its professional manpower as a means of accelerating development and strengthening its own institutions of higher education, Africa can be expected to rely on foreign universities to supplement its own tertiary facilities for some time to come. Thus the question to be addressed is not whether overseas training has a role to play in Africa's development process but in which ways such programs can be usefully integrated with national and regional training and skills requirements to achieve objectives for a more productive and equitable society.

Issues and Questions Related to the Effective Provision of Overseas Study

As international assistance agencies and African governments continue to think about the consistency of overseas study with national development objectives, it may be worth noting a number of implications that derive from the preceding discussion.

a) Insufficient attention is given by home and host governments and assistance agencies to the pattern of overseas education and its compatibility with overall development objectives and changing circumstances in sub-Saharan Africa.

b) The prevalent assumption that training abroad inculcates inappropriate attitudes and values, raises false expectations, or creates intellectual dependence on development theories and strategies unsuitable for African conditions has not been closely examined. On the other hand, the notion that African development can be accelerated by producing African professionals with conventional academic training and skills replicating those of expatriate predecessors needs careful reevaluation.

c) Given our fragmentary understanding of current trends in overseas study for African students, more information would be welcome about the types of students and institutions involved, levels and fields of study, sources of financial support, and utilization of acquired skills on return. Such documentation should then be compared with data derived from similar efforts in mapping the provision of tertiary education within Africa.

d) Since there is greater likelihood of designing relevant overseas training programs when African students can work with faculty who are knowledgeable about the home country, it would be worth exploring ways of increasing opportunities for professors in industrial nations to gain research and teaching experience in Africa. One such possibility might be the establishment or reinforcement of cooperative programs between

181

African universities and selected institutions abroad. This type of arrangement can also be used to facilitate reciprocal teaching schemes, dissertation research in the home country, intensive short-term training overseas combined with a home country degree, or joint research projects.

e) In view of the fact that Africa requires more *educated* and *not merely trained* people to cope with the complexities and social instabilities of transitional economies, greater attention needs to be given to the actual content of overseas training courses. As part of this review, curriculum innovations, such as supplementation of technical training with liberal arts or management courses, construction of core courses in development problems and processes, exposure to the range of methodological approaches used by the various academic disciplines, and provision of apprenticeships or practical learning-by-doing experiences merit serious consideration.

f) Too few of the students who get into overseas training programs are sufficiently prepared for the host environment and its modes of instruction. The use of transitional programs to orient students to their new university and community life and efforts by the home government to maintain contacts with trainees during the period of study away from home are likely to facilitate a positive experience abroad and to stimulate commitment to national development on return.

g) Overseas education, for better or worse, is only one factor in a complex set of social and economic phenomena in Africa, and tighter control over policies affecting foreign study cannot in itself be expected to strengthen economic development if other national policies run in a counter direction.

h) Little is known about relationships among different types of educational provision, job performance, and socioeconomic outcomes. In this regard, longitudinal case studies are needed which can capture the operational dynamics of the labor market and identify deficiencies in the structure of opportunities and incentives for professional work.

i) While past efforts at establishing regional or subregional training programs in Africa have not met with much success as alternatives to foreign study, Africa's current development problems may provide new incentives for regional cooperation. In the interests of creating economies of scale among neighboring countries in the provision of higher education, possibilities for developing megauniversities or broadening regional exchange deserve to be reexamined.

j) Efforts to improve the consistency between the world of work and current training policies and practices are most likely to be effective when countries or at least international donors take a long-term perspective on development issues and are able to plan beyond the pressing needs of the moment in establishing educational strategies and objectives.

k) In the interest of equality of opportunity, governments and assistance agencies might consider provision of economic incentives through special bursaries both at the tertiary level and lower to encourage women and others from relatively disadvantaged backgrounds to further their educational careers.

Overseas training continues to play an important role in building the professional elite of Africa, an elite which tends to equate its needs and interests with those of the nation. While it is important to seek the African ideal of higher education in new local and regional training configurations, ways of assisting foreign study to conform to national needs should still be explored. It is precisely because foreign study is inevitably selective and its products highly influential in the development process that it should not be allowed to proceed haphazardly.

The Political Dilemmas of Foreign Study

HANS N. WEILER*

There is a fundamental ambivalence in the relationship between the universities of North America and the countries of the Third World. This ambivalence is reflected in serious dilemmas for both the institutions of higher education in the United States and the political and professional leadership in the countries of the Third World. This article argues that, as the enrollment of foreign students in U.S. institutions, especially at the graduate level, continues to increase, these dilemmas will tend to become more rather than less acute.

The American Dilemma

On the North American side, academia and academics have long discovered the many benefits to be derived from being involved in training, consulting, or other technical assistance programs for underdeveloped countries in Africa, Asia, and Latin America: students from abroad form an increasingly welcome source of enrollment and tuition in universities where the decrease in the American graduate student population (caused by demographic as well as labor-market conditions) has often brought both enrollment and tuition levels to below a critical mass level.[1] Considerations of efficiency in the use of an institution's resources and capacities make increments of foreign students attractive where declining domestic student populations tend to drive up the unit costs per student. At the same time, many foreign students, especially from Third World countries, tend to come with full or major financial support from their governments, international assistance agencies, or philanthropic organizations, thus sparing their American host institutions the problem of financial support. Problems of "brain drain" in the case of some countries notwithstanding, the majority of foreign students tend to return to positions in their home countries, relieving the U.S. institution of yet another headache, that of placement in a shrinking labor market for graduates in most disciplines.

An earlier version of this article was presented as the keynote address at the Western Regional Conference of the Comparative and International Education Society, Los Angeles, October 19, 1978. I thank David Lansdale, Ramadhani Ntuah, and Jeff Unsicker for much help and advice in the revision of this material.

* Professor and director of the Stanford International Development Education Center at Stanford University.

[1] American Council on Education, *Foreign Students and Institutional Policy: Toward an Agenda for Action* (Washington, D.C.: American Council on Education, 1982), pp. 39–43; Craufurd D. Goodwin and Michael Nacht, *Absence of Decision: Foreign Students in American Colleges and Universities* (New York: Institute of International Education, 1983), pp. 12–17.

Faculty in North American universities cherish the opportunities for travel and consultancies that often go with their universities' involvement in human resource development projects of one kind or another, especially since other funds for research overseas, which once flowed so amply, have all but dried up. And last, there seems to have developed, particularly among faculty, an increasingly articulate feeling of appreciation for the intellectual and cultural richness which the presence of foreign students can contribute to a university or program.[2]

While these benefits are, at least for some institutions, real enough, it turns out that they are accompanied by equally real costs and dilemmas. One problem lies strictly in the financial realm and has to do with the question of how much of the cost of training foreign students at North American universities is actually covered by fees, be they in the form of private-institution tuition or out-of-state fees in public schools. This question is difficult to answer with any precision, but the overall conclusion from studies of the matter is that, under whatever fee-paying arrangement, only a more or less limited portion of the actual cost of training a foreign (or, for that matter, a U.S.) student is covered by fees. In times of financial constraints, this issue of "hidden scholarships"[3] very easily becomes a matter of considerable contention between public institutions and their legislatures or between private institutions and their financial administrators and trustees.[4] Another ingredient in this discussion that is even more difficult to assess with any precision has to do with the contribution of foreign students' spending to a local, regional, or national economy, but it seems clear that the significance of this factor is far from negligible.[5]

Beyond these considerations of cost-benefit ratios, however, lies another source of apprehension and exasperation over the increasing presence of foreign students on North American campuses. This has to do more with the intellectual and instructional mandate of U.S. institutions of higher education and with the frame of reference within which this mandate has traditionally been defined. As in all societies—ceremonial rhetoric about the fundamentally international quality of knowledge, research, and education notwithstanding—institutions of higher learning in the United States derive their intellectual agenda and instructional orientation first and foremost from the society within which they function, from which they receive material and political support, and the future leadership for

---

[2] Goodwin and Nacht, p. 18.

[3] American Council on Education, pp. 41–43.

[4] Goodwin and Nacht, pp. 8, 16–17; for an analysis of this issue in the British context, see Peter Williams, ed., *The Overseas Student Question: Studies for a Policy* (London: Heinemann, 1981), pp. 47–90.

[5] For an assessment of this factor in the case of the San Francisco Bay Area, see Susan J. Duggan and Peter A. Wollitzer, *The World's Students in Bay Area Universities* (San Francisco: Bay Area and the World, 1983).

which they are expected to prepare. While different disciplines and fields of professional training are bound to these frames of reference to different degrees—statistics less than educational administration, mechanical engineering less than industrial engineering, linguistics less than history—there is a clear and understandable propensity on the part of North American universities to gear their instructional programs foremost to the needs and conditions of the North American society and economy. Syllabi, texts, exercises, and examinations all reflect this orientation, as do, more importantly, the conceptual and theoretical paradigms within which such subjects as public administration, organizational behavior, macroeconomics, or educational sociology have been conceived for purposes of academic and professional training. This created no problems as long as the vast majority of students at American universities were American or came from societies with similar characteristics, such as Canada or Western Europe. The growing and, in some cases, dramatically increasing presence of students from non-Western societies, however, has begun to create a formidable challenge to the nature and the relative homogeneity of this framework for graduate training at U.S. universities. Faculty members are beginning to become apprehensive and, in some cases, defensive about what they perceive either as their lack of ability to gear their teaching to the needs of students from a much wider range of cultural and intellectual backgrounds, or as those students' inability to relate to their teaching, or as both. Whatever the individual faculty's interpretation of the problem, however, there is increasing evidence that a problem is believed to exist and that present reality in American higher education with regard to the training of foreign students is far from having solved it.[6] Time-honored and demonstrably successful ways of training superintendents of schools for U.S. school districts become patently irrelevant in training ministerial or para-statal planning officers for Tanzania or Sri Lanka; theories of the market as the basis for economic decision making serve poorly where markets are either artificial, nonexistent, or externally dominated; venerable models of public management prove unable to cope with the tremendous differences between urban and rural areas in underdeveloped societies:[7] the list of potential or real mismatches between the concepts and practices prevailing in American university classrooms and the kinds of problems and conditions which students from developing countries bring to their North American training institutions could be extended considerably by anyone with experience in the increasing number of U.S. graduate or

---

[6] National Association for Foreign Student Affairs (NAFSA), *The Relevance of U.S. Graduate Programs to Foreign Students from Developing Countries* (Washington, D.C.: NAFSA, 1979); Goodwin and Nacht, pp. 9–10.

[7] Lawrence D. Stifel, Joseph E. Black, and James S. Coleman, eds., *Education and Training for Public Sector Management in Developing Countries* (New York: Rockefeller Foundation, 1977).

professional schools where between 30 and 40 percent of students are foreign and where every fourth or fifth student comes from a country in the Third World.[8]

Academics have different ways of reacting to such a challenge. Some ignore it and penalize deviations from the established frame of reference. Others leave it to the foreign students in their classes to work out for themselves how the course material might be adapted and applied to the students' background and needs. Still others seek, sometimes at considerable expense of time and energy, to broaden their own professional outlook and basis in order to provide a broader range of conceptual and practical options in their teaching. Whatever the reaction, it tends to incur uneasiness and costs of various kinds; the attractiveness of larger enrollments of foreign students from the point of view of efficiency and material as well as cultural enrichment seems to be at least in part offset by the challenge to the American university's identity and social definition and the kinds of intrainstitutional conflicts that this challenge produces—from controversies over whether "hidden scholarships" for foreign students are worthwhile to debates over curricula, texts, and examination requirements.

The Third World Dilemma

If the North American university faces a dilemma, on the one hand, in finding the opportunity of training foreign students attractive while, on the other hand, realizing the considerable difficulties involved in adequately accommodating these students' training needs, the dilemma which Third World countries face with regard to the training of their students in North America is different, but no less serious.

Both governments and individuals in countries of the Third World consider university training in North America to be a source of considerable knowledge, skills, and prestige and go to considerable lengths to secure opportunities for such training. There is an implicit assumption in this orientation that the training which American institutions of higher education have to offer has something to do with the level of scientific, technological, economic, military, and political power that the United States has attained and that, by partaking in the former, a little of the latter will accrue to the country that sends its students to U.S. universities. In addition, there are many areas of rather highly specialized professional training (specialized surgery, high-speed computer technology, experimental psychology, etc.) in which only North America has training facilities of adequate size, sophistication, and flexibility to accommodate foreign trainees in any significant number.

---

[8] Institute of International Education (IIE), *Open Doors, 1979/80: Report on International Educational Exchange* (New York: IIE, 1981).

If training professionals in North America is so attractive, then where, from the point of view of the developing country, is the dilemma? The problem arises from two different but related issues. One of these has to do with the difference in training needs between North American students and students from countries at the periphery of the world system. As I have already indicated, graduate training in American universities in such fields as education, public administration and management, industrial engineering, economics, and most of the other social sciences is based on a body of research and predicated on a set of corresponding paradigms which are not necessarily applicable or relevant to the social, economic, and political reality of an underdeveloped country. It is difficult to see how training in economics in the framework of neoclassical theory is to prepare an African graduate student for playing a role of professional leadership in a country whose socioeconomic system is characterized by a great deal of state control and by a more or less deliberate movement of the economy to more socialist patterns of production and ownership. It is even more difficult to see, however, how such a student could arrive at a reasonable examination of which conception of economic analysis may be relevant to his or her future professional tasks if the training to which the student is exposed does not provide an opportunity to study, for example, any of the many theoretical variations on the basic Marxist paradigm of economic analysis.

The field of curriculum development, to take another example, has come to loom large on the list of priorities of many developing countries for professional training. This has a great deal to do with the political determination of many Third World countries to overcome the colonial traces in the content and substance of their educational systems and to replace them with a more independent, autochthonous educational message. The task is clear and important enough; what remains problematic, however, is whether graduate instruction in our typical North American school of education conveys the kinds of skills and conceptual categories necessary to understand, anticipate, and influence the dynamics of the political process that is involved in this decolonization of curriculum in developing countries. Not much of either attention or expertise in this matter appears to be forthcoming.

There is no shortage of further examples of this kind. However, the lack of relevance in the subject matter and in the frame of reference is only one side of the dilemma which developing countries face in viewing graduate training for their professional leadership at North American institutions. For many underdeveloped countries, behind the question of relevance lies a more fundamental concern with their existing degree of cultural dependence on the countries at the center of the world system and with the prospect of becoming more dependent all the time. This concern reflects one of the most critical aspects of underdevelopment, namely, that underdeveloped countries are dependent not only on the mechanisms of economic control that are built into the international system by the countries at the system's center but also—albeit in more subtle ways—on models of cultural, scientific, and professional activity that have been generated and sustained by systems of knowledge production and higher education in the center countries. As part of the process of precolonial as well as postcolonial domination, these models have been imposed on the emerging systems of higher education in the countries of the periphery; their staying power is reinforced by the intricate web of relationships between knowledge, technology, production, and power.[9]

Fuenzalida describes this phenomenon, with special but not exclusive reference to Latin America, as the "incorporation" of the scientific-technological infrastructure in general, and the university in particular, into the cultural superstructure of transnational capitalism.[10] This "cultural superstructure" is shaped and guided by the philosophical and epistemological tenets of the North American and European universities; the incorporation of universities from underdeveloped, dependent societies has the dual effect of assimilating their institutional culture to these tenets while at the same time dissociating institutions of higher education from the national context within which they were established. Looking at higher education in many Third World countries provides ample evidence of that dissociation, of a widening gap between the preoccupations and agendas of academies and academicians and the needs and concerns of the masses of the country. Talking about the Africanization of university faculties in Africa, Babs Fafunwa from Nigeria concludes: "The local staff member differs only in color, not in attitude, from his expatriate counterpart. Both were probably trained in the same overseas institution, and both have imbibed the same idea of what a university is in an affluent society. Their research orientation and their attitude to teaching and curriculum are those of a developed economy."[11]

Whether what Fafunwa says about African universities is true for universities throughout the Third World may well be open to further discussion, but it seems to be true enough in a large enough number of countries to have become a matter of considerable concern to a generation

---

[9] Hans N. Weiler, "Knowledge and Legitimation: The National and International Politics of Educational Research" (Claude A. Eggertsen Lecture at the annual meeting of the Comparative and International Education Society, Atlanta, March 18, 1983).

[10] Edmundo Fuenzalida, "The Problem of Technological Innovation in Latin America," in *Transnational Capitalism and Development,* ed. José Villamil (London: Harvester, 1978).

[11] A. Babs Fafunwa, "The Role of African Universities in Overall Educational Development," in *Higher Education and Social Change: Promising Experiments in Developing Countries,* vol. 2, *Case Studies,* ed. Kenneth W. Thompson, Barbara R. Fogel, and Helen E. Danner (New York: Praeger, 1977), p. 512.

of political leaders for whom genuine self-reliance and independence in more than just name has become a powerful political mandate. Training abroad is obviously one of the prime factors in bringing about and sustaining the kind of cultural dependence that has given rise to these concerns. The vast majority of academics in the Third World, and a large number of professionals in influential nonacademic positions, have been trained either at universities in center countries themselves or in their own country by foreign-trained expatriates or fellow nationals. The cultural and intellectual ancestry is thus virtually intact: universities and academics in the Third World have, by and large, emulated the professional model of the center of the transnational system, and, given the historical development of higher education in developing countries, it could hardly have been otherwise.

If there is ambivalence on the part of both partners in this uneasy relationship, then where does the future of this relationship lie? Clearly, there is a considerable and growing tension between, on the one hand, a set of gravitational forces that pull the transnational structure of knowledge production and higher learning ever closer to the modes and norms of the institutions at the structure's center and, on the other hand, a set of "centrifugal" forces that seek to move the countries at the periphery to greater independence and cultural autochthony. For the future of the relationship between North American universities and the countries of the Third World, it is crucial to know whether and how this tension can be resolved. To the extent that the training, research, and consultative capacity of North American universities can make a contribution to solving some of the key problems of underdevelopment without necessarily perpetuating and further reinforcing the "centripetal" trend toward an ever more homogeneous transnational system of higher learning, science, and research, there may be a viable future for this relationship. To assess the prospects of what kind of relationship is realistically feasible, however, we need to develop a better understanding of the political issues which, in many countries of the Third World, are associated with the question of training academic and political elites in the universities of North America or other center countries. These issues, as I will argue in the remainder of this article, have primarily to do with equity and self-reliance, and it is with regard to these issues and their political salience in the Third World that we will have to reexamine the possible future of the relationship between higher education in the United States and its potential foreign student population.

Equity and the Training of Elites

In view of ever-widening inequities both within and between societies, it is difficult to take much of today's equity rhetoric seriously—in any society. It often seems as if talking about redistribution is taking the place of doing something about it—rhetoric as a source of remedial legitimation.

Yet, there are enough serious people in all of these societies who are seriously preoccupied with the problem of equity in the access to and the utilization of life chances and who are particularly concerned with the inordinately greater difficulty of achieving equity in a dependent society. Even in a country like the United States, which is very much the master of its own destiny, it proves difficult enough to move toward greater equity in, say, the distribution of income, the provision of social services, or the utilization of educational opportunities. How much more difficult must it be to accomplish a major redistributive effort in the countries of the world's periphery, where existing inequalities of wealth, status, and power are buttressed and sustained by the web of interests, dependencies, and controls that ties the periphery of the international system to its center and in which the multinational corporation plays such a key role.

By all accounts, the gap between urban and rural quality of life, between the economically privileged and the poor, is widening in most countries of the Third World, and the determination on the part of those at the top not to share with those at the bottom seems to become stronger all the time. Those who have made their way through the higher echelons of academic training at home or abroad not only occupy key positions in the political, economic, and academic life of their country but have also managed to obtain and retain the perquisites of rather comfortable life styles—not at all, of course, unlike their colleagues in both the West and the East.

Whether we like it or not, and whether or not it was intended that way, the North American university has made an important contribution to this state of affairs. Because of its technical prestige, graduate training at a U.S. university has been considered the pinnacle of successful mobility through education and has been correspondingly rewarded in the trainee's home country. Graduates of U.S. universities and professional schools now occupy key positions near the top of the social hierarchy and, what is at least as important, tend to play a critical role in determining who the next generation of U.S.-trained elites is going to be. Co-optation to elite status functions as an effective means of system maintenance, and the process of recruiting and selecting holders of fellowships for study abroad is a case in point.

We might as well face it: as long as, in the present international order, North American universities continue to train academics and professionals from the countries of the world's periphery, they will continue to confer on them statuses which make those students part of a very distinct and remarkably persistent upper class in their own countries and will thus help exacerbate the already intractable problem of social equality in those countries. Are then the only alternatives either to cut off the flow of foreign students into our universities or to pursue "business as usual" in our graduate and professional schools and let the effects on the students' home countries be what they may? I think not. Given the important role that our universities play in affecting the social structure of the countries from which our students come, there is a case for much more of a mutually critical interaction between the North American university and the Third World. The fact that academic institutions in North America are an important element in creating and sustaining class structures both in their own society and in other societies is much too crucial to be swept politely under the rug and ought to be a much more prominent and explicit feature in orienting both ourselves and our foreign student colleagues to the peculiar quality of the relationship between U.S. higher education and the Third World.

Self-Reliance and Cultural Authenticity

It was Amadou Mahtar M'Bow, the distinguished Senegalese educator and now director-general of Unesco, who concluded the Lagos Conference of African Ministers of Education in 1976 by saying that "present day systems of education are a means of perpetuating ways of thought and life that are different from those of the African societies" and that "the full development of cultural identity cannot be ensured unless the educational systems inherited from colonial days are called in question."[12] Joseph Ki-Zerbo of Upper Volta speaks, in typical eloquence, of the need for the "liberation of the long inhibited indigenous creative genius" and demands of the African university that it "must not be a mirror diffusing a reflected light but a torch that . . . is fueled primarily in the hearths and homes of the people."[13]

The reality of the countries at the periphery, however, resembles more the mirror than the torch and nowhere more so and more consequentially so than in the academic and scientific establishment of the Third World. The factors that militate against genuine cultural authenticity in education are powerful indeed: an inherited colonial system of education geared to a structure of qualifications that remains metropolitan in nature and origin; a postcolonial pattern of cultural and educational relationships that reflects the dominant nature of the transnational system and its origin in the center countries; the consolidation of a social order that is at once a reflection of the unequal distribution of educational opportunities and the principal mechanism for sustaining it; and, as if that were not enough,

---

[12] Unesco, Conference of Ministers of Education of African Member States, Lagos, January 27–February 4, 1976, *Final Report* (Paris: Unesco, 1976), p. 74.

[13] Quoted in Aimé Damiba, *Education in Africa in the Light of the Lagos Conference (1976)* (Paris: Unesco, 1977), p. 26.

conditions of extreme and persistent resource constraints in which any further developments in education are heavily dependent on outside funds and on the multiple agendas associated with the various sources of such funds. As the official in charge of educational planning in a West African country put it: "When outside aid has to supply 74% of the finance required, planning becomes meaningless and is reduced to a matter of preparing dossiers for potential external funding and of participating in a series of negotiations where the money obtained bears no relationship to what is lost in terms of independence and coherent national policy."[14]

But it is not just the funds. Perhaps the more significant obstacle to cultural authenticity is the dependence—real or perceived—of many Third World countries on the academic training capacity of center countries such as the United States and the resulting perpetuation of the "international model" that has characterized higher education and the socialization of professionals in periphery countries. Some Third World countries have made serious efforts toward reinstating some key elements of their cultural tradition, notably in terms of the use of national languages and of changes in the curriculum. While these attempts at change reflect in many instances a serious political will in the direction of greater independence, it is difficult to anticipate their success while the pinnacle of the cultural and educational system, the university and the professional community in its orbit, remains so closely tied to the pervading and essentially Western model of the transnational system. In a bold move, backed by a remarkable political will for self-reliance in more than words, Tanzania's "Musoma policy" has begun to change the nature and the social identity of its university by radically changing the criteria for university admission. The difficulties which this policy is encountering even under largely favorable political conditions provide an instructive commentary on the tenacity with which the existing academic culture retains its hold on the institution.

Exceptions such as Tanzania aside, the overall picture in the countries of the periphery consists of an academic-professional establishment that exists at considerable (and, it seems, increasing) distance from the masses of the people and their concerns and that is sustained in its social role and identity by new recruits who have been trained at the universities of North America and other center countries. This involvement of the American university is one of the most important mechanisms for sustaining the relationship of cultural dependence between center and periphery. There are some things, however, which can potentially moderate this role and introduce elements into the relationship which would move it more toward one of interdependence than dependence. By way of concluding this discussion, I will offer some propositions on what those elements might be.

[14] Hans N. Weiler, *Educational Planning and Social Change* (Paris: Unesco, 1980), p. 73.

193

The Future of a Difficult Relationship

A good many interesting and encouraging examples to the contrary notwithstanding, much of our academic subculture in professional training is still very strongly oriented toward a belief in technical solutions for human and social problems. In the history of Western man, there is indeed ample evidence on what such devices as railroads, fertilizer, airplanes, immunizations, et cetera can do and have done for the quality of individual and collective life. At the same time, historical success in the utilization of technical solutions has tended to make us oblivious to their limitations, especially in the context of solving problems of underdevelopment in today's world. Two examples from the field of education illustrate my point: our belief in planning and our belief in the role of electronic media in education. Both beliefs have played a major role in our thinking about the development of education in Third World countries, in the design of research, training, and consulting programs, and, to be sure, in programs of international assistance. Yet both beliefs have turned out to be grossly oversimplified and have attributed much more effectiveness to particular techniques and devices than turns out realistically to be justified. What has become necessary as a result is the demystification of the autonomous power of such techniques as planning or media use, a clarification of the contingent nature of their effectiveness, and a better understanding of the nontechnical, political conditions of development and underdevelopment.[15]

A second point relates to another tendency in our North American academic subculture, the tendency to be mono-paradigmatic, that is, to adhere to a particular frame of reference to the exclusion or neglect of other, alternative paradigms. If this observation is correct, it would indeed explain why intellectual and cultural traditions in the periphery (which do espouse different paradigms) have so little impact on the center. It must be very difficult and frustrating for a Third World student at one of our universities to be told that Samir Amin or Osvaldo Sunkel or Rajni Kothari are some interesting but marginal phenomena at the fringe of scholarship—just as difficult and frustrating, incidentally, as I find the narrow-mindedness of dusty Marxist orthodoxy in many Eastern European universities.

The very involvement of the American university, through training and otherwise, in a world which is evidently capable of generating a rich variety of paradigms for the analysis and understanding of human and social problems, and especially for the study of social change, imposes on

---

[15] Hans N. Weiler, "The Politics of Educational Planning: Notes on the Political Economy of Education and Development," Working Paper (Paris: International Institute for Educational Planning, 1983).

us the obligation to take this diversity much more seriously than we have done so far. Indeed, there is every reason actively to seek out this diversity, rather than merely to tolerate it, and to develop both more independence and more skills in assessing the relative strengths and weaknesses of alternative frames of reference.

Last, I would suggest that the involvement of the North American university in "human resource development" for the Third World, its present "boom" notwithstanding, ought to be a declining business over the long run. There are and will be powerful forces—both here and in the developing world—to maintain or even increase the level of involvement over time. But ultimately, and sooner rather than later, the countries of the periphery will need to have the capacity to do their own human resource development and to design, organize, and evaluate their own training programs. To be sure, most international assistance language has always shared this view, but the results are rather limited. We still train engineers rather than the trainers of engineers, planners rather than the trainers of planners, and while "institution building" and "capacity building" are a prominent part of the development vocabulary these days, there is still a preference for having a particular task in a developing country done properly by an expert foreign consultant rather than, perhaps somewhat less properly, by an emerging local institution.

What is needed are centers for research and training in the periphery, not carbon copies of ourselves, but healthy antibodies in the international bloodstream of discovery: centers which are capable and independent enough to create, maintain, and disseminate a more authentic knowledge base for coping with the specific needs of their country within the framework of its own intellectual and cultural traditions. To the extent that our training programs contribute to the emergence and strengthening of such centers of critical thought and action in the periphery, we will have made a significant contribution to the advancement of both discovery and independence. To the extent that, instead of making such a contribution, we continue to reproduce our own kind, we remain part of the problem rather than part of the solution.

Institutional Culture and Third World Student Needs at American Universities

DAVID LANSDALE*

Introduction

Universities in the United States face a delicate challenge in educating an increasing number of Third World nationals. One of the inevitable dilemmas is the potential mismatch between the instructional capacities and objectives of the university—the "institutional culture"—on the one hand and the perceptions, expectations, and needs of Third World students on the other. The research project described in this article was designed to compare the institutional culture and Third World student expectations in the school of engineering of a large, private research university.[1] I expected that the institution studied might be embracing a U.S.-centered orientation to the exclusion of the needs and interests of Third World students.

"Institutional culture" was defined as the shared values and perceptions of the members of the institution that in part determine both the behavior (teaching, conducting research, and advising students) of its members as well as the visible artifacts of the institution (programs, courses, and materials).[2] In an academic setting the key actors (faculty) interact in several subcultures: the discipline or profession (sociology, engineering) through associations and journals; the school or department in which they work (education, civil engineering); and the institution for which they work (university). For the purposes of the project, the focus was on one school and its departments, and professors were identified as the key carriers of the culture of the institution at that level.

I was interested in the perceptions of faculty regarding Third World students and their integration into the program offered by their department and in the perceptions Third World students held of both faculty and the program in which they were involved. I determined the extent to which faculty saw Third World students as having needs different from

This research was conducted in cooperation with Hans Weiler, Ramadhani Ntuah, Jeff Unsiker, and June Yamashita. It was supported by a grant from the Institute of International Education. While the article was written by one person, the conceptualization and implementation of the project was a group effort.

* Doctoral student at the Stanford International Development Center, Stanford University.

[1] Third World countries were defined as all countries that were not industrial market economies or East European nonmarket economies, with the exception of Greece (see *World Development Report* [New York: Oxford University Press, 1982], p. ix).

[2] For an introduction to organizational culture, see Linda Smircich, "Concepts of Culture and Organizational Analysis," *Administrative Science Quarterly* 28 (September 1983): 339–58.

those of domestic students and the efforts being made to respond to those needs.[3] I considered the availability and responsiveness of faculty to Third World students as an indicator of faculty commitment to understanding the culture of those students and to interpreting the institution's culture to them. We also identified the perceptions of the students from the Third World along similar lines with the purpose of comparing the two groups.[4]

The first part of the article presents the data gathered from Third World students in the school of engineering. The second part introduces data gathered from faculty, including three department chairmen. The third part compares and contrasts findings from the two groups. The conclusion suggests that future research should probe further into the dynamic of the relationship between faculty and students from Third World countries, using the department within the school or college as the most appropriate unit of analysis.

The school of engineering was chosen for the study for the following reasons: (1) engineering draws the largest proportion of foreign students studying in the United States (19 percent of all foreign students in the United States in 1982–83, up .2 percent from the previous year)[5] and (2) the school of engineering has the highest percentage of foreign students in the university (37 percent of all graduate students in engineering in 1982–83, when the study was conducted).[6] A breakdown of the populations in the school indicated that over one-third of all students enrolled were from other countries and that over two-thirds of the foreign students were from Third World countries.

Third World Students' Perceptions

Third World students were asked how many of their professors used reading materials, assignments, or teaching methods in their classes that were relevant to situations in their home countries. More than half (54

---

[3] For a typology of needs, I used one developed by Motoko Y. Lee et al., *Needs of Foreign Students from Developing Nations at U.S. Colleges and Universities* (Washington, D.C.: National Association for Foreign Student Affairs, April 1981), pp. 23–25. I focused specifically on academic needs, including information, degree program, and degree program relevancy needs. Linguistic needs were included as an important predictor of integration into academic and institutional culture.

[4] Questionnaires that evolved through open-ended interviews with Third World students were mailed to all Third World students in engineering during the winter quarter of 1983. The response rate was 49 percent. Questionnaires were also sent to a comparison group of American students in engineering, with 56 percent responding. Nineteen faculty were interviewed during the winter and spring quarters of 1983. The sample was randomly drawn within each academic rank. Five departments were chosen for analysis: three were highly technical, two of which had the lowest ratio of Third World students to domestic students, while the third had the highest; the other two departments were more oriented toward planning and management. The number of faculty interviewed in each department was proportional to the number of foreign students in that department.

[5] Figures quoted from International Institute of Education releases in "Foreign Students in U.S. Institutions," *Chronicle of Higher Education* (November 9, 1983), p. 21.

[6] Statistics on the school and its departments were provided by the registrar's office of the university where the study was conducted.

percent) claimed that none of their professors used such materials, almost a third stated that some used such materials, and only 16 percent said that many professors were doing so (table 1). The breakdown by department (electrical engineering, material sciences engineering, and mechanical engineering are more technical, while civil engineering and engineering economic systems are less so) shows that faculty in the less technical departments were perceived as adapting their classes more to Third World students, with the exception of material sciences engineering, in which 33 percent of the students said that many professors used materials relevant to their country (material sciences had the highest proportion of Third World to domestic students).

TABLE 1

PROFESSORS USING MATERIALS RELEVANT TO THIRD WORLD COUNTRIES, RATED BY STUDENTS FROM THOSE COUNTRIES

Department	Many	Some	None
Civil engineering	5 (16)	11 (35)	15 (48)
Electrical engineering	5 (9)	18 (34)	30 (57)
Engineering economic systems	1 (8)	6 (50)	5 (42)
Material sciences engineering	8 (20)	8 (20)	24 (60)
Mechanical engineering	7 (33)	4 (19)	10 (48)
Total	26 (16)	47 (30)	84 (54)

NOTE.—Figures in parentheses represent percentage.

Students were asked how adequate they found their department's program in terms of the number of courses or other activities meeting their unique interests and needs as students from developing countries (table 2). The technical departments were evaluated more favorably, while students were more critical in those engineering departments where planning and economics play an important role. For the entire school, just over half the students felt their program could be improved to meet their needs, 19 percent said their program was inadequate, and 28 percent claimed their program to be adequate (with most of the responses in the last group coming from students in two of the larger, more prestigious, highly technical departments).

The availability of the faculty adviser is critical to students from Third World countries. The adviser provides an important link for the student to the profession's and department's academic norms and expectations. The majority of students who responded to the questionnaire claimed that their advisers were either "readily available" or "available" to them. Master's students found it more difficult to see their advisers than doctoral students, and 19 percent of the total sample found it "very difficult" to

TABLE 2

ADEQUACY OF PROGRAM TO MEET THE NEEDS AND INTERESTS OF STUDENTS FROM THIRD WORLD
COUNTRIES, RATED BY STUDENTS FROM THOSE COUNTRIES

Department	Adequate	Needs Improvement	Not Adequate
Civil engineering	5 (18)	15 (56)	7 (26)
Electrical engineering	21 (39)	22 (41)	11 (20)
Engineering economic systems	2 (17)	6 (50)	4 (33)
Material sciences engineering	10 (26)	24 (61)	5 (13)
Mechanical engineering	5 (22)	15 (65)	3 (13)
Total	43 (28)	82 (53)	30 (19)

NOTE.—Figures in parentheses equal percentage.

see their advisers. The ratio of availability to unavailability was roughly two-thirds to one-third.

Third World students were asked how responsive they found faculty to be to them relative to American students. Over two-thirds felt that professors were equally responsive to them, but of the remaining one third, most (26 percent compared to 5 percent) found faculty to be more responsive to American students. Most (80 percent) of the comparison group of American students found the faculty to be equally responsive to the two groups of students, though again more of the remaining students (15 percent compared to 5 percent) found faculty favoring American over Third World students.

Faculty Perceptions of Third World Students

Ten of the nineteen faculty interviewed felt that Third World students had special needs (table 3). Two of the professors suggested that the needs and interests of these students were different from those of the American students but felt uncomfortable calling them "special." Faculty were asked if their departments provided any special courses or other academic services and activities addressing the concerns and needs of Third World students. Fifteen of the nineteen professors responded that they did not. Asked if any arrangements should be made to accommodate these needs, eleven said no arrangements should be made, while eight suggested that such arrangements should be made. The technical orientation of the engineering profession may account for this breakdown, given that, of the four who responded that their departments did provide for Third World student needs, all four were in the less technical (planning and economics-oriented) departments.

Professors were asked how available they were to meet the advising needs of Third World students. Three felt they were "difficult to see," one professor stated that he was "very difficult to see," with the rest

TABLE 3
FACULTY RESPONSES TO WHETHER THIRD WORLD STUDENTS HAVE SPECIAL NEEDS, SPECIAL
COURSES IN THE DEPARTMENT TO MEET THOSE NEEDS, WHETHER ARRANGEMENTS SHOULD BE MADE
TO MEET THOSE NEEDS

Department	Special Needs		Special Courses		Arrangements	
	Yes	No	Yes	No	Yes	No
Civil engineering	3	1	3	1	2	2
Electrical engineering	1	5	0	6	2	4
Engineering economic systems	1	1	1	1	1	1
Material sciences engineering	2	1	0	3	1	2
Mechanical engineering	3	1	0	4	2	2
Total	10	9	4	15	8	11

distributed between "readily available" and "available" (eight and seven, respectively). Approximately half of the professors said they spent more time advising Third World students than they did American students, with almost all the others claiming that they spent equal time advising both groups of students. Only one professor said he spent more time advising American students.

Most of the faculty interviewed had encountered language problems with Third World students. Specifically, 13 of the sample said they had to negotiate the language problem "sometimes" or "often." Six professors claimed "rarely" to have to deal with such problems, often because the nature of their work was extremely technical so that language problems were less likely to arise.

Faculty interviewees were asked whether they felt the percentage of students from developing countries in their departments should be higher, lower, or remain the same. Table 4 lists the distributions of students by department, and table 5 shows the preference of the faculty. In the two less technical departments, faculty seemed to favor having fewer Third World students because the ratios in these two departments were already slightly higher than in the more technical departments, which tended to be more selective because of larger applicant pools (material sciences was an exception, as noted earlier). In the total distribution, seven felt the ratios should stay the same, and eight suggested they should decrease, while three of the faculty had no opinion on the matter.

The faculty were asked several open-ended questions about the advantages and disadvantages of having students from the Third World in their departments and classes. Advantages, in order of frequency mentioned, included cultural diversity, international understanding, connections with Third World leaders, broader perspectives, the chance to verify materials on the Third World, and increased political awareness. Many students

TABLE 4
DISTRIBUTION OF FOREIGN AND THIRD WORLD STUDENTS BY DEPARTMENT (%)

Department	All Foreign	All Third World	Third World/Foreign
Civil engineering	46	34	73
Electrical engineering	36	23	80
Engineering economic systems	41	33	80
Material sciences engineering	29	23	78
Mechanical engineering	41	37	90

from the Third World were also credited with being extremely hardworking and well prepared, which in turn increased competition with American students and in general helped promote the academic quality of work in the department.

The most frequently mentioned disadvantage was language problems. Others were that Third World students needed special materials to familarize them with subjects covered in class, had problems with note taking, slowed down instruction, needed remedial programs, and demonstrated different ethics.

Evaluating the Data: A Problem of Numbers as Well as Accommodation

The data suggest that (1) most Third World students, while recognizing some efforts by faculty to respond to their needs, felt that their departments' programs could be improved; (2) faculty response to the interests and needs of those students was limited and varied, the best predictor being the degree of technical emphasis within a given department and the proportion of Third World to American students in the department; and (3) faculty were both affected by and concerned about the presence of substantial numbers of students from developing countries.

Faculty Response to Third World Student Expectations

Professors in the less technical departments appeared to be more

TABLE 5
FACULTY PREFERENCE FOR PERCENTAGE OF THIRD WORLD STUDENTS IN DEPARTMENT

Department	Higher	Same	Lower
Civil engineering	1	1	1
Electrical engineering	0	4	1
Engineering economic systems	0	0	2
Material sciences engineering	0	2	0
Mechanical engineering	0	0	4
Total	1	7	8

NOTE.—No opinion: $N = 3$.

responsive to Third World student needs, in that more than half the students said that professors in those two departments used relevant materials. At the same time, students in those departments expected the programs to be more relevant to their interests and needs. This phenomenon may be attributed to the following reasons: (1) the less technical departments are also the less prestigious, drawing fewer top-quality American applicants, and consequently end up with higher proportions of Third World students whose needs are more likely to be met when their numbers are high; (2) the less technical departments are also smaller in numbers of students so that Third World students tend to be more visible; and (3) material presented in less technical departments is more applicable to the home country situation of students from developing countries: projecting growth through economic modeling, for example, is just as appropriate an exercise for a developing country's economy as it is for the economy of the United States.

Third World students were critical of their programs in all the departments studied. This suggests that, while some professors may be making an effort to use materials relevant to Third World student needs, the prevailing institutional culture precludes fundamental curricular modifications in response to those needs. Only one department was rated as adequate in meeting the needs of Third World students by more than a third of those students. Even in this department, however, 41 percent of the respondents felt there could be improvements to make the program more relevant for Third World students, and 20 percent felt the program was not adequate to meet the needs of those students. From the students' point of view, the effort by some faculty to incorporate their needs was incidental in the context of an institutional culture reflecting a predominately Western orientation.

The faculty responses tended to support the conclusion that little was being done to respond to Third World student interests and needs. Students from the Third World were recognized by most professors as having special needs. Further probes indicated, however, that these needs were perceived to be primarily linguistic. Professors tended to respond to those needs by slowing down the instruction pace. Several professors suggested writing courses be made available in the department. In the technical departments, none of the professors were aware of courses being offered to meet the needs of Third World students. Five of these felt, however, that arrangements should be made by the department to meet those needs. This supports the students' responses: even the technical departments could make arrangements in their course offerings and curricula to respond better to the needs of students from Third World countries.

A professor who was also chairman of one of the less technical departments pointed out that "we stress the fundamentals, because the applications can be made anywhere. We could add a course or two on special problems of developing countries, which might be useful for American as well as foreign students due to the involvement of the United States abroad; unfortunately, there are limited faculty resources and any change would be contingent on new faculty resources." The same interviewee continued by emphasizing the importance of appropriate technology. The problem, he suggested, lay in that "the desire for high technology comes from Third World students as well as through the imposition of the industrialized world on those countries. Students and governments of Third World countries don't want second rate solutions." He concluded by pointing out that different countries faced different problems: "In China, they use a lot of appropriate technology, but have a limited knowledge of the underlying fundamentals; thus they are eager to apply without much caution and can ultimately only take the application so far. In India, the situation is the opposite: they have the understanding, and the trained engineers, but not what it takes to apply the knowledge."

Feedback from other interviews suggested that most of the faculty in the less technical departments were aware of the needs of students from Third World countries and that professors in the more technical departments were less aware of, or at least did not acknowledge, those needs. Awareness of those needs does not necessarily result in arrangements to provide for them, however. While some faculty were responsive, the institutional culture in which they operate provides carefully prescribed guidelines embracing a Western orientation both in the substance and in the method of what is taught. Resources are allocated along these guidelines. Much of this orientation may be the result of a perceived mandate, a charter from American society, to promote technological advances that would be compromised if adjustments were made to accommodate the needs of students from the Third World.

Third World students also have needs related to their adjustment as members of their respective departments. Some interesting discrepancies emerged from the data. Faculty rated themselves as being more available to Third World students than the latter perceived them to be. Moreover, faculty felt they spent more time advising Third World than American students, while both Third World and American students thought the faculty were more responsive to American than to Third World students. This discrepancy may reflect the following tension: faculty feel more comfortable with and respond more readily to American students. Third World students, however, require more time as advisees because of the information they need as an introduction to and for transition through the institutional culture. Consequently, while some students from the Third World may have felt that their advisers were not available, most of the faculty perceived themselves correctly as giving readily of their time because the commitment required from those students was greater than it was for Americans who make the transition into the institutional culture more smoothly.

One professor, also a department chairman, described an introductory-level course he had taught that might provide a model for other departments. Recognizing that incoming students, particularly those from the Third World, needed a special introduction and orientation to what I have called the institutional culture, he developed his course to address the needs and interests of the students as he perceived them. The first class sessions focused on explaining the academic culture into which the students were entering. Expectations and guidelines concerning the university's "honor code" in particular were explicitly outlined. In handling the material covered in class, the professor assigned students to groups, distributing those from the same countries and regions of the world across groups. Students were encouraged to draw heavily from their own experiences and knowledge in the class projects and discussions. The professor responsible seemed to be particularly pleased with the effort and its results, claiming considerable success with the approach for each year he had used it. Feedback from students who had taken the course suggested that it had been quite helpful to them.

While some of the faculty were making efforts to respond to the needs of Third World students, almost half did not perceive those students as having special needs. Even the faculty who were responsive were unable to effect the kind of modifications that would be acceptable to Third World students, given the parameters outlined by the institutional culture.

Striking the Delicate Balance

The findings of this research indicate a definite mismatch between the needs of Third World students and the institutional culture as embodied in department programs, even though there is considerable variation across the members of the faculty. The problem appears to intensify when the ratio of Third World to American students passes a certain threshold.

The school in which the study was conducted is one of the more competitive in the field and as such can afford to be selective in its admissions. Why did so many of the professors (eight out of 19) express concern about the proportion of Third World students when they themselves make the admissions decisions through committees in each department?

The reason behind the discrepancy is a combination of the structural composition of the department admissions process and market forces. Students apply to a department at either the master's or the postmaster's level. At the master's level, the selection process is rigorous, and domestic students are favored over foreign students, who are evaluated on the basis of more stringent criteria. During the course of their master's program, all students have the option of qualifying for the doctoral program. The majority of domestic master's students prefer to take lucrative jobs in industry, however, leaving a much higher percentage of foreign students, the brightest of their cohort, to move into the doctoral pool. Students are also admitted to the doctoral pool by applying as doctoral candidates to the department. Regardless of how selective the admissions committee is, however, it has virtually no control over the flow of Third World students into the doctoral program from the master's program, the result being that most of the departments have approximately 50 percent of their doctoral students from foreign countries, primarily of the Third World.

The lack of control by faculty over the proportion of Third World students in their department at the doctoral level is seen as problematic for the following reasons: (1) classroom instruction slows down; (2) faculty need to spend more time advising; (3) more time is invested helping students with language problems, particularly on dissertations; and (4) Third World students feel more frustrated in their effort to understand and become part of the institutional culture. One professor interviewed, the chairman of the department's admissions committee, pointed out that, "when the number of Third World students gets too high, it changes the flavor of the class." Yet the faculty, acting as gatekeepers monitoring entry to the culture, are limited in their control over access because of market forces and structural elements in the admissions process. The data suggest that higher proportions of Third World students introduce a tension into the institutional culture once a certain threshold is reached. More information is necessary to provide better understanding of this tension, which in turn might suggest options for reconciling it to the benefit of both faculty and Third World students.

Conclusion: Future Research

The research described in this article was conceived as a pilot study to explore the match or mismatch between institutional culture and Third World student needs and expectations in a competitive school of engineering. The small number of professors sampled, coupled with the standing of the school as a leader and consequently an outlier in its field, allows for tentative generalizations at best. While the findings do suggest a definite mismatch, a more extensive sample of schools or departments, faculty, and administrators is needed to substantiate the conclusions drawn from the data.

Future research should concentrate on the dynamic between faculty and Third World students, with special consideration given to the respective ideological orientation of the two groups. The former play an important role both as gatekeepers to and carriers of the institutional culture hosting increasing numbers of students from the Third World. The latter arrive with expectations that most probably will be modified to match what the institution offers, a compromise that makes it difficult when the time comes for the students to return to their home country and apply what was learned. Both faculty and Third World students experience the tensions that are aggravated by increasing numbers of Third World students.

These tensions need to be identified and articulated. Faculty play central roles in the admission, orientation, training, and preparation of students from Third World countries. Each one of these processes represents one component of the integration of Third World students into the institutional culture of the department, school, and university. Further research should seek to determine the values underlying an institution's culture, suggesting in turn possible options for modifying both the content and methods in existing department programs in response to the needs of a sizable proportion of Third World students.

The tensions being played out in the microcosm of the American university are an interesting reflection of ideological differences at a macro socioeconomic and international level. The task of articulating these tensions is a prerequisite to the formulation of possible options for reconciling the differences. Of particular interest would be the explicit articulation of the ideological orientation of Third World students in the context of an institutional culture founded on basic assumptions of a completely different nature. This article will, it is hoped, encourage others to probe more deeply into this phenomenon, particularly at the department level, where faculty, students, and the institutional culture can be studied most fruitfully.

International Students and Study-Abroad Programs: A Select Bibliography

Y. G-M. LULAT*

ASSISTED BY J. CORDARO

Overview

Hugh M. Jenkins, a long-time authority on affairs pertaining to international students, states in his recent book *Educating Students from Other Nations* (reviewed in this issue; see also Sec. 3*b* below) that a "superabundance" of information exists on the subject of international students and study-abroad programs. While this is so, the quality and scope of this literature leaves much to be desired. As this bibliography shows, despite the phenomenal four fold increase in the number of international students throughout the world, from approximately 250,000 in 1960 to a million-plus today (flowing mostly from the South to the North), the traditional research concerns in the literature on international students, identified almost a decade ago by Spaulding and Flack in their authoritative book (see Sec. 1 below), have to date by and large continued to hold sway. Thus, overwhelmingly, the literature continues to be dominated by two principal sets of research concerns: those of a sociopsychological character, exemplified by studies pertaining to the cross-cultural consequences of studying abroad, and those dealing with how best to help international students to adapt and to succeed in an alien institutional and cultural environment.

Although a beginning has been made, there are still relatively very few studies that examine the consequences of large international student flows from the perspective of the home country, the host country, or even the host institution—that is, from a perspective other than that of the student. Hence for future research, among the more pressing questions pertaining to international students and study-abroad programs, the following questions are suggested as meriting attention:

1. International students constitute a severe drain on scarce foreign exchange reserves of their countries (especially those in the Third World). Under this circumstance, do the benefits, in terms of social rates of return, outweigh the costs of sending students abroad?

2. What consequences result for the social structures of societies of the Third World from the presence of significantly increasing numbers of foreign-credentialed persons—especially from the perspective of equality issues?

I am greatly indebted to the following for assisting in the preparation of this bibliography: José Agudelo, J. Cordaro, Marilyn Haas, Andrea Hubal, Charlene Capwell, and Karen Smith. Special thanks are also due to Dan Walsh, the night janitor. This bibliography is part of an ongoing bibliography project on international students under the directorship of Philip G. Altbach and funded in part by the Exxon Foundation, the Institute of International Education, and the National Association for Foreign Student Affairs. Correspondence from readers is invited, especially on new entry suggestions.

* Doctoral student in the Comparative Education Center, State University of New York at Buffalo.

3. What are the economic implications (especially in terms of technology and industry) of training students in institutions of the advanced industrial nations with curricula not modified to suit the circumstances of the Third World home countries?

4. What are the consequences for the educational systems of Third World nations that send a large proportion of their undergraduate-level students for study abroad—especially in terms of matters such as educational reform?

5. What are the economic costs and benefits of large numbers of international students for the host country?

6. What are the policy alternatives with regard to international students (in view of their ever-increasing numbers) for the host countries?

7. What impact does the presence of large numbers of international students in host-country institutions have on the curriculum and on the general orientation of departments in which international students are a major force?

8. Does the presence of international students affect the interests of minority students in any way?

9. What is the optimum number of international students that a host institution can constructively accommodate?

10. Does the presence of a large number of international students encourage the host institution to develop international programs—training, consultancy, et cetera—and does such encouragement come from alumni contacts?

In addition to these questions there is also a strong need for research attention to be directed toward the following areas, where information of almost any kind (including the sociopsychological and adaptation variety) pertaining to international students is severely lacking in the literature: (*a*) international students studying in the Third World, that is, students from Third World countries studying in other Third World countries, (*b*) international students studying in China and Eastern bloc countries, and (*c*) female international students, that is, students who, by virtue of their gender, encounter special problems both in the host country and, on returning, in the home country. Mention must also be made of the need to develop research methods that can come to grips with such traditionally accepted claims made for study-abroad programs as that they promote international understanding, that they have long-term trade and political benefits for the host country, and so on.

Turning to the organizational aspects of the bibliography, the material covered in it was published from 1975 to November 1983. The 1975 cutoff date was determined on the basis of the fact that Spaulding and Flack's excellent bibliography covers the period up to 1974. Two sets of concerns that are sometimes associated with international students have been largely ignored in this bibliography: those pertaining to the phenomenon of brain drain, that is, the migration of talent (usually from the Third World to the advanced industrial nations), and those pertaining to the teaching of English (or any other language) as a second language. The reason for the omission of material relating to these two areas is that neither area concerns international students exclusively. Brain drain and second language issues may or may not involve international students. In other words, the material covered in this bibliography is limited to issues that are intrinsic to the condition of being an international student. Also left out of the bibliography are dissertations, for outside the United States there are very few dissertations that have been done on international students, and those within the United States (mostly on either attitudes or needs of international students in the United States) are easily accessible in *Dissertation Abstracts International*. Unpublished conference papers have not been included either—some of these can be found in the *Resources in Education* index.

The bibliography has been divided into the following sections and each section further divided, where necessary, into two subsections: articles and monographs (books, reports, etc.).

1. Reference—Bibliographies
2. References—Statistical Sources
3. General
4. Historical Studies
5. Policy—Home Country
6. Policy—Host Country
7. International Students and Host Country (General Issues)
8. Institutional Policy
9. Economics: Costs and Benefits—Home Country
10. Economics: Costs and Benefits—Host Country
11. Legal Issues (Visas, etc.)
12. Recruitment (Policies and Procedures)
13. Admission (Policies and Procedures)
14. Administration (Programs and Services)
15. Finances (Sources, Problems, etc.)
16. Health
17. Counseling Services
18. Adaptation Problems (The Alien Institutional and Cultural Environment)
19. Academic Performance (Constraints and Success Factors)
20. Attitudinal and Behavioral Studies
21. Cross-cultural Issues and Activities
22. Curricula and Programs of Study (Including Relevance of Curricula)
23. International Educational Exchange and Study-Abroad Programs
24. Disciplinary Studies (Engineering, Law, Medicine, etc.)
25. Specific Student Nationality Studies
26. Specific Institution Studies
27. Female International Students
28. China and Eastern Bloc Countries
29. International Students Studying in Third World Countries
30. Foreign Aid for Study Abroad
31. Overseas Training and National Development
32. Poststudy Matters (Practical Training, Returning Home, etc.)
33. Alumni Issues

1. Reference—Bibliographies

Monographs

American Association of Collegiate Registrars and Admissions Officers. *Bibliography of Reference Materials for Evaluating Foreign Student Credentials.* 3d ed. Washington, D.C.: American Association of Collegiate Registrars and Admissions Officers, 1982.

Ausländerstudium in der BRD: Bestandsaufnahme und Bewertung der Literatur. Baden-Baden: Nomos, 1982.

Espinosa, J. Manuel. *A Selected Bibliography on Educational and Cultural Exchange: With Special Reference to the Programs of the United States Department of State.* Washington, D.C.: Department of State, Bureau of Educational and Cultural Affairs, 1975.

Jones, Valarie A., and Stalker, John., comps. *Interpreting the Black Experience in America to Foreign Students: A Guide to Materials—Preliminary Edition.* Washington, D.C.: National Association for Foreign Student Affairs, 1976.

National Association for Foreign Student Affairs. *Bibliography on Study, Work and Travel Abroad.* Washington, D.C.: National Association for Foreign Student Affairs, Section on U.S. Study Abroad, 1982.

National Association for Foreign Student Affairs. *Foreign Student Admissions, Credentials Bibliography.* Washington, D.C.: National Association for Foreign Student Affairs, 1979.

Paget, Roger. *International Educational Exchanges: Selected Bibliography of Recent Materials.* Washington, D.C.: U.S. Information Agency, U.S. International Communication Agency, 1980.

Spaulding, Seth, and Flack, Michael J. *The World's Students in the United States: A Review and Evaluation of Research on Foreign Students.* New York: Praeger, 1976.

Spencer, Charles S., and Stahl, Vivian R. *Bibliography of Research on International Exchanges.* Washington, D.C.: U.S. Information Agency, Office of Research, 1983.

Tysse, Agnes N. *International Education: The American Experience— A Bibliography.* Vol. 1, *Dissertations and Theses.* Metuchen, N.J.: Scarecrow, 1974.

Tysse, Agnes N. *International Education: The American Experience—A Bibliography.* Vol. 2, *Periodicals.* Metuchen, N.J.: Scarecrow, 1977.

2. Reference—Statistical Sources

a) Articles

Cerych, L., and Colton, S. L. "Summarising Recent Student Flows," *European Journal of Education* 15, no. 1 (1980): 15–35.

Jenkins, Hugh M., et al. "Data Collection Project on Foreign Student Enrollments in U.S. Colleges and Universities," *College and University* 53 (Summer 1978): 512–17.

"Overall Picture of the Distribution of Foreign Students in the Countries of the Unesco European Region," *Higher Education in Europe* 4 (April/June 1979): 13–17.

Teichler, Ulrich. "Trends in Higher Education with Respect to Student Population" [Foreign students], *Higher Education in Europe* 5 (February 1980): 24–34.

b) Monographs

Brown, George H. *Earned Degrees by Racial/Ethnic Status, 1978/79.* American Statistical Index accessions no. 4828-13. Washington, D.C.: Department of Education, National Center for Education Statistics, 1982.

Canadian Bureau for International Education. *Statistics on Foreign Students.* Ottawa: Canadian Bureau for International Education, 1981.

Imbert, Jacques. *Les Etudiants étrangers en France.* Paris: Centre des oeuvres universitaires et scolaires, 1980.

Institute of International Education. *Open Doors: Report on International Educational Exchange.* New York: Institute of International Education, 1956–. (Published annually.)

Institute of International Education. *Profiles: The Foreign Student in the United States.* New York: Institute of International Education, 1981.

National Association for Foreign Student Affairs. Interassociational Committee on Data Collection. *Guide to Data Collection on International Students.* Washington, D.C.: National Association for Foreign Student Affairs, 1982.

Service des études informatiques et statistiques. Ministère de l'éducation France. *Statistique des étudiants de nationalité étrangère dans les universités.* Paris: Service des études informatiques et statistiques, Ministère de l'éducation. (Published annually.)

Statistical Office of the European Communities. *Eurostat: Education and Training.* Luxembourg: Office of the Official Publications of the European Communities, 1977–. (Published annually.)

Unesco. *Statistics of Students Abroad, 1962–1968.* Paris: Unesco, 1972.

Unesco. *Statistics of Students Abroad, 1969–1973.* Paris: Unesco, 1976.

Unesco. *Statistics of Students Abroad, 1974–1978.* Paris: Unesco, 1982.

United Kingdom. British Council. *Statistics of Overseas Students in Britain.* London: British Council, 1950–. (Published annually.)

United States. Central Intelligence Agency. *Communist Aid Activities in Non-Communist Less-developed Countries, 1979, and 1954–1979: A Research Paper.* Washington, D.C.: Central Intelligence Agency, National Foreign Assessments Center, 1980.

von Zur-Muehlen, Max. *Foreign Students in Canada: A Preliminary Documentation for 1981–82.* Ottawa: Statistics Canada, Education, Science and Culture Division, 1981.

3. General

a) Articles

Berendzen, Richard. "Ethics in International Higher Education." In *Ethical Principles, Practices and Problems in Higher Education,* edited by M. C. Baca and R. H. Stein, pp. 80–98. Springfield, Ill.: Thomas, 1983.

Blaug, Mark, and Woodhall, Maureen. "A Survey of Overseas Students in British Higher Education, 1980." In Williams, ed. (Sec. 6*b* below), pp. 239–64.

Crewson, John W. "International Students and American Higher Education: An Interview with Richard Berendzen," *Trends 2000* 1, no. 4 (1979): 15–24.

Dahl, O., and Denninger, E. "Un Voyage d'études à Berlin," *Education et développement,* no. 111 (1976), pp. 32–41.

Derham, D. T. "Mobility of Students and Staff Internationally." In *Pressures and Priorities,* edited by T. Craig, pp. 359–64. London: Association of Commonwealth Universities, 1979.

Diener, Thomas J. "Foreign Students and U.S. Community Colleges," *Community College Review* 7, no. 4 (1980): 58–65.

Diener, Thomas J. "Profile of Foreign Students in United States Community and Junior Colleges." In Gleazer, Jr., et al. (Sec. 3*b* below), pp. 14–31.

"Dossier" [Foreign students in Europe], *CRE-Information,* no. 57 (1st Quarter 1982), pp. 68–80.

Fontaine, R. "Echanges d'élèves, sejours et voyages à l'étranger," *Inrap,* no. 45 (1980), pp. 29–49.

Michel, J. M. "Le Voyage à l'étranger: Errance ou moyen de formation pour les jeunes," *Vers l'éducation nouvelle,* no. 297 (1975), pp. 24–34.

Perkins, J. A. "Mobility of Students and Staff Internationally." In *Pressures and Priorities,* edited by T. Craig, pp. 365–71. London: Association of Commonwealth Universities, 1979.

Robert, Jacques. "Rapport final" [Accueillir l'étudiant étranger], *CRE-Information,* no. 57 (1st Quarter 1982), pp. 60–67.

Schulte, Hansgerd. "Réflexions sur le problème de la mobilité des étudiants en Europe," *CRE-Information,* no. 34 (2d Quarter 1976), pp. 11–29.

Smith, I. M. "Spatial Ability, Field Independence and Climate: Some Thoughts on the Testing of Overseas Students," *Vocational Aspect* 26 (Autumn 1974): 121–25.

Thistlethwaite, F. "Mobility of Students and Staff Internationally." In *Pressures and Priorities,* edited by T. Craig, pp. 372–86. London: Association of Commonwealth Universities, 1979.

Woodhall, Maureen. "Overseas Students." In *Access to Higher Education,* pp. 192–201. Guildford: Society for Research into Higher Education, 1981.

b) Monographs

Australian Committee of Directors and Principals of Advanced Education. *Overseas Students in Colleges of Advanced Education.* Canberra: Australian Committee of Directors and Principals of Advanced Education, 1983.

Australian Vice Chancellors' Committee. *Overseas Students Enrolled at Australian Universities.* Canberra: Australian Vice Chancellors' Committee, 1983.

Blaug, Mark, and Woodhall, Maureen. *A Survey of Overseas Students in British Higher Education, 1980.* London: Overseas Students Trust, 1981.

Council of Europe. *The Conference on Academic Mobility in Europe (Strasbourg, 17–19 March 1981): Dossier.* Strasbourg: Council of Europe, 1981.

Council of Graduate Schools. *The Foreign Student in American Graduate Schools.* Washington, D.C.: Council of Graduate Schools, 1980.

East Sussex County Planning Department. *Foreign Students in East Sussex: Report of Proceedings at Seminar at East Sussex College of Higher Education, Eastbourne, on 8 April 1978.* Lewes: East Sussex County Planning Department, 1978.

Gleazer, Edmund J., Jr., et al. *The Foreign Student in United States Community and Junior Colleges.* New York: College Entrance Examination Board, 1978.

Jarousse, Jean-Pierre. *Foreign Students in France.* Paris: Institute of Education of the European Cultural Foundation, 1980.

Jenkins, Hugh M. *A Glance Back, A Glimpse Forward: Leafing through the History and Future of the National Association for Foreign Student Affairs.* Washington, D.C.: National Association for Foreign Student Affairs, 1979.

Jenkins, Hugh M., et al. *Educating Students from Other Nations: American Colleges and Universities in International Educational Interchange.* San Francisco: Jossey-Bass, 1983.

Masclet, J. C. *The Intra-European Mobility of Undergraduate Students.* Paris: Institute of Education of the European Cultural Foundation, 1975.

Miller, Vincent A. *The Guidebook for International Trainers in Business and Industry.* New York: Van Nostrand Reinhold, 1979.

National Association for Foreign Student Affairs. *Selected Speeches: 27th Annual Conference of the National Association for Foreign Student Affairs, Washington, D.C., May 7–11, 1975.* Washington, D.C.: National Association for Foreign Student Affairs, 1975.

Nelson, Donald N. *Crucial Issues in Foreign Student Education.* Washington, D.C.: National Association for Foreign Student Affairs, 1975.

Niece, David C., and Braun, Peter H. *A Patron for the World? A Descriptive Report of the C.B.I.E. Survey of Foreign Students in Post-Secondary Institutions in Canada, 1977.* 2 vols. Ottawa: Canadian Bureau for International Education, 1977.

Rao, G. Lakshmana. *Overseas Students in Australia: Some Major Findings from a Nation-wide Survey.* Canberra: Australian National University, Research School of Social Sciences, Education Research Unit, 1977.

Thompson, Mary A. *Unofficial Ambassadors: The Story of International Student Service.* New York: International Student Service, 1982.

von Zur-Muehlen, Max. *Foreign Students in Canada and Canadian Students Abroad.* Ottawa: Canadian Bureau for International Education, 1978.

von Zur-Muehlen, Max. *Foreign Students' Patterns in Canadian Universities in 1980.* Ottawa: Canadian Bureau for International Education, 1980.

4. Historical Studies

a) Articles

Billigmeier, R. H., and Forman, D. C. "Göttingen in Retrospect: A Longitudinal Assessment of the University of California's Education Abroad Program in Göttingen by 1965–66 Participants," *International Review of Education* 21, no. 2 (1975): 217–30.

Carroll, L. "Seavoyage Controversy and the Kayasthas of North India, 1901–1909: Indic Students in England," *Modern Asian Studies* 13 (April 1979): 265–99.

Cross, A. G. "Russian Students in Eighteenth-Century Oxford," *Journal of European Studies* 5 (June 1975): 91–110.

Cunningham, R. J. "German Historical World of Herbert Baxter Adams: 1874–1876," *Journal of American History* 68 (September 1981): 261–75.

Diehl, Carl. "Innocents Abroad: American Students in German Universities, 1810–1870," *History of Education Quarterly* 16, no. 3 (1976): 321–41.

Evans, B. "China-Canada Student Exchange—1st 20," *Pacific Affairs* 49, no. 1 (1976): 93–101.

Frijhoff, Willem. "Etudiants étrangers à l'academie d'angers au 17ᵉ siècle," *Lias* (Amsterdam) 4, no. 1 (1977): 13–84.

Frijhoff, Willem. "Etudiants hollandais dans les collèges français, 17ᵉ et 18ᵉ siècles," *Lias* (Amsterdam) 3, no. 2 (1976): 301–12.

Jenkins, Hugh M. "International Education and the National Association for Foreign Student Affairs, 1948–1978," *International Educational and Cultural Exchange* 14, no. 1 (1978): 17–21.

Jewsbury, George F. "Russian Students in Nancy, France, 1905–1914: A Case Study," *Jahrbücher für Geschichte Osteuropas* 23, no. 2 (1975): 225–28.

Joshi, Joan H., et al. "Fulbright Act of 1946," *College and University* 51 (Summer 1976): 555–60.

Ninkovich, F. "Cultural Relations and American China Policy, 1942–1945" [Chinese students in the United States], *Pacific Historical Review* 49 (August 1980): 471–98.

Plattard, J. "Un Etudiant écossais en France en 1665–1666," *Bulletin de l'Association Guillaume Budé*, no. 2 (1981), pp. 215–23.

Silvera, Alain. "The First Egyptian Student Mission to France under Muhammed Ali," *Middle Eastern Studies* 16 (May 1980): 1–22.

Stewart, Gordon M. "British Students at the University of Göttingen in the Eighteenth Century," *German Life and Letters* 33, no. 1 (1979): 24–41.

Valdes, Dennis Nodin. "Perspiring Capitalists: Latinos and the Henry Ford Service School, 1918–1928," *Aztlan: International Journal of Chicano Studies Research* 12, no. 2 (1981): 227–39.

Watt, D. E. R. "Scottish Student Life Abroad in the Fourteenth Century," *Scottish Historical Review* 59 (April 1980): 3–21.

Williams, W. L. "Ethnic Relations of Africa Students in the United States with Black Americans, 1870–1900," *Journal of Negro History* 65 (Summer 1980): 228–49.

Yates, B. A. "Educating Congolese Abroad: An Historical Note on African Elites," *International Journal of African Historical Studies* 14, no. 1 (1981): 34–64.

b) Monographs

Buchloh, Paul G., and Rix, Walter T., eds. *American Colony of Göttingen: Historical and Other Data Collected between the Years 1855 and 1888*. Göttingen: Vandenhoeck & Ruprecht, 1976.

Byrnes, Robert Francis. *Soviet-American Academic Exchanges, 1958–1975*. Bloomington: Indiana University Press, 1976.

Chadwick, John. *The Unofficial Commonwealth: The Story of the Commonwealth Foundation* [Fund to promote professional exchange within the British Commonwealth]. London: Allen & Unwin, 1982.

Diehl, Carl. *Americans and German Scholarship, 1770–1870.* New Haven, Conn.: Yale University Press, 1978.

Espinosa, J. Michael. *Inter-American Beginnings of U.S. Cultural Diplomacy, 1936–1948.* Washington, D.C.: Department of State, Bureau of Educational and Cultural Affairs, 1976.

Kellermann, Henry J. *Cultural Relations as an Instrument of U.S. Foreign Policy: The Educational Exchange Program between the United States and Germany, 1945–1954.* Washington, D.C.: Department of State, Bureau of Educational and Cultural Affairs, 1978.

Munro, Dana Gardner. *A Student in Central America, 1914–1916.* New Orleans: Tulane University, Middle American Research Institute, 1983.

Roth, Lois. *Public Diplomacy and the Past: The Studies of United States Information and Cultural Programs, 1952–1975.* Washington, D.C.: Department of State, Foreign Service Institute, 1981.

5. Policy—Home Country

a) Articles

Adam, H. M. "Somali Policies towards Education, Training and Manpower." In Maliyamkono, ed. (Sec. 5*b* below), pp. 99–122.

Hunter, Guy. "The Needs and Desires of Developing Countries for Foreign Study Facilities: Some Reflections." In Williams, ed. (Sec. 6*b* below), pp. 135–49.

Kinyanjui, K.; Adholla, M.; and Anaminyi, P. "Evolution of Overseas Training Policy in Kenya." In Maliyamkono, ed. (Sec. 5*b* below), pp. 58–79.

Koloko, E. M. "Origins of Overseas Training for Zambians, 1900–1975." In Maliyamkono, ed. (Sec. 5*b* below), pp. 80–98.

Similane, V. M. "Analysis of Training Policies in Swaziland." In Maliyamkono, ed. (Sec. 5*b* below), pp. 123–30.

Sumra, S., and Ishumi, A. G. "Trends in Tanzania's Policies towards Higher Training." In Maliyamkono, ed. (Sec. 5*b* below), pp. 38–57.

b) Monograph

Maliyamkono, T. L., ed. *Policy Developments in Overseas Training.* Dar es Salaam: Black Star Agencies and Eastern African Universities Research Project, 1980.

6. Policy—Host Country

a) Articles

Kahne, Stephen. "Does the U.S. Need a National Policy on Foreign Students," *Engineering Education* 74 (October 1983): 54–56.

O'Leary, J. "Britain Puts Up the Fees for Overseas Students," *Round Table,* no. 278 (1980), pp. 167–71.

Smith, Alan; Woesler de Panafieu, Christine; and Jarousse, Jean-Pierre. "Foreign Student Flows and Policies in an International Perspective." In Williams, ed. (Sec. 6*b* below), pp. 165–223.

Spaulding, S., and Coelho, G. V. "Research on Students from Abroad—the Neglected Policy Implications." In *Uprooting and Development,* edited by G. V. Coelho and P. I. Ahmed, pp. 321–39. New York: Plenum, 1980.

Vaudiaux, Jacques. "Les Politiques nationales d'access des étudiants étrangers," *CRE-Information,* no. 57 (1st Quarter 1982), pp. 7–24.

Williams, Peter. "The Emergence of the Problem." In Williams, ed. (Sec. 6*b* below), pp. 1–21.

Williams, Peter. "Overseas Students in Britain: The Background." In Williams, ed. (Sec. 6*b* below), pp. 22–46.

Williams, Peter. "The Way Ahead." In Williams, ed. (Sec. 6*b* below), pp. 223–38.

b) Monographs

Australian Government. *Overseas Students Charge Collection Act.* AGPS catalog no. 79 5214 9. Canberra: Australian Government Publishing Service, 1979.

Bristow, R., and Thornton, J. E. C. *Overseas Students and Government Policy, 1962–1979.* London: Overseas Students Trust, 1979.

Canadian Bureau for International Education. *A Question of Self-Interest: A Statement on Foreign Students in Canada.* Ottawa: Canadian Bureau for International Education, 1977.

Carrigan, Owen. *The Right Mix: The Report of the Commission on Foreign Student Policy in Canada.* Ottawa: Canadian Bureau for International Education, 1981.

New Zealand. Department of Education. *Educating Pacific Islanders in New Zealand: A Report of a Conference at Lapdell House, Wellington, 7–12 July 1974.* Wellington: Department of Education, 1975.

New Zealand Students Association. *Submission to the Minister of Education on the Effects of the $1500 Discriminatory Fee for Private Overseas Students.* Wellington: New Zealand Students Association, 1980.

Overseas Students Trust. *Overseas Students and Government Policy.* London: Overseas Students Trust, 1979.

United Kingdom. Department of Education and Science. *Government Observations on the First Report from the Education, Science and Arts Committee* [Of the House of Commons]. H.C. 552-1. Command Paper 8011. London: Her Majesty's Stationery Office, 1980.

United Kingdom. House of Commons. Education, Science and Arts Committee. *The Funding and Organization of Courses in Higher Education: Interim Report on Overseas Student Fees (HC 552-1).* London: Her Majesty's Stationery Office, 1980.

Williams, Peter. *A Policy for Overseas Students.* London: Overseas Students Trust, 1982.

Williams, Peter, ed. *The Overseas Student Question: Studies for a Policy.* London: Heinemann, 1981.

World University Service. *Overseas Students: The Dramatic Decline—the WUS Report.* London: World University Service, 1981.

7. International Students and Host Country (General Issues)

a) Articles

Dahrendorf, Ralf. "Overseas Students—Whither Now?" *Political Quarterly* 53 (October/December 1982): 449–51.

Dickson, D. "New Pentagon Rules on Overseas Students—Secrecy Threat to Sensitive Research Plans," *Nature* 289, no. 5800 (February 26, 1981): 736.

Dickson, D. "Universities Complain at Pentagon Policy—Restrictions on Foreign Students Cause Alarm," *Nature* 290, no. 5806 (April 9, 1981): 435–36.

Edgerton, Wallace B. "Number of Foreign Students Continues to Increase, But at a Slower Rate," *Change* 14 (November/December 1982): 49–51.

Enarson, Harold L. "Response of U.S. Higher Education to Educational Needs of Foreign Students," *Higher Education in Europe* 4 (April/June 1979): 20–23.

Farmer, Richard N., and Hoyt, Ronald E. "Foreign Students in Indiana," *Indiana Business Review* 50 (March/April 1975): 7–9.

Florin, Frits. "Refugee Students in the Netherlands," *Higher Education and Research in the Netherlands* 19, no. 3 (1975): 19–23.

Huang, Lucy Jen. "The Imported Marriage: The Case of Nigerian Student Marriage in the United States," *International Journal of the Sociology of the Family* 8, no. 1 (1978): 37–51.

"Italy: Reprieve for Foreign Students," *Newsletter* (Council of Europe), no. 3 (1977), pp. 24–26.

Lamarsh, J. R., and Miller, M. M. "Weapons Proliferation and Foreign Students," *British Atomic Scientist* 36, no. 3 (1980): 25–30.

Mayol, P., et al. "Les Etudiants," *Esprit, changer la culture et la politique,* no. 11/12 (1978), pp. 188–223.

Øyen, Ørjar. "The Integration of Foreign Students," *CRE-Information,* no. 57 (1st Quarter 1982), pp. 45–59.

Phipps, Michael. "American Society and the Foreign Student," *Community College Social Science Quarterly* 6, no. 3 (1976): 19–23.

Pratt, Alice Reynolds. "Citizen Diplomat: The Community's Role Today" [In educational exchange], *Annals of the American Academy of Political and Social Science* 424 (March 1976): 96–106.

Pratt, Cornelius. "How Media Credibility Ratings of African and U.S. Students Compare," *Journalism Quarterly* 59, no. 4 (1982): 581–87.

Semlak, William D. "Effect of Media Use on Foreign Student Perceptions of U.S. Political Leaders," *Journalism Quarterly* 56, no. 1 (1979): 153–56, 178.

Wallace, William. "Overseas Students: The Foreign Policy Implications." In Williams, ed. (Sec. 6*b* above), pp. 111–34.

b) Monographs

Grieswelle, Detlaf. *Studenten aus Entwicklungsländern: Eine Pilot-Studie.* Munich: Minerva, 1978.

Grubb Institute. *Freedom to Study: Requirements of Overseas Students in the U.K.* London: Overseas Students Trust, 1978.

Jarousse, Jean-Pierre; Smith, Alan; and Woesler, Christine. *Les Etudiants étrangers: Comparaison internationale des flux et des politiques.* Paris: Institut Europeen d'éducation et de politique sociale, 1982.

8. Institutional Policy

a) Articles

Adams, A. H.; Ellyson, G.; and Greene, W. "Effective Programming for Foreign Students in Community and Junior Colleges." In Gleazer, Jr., et al. (Sec. 3*b* above), pp. 53–74.

Diener, Thomas J., and Kerr, L. "Institutional Responsibilities to Foreign Students," *New Directions for Community Colleges,* no. 26 (1979), pp. 49–56.

Gleazer, Edmund J., Jr., "To Transcend the Boundaries." In Gleazer, Jr., et al. (Sec. 3*b* above), pp. 4–13.

Lobkowicz, Nikoloaus. "La Responsibilité éducative de l'université vis-à-vis des étudiants étrangers," *CRE-Information,* no. 57 (1st Quarter 1982), pp. 27–43.

Martorana, S. V. "Constraints and Issues in Planning and Implementing Programs for Foreign Students in Community and Junior Colleges." In Gleazer, Jr., et al. (Sec. 3*b* above), pp. 32–51.

Pyle, C. A. "Graduate Education for International Students." In *Proceedings of the Eighteenth Annual Meeting of the Council of Graduate Schools in the United States: Changing Patterns in Graduate Education,* edited by J. W. Ryan, pp. 120–30. Washington, D.C.: Council of Graduate Schools, 1979.

Rix, J. A. "Impact of Foreign Students on Graduate Education." In *Proceedings of the Eighteenth Annual Meeting of the Council of Graduate Schools in the United States: Changing Patterns in Graduate Education,* edited by J. W. Ryan, pp. 131–33. Washington, D.C.: Council of Graduate Schools, 1979.

b) Monographs

American Council on Education. *Foreign Students and Institutional Policy.* Washington, D.C.: American Council on Education, 1982.

Burn, Barbara B. *Higher Education Reform: Implications for Foreign Students.* New York: Institute of International Education, 1978.

Canadian Bureau for International Education. *Existing Institutional Policies and Practices regarding Foreign Students.* Ottawa: Canadian Bureau for International Education, 1981.

Canadian Bureau for International Education. *Foreign Student Policies in Canadian Universities and Colleges.* Ottawa: Canadian Bureau for International Education, 1981.

College Entrance Examination Board. *The Foreign Undergraduate Student: Institutional Priorities for Action.* New York: College Entrance Examination Board, 1975.

Council of Ontario Universities. *Tuition Fees for Foreign Students: Brief to the Ontario Council on University Affairs, 1977.*

Goodwin, Craufurd D., and Nacht, Michael. *Absence of Decision: Foreign Students in American Colleges and Universities: A Report on Policy Formation and Lack Thereof.* New York: Institute of International Education, 1983.

Hood, Mary Ann G. *235,000 Foreign Students in U.S. Colleges and Universities: Impact and Response.* Washington, D.C.: National Association for Foreign Student Affairs, 1979.

Hubbard, J. R. *Higher Education and the International Student.* Los Angeles: University of Southern California, 1978.

Institute of International Education. *Report on the Survey of Policy Changes toward Foreign Students in Public Institutions of Higher Education.* New York: Institute of International Education, 1981.

Institute of International Education. *Survey of U.S. Public Institutional Policies regarding Foreign Students.* New York: Institute of International Education, 1981.

National Association for Foreign Student Affairs. *The College, the University and the Foreign Student.* Washington, D.C.: National Association for Foreign Student Affairs, 1979.

9. Economics: Costs and Benefits—Home Country

Article

Maliyamkono, T. L., and Wells, S. "Impact Surveys on Overseas Training." In Maliyamkono, ed. (Sec. 5*b* above), pp. 1–37.

10. Economics: Costs and Benefits—Host Country

a) Articles

Blaug, Mark. "The Economic Costs and Benefits of Overseas Students." In Williams, ed. (Sec. 6*b* above), pp. 47–90.

Jenkins, Hugh M. "Economics: Analysing Costs and Benefits." In Jenkins et al. (Sec. 3*b* above), pp. 237–50.

Overseas Students Trust. "Overseas Students and British Commercial Interests." In Williams, ed. (Sec. 6*b* above), pp. 91–110.

Ulivi, Ricardo M., and Jones, Thomas W. "The Economic Impact of International Students on Northwest Arkansas, 1977," *Arkansas Business and Economic Review* 12 (Spring 1979): 22–31.

b) Monographs

Limbird, H. M. *Foreign Students in Iowa: A Preliminary Estimate of Social and Economic Benefits and Costs.* Ames: Iowa State University, Office of International Educational Services, 1979.

London Conference on Overseas Students. *Overseas Students: A Subsidy to Britain (Report of the Working Party on the Costs and Benefits of Overseas Students in the U.K.).* London: London Conference on Overseas Students, 1979.

Sims, W. A., and Stelcner, M. *The Costs and Benefits of Foreign Students in Canada: A Methodology.* Ottawa: Canadian Bureau for International Education, 1981.

Winkler, D. R. *The Economic Impacts of Foreign Students in the United States.* Los Angeles: University of Southern California, School of Public Administration, 1981.

Winkler, D. R. *The Fiscal Consequences of Foreign Students in Public Higher Education: A Case Study of California.* Los Angeles: University of Southern California, School of Public Administration, 1982.

11. Legal Issues (Visas, etc.)

a) Articles

Anthony, Mark W. "Suspension of Deportation: A Revitalized Relief for the Alien (*Kamheangpatiyooth* vs. *Immigration and Naturalization Service*)," *San Diego Law Review* 18 (December 1980): 65–88.

Bedrosian, Alex. "Alien Status: Legal Issues and Institutional Responsibilities." In Jenkins et al. (Sec. 3*b* above), pp. 163–83.

Cooper, Timothy T. "Educating the Foreign and Illegal Alien Student." In *School Law in Contemporary Society,* edited by M. A. McGheney. Topeka, Kans.: National Organization on Legal Problems of Education, 1980.

Dilley, S. C., and McGilskey, D. E. "United States and Foreign Tax Ramifications for a Student Studying or Working Abroad," *Taxes* 57, no. 3 (1979): 170–73.

Fortunato, Joseph A. "Constitutional Law—Equal Protection Does Not Protect Nonimmigrant Iranian Students from Selective Deportation—*Narenji* v. *Civiletti,*" *Seton Hall Law Review* 11, no. 2 (1980): 230–42.

Gray, Julius H. "The Status of Foreign Students under the Immigration Act, 1976" [Canada], *McGill Law Journal* 27 (Summer 1982): 556–62.

McDonald, Nancy J. "Selective Enforcement of Immigration Laws on the Basis of Nationality as an Instrument of Foreign Policy" [With reference to the case of *Narenji* v. *Civiletti,* a class action filed on behalf of nonimmigrant Iranian students], *Notre Dame Lawyer* 56 (April 1981): 704–18.

Maxwell, Janette Fenn. "An Alien's Constitutional Right to Loan, Scholarship and Tuition Benefits of State Supported Colleges and Universities," *California Western Law Review* 14, no. 3 (1979): 514–62.

Olson, Heather. "Immigration Regulations Affecting Practical Training" [Of foreign students]. In National Association for Foreign Student Affairs (Sec. 32*b* below), pp. 15–20.

Smith, Shelagh Kiley. "Alien Students in the United States: Statutory Interpretation and Problems of Control," *Suffolk Transnational Law Journal* 5 (June 1981): 235–50.

Watson, Roy J., Jr. "The Simpson-Mazzoli Bill: An Analysis of Selected Economic Policies," *San Diego Law Review* 20 (December 1982): 97–116.

b) Monographs

Comptroller General of the United States. *Report to the Congress: Better Controls Needed to*

Prevent Foreign Students from Violating the Conditions of Their Entry and Stay While in the United States. Washington, D.C.: General Accounting Office, 1975.

National Association for Foreign Student Affairs. *Adviser's Manual of Federal Regulations Affecting Foreign Students and Scholars.* Rev. ed. Washington, D.C.: National Association for Foreign Student Affairs, 1982.

Smith, Eugene H., and Baron, Marvin. *Faculty Member's Guide to U.S. Immigration Law.* Washington, D.C.: National Association for Foreign Student Affairs, 1980.

12. Recruitment (Policies and Procedures)

a) Articles

Armenio, Joseph A. "Back to the Agora: Marketing Foreign Admissions," *Journal of the National Association of College Admissions Counselors* 22, no. 4 (1978): 30–34.

Fiske, Edward B. "Ethical Issues in Recruiting Students," *New Directions for Higher Education* 9, no. 1 (1981): 41–48.

Jenkins, Hugh M. "Recruitment: Ensuring Educational and Ethical Standards." In Jenkins et al. (Sec. 3*b* above), pp. 113–34.

b) Monographs

College Entrance Examination Board. *Guidelines for the Recruitment of Foreign Students.* New York: College Entrance Examination Board, 1978.

Jenkins, Hugh M., ed. *Foreign Student Recruitment: Realities and Recommendations.* New York: College Entrance Examination Board, 1980.

13. Admission (Policies and Procedures)

a) Articles

Abadzi, Helen. "The Use of Multivariate Statistical Procedures in International Student Admissions," *Journal of College Student Personnel* 21, no. 3 (1980): 195–201.

Arrighi, P. "Recognition of Diplomas in the European Community," *Western European Education* 14 (Spring/Summer 1982): 131–36.

Dixon, Rebecca, et al. "Controversial Issues in Interpreting Foreign Academic Records," *College and University* 51 (Summer 1976): 462–68.

Griff, E. R., et al. "Foreign Credential Evaluation," *College and University* 51 (Summer 1976): 474–82.

Haas, G. J. "Foreign Student Admissions," *College and University* 50 (Summer 1975): 505–12.

Haas, G. J. "Undergraduate Transfer Credits from Abroad," *College and University* 57, no. 2 (1982): 218–25.

Johnson, A. W., and Gotcher, J. R. "Priorities System for Admitting International Students," *International Education and Cultural Exchange* 13 (Spring 1978): 41–47.

Palmer, L. A., and Woodford, P. E. "English Tests: Their Credibility in Foreign Student Admissions," *College and University* 53 (Summer 1978): 500–510.

Patrick, William S. "Admissions: Developing Effective Selection Practices," in Jenkins et al. (Sec. 3*b* above), pp. 135–62.

Ruiz-Fornells, E. "Study in Spain and the Problem of Credit Transfer," *Hispania* 66 (March 1983): 69–74.

Silny, J., and Young, N. W. "Fraudulent Foreign Student Credentials," *College and University* 53 (Summer 1978): 490–98.

b) Monographs

Fisher, S. H., and Dey, W. J. *Forged Educational Credentials: A Sorry Tale.* New York: World Education Services, 1979.

Institute of International Education. *Evaluating Foreign Students' Credentials*. New York: Institute of International Education, 1981.

Merva, George E. *Admissions Criteria for Foreign Students and Graduates of Curricula Other than Agricultural Engineering*. St. Joseph, Mich.: American Society of Agricultural Engineers, 1978.

National Association for Foreign Student Affairs. *Guidelines: English Language Proficiency*. Washington, D.C.: National Association for Foreign Student Affairs, 1977.

National Association for Foreign Student Affairs. *Selection and Admission of Foreign Students*. Washington, D.C.: National Association for Foreign Student Affairs, 1978.

Powers, Donald E. *The Relationships between Scores on the Graduate Management Admission Test and the Test of English as a Foreign Language*. Princeton, N.J.: Educational Testing Service, 1980.

Turner, Solveig M., ed. *Evaluation of Foreign Educational Credentials and Recognition of Degree Equivalences*. Boston: Northeastern University, Center for International Higher Education Documentation, 1979.

Woolston, Valerie, ed. *Foreign Educational Credentials Required for Consideration of Admission to Universities and Colleges in the United States*. Washington, D.C.: U.S. Agency for International Development, Office of International Training, 1981.

14. Administration (Programs and Services)

a) Articles

Garrett, Larry, and Garrett, C. Joanne. "The International Student and Academic Advisement: The Bus Stops Here," *International Education* 10 (Spring 1981): 20–24.

Hansen, Evelyn Unes. "A Brief Statement of Some Needs of Nontraditional Foreign Students in American Colleges and Universities," *Alternative Higher Education* 6, no. 3 (1982): 139–41.

MacArthur, James D. "Career Services for University International Students," *Vocational Guidance Quarterly* 29, no. 2 (1980): 178–81.

Ryan, A. "Welfare Problems and Induction of Overseas Students," *Coombe Lodge Reports* 10, no. 6 (1977): 256–60.

Sharp, T. E. "Institutional Administration and the Foreign Student Program," *College and University* 57, no. 3 (1982): 323–26.

Weill, L. V. "Advising International Students at Small Colleges," *NACADA Journal* 2, no. 1 (1982): 52–56.

Woolston, Valerie. "Administration: Coordinating and Integrating Programs and Services." In Jenkins et al. (Sec. 3*b* above), pp. 184–209.

b) Monographs

Australian Development Assistance Agency. *Interstate Conference of Coordinating Committees and Welfare Officers: Welfare Work with Foreign Students: Conference Proceedings*. Canberra: Australian Government Publishing Service for Australian Development Assistance Agency, 1975.

Baron, M. J., ed. *Advising, Counseling, and Helping the Foreign Student*. Washington, D.C.: National Association for Foreign Student Affairs, 1975.

Canadian Bureau for International Education. *Cross-Canada Survey of Foreign Student Services*. Ottawa: Canadian Bureau for International Education, 1977.

National Association for Foreign Student Affairs. *Guidelines: Academic and Personal Advising*. Washington, D.C.: National Association for Foreign Student Affairs, 1975.

National Association for Foreign Student Affairs. *Orientation of Foreign Students*. Washington, D.C.: National Association for Foreign Student Affairs, 1980.

15. Finances (Sources, Problems, etc.)

a) Articles

Baumer, E. F. "Visas, Financial Support, and Fees for International Students." In *Proceedings of the Eighteenth Annual Meeting of the Council of Graduate Schools in the United States: Changing Patterns in Graduate Education,* edited by J. W. Ryan, pp. 271–77. Washington, D.C.: Council of Graduate Schools, 1979.

Dickey, K. N., and Lovelace, H. D. "Financial Verification for Foreign Students," *College and University* 53 (Summer 1978): 477–81.

Joshi, Joan H. "Finances: Finding the Funds for International Study." In Jenkins et al. (Sec. 3*b* above), pp. 91–112.

b) Monographs

Institute of International Education. *Costs at U.S. Educational Institutions.* New York: Institute of International Education. (Published annually.)

Layard, Richard, and Petoussie, E. *Overseas Students' Fees and the Demand for Education.* London: London School of Economics, Centre for Labour Economics, 1982.

Lurie, Joe, and Miller, Jonathan. *A Foreign Students' Selected Guide to Financial Assistance for Study and Research in the United States.* Adelphi, N.Y.: Adelphi University, 1983.

Phillips, A. *British Aid for Overseas Students.* London: World University Service, 1980.

16. Health

Articles

Cole, J. B.; Allen, F. C. L.; and Green, J. S. "Survey of Health Problems of Overseas Students," *Social Science and Medicine.* Pt. A, *Medical Sociology* 14, no. 6A (1980): 627–31.

Furnham, Adrian, and Tresize, L. "The Mental Health of Foreign Students," *Social Science and Medicine* 17, no. 6 (1983): 365–70.

Henry, C. J., and Wheeler, E. F. "Dietary Patterns among Overseas Students in London," *Proceedings of the Nutrition Society* 39, no. 2 (1980): A47.

Huang, Ken. "Campus Mental Health: The Foreigner at Your Desk," *Journal of the American College Health Association* 25 (February 1977): 216–19.

Itouanga, A. F. "Study of Digestive Parasitism in Lille among Foreign Students" (in French), *Lille Medical* 23, no. 1 (1978): 25–32.

Ko, Y. H. "Mental Health of the Overseas Chinese Students in the New Environment," *Acta Psycologica Taiwanica* 20, no. 2 (1978): 1–7.

Miller, D. F., and Harwell, D. J. "International Students at an American University: Health Problems and Status," *Journal of School Health* 53 (January 1983): 45–49.

Opalka, J.; Mitchell, J.; and Martin, R. "Introducing International Students to the American Food Supply," *Journal of the American Dietetic Association* 82, no. 5 (1983): 531–33.

17. Counseling Services

Articles

Alexandar, A. A.; Klein, Marjorie H.; Workneh, Fikre; and Miller, Milton H. "Psychotherapy and the Foreign Student." In *Counseling across Cultures—Revised and Expanded Edition,* edited by Paul B. Pedersen, Juris G. Draguns, Walter J. Lonner, and Joseph E. Trimble, pp. 227–46. Honolulu: University Press of Hawaii, 1981.

Childs, J. A. "Counseling and the Training of Counselors" [For foreign students], *Coombe Lodge Reports* 10, no. 6 (1977): 261–67.

Dadfar, Sohrabi, and Friedlander, Myran L. "Differential Attitudes of International Students toward Seeking Professional Psychological Help." *Journal of Counseling Psychology* 29, no. 3 (1982): 335–38.

Dillard, John M., and Chisolm, Grace B. "Counseling the International Student in a Multicultural Context," *Journal of College Student Personnel* 24, no. 2 (1983): 101–5.

Higginbotham, H. N. "Cultural Issues in Providing Psychological Services for Foreign Students in the United States," *International Journal of Intercultural Relations* 3 (1979): 49–85.

Ruiz, R. A., and Padilla, A. M. "Counseling Latinos," *Personnel and Guidance Journal* 55 (March 1977): 401–8.

Story, Kathryn E. "The Student Development Professional and the Foreign Student: A Conflict of Values," *Journal of College Student Personnel* 23, no. 1 (1982): 66–70.

Vigushin, Joan. "Helping Campus Personnel Help Foreign Students: A Counseling Simulation," *Humanist Educator* 20, no. 3 (1982): 134–42.

Walter-Samli, Jane H., and Samli, A. Coskun. "A Model of Career Counseling for International Students," *Vocational Guidance Quarterly* 28, no. 1 (1979): 48–55.

Yuen, Rhoda Ka-Wai, and Tinsley, Howard E. A. "International and American Students' Expectancies about Counseling," *Journal of Counseling Psychology* 28, no. 1 (1981): 66–69.

18. Adaptation Problems (The Alien Institutional and Cultural Environment)

a) Articles

Boer, Edward E. "Some Psychosocial Factors Affecting Adaptation and Orientation of Foreign Students." In Dunnett, ed. (Sec. 18*b* below), pp. 34–58.

Bork, Uwe. "The Shock of Studying in Germany: Students from Developing Countries in Germany," *Western European Education* 13, no. 3 (1981): 57–64.

Carey, Philip, and Mariam, Alemaheyu. "Minoritization: Toward an Explanatory Theory of Foreign Student Adjustment in the United States," *Negro Educational Review* 31, nos. 3–4 (1980): 127–36.

Chevrolet, Daniel, et al. "Les Problemes d'adaptation des étudiants étrangers au système universitaire français," *Revue français de pédagogie* 40, no. 3 (1977): 30–44.

Church, A. T. "Sojourner Adjustment," *Psychological Bulletin* 91 (May 1982): 540–72.

Coelho, G. V. "The Foreign Student's Sojourn as a High-Risk Situation—the Culture Shock Phenomenon Re-examined." In *Uprooting and Surviving: Adaptation and Resettlement of Migrant Families and Children,* edited by R. C. Nann, pp. 101–8. Dordrecht: D. Reidel, 1982.

Ebbers, K. DeLyte, and Petersen, Dennis M. "The Seductivity of Stereotypes: Examining American Attitudes toward Foreign Students." In Dunnett, ed. (Sec. 18*b* below), pp. 176–90.

Furnham, Adrian, and Bochner, Stephen. "Social Difficulty in a Foreign Culture: An Empirical Analysis of Culture Shock." In *Cultures in Contact: Studies in Cross-cultural Interaction,* edited by Stephen Bochner, pp. 161–98. Oxford and New York: Pergamon, 1982.

Graham, Morris A. "Acculturative Stress among Polynesian, Asian and American Students on the Brigham Young University—Hawaii Campus," *International Journal of Intercultural Relations* 7, no. 1 (1983): 79–104.

Hojat, Mohammadreza. "Loneliness as a Function of Selected Personality Variables," *Journal of Clinical Psychology* 38, no. 1 (1982): 137–41.

Hull, W. Frank, IV, and Finney, Kevin P. "Longitudinal Case Studies of Foreign Students during Their Initial Educational Sojourn." In Hull (Sec. 18*b* below), pp. 196–224.

Idrus, Faridah K., and Hendry, L. B. "Student Problems in Further Education: Some Home-Overseas Comparisons," *Journal Pendidikan*, no. 4 (October 1976), pp. 39–45.

Johnson, K., and Morrow, K. "Meeting Some Social Language Needs of Overseas Students," *Canadian Modern Languages Review* 33, no. 5 (1977): 694–707.

Kedem, Peri, and Bar-Lev, Mordechai. "Is Giving Up Traditional Religious Culture Part of the Price to Be Paid for Acquiring Higher Education? Adaptation of Academic Western Culture by Jewish Israeli University Students of Middle Eastern Origin," *Higher Education* 12, no. 4 (1983): 373–88.

Kertis, Joan, and O'Driscoll, James. "International Students and Sponsored Programs: Some Considerations." In Dunnett, ed. (Sec. 18*b* below), pp. 141–48.

Klein, Marjorie H. "Adaptation to New Cultural Environments." In *Overview of Intercultural Education, Training and Research*. Vol. 1, *Theory*, edited by David S. Hoopes, Paul B. Pedersen, and George W. Renwick, pp. 49–55. Washington, D.C.: Georgetown University, Society for Intercultural Education, Training and Research, 1977.

Klineberg, Otto. "Practical Implications of Research on International Student Exchange." In Dunnett, ed. (Sec. 18*b* below), pp. 1–15.

Klineberg, Otto, "Stressful Experiences of Foreign Students at Various Stages of Sojourn: Counseling and Policy Implications." In *Uprooting and Development*, edited by G. V. Coelho and Paul I. Ahmed, pp. 271–94. New York: Plenum, 1980.

Michii, Takako N. "Problems of the Cross-cultural Education: The Japanese Case." In Dunnett, ed. (Sec. 18*b* below), pp. 126–36.

Morgan, E. E., Jr. " 'Study Abroad': A Process of Adaptation and Change," *International Review of Education* 21, no. 2 (1975): 207–15.

Pedersen, Paul. "Personal Problem Solving Resources Used by University of Minnesota Foreign Students." In *Topics in Culture Learnings*. Vol. 3, edited by Richard W. Brislin, pp. 55–65. Honolulu: East-West Center, 1975.

Pedersen, Paul. "Role Learning as a Coping Strategy for Displaced Foreign Students." In G. V. Coelho, *Uprooting and Development*, edited by G. V. Coelho and Paul I. Ahmed, pp. 296–320. New York: Plenum, 1980.

Perkins, Carolyn S., et al. "A Comparison of the Adjustment Problems of Three International Student Groups," *Journal of College Student Personnel* 18 (September 1977): 382–88.

Thomas, H., Jr., et al. "Adjustment of International Students," *National Association of Student Personnel Administrators Journal* 18, no. 1 (1980): 40–45.

White, Sheida, and White, Thomas G. "Acculturation of Foreign Graduate Students in Relation to Their English Language Proficiency." In Dunnett, ed. (Sec. 18*b* below), pp. 59–77.

Williams, Joseph F. "A Peer Assistance Program: An Asset for Foreign Student Adaptation." In Dunnett, ed. (Sec. 18*b* below), pp. 149–59.

b) Monographs

Australia. Department of Foreign Affairs. Australian Development Assistance Bureau. *Conference on Educational Difficulties of Overseas Students, 11–12 December, 1980, Canberra.* Canberra: Australian Development Assistance Bureau, 1980.

Claire, E. *Foreign Students' Guide to Dangerous English.* Rochelle Park, N.J.: Eardley, 1980.

Dunnett, Stephen Charles. *A Study of the Effects of an English Language Training and Orientation Program on Foreign Student Adaptation at the State University of New York at Buffalo.* Buffalo: State University of New York at Buffalo, Council on International Studies, 1977.

Dunnett, Stephen Charles, ed. *Factors Affecting the Adaptation of Foreign Students in Cross-cultural Settings.* Special Studies no. 134. Buffalo: State University of New York at Buffalo, Council on International Studies, 1981.

Hull, W. Frank, IV. *Foreign Students in the United States of America: Coping Behaviour within the Educational Environment*. New York: Praeger, 1978.

Lee, Motoko; Adb-Ella, Mokhtar; and Thomas, Linda Burks. *Need Assessment of Foreign Students from Developing Nations: A Research Design: The Final Report of Phase I*. Sociology Report no. 144. Ames: Iowa State University, 1979.

19. Academic Performance (Constraints and Success Factors)

a) Articles

Bejoint, H. "The Foreign Student's Use of Monolingual English Dictionaries—a Study of Language Needs and Reference Skills," *Applied Linguistics* 2, no. 3 (1981): 207–22.

Bie, Karen Nossum. "Norwegian Students at British Universities—a Case Study of the Academic Performances of Foreign Students," *Scandinavian Journal of Educational Research* 20, no. 1 (1976): 1–24.

Brew, A. "Responses of Overseas Students to Differing Teaching Styles." In Greenall and Price, eds. (Sec. 19*b* below), pp. 115–25.

Fox, J., and Hammond, D. "Report of Competency-based Teaching of International Students." In *Improving University Teaching*, pp. 1013–23. College Park: University of Maryland, University College, 1979.

Franck, Marion R., and DeSousa, Michael A. "Foreign T.A.s: A Course in Communication Skills," *Improving College and University Teaching* 30, no. 3 (1982): 111–14.

Hendel, D. D., and Doyle, K. O. "Predicting Success for Graduate Study in Business for English-Speaking and Non–English Speaking Students," *Educational and Psychological Measurement* 38 (Summer 1978): 411–14.

Howes, R.; MacFarlane, Smith; and Shepherd, K. "A Study of the Validity of a Battery of Tests for Predicting the Success of Overseas Students Attending Institutions of Further Education," *Vocational Aspect* 29 (December 1977): 119–25.

Mood, T. A. "Foreign Students and the Academic Library," *RQ [Reference Quarterly]* 22, no. 2 (1982): 175–80.

Saigh, Philip A. "The Validity of the Lorge Thorndike Nonverbal Battery as a Predictor of the Academic Achievement of International Students," *Educational and Psychological Measurement* 41 (Winter 1981): 1315–18.

St. George, R. "Language Achievement for Overseas Students—LATOS: A Kiwi Controversy," *New Zealand Journal of Education* 16, no. 2 (1981): 111–27.

Smith, I. M., et al. "Study of the Abilities and Interests of Overseas Students," *Vocational Aspect of Education* 28 (August 1976): 55–65.

Thomas, Ronald E., and Richardson, John W. "Study of English Proficiency Standards for Foreign Graduate Students," *College and University* 53, no. 2 (1978): 201–8.

b) Monographs

Australia. Commonwealth Department of Education. Education Planning Group. *Academic Progress of Private Overseas Students Who First Enrolled in a Tertiary Course in 1977*. Canberra: Commonwealth Department of Education, Education Planning Group, 1982.

Greenall, G. M., and Price, J. E., eds. *Study Modes and Academic Development of Overseas Students*. ELT [English language teaching] Document 109. London: British Council, 1980.

Mestenhauser, Josef A., et al. *Report of a Special Course for Foreign Student Teaching Assistants to Improve Their Classroom Effectiveness*. Minneapolis: University of Minnesota, International Student Advisor's Office, 1980.

20. Attitudinal and Behavioral Studies

a) Articles

Alexander, Neville. "Alienation from the Second Homeland: German Difficulties in Dealing with Foreigners," *Western European Education* 13, no. 3 (1981): 65–69.

Bochner, Stephen; Buker, Eloise A; and McLeod, Beverly M. "Communication Pattern in an International Student Dormitory: A Modification of the Small World Method," *Journal of Applied Social Psychology* 6, no. 3 (1976): 275–90.

Bochner, Stephen; McLeod, B. M.; and Lin, A. "Friendship Patterns of Overseas Students: A Functional Model," *International Journal of Psychology* 12, no. 4 (1977): 227–94.

Bochner, Stephen, and Orr, Fred E. "Race and Academic Status as Determinants of Friendship Formulation: A Field Study," *International Journal of Psychology* 14, no. 1 (1979): 37–46.

Bowman, J. S. "Learning about American Government: Attitudes of Foreign Students," *Teaching Political Science* 5, no. 2 (1978): 181–91.

Carsello, Carmen, and Creaser, James. "How College Students Change during Study Abroad," *College Student Journal* 10, no. 3 (1976): 276–78.

Cowser, R. L., Jr. "Foreign Student: New Nigger on Campus," *Community College Review* 6 (Summer 1978): 4–7.

Driedger, Leo. "Ethnic Self-Identity: A Comparison of In-Group Evaluations," *Sociometry* 39, no. 2 (1976): 131–41.

Drury, D. W., and McCarthy, J. D. "Social Psychology of Name Change: Reflections on a Serendipitous Discovery" [American students in Denmark], *Social Psychology Quarterly* 43 (September 1980): 310–20.

Hensley, T. R., and Sell, D. K. "Study Abroad Program: An Examination of Impacts on Student Attitudes," *Teaching Political Science* 6 (July 1979): 387–411.

Katz, A. N. "Changing Indian Perceptions of the Indian Government," *Asian Survey* 17 (March 1977): 264–74.

Kelman, Herbert C. "International Interchanges: Some Contributions from Theories of Attitude Change," *Studies in Comparative International Development* 10 (Spring 1975): 83–99.

Marion, Paul B., Jr. "Relationships of Student Characteristics and Experiences with Attitude Changes in a Program of Study Abroad," *Journal of College Student Personnel* 21, no. 1 (1980): 58–64.

Marion, Paul B., Jr., and Thomas, H., Jr. "Residence Hall Proximity to Foreign Students as an Influence on Selected Attitudes and Behaviours of American College Students," *Journal of College and University Student Housing* 10, no. 1 (1980): 16–19.

Matross, Ronald, et al. "American Student Attitudes toward Foreign Students before and during an International Crisis," *Journal of College Student Personnel* 23, no. 1 (1982): 58–65.

Owie, Ikponmwosa. "A Comparative Study of Alienation: American versus Foreign Students," *International Education* 11, no. 2 (1982): 35–38.

Sell, Deborah K. "Research on Attitude Change in U.S. Students Who Participate in Foreign Study Experiences: Past Findings and Suggestions for Future Research," *International Journal of Intercultural Relations* 7, no. 2 (1983): 131–48.

Smith, R. J., et al. "When Is a Stereotype a Stereotype?" [American students in West Germany], *Psychological Report* 46 (April 1980): 599–608.

Suzuki, Eisuki. "Foreign Students and the American Dream," *Yale Review* 68 (Spring 1979): 369–82.

b) Monograph

Klineberg, Otto, and Hull, W. Frank, IV. *At a Foreign University: An International Study of Adaptation and Coping.* New York: Praeger, 1979.

21. Cross-cultural Issues and Activities

a) Articles

Alexander, F. Q. "Foreign Students in the U.S.: New Help for High Schools," *College Board Review,* no. 116 (Summer 1980), pp. 2–6.

Barnes, Leslie R. "Cross-cultural Exchange: How Students Can Frustrate the Aims of Study Abroad Programs," *International Review of Education* 28, no. 3 (1982): 373–76.

Batchelder, Donald. "Training U.S. Students Going Abroad." In *Overview of Intercultural Education, Training and Research.* Vol. 2, *Education and Training,* edited by David S. Hoopes, Paul B. Pedersen, and George W. Renwick, pp. 45–63. Washington, D.C.: Georgetown University, Society for Intercultural Education, Training and Research, 1978.

Baty, R. M., and Dold, E. "Cross-cultural Homestays: An Analysis of College Students' Responses after Living in an Unfamiliar Culture," *International Journal Intercultural Relations* 1, no. 1 (1977): 61–76.

Baumann, Cecilia C. "Enriching the Classroom Experience: International Resources in Your Own Backyard," *Bulletin of the Association of Departments of Foreign Languages* 10, no. 3 (1979): 39–43.

Bochner, Stephen. "Cultural Diversity: Implications for Modernization and International Education." In *Bonds without Bondage: Explorations in Transcultural Interactions,* edited by Krishna Kumar, pp. 231–56. Honolulu: University Press of Hawaii, 1979.

Brislin, Richard W., and Pedersen, Paul. "Potential Audiences for Cross-cultural Orientation Programs: Foreign Students in the United States." In *Cross-cultural Orientation Programs,* edited by Richard W. Brislin and Paul Pedersen, pp. 133–38. New York: Gardner, 1976.

Brislin, Richard W., and Pedersen, Paul. "Potential Audiences for Cross-cultural Orientation Programs: United States Students and Faculty Abroad." In *Cross-cultural Orientation Programs,* edited by Richard W. Brislin and Paul Pedersen, pp. 138–42. New York: Gardner, 1976.

Bulhan, Hussein Abdilahi. "Dynamics of Cultural In-Betweenity: An Empirical Study," *International Journal of Psychology* 15, no. 2 (1980): 105–21.

Christensen, George C., and Thielen, Thomas B. "Cross-cultural Activities: Maximising the Benefits of Educational Interchange." In Jenkins et al. (Sec. 3*b* above), pp. 210–36.

Eng-Kung, Yeh, et al. "Psychiatric Implications of Cross-cultural Education: Chinese Students in the United States." In *The Mediating Person: Bridges between Cultures,* edited by Stephen Bochner, pp. 136–68. Cambridge, Mass.: Schenkman, 1981.

Foust, Stephen, et al., eds. "Dynamics of Cross-cultural Adjustment: From Pre-arrival to Re-entry." In Althen, ed. (Sec. 21*b* below), pp. 7–29.

Hecht, Kathryn A. "Challenging Evaluation to the Cross-cultural Test: Program Evaluation in Cross-cultural Settings," *International Journal of Intercultural Relations* 3, no. 3 (1979): 315–26.

Horner, David, et al., eds. "Cross-cultural Counseling." In Althen, ed. (Sec. 21*b* below), pp. 30–50.

Hull, W. Frank, IV. "Cross-cultural Experimental Programming," *International Review of Education* 27, no. 1 (1981): 64–75.

Kagitcibasi, Cigdim. "Cross-national Encounters: Turkish Students in the United States," *International Journal of Intercultural Relations* 2, no. 2 (1978): 141–60.

Kahne, Merton J. "Cultural Differences: Whose Troubles Are We Talking About?" *International Educational and Cultural Exchange* 11, no. 4 (1976): 36–40.

King, Maxwell C., and Fersh, Seymour C. "General Education through International Intercultural Dimensions," *New Directions for Community Colleges* 10, no. 4 (1982): 49–57.

Klineberg, Otto. "The Role of International University Exchanges." In *The Mediating Person: Bridges between Cultures,* edited by Stephen Bochner, pp. 113–35. Cambridge, Mass.: Schenkman, 1981.

Mashiko, Ellen E. "Preparing Students for Study Outside Their Home Countries." In Jenkins et al. (Sec. 3*b* above), pp. 31–64.

Mestenhauser, Josef A. "Foreign Students as Teachers: Lessons from the Program in Learning with Foreign Students." In Althen, ed. (Sec. 21*b* below), pp. 143–50.

Moran, Robert. "Learning Cross-culturally: The Case Study of Management." In Althen, ed. (Sec. 21*b* below), pp. 138–42.

Nash, D. "The Stranger Group in an Overseas Study Program," *French Review* 49, no. 3 (1976): 366–73.

Nilan, Michael S. "Development of Communication Expectations in Occupational Contexts: A Comparison of U.S. and Foreign Graduate Students," *International Journal of Intercultural Relations* 6, no. 3 (1982): 185–210.

Paige, R. Michael. "Cultures in Contact: On Intercultural Relations among American and Foreign Students in the U.S. University Context." In *Handbook of Intercultural Training.* Vol. 3, *Area Studies in Intercultural Training,* edited by Dan Landis and Richard W. Brislin, pp. 102–3. New York: Pergamon, 1983.

Paige, R. Michael. "Foreign Students as Learning Resources." In *Proceedings of the Central Region Conference on International Agricultural Training.* Urbana-Champaign: University of Illinois, 1978.

Penn, J. R., and Durham, M. L. "Dimensions of Cross-cultural Interaction," *Journal of College Student Personnel* 19 (May 1978): 264–67.

Pusch, Margaret, et al., eds. "Cross-cultural Training." In Althen, ed. (Sec. 21*b* below), pp. 72–103.

Pyle, K. R. "International Cross-cultural Service/Learning: Impact on Student Development" [American students in Jamaica], *Journal of College Student Personnel* 22 (November 1981): 509–14.

Robinson, Beatrice E., and Hendel, Darwin D. "Foreign Students as Teachers: An Untapped Educational Resource," *Alternative Higher Education* 5, no. 4 (1981): 256–69.

Sepmeyer, Inez H., and Sharp, T. E. "What's His Other Name? A Guide to the Usage of Names in 112 Countries of the World," *College and University* 56, no. 3 (1981): 292–98.

Shanaa'a, Joyce. "The Foreign Student: Better Understanding for Better Teaching," *Improving College and University Teaching* 26, no. 4 (1978): 234–46.

Smart, Reginald. "Intercultural Dimensions of Foreign Student Affairs." In *Overview of Intercultural Education, Training and Research.* Vol. 3, edited by David S. Hoopes, Paul B. Pedersen, and George W. Renwick, pp. 44–65. Washington, D.C.: Georgetown University, Society for Intercultural Education, Training and Research, 1978.

b) Monographs

Althen, Gary, ed. *Learning across Cultures: Intercultural Communication and International Educational Exchange.* Washington, D.C.: National Association for Foreign Student Affairs, 1981.

Mestenhauser, Josef A. *Learning with Foreign Students.* Minneapolis: University of Minnesota, International Student Adviser's Office, 1976.

Mestenhauser, Josef A., and Barsig, Dietmar. *Foreign Student Advisers and Learning with Foreign Students.* Washington, D.C.: National Association for Foreign Student Affairs, 1977.

Mestenhauser, Josef A., and Barsig, Dietmar. *Foreign Students as Teachers: Learning with*

Foreign Students. Washington, D.C.: National Association for Foreign Student Affairs, 1978.

Miller, Olive. *Creating a World of Friends: A Twenty Year History of the Community Section of the National Association for Foreign Student Affairs.* Washington, D.C.: National Association for Foreign Student Affairs, 1981.

Neff, Charles B., ed. *New Directions for Experiential Learning: Cross-cultural Learning, no. 11.* San Francisco: Jossey-Bass, 1981.

22. Curricula and Programs of Study (Including Relevance of Curricula)

a) Articles

Cooper, Kenneth J. "Increasing the International Relevance of U.S. Education." In Jenkins et al. (Sec. 3*b* above), pp. 277–94.

Fitterling, Dorothea. "Curricula for Foreigners?" *Western European Education* 13, no. 3 (1981): 38–48.

Fuenzalida, Edmund F. "U.S. Education for the Third World: How Relevant?" *World Higher Education Communiqué* 4 (1981): 15–19.

Kaplan, Robert B. "Meeting the Educational Needs of Other Nations." In Jenkins et al. (Sec. 3*b* above), pp. 253–76.

Ngong-Nassah, E. N. "They Don't Need Ivy in the Third World: Some Thoughts on International Student Training," *Journal of Geography* 81 (September/October 1982): 192–94.

Rawls, James R., and Akpanudo, Moses. "Training Obtained in Developed Countries and Needs of a Developing Country," *International Review of Applied Psychology* 30, no. 4 (1981): 535–52.

Schuh, G. Edward. "The Impact of Foreign Students on U.S. Economic Curricula." In *Higher Education in Economics: The International Dimensions,* edited by Wyn F. Owen et al., pp. 39–45. Boulder, Colo.: Economics Institute, 1981.

Shaner, Willis W. "Instruction in Project Analysis for the LDCs: An Unfilled Need," *Technos* 4, no. 3 (1975): 13–24.

Will, W. Marvin. "American Politics in Comparative Perspective: Thoughts on Teaching the Basic Course to International Students," *Teaching Political Science* 7, no. 4 (1980): 473–80.

Worley, James S. "International Dimensions of Economic Education: A Comment." In *Higher Education in Economics: The International Dimensions,* edited by Wyn F. Owen et al., pp. 46–52. Boulder, Colo.: Economics Institute, 1981.

b) Monographs

Dunnett, Stephen C. *Management Skills Training for Foreign Engineering Students: An Assessment of Need and Availability.* Washington, D.C.: National Association for Foreign Student Affairs, 1982.

Hedges, Bob A. *A Critique of A.I.D./N.A.F.S.A. Workshop: "Appropriate Technology in the Graduate Curriculum."* Washington, D.C.: National Association for Foreign Student Affairs, 1979.

Jenkins, Hugh M. *The Relevance of U.S. Education to Students from Developing Countries: A Report of the Agency for International Development and National Association for Foreign Student Affairs Workshop* [Fourth workshop]. Washington, D.C.: National Association for Foreign Student Affairs, 1980.

Myers, R. B. *Curriculum: U.S. Capacities, Developing Countries' Needs.* New York: Institute of International Education, 1979.

Taylor, Mary Louise, ed. *Curriculum: U.S. Capacities, Developing Countries' Needs: A Study of How Well U.S. Colleges and Universities Are Meeting the Needs of Students from Developing Countries in Selected Fields of Science, Technology Administration and Social Sciences.* New York: Institute of International Education, 1979.

23. International Educational Exchange and Study-Abroad Programs

a) Articles

Barnes, Leslie R. "A Sociological Analysis of an Educational Exchange Programme," *Derham and Newcastle Research Review* 10 (Autumn 1982): 4–8.

Bhasin, K. "Exchange Visits: An Effective Way to Learning," *Convergence* 15, no. 1 (1982): 38–44.

Burn, Barbara B. "Prospects for Student Exchange and Studies Abroad in the Countries of Western Europe," *Higher Education in Europe* 4 (April/June 1979): 17–20.

Burn, Barbara B. "Study Abroad and International Exchanges," *Annals of the American Academy of Political and Social Science* 449 (May 1980): 129–40.

Carter, William D. "Study and Training Abroad in the United Nations," *Annals of the American Academy of Political and Social Science* 424 (March 1976): 67–77.

Davis, Dorothy. "Study Abroad: A Case Study and Some Implications," *International Journal of University Adult Education* 17 (April 1978): 14–23.

Deutsch, K. W., and Merritt, R. L. "Transnational Communications and the International System," *Annals of the American Academy of Political and Social Science* 442 (March 1979): 85–97.

Edgerton, Wallace B. "Who Participates in Educational Exchange?" *Annals of the American Academy of Political and Social Science* 424 (March 1976): 6–15.

Flack, Michael J. "The International Realm as Experience: Experiential Learning in Transnational Contexts." In *Research on Exchanges: Proceedings of the German-American Conference at Wissenschaftzentrum,* by German Academic Exchange Service. Bonn: German Academic Exchange Service (DAAD), 1980.

Flack, Michael J. "Results and Effects of Study Abroad," *Annals of the American Academy of Political and Social Science* 424 (March 1976): 107–18.

Fulbright, I. William. "The Most Significant and Important Activity I Have Been Privileged to Engage in during My Years in the Senate" [The Fulbright Scholarship Program], *Annals of the American Academy of Political and Social Science* 424 (March 1976): 1–5.

Gaer, Felice D. "Scholarly Exchange Programs with Countries Abroad: Should Learning and Politics Mix?" *Vital Issues* 29, no. 10 (1980): 1–6.

Hull, W. Frank, IV, and Lemke, W. H., Jr. "Assessment of Off-Campus Higher Education," *International Review of Education* 21, no. 2 (1975): 195–206.

Hull, W. Frank, IV, and Lemke, Walter H., Jr. "Retrospective Assessment of the United States Senior Fulbright-Hays Program," *International Educational and Cultural Exchange* 13, no. 2 (1978): 6–9.

Hull, W. F., IV, and Van Wart, M. R. "Affordable and Quality International Programing for the 1980s," *Liberal Education* 68 (Fall 1982): 193–99.

"International Educational Relations and Exchange," *College and University* 52, no. 4 (1977): 497–557.

"International Educational Relations and Exchange," *College and University* 55, no. 4 (1980): 323–429.

"International Educational Relations and Exchange," *College and University* 56, no. 4 (1981): 309–425.

"International Exchange and the Future: Symposium," *International Educational and Cultural Exchange* 11 (Summer 1975): 3–44.

James, N. E. "Students Abroad: Expectations versus Reality," *Liberal Education* 62 (December 1976): 599–607.

Jenkins, Hugh M. "Growth and Impact of Educational Interchanges." In Jenkins et al. (Sec. 3*b* above), pp. 4–30.

Joshi, Joan H. "International Exchange in the Arts" [Educational exchange], *Annals of the American Academy of Political and Social Science* 424 (March 1976): 78–84.

Nash, D. "Personal Consequences of a Year of Study Abroad," *Journal of Higher Education* 47 (March 1976): 191–203.

Reichard, John F. "Summary and Agenda for Future Interchanges." In Jenkins et al. (Sec. 3*b* above), pp. 259–318.

Roeloffs, Karl. "International Mobility in Higher Education: The Experience of an Academic Exchange Agency in the Federal Republic of Germany," *European Journal of Education* 17, no. 1 (1982): 37–48.

Smith, Alan. "International Communication through Study Abroad: Some Priorities and Pitfalls for Future Research," *European Journal of Education* 18, no. 2 (1983): 139–50.

Smuckler, Ralph H. "Institutional Linkages: A Key to Successful International Exchanges," *Annals of the American Academy of Political and Social Science* 424 (March 1976): 43–51.

Thiel, F. "Sights, Sounds and Scents—the Physical Side of Foreign Study," *Modern Languages Journal* 64, no. 4 (1980): 434–40.

Tierney, James F., et al. "Exchange, International." In *International Encyclopaedia of Higher Education*. Vol. 4, pp. 1505–98. Los Angeles: Jossey-Bass, 1977.

Wolfson, R. G. "Innovative Living Experience in Israel," *Jewish Education* 44 (Spring 1976): 68–80.

b) *Monographs*

Batchelder, Donald, and Warner, Elizabeth G., eds. *Beyond Experience: The Experiential Approach to Cross-cultural Education*. Brattleboro, Vt.: Experiment in International Living, 1977.

Burn, Barbara B. *Expanding the International Dimension of Higher Education*. San Francisco: Jossey-Bass, 1980.

Crespi, Leo P. *The Effectiveness of the Exchange Program*. Washington, D.C.: U.S. Information Agency, Office of Research, 1978.

Hess, Gerhard. *Freshmen and Sophomores Abroad: Community Colleges and Overseas Academic Programs*. New York: Teachers College Press, 1982.

Hull, W. Frank, IV; Lemke, W. H., Jr.; and Houang, R. T. *The American Undergraduate, Off-Campus and Overseas: A Study of the Educational Validity of Such Programs*. New York: Council on International Educational Exchange, 1977.

International Educational Exchange Liaison Group. *Enhancing American Influence Abroad: International Exchanges in the National Interest*. Washington, D.C.: National Association for Foreign Student Affairs, 1981.

Kadushin, C.; Denitch, B.; and Genevia, L. *An Evaluation of the Experiences of Exchange Participants, 1969/70 through 1974/75*. New York: International Researches and Exchanges Board, 1977.

Klineberg, Otto. *International Educational Exchange*. Paris: Mouton, 1976.

National Association for Foreign Student Affairs. *NAFSA Principles for International Educational Exchange*. Washington, D.C.: National Association for Foreign Student Affairs, 1981.

National Association for Foreign Student Affairs. *Standards and Responsibilities in International Educational Exchange*. Washington, D.C.: National Association for Foreign Student Affairs, 1979.

National Association for Foreign Student Affairs. *Study Abroad: Handbook for Advisers and*

Administrators. Washington, D.C.: National Association for Foreign Student Affairs, 1979.

Rose, Peter Q. *Academic Sojourners: A Report on the Senior Fulbright Programs in East Asia and the Pacific.* Washington, D.C.: Department of State, Bureau of Educational and Cultural Affairs, Office of Policy and Plans, 1976.

Ruiz-Fornells, Enrique, and Ruiz-Fornells, Cynthia Y. *Symposium on American Academic Programs in Mexico, Spain and Other Spanish and Portuguese Speaking Countries, Madrid, 1978.* Madrid: Sociedad general española de librería, 1979.

United States. General Accounting Office. *Flexibility—Key to Administering Fulbright-Hays Exchange Program: Report to Congress.* Government Printing Office monthly catalog no. 80-10351. Washington, D.C.: Government Printing Office, 1979.

Winks, Robin W. *A Report on Some Aspects of the Fulbright-Hays Program.* New Haven, Conn.: Yale University Press, 1977.

Woodrow Wilson International Center for Scholars. *The Fulbright Program in the Eighties: Summary of Conference Proceedings.* Washington, D.C.: Woodrow Wilson International Center for Scholars, 1980.

Yarrington, Roger, ed. *Internationalizing Community Colleges.* Washington, D.C.: American Association of Community and Junior Colleges, 1978.

24. Disciplinary Studies (Engineering, Law, Medicine, etc.)

a) Articles

Abu-Saad, H., et al. "Asian Nursing Students in the United States," *Journal of Nursing Education* 21 (September 1982): 11–15.

Abu-Saad, H., et al. "Latin American Nursing Students in the United States," *Journal of Nursing Education* 21 (September 1982): 16–21.

Abu-Saad, H., and Kayser-Jones, J. S. "Middle-Eastern Nursing Students in the United States," *Journal of Nursing Education* 21 (September 1982): 22–25.

Adams, M. "Teaching Students from Other Cultures," *Journal of Chemical Education* 58 (December 1981): 1010–12.

Ahimaz, F. J. "Organizational Need—Institutional Triumvirate to Structure and Offer Relevant Engineering Education at United States Universities for International Students." In *Proceedings: 1979 Frontiers in Education Conference,* edited by L. P. Grayson and J. M. Biedenbach, pp. 194–97. Washington, D.C.: American Society for Engineering Education, 1979.

Allen, M. E. M. "Problem of Communication in a Summer Workshop for Foreign Nurses: Psychiatric Nursing," *Journal of Nursing Education* 19 (January 1980): 8–12.

Ayers, Jerry B., and Peters, R. Martin. "Predictive Validity of the Test of English as a Foreign Language for Asian Graduate Students in Engineering, Chemistry or Mathematics," *Educational and Psychological Measurement* 37, no. 2 (1977): 461–63.

Babiker, I. E.; Cox, J. L.; and Miller, P. M. "The Measurement of Cultural Distance and Its Relationship to Medical Consultations, Symptomatology and Examination Performance of Overseas Students at Edinburgh University," *Social Psychiatry* 15, no. 3 (1980): 109–16.

Baume, C. A. "United States University and the Foreign Student." In *Proceedings: 1979 Frontiers in Education Conference,* edited by L. P. Grayson and J. M. Biedenbach, pp. 65–68. Washington, D.C.: American Society for Engineering Education, 1979.

Berendt, H. "Issue of Change: Its Relationship to Teaching Foreign Nursing Students: Attitudes toward Mental Illness and Psychiatric Patients," *Journal of Nursing Education* 19 (January 1980): 4–7.

Brook, P. "Training Opportunities for Overseas Psychiatrists," *British Journal of Psychiatry* 127 (August 1975): 179–84.

Browder, Halbert C. "Foreign Dental Graduates: Admission Criteria and Predicted Success in an American Dental School," *Journal of Dental Education* 44, no. 10 (1980): 580–84.

Bugliarello, George. "International Concerns in Engineering Education," *Engineering Education* 72 (January 1982): 266–68.

Burris, Conrad T., and Crewe, Colin. "International Co-operation between Industry and Education," *Engineering Education* 72 (January 1982): 317–19.

Carter, Jane Robbins. "Multi-cultural Graduate Library Education," *Journal of Education for Librarianship* 18, no. 4 (1978): 295–314.

Chandra, Suresh. "Junior Year Abroad: An International Dimension to Engineering Education," *Engineering Education* 72 (January 1982): 280–83.

Chen, R. M. "Education and Training of Asian Foreign Medical Graduates in the United States," *American Journal of Psychiatry* 135, no. 4 (1978): 451–53.

Chesson, Eugene. "The Future Shortage of Faculty: A Crisis in Engineering," *Engineering Education* 70 (April 1980): 731–38.

Chiang, Shing Ho, and Andersen, Hans O. "Perception of Undergraduate Education in Physics by Chinese Physics Graduate Students Studying in Taiwan and the United States," *School Science and Mathematics* 82, no. 6 (1982): 470–77.

Clapper, T. H. "Teaching American Government to Foreign Students," *Teaching Political Science* 3, no. 3 (1976): 311–16.

Cornish, D. "British Councils Role in Education and Training in the Library and Information-Science Field." In *Education and Training Theory and Provision,* pp. 85–87. The Hague: Fédération internationale de documentation, 1979.

Cox, J. L.; Babiker, I. E.; and Miller, P. M. "Psychiatric Problems and 1st Year Examinations in Overseas Students at Edinburgh University," *Journal of Adolescence* 4, no. 3 (1981): 261–70.

Damarin, S., and West, G. "Preparation of Foreign Graduate Students to Teach Mathematics: An Experimental Course," *American Mathematical Monthly* 86 (June/July 1979): 494–97.

Dhillon, Gita L., and Litwack, Lawrence. "Study Programs for Foreign Nurses," *Nursing Outlook* 24 (January 1976): 41–44.

Dickinson, John C., and Stump, John E. "Transfer of Students from U.S. and Foreign Veterinary Schools—Admissions and Performance," *Journal of Veterinary Medical Education* 7, no. 2 (1980): 91–93.

Drury, R. K., and Dhillon, Gita L. "Study Programs for Foreign Nurses," *Nursing Outlook* 24 (January 1976): 41–44.

Evett, Jack B. "Cozenage: A Challenge to Engineering Instruction" [Foreign students], *Engineering Education* 70 (February 1980): 434–36.

Fitch, R. K. "Experiences of a Postgraduate Physics Course Tutor with Overseas Students." In Greenall and Price, eds. (Sec. 19*b* above), pp. 44–49.

Fouad, A. A., and Jones, E. C. "Electrical-Engineering Curriculum and the Education of International Students," *IEEE Transactions on Education* 22, no. 2 (1979): 95–98.

Giorgis, Tedla W., and Helms, Janet E. "Training International Students from Developing Nations as Psychologists: A Challenge for American Psychology," *American Psychologist* 33, no. 10 (1978): 945–51.

Goodyear, A. "International Co-operation in Engineering Education." In *Proceedings: 1979 Frontiers in Education Conference,* edited by L. P. Grayson and J. M. Biedenbach, pp. 238–43. Washington, D.C.: American Society for Engineering Education, 1979.

"Guidelines for Schools Offering a Health Education Major Which Accept International Students," *Journal of School Health* 49, no. 5 (1979): 267–74.

Haak, A. H. "The International Agricultural Centre (IAC)" [And foreign students], *Higher Education and Research in the Netherlands* 20, no. 2 (1976): 19–23.

Hammond, S. B., and Kanter, M. A. "Nuclear Power Project Training for Engineers from Developing Countries," *Engineering Education* 72 (January 1982): 314–16.

Iverson, S. C. "Developmental Engineering Science Program for International Students." In *Proceedings: 1979 Frontiers in Education Conference*, edited by L. P. Grayson and J. M. Biedenbach, pp. 231–34. Washington, D.C.: American Society for Engineering Education, 1979.

Johnson, David. "Engineering Studies in Britain for Students from Commonwealth Developing Countries," *European Journal of Engineering Education* 6, no. 3/4 (1981): 253–62.

Jonas, S. "State Approval of Foreign Medical Schools—Ensuring the Quality of the Training of the Students and Graduates from Foreign Medical Schools Entering New York State," *New England Journal of Medicine* 305, no. 1 (1981): 45–48.

Kay, J. M. "Veterinary Education Abroad: An Alternative for American Students—or Exile?" *Modern Veterinary Practice* 61, no. 6 (1980): 492–95.

Kayser-Jones, J. S., et al. "Canadian and European Students in the United States," *Journal of Nursing Education* 21 (September 1982): 26–31.

Kelly, Judith. "Latin American Business Students Learn the Harvard Hustle," *Change* 8, no. 8 (1976): 13–17.

Kim, Hae A. "Transplantation of Psychiatrists from Foreign Cultures," *Journal of the American Academy of Psychoanalysis* 4, no. 1 (1976): 105–12.

Lancour, H., et al. "Comparative Education: The International Student—an Asset to the Graduate Library School." In *Administrative Aspects of Education for Librarianship: A Symposium*, edited by Mary B. Cassata and Herman L. Totten, pp. 339–49. Metuchen, N.J.: Scarecrow, 1975.

Leone, L. P. "Orienting Nurses from Other Countries to Graduate Education in the United States," *Journal of Nursing Education* 21 (September 1982): 45–47.

Levinson, R. M. "Experiential Education Abroad: Comparative Health Care Systems Program," *Teaching Sociology* 6, no. 4 (1979): 415–19.

Levinson, R. M. "Potentials of Cross Cultural Field Study: Emory's Comparative Health Care Systems Program in London," *Journal of Nursing Education* 18 (November 1979): 46–52.

Lipson, C. S. "Preparing for an Influx of Foreign Students in Technical Writing Courses—Understanding Their Background." In *Technical Communication: Perspectives for the Eighties*. Pt. 1, edited by J. C. Mathes and T. E. Pinelli, pp. 173–80. Washington, D.C.: National Aeronautics and Space Administration, 1981.

Luxenberg, M. N. "Present and Future Training of Foreign Ophthalmologists in the U.S.A.—Perspective of Association of University Professors of Ophthalmology," *Ophthalmology* 90, no. 2 (1983): 59A–63A.

McDermott, John F., and Maretzki, Thomas W. "Some Guidelines for the Training of Foreign Medical Graduates: Results of a Special Project," *American Journal of Psychiatry* 132, no. 6 (1975): 658–61.

Maloney, J. O. "Broader Training for Foreign Engineering Students," *Technos* 5 (July/September 1976): 41–51.

Mason, Hugh, and Tunbridge, John. "Academic Exchange: A Practical Guide to Promise, Planning and Pitfalls," *Journal of Geography of Higher Education* 4 (Spring 1980): 23–30.

Mick, S. S. "Los médicos graduados en el extranjero," *Universidades* 16, no. 3 (1976): 48–61.

Mitchell-Bateman, Mildred. "The Foreign Medical Graduate in American Psychiatry: The Viewpoint of a Psychiatric Administrator," *Psychiatric Opinion* 13, no. 4 (1976): 24–30.

Mittel, Neuman S. "The Foreign Medical Graduate in American Psychiatry: Perspectives, 1976," *Psychiatric Opinion* 13, no. 4 (1976): 6–13.

Morrison, B. L. "Conflicts and Frustration Influencing Nurses from Other Countries," *Journal of Nursing Education* 19 (January 1980): 12–19.

Mura, Elaine L., et al. "Medical Competence: Is the ECFMG Examination a Relevant Measure?" *Journal of Medical Education* 51, no. 2 (1976): 127–29.

Ndegwa, Eric. "The Pitfalls of Library Education in the U.K.: A Personal View of a Foreign Student," *Assistant Librarian* 73 (July/August 1980): 99–101.

Okanes, M. M., and Murray, L. W. "Machiavellian and Achievement Orientations among Foreign and American Master's Students in Business Administration," *Psychological Reports* 50, no. 2 (1982): 519–26.

Ordonez, J. "Problems of Foreign Graduate Students and Factors Limiting Their Expectations," *Journal of Animal Science* 45, no. 4 (1977): 919–22.

"Over There! Over There! Summer Law Programs Abroad," *Student Law* 10 (February 1982): 29–34.

Peuse, H. Gene. "Training Foreign Students—Implications for Teachers and Agricultural Programs," *National Association of College Teachers of Agriculture Journal* 27, no. 1 (1983): 31–34.

Reyesguerra, D. R. "Quality of United States Engineering Education vs. the Needs of Less Developed Countries." In *Proceedings: 1979 Frontiers in Education Conference,* edited by L. P. Grayson and J. M. Biedenbach, p. 237. Washington, D.C.: American Society for Engineering Education, 1979.

Richert, J. A.; Schimpfh, F.; and Papp, K. "Prescription-based Educational Training Program for United States Students Returning from Foreign Medical Schools," *New York State Journal of Medicine* 80, no. 5 (1980): 811–15.

Russo, Celia. "The European Engineering Programme: A Joint Venture," *European Journal of Education* 17, no. 1 (1982): 59–64.

Saracevic, T. "The United States Information Science Programs and Foreign Students—One-Way or Two-Way Street." In *Proceedings of the American Society for Information Science.* Vol. 19, *1982,* edited by Anthony E. Petrarca, Celianna I. Taylor, and Robert S. Kohn, pp. 265–67. Washington, D.C.: American Society for Information Science, 1982.

Saurwein, V. "Evaluation and Placement of International Engineering Students in the United States Universities—United Nations Connections." In *Proceedings: 1979 Frontiers in Education Conference,* edited by L. P. Grayson and J. M. Biedenbach, pp. 69–72. Washington, D.C.: American Society for Engineering Education, 1979.

Schmiedeck, Raoul A. "The Foreign Medical Graduate and the Nature of Emigration," *Psychiatric Opinion* 15, no. 3 (1978): 38–40.

Shaner, W. W. "Teaching Engineering Students from Developing Countries," *Engineering Education* 69 (November 1978): 214–15.

Shaw, Robert A. "The Stranger in Our Midst: Liability or Asset?" *Engineering Education* 72 (January 1982): 310–13.

Sprinkle, Robert M. "International Work Assignments for Co-op Students: Some Issues to Be Considered," *Journal of Cooperative Education* 17, no. 3 (1981): 99–108.

Suzuki, N. "Chase of the Wild Geese Flying Pattern of Foreign Business Students at United States Business Schools—Why It Has Happened," *Management International Review* 19, no. 4 (1979): 95–110.

Trakman, L. E. "Need for Legal Training in International Comparative and Foreign

Law—Foreign Lawyers at American Law Schools," *Journal of Legal Education* 27, no. 4 (1976): 509–51.

Turack, Daniel C. "Access to the State Bar Examination for Foreign Trained Graduates: The Ohio Experience," *Ohio Northern University Law Review* 8 (April 1981): 265–98.

Tyler, Varro E. "Admission and Placement of Foreign Graduate Students," *American Journal of Pharmaceutical Education* 41, no. 4 (1977): 385–88.

Watt, J. C. "Performance of Overseas Postgraduate Students: A Management Teacher's View." In Greenall and Price, eds. (Sec. 19*b* above), pp. 38–43.

Way, P. O.; Jensen, L. E.; and Goodman, L. J. "Foreign Medical Graduates and Issue of Substantial Disruption of Medical Services," *New England Journal of Medicine* 299, no. 14 (1978): 745–51.

Weinstein, Sanford A.; Barthalow, Patricia; and Hamburg, Marian V. "The Effects of Study Abroad on Health Educators' Attitudes toward International Health Efforts," *Journal of School Health* 46 (December 1976): 599–601.

Weiss, James M., and Davis, David. "Predicting Success in Psychiatric Training for Foreign Medical Graduates. II. Patterns in Course," *Psychological Medicine* 7, no. 2 (1977): 311–16.

Wise, M. "Visitors to Britain" [Foreign students studying librarianship], *Library Review* 28 (Winter 1979): 254–58.

Wotiz, J. H. "Education of Foreign Chemists in America," *Journal of Chemical Education* 54, no. 7 (1977): 413–16.

b) Monographs

Bennett, John Makepeace. *Effectiveness of Australian Tertiary Educational Training for South East Asia over Last Quarter Century.* Technical Report no. 108. Sydney: University of Sydney, Basser Department of Computer Science, 1976.

Dubé, W. F. *Characteristics of U.S. Citizens Seeking Transfer from Foreign to U.S. Medical Schools in 1975 via the Coordinated Transfer Application System (COTRANS)* [Final report]. Washington, D.C.: Association of American Medical Colleges, 1977.

Dubé, W. F. *Trend Study of Coordinated Transfer Application System (COTRANS) Participants, 1970 through 1976: Final Report.* Washington, D.C.: Association of American Medical Colleges, Division of Student Studies, 1977.

Mejia, Alfonso; Pizurki, Helena; and Royston, Erica. *Foreign Medical Graduates: The Case of the United States.* Lexington, Mass.: Lexington Books, 1980.

National Science Foundation. *Foreign Participation in U.S. Science and Engineering Higher Education and Labor Markets.* American Statistical Index accessions no. 9626-6.7; Government Printing Office monthly catalog no. 82-19618. Washington, D.C.: National Science Foundation, 1981.

National Science Foundation. *Scientists and Engineers from Abroad: Trends of the Past Decade: 1966–1975.* National Science Foundation publication no. 28. Government Printing Office monthly catalog no. 77-15369; American Statistical Index accessions no. 9626-1.28. Washington, D.C.: Government Printing Office, 1977.

Pfau, Richard H. *Teaching Expectations and Related Backgrounds of Foreign Science and Engineering Students at the University of Pittsburgh.* Pittsburgh: University of Pittsburgh, University Center for International Studies, 1976.

United States. General Accounting Office. *Policies on U.S. Citizens Studying Medicine Abroad Need Review and Reappraisal: Report to the Congress by the Comptroller General of the United States.* Washington, D.C.: General Accounting Office and Government Printing Office, 1980.

United States. House of Representatives. Committee on Interstate and Foreign Commerce. Sub-committee on Health and the Environment. *Oversight—GAO Report on U.S. Foreign*

Medical Graduates: Hearing before the Sub-committee on Health and the Environment of the Committee on Interstate and Foreign Commerce, House of Representatives, Ninety-sixth Congress, Second Session, on Quality of Medical Education Received by U.S. Citizens Studying Abroad, November 21, 1980. Y.4In8/4:96–221. Washington, D.C.: Government Printing Office, 1981.

25. Specific Student Nationality Studies

a) Articles

Bourne, Peter G. "The Chinese Student: Acculturation and Mental Illness," *Psychiatry* 38, no. 3 (1975): 269–77.

Bowers, R. "The Background of Students from the Indian Sub-Continent." In Greenall and Price, eds. (Sec. 19*b* above), pp. 104–13.

Brown, Carole, et al. "Reasoning about Implication: A Comparison of Malaysian and Australian Subjects" [University students], *Journal of Cross-cultural Psychology* 11 (December 1980): 395–410.

Brown, M. Archer. "U.S. Students Abroad." In Jenkins et al. (Sec. 3*b* above), pp. 65–86.

Bulhan, Hussein Abdilahi. "Reactive Identification, Alienation, and Locus of Control among Somali Students," *Journal of Social Psychology* 104 (February 1978): 69–80.

Castillo, Leonel J. "I.N.S. Arrests and Detention of 180 Unidentified Iranian Students in Chicago, Illinois (May 1978 Memo)." In *Departments of State, Justice, and Commerce: The Judiciary and Related Agencies Appropriations for 1980.* Pt. 5, *Department of Justice* [Congressional hearings], pp. 565–71. Government Printing Office monthly catalog no. 79-18889. Washington, D.C.: Government Printing Office, 1979.

Chunnual, N., and Marsella, A. J. "Convergent and Discriminant Validation of a Traditionalism-Modernism Attitude Questionnaire for Thai Exchange Students," *Journal of Social Psychology* 96, no. 1 (1975): 21–26.

Dalheimer, R. "FH Special—to Portsmouth for the Bachelor's Degree: Experiences with Study Abroad" [German students], *Western European Education* 13 (Fall 1981): 49–56.

Djao, A. W. "Industrialism and Education: Influx of Hong Kong Students to Canadian Universities," *Journal of Contemporary Asia* 12, no. 2 (1982): 216–25.

Drettakis, E. G. "Greek Students in Foreign Universities," *European Journal of Education* 13, no. 3 (1978): 85–106.

Dudley-Evans, A., and Swales, J. "Study Modes and Students from the Middle East." In Greenall and Price, eds. (Sec. 19*b* above), pp. 91–103.

Hasan, R. "Socialization and Cross-cultural Education" [Indo-Pakistani students studying in Britain], *Linguistics,* no. 175 (1976), pp. 7–25.

Hawkey, R., and Nakornchai, C. "Thai Students Studying." In Greenall and Price, eds. (Sec. 19*b* above), pp. 70–78.

Hodgkin, Mary C. "Acculturative Stress among Asian Students in Australia," *Australian Journal of Social Issues* 13 (May 1978): 139–50.

Hojat, Mohammadreza. "Psychometric Characteristics of the UCLA Loneliness Scale: A Study with Iranian College Students," *Educational and Psychological Measurement* 42, no. 3 (1982): 917–25.

Kumagai, Fumie. "The Effects of Cross-cultural Education on Attitudes and Personality of Japanese Students," *Sociology of Education* 50 (January 1977): 40–47.

Kuo, H. K., and Marsela, A. J. "Meaning and Measurement of Machiavellianism in Chinese and American College Students," *Journal of Social Psychology* 101 (April 1977): 165–73.

Kurlansky, M. J. "Students and Colleges Profit from American Study Abroad in France," *Change* 13 (March 1981): 48–51.

Liebesny, H. J. "Lawyers from Developing Countries in the United States: A Special Cultural Shock" [Afghan students in United States], *Middle Eastern Journal* 34 (Spring 1980): 205–13.

McNown, John S. "African Students of Engineering at Home and in the U.S.," *Technos* 4 (July/September 1975): 43–56.

Meleis, Afaf I. "Arab Students in Western Universities: Social Properties and Dilemmas," *Journal of Higher Education* 53, no. 4 (1982): 439–47.

Mellor, W. L., and Begum, Z. "Bangladeshi Students in Australia: Some Background," *Unicorn* 4 (July 1978): 142–56.

Nassefat, Morteza, and Madani-Wells, Joy. "Iranian Students Abroad," *Iranian Review of International Relations* (Spring 1976), pp. 19–47.

Ntiri, Daphne Williams. "Continuing Education Efforts of African Students' Wives in the United States," *Journal of the National Association for Women Deans, Administrators, and Counselors* 42 (Summer 1979): 16–21.

Onwere, Godfrey O. "Factors Associated with Interest in Science of West African Students in Washington, D.C." [University students], *Journal of Negro Education* 49, no. 2 (1980): 207–14.

Oshodin, Osayuki G. "Alcohol Abuse among Nigerian College Students in New York Area of the United States," *College Student Journal* 16, no. 2 (1982): 153–57.

Parker, Orin D. "Cultural Clues to the Middle Eastern Student," *International Educational and Cultural Exchange* 12, no. 2 (1976): 12–18.

Payind, Mohammad Alam. "Academic, Personal and Social Problems of Afghan and Iranian Students in the United States," *Educational Research Quarterly* 4 (Summer 1979): 3–11.

Peuse, H. Gene. "Agricultural Education in a Cross-national Context: Problem Solving among Nigerian Students," *Journal of the American Association of Teacher Educators in Agriculture* 24, no. 2 (1983): 30–33, 39.

Pruitt, France J. "The Adaptation of African Students to American Society," *International Journal of Intercultural Relations* 2, no. 1 (1978): 90–118.

Rahn, H. "Aid to Study Abroad: Experiences and Implications" [German students], *Western European Education* 11 (Fall/Winter 1979–80): 150–64.

Sabato, L. "Yank at Oxford in the Bicentennial Year," *Virginia Quarterly Review* 52 (Summer 1976): 476–85.

Smith, P. C. "Work as Education: A Polynesian Illustration" [Polynesian students in the United States], *Journal of Cooperative Education* 17 (Spring 1981): 64–73.

Tan, A. S. "Television Use and Social Stereotypes" [Chinese students in the United States], *Journalism Quarterly* 59 (Spring 1982): 119–22.

Thomas, Katrina, and Tracy, William. "America as Alma Mater" [A study of Arab students in the United States and Saudi Arabian alumni of American universities who have returned home], *Aramco World Magazine* 30 (May/June 1979): 1–32.

Vanegas, Luz M. "An Overview of the Adaptation Problems of Latin American Students." In Dunnett, ed. (Sec. 18*b* above), pp. 137–40.

Walgren, Doug, et al. "Taiwan Surveillance and Harassment of Taiwanese University Students in the U.S." In *Taiwan Agents in America and the Death of Professor Wen-Chen Chen* [Congressional hearings], pp. 22–59. Government Printing Office monthly catalog no. 82–15117. Washington, D.C.: Government Printing Office, 1981.

Watkins, David, and Astilla, Estela. "Self-Esteem and Causal Attribution of Achievement: A Filipino Investigation," *Australian Psychologist* 15, no. 2 (1980): 219–25.

Watson, Barbara M., and Crosland, David W. "Review of U.S. Policy on Iranian Immigration in Light of November 1979 Takeover of the American Embassy in Iran" [Includes students]. In *U.S. Immigration Policy regarding Iranian Nationals,* pp. 2–33. Government

Printing Office monthly catalog no. 81-5285. Washington, D.C.: Government Printing Office, 1980.

Wicks, P. "Asian Students in Australia: Policies and Issues," *Unicorn* 4 (July 1978): 135–41.

Williams, Peter. "Look West? Asian Attitudes to Study Abroad and Britain's Response," *Asian Affairs* 14 (February 1983): 15–26.

Yao, Esther Lee. "Chinese Students in American Universities," *Texas Tech Journal of Education* 10, no. 1 (1983): 35–42.

Yavas, U. "Attitudes of Turkish Students toward International Business and Foreign Firms," *Akron Business and Economic Review* 11, no. 1 (1980): 34–38.

Yeh, Eng-Kung, et al. "Psychiatric Implications of Cross-cultural Education: Chinese Students in the U.S.A.," *Acta Psychologica Taiwanica* 21, no. 1 (1979): 1–26.

b) Monographs

African American Institute. *Annual Report.* New York: African American Institute, 1954–. (Published annually.)

Al-Banyan, A. S. *Saudi Students in the United States.* London: Ithaca Press, 1980.

Althen, Gary L., ed. *Students from the Arab World and Iran.* Washington, D.C.: National Association for Foreign Student Affairs, 1978.

American Council on Education. Overseas Liaison Committee. *An Analysis of the U.S.-Iranian Cooperation in Higher Education.* Washington, D.C.: American Council on Education, 1976.

American Council on Education. Overseas Liaison Committee. *Future Nigerian-U.S. Linkages in Higher Education.* Washington, D.C.: American Council on Education, 1977.

Chu, Jennings P. *Chinese Students in America: Qualities Associated with Their Success.* New York: AMS Press, 1978.

Cracknell, B. E.; Stonemann, R.; and Haines, R. B. W. *An Evaluation of the Training Received by the Bangladesh Study Fellows in the U.K.* London: Ministry of Overseas Development, 1977.

Jenkins, Hugh M., and Lockyear, Frederick. *Iranian Students in the United States: Status Report.* Washington, D.C.: National Association for Foreign Student Affairs, 1979.

Pfau, Richard H. *Education Skills Training Project—Nepal: Final Report and Process Evaluation.* Storrs: University of Connecticut, Institute of Public Service, 1981.

Pruitt, France J. *The Adaptation of African Students to American Education.* Buffalo: State University of New York at Buffalo, 1977.

Thomas, Katrina, and Tracy, William. *Arab Students in the United States.* Brooklyn, N.Y.: Revisionist Press, 1979.

26. Specific Institution Studies

a) Articles

Abrams, Irwin. "The Impact of Antioch Education through Experience Abroad," *Alternative Higher Education: Journal of Nontraditional Studies* 3 (Spring 1979): 176–87.

Hsiao, Kung-ch'üan. "Pursuit of Learning on a New Continent. I. Three Years at the University of Missouri," *Chinese Studies in History* 12, no. 2 (1978–79): 3–24.

b) Monographs

Bailey, Robert L., and Powell, Frances. *Undergraduate Foreign Student Review.* Berkeley: University of California, Berkeley, Office of Admissions and Records, 1978.

Brusick, Kathleen. *Report on International Students Enrolled Fall Semester 1974, Rockville Campus.* Rockville, Md.: Montgomery Community College, Office of Institutional Research, 1975.

Dalili, Farid. *The International Student Office at the University of Akron: From People Processing to People Changing.* Akron, Ohio: University of Akron, International Student Office, 1982.

Duggan, Susan J., and Wollitzer, Peter A. *The World's Students in Bay Area Universities.* San Francisco: Bay Area and the World, 1983.

Hendricks, Glenn L., and Skinner, Kenneth A. *Economic and Social Coping Strategies of Foreign Students.* Research Bulletin, vol. 15, no. 23. Minneapolis: University of Minnesota, Office for Student Affairs, 1975.

Hendricks, Glenn L., and Zander, David. *Impact of an Orientation Program for Foreign Students.* Research Bulletin, vol. 16, no. 4. Minneapolis: University of Minnesota, Office for Student Affairs, 1975.

International Education at Michigan State University in an Interdependent World. East Lansing: Michigan State University, 1980.

Leong, Frederick T. L., and Sedlacek, William E. *A Survey of Incoming International Students.* Research Report no. 6-82. College Park: University of Maryland College Park, Counseling Center, 1982.

Overall, J. U. *First-Time International and Domestic Freshmen: Enrollment Trends and Characteristics* [At the University of Southern California]. Report no. UCS-OIS-RM-81-103. Los Angeles: University of Southern California, Office of Institutional Studies, 1981.

Overall, J. U. *International and Domestic Undergraduates: Enrollment Trends and Characteristics.* Report no. UCS-OIS-RM-81-105. Los Angeles: University of Southern California, Office of Institutional Studies, 1981.

Report on the Task Force on Visiting International Students in Alberta. Edmonton: University of Alberta, 1979.

Robertson, Daniel L. *Evaluation of 1981 Nihon University Overseas Summer Training Program: Final Report* [Japan]. Urbana-Champaign: University of Illinois at Urbana-Champaign, Office of the Program of Overseas University Collaboration, 1981.

Rust, Val D. *The Foreign Student at the UCLA Graduate School of Education.* Los Angeles: University of California, Los Angeles, Graduate School of Education, 1981.

State University of New York at Buffalo. International Student Affairs. Task Force on International Programming. *Report of the Sub-committee on Foreign Students, Foreign Scholars and Exchange Programs.* Buffalo: State University of New York at Buffalo, International Student Affairs, 1982.

University of New South Wales. *Overseas Students at the University of New South Wales.* Sydney: University of New South Wales, Office of the Registrar, 1983.

27. Female International Students

a) Articles

Dieffenbacher, T.; Etish-Andrews, J.; and Rowe, L. "Female/Male Dimensions of Cross-cultural Counseling: A Workshop for Advisers of International Students." In Rowe and Sjoberg, eds. (Sec. 27*b* below), pp. 49–59.

Ekou-Pondza, Hazel. "Problems of the Educated Woman on Returning Home: A Case Review of Jamaica." In Rowe and Sjoberg, eds. (Sec. 27*b* below), pp. 40–43.

Helm, Ann. "Task Force on Women: International Training Program for Regional Coordinators and Students." In Rowe and Sjoberg, eds. (Sec. 27*b* below), pp. 98–100.

Ibrahim, Farah I. "A Survey of International Students' Perceptions of Male/Female Relationships in the United States." In Rowe and Sjoberg, eds. (Sec. 27*b* below), pp. 60–66.

Lee, Motoko. "Needs of International Women Students: Report on Findings of the National

Association for Foreign Student Affairs/United States Agency for International Development National Survey." In Rowe and Sjoberg, eds. (Sec. 27*b* below), pp. 90–97.

Sjoberg, Steve. "A Re-entry Workshop for International Women Students." In Rowe and Sjoberg, eds. (Sec. 27*b* below), pp. 81–89.

White, Merry I. "The Social and Economic Context of the Overseas-educated Woman." In Rowe and Sjoberg, eds. (Sec. 27*b* below), pp. 22–26.

b) Monographs

Rowe, Leslie, and Sjoberg, Steve, eds. *International Women Students: Perspectives for the 80s. Report of the International Women Student Conference (Boston, Mass., August 1981)*. Washington, D.C.: National Association for Foreign Student Affairs, 1981.

Unesco. *Evaluation of Unesco Fellowships with Particular Reference to Women*. Paris: Unesco, 1978.

28. China and Eastern Bloc Countries

a) Articles

Bannov, B., and Nikolayeva, T. "University Graduates from Moscow" [Foreign university graduates], *Soviet Literature*, no. 9 (1980), pp. 149–53.

Brook, T., and Wagner, R. "Teaching of History to Foreign Students at Peking University," *China Quarterly*, no. 71 (1977), pp. 598–607.

"Chinese Studying Abroad," *Beijing Review* 25 (December 6, 1982): 25–27.

Diaconescu, M. "Foreign Students in Romania—a Short Historical Survey," *Romanian Review*, no. 12 (1980), pp. 103–11.

Dolmatovsky, E. "Pupil and Teacher" [Ethiopian student in Russia], *Soviet Literature*, no. 3 (1977), pp. 163–67.

Fitzpatrick, S. "Student in Moscow," *Wilson Quarterly* 41 (Summer 1982): 132–41.

Henry, N. "African in Peking" [Tanzanian students in China], *Crisis* 83 (December 1976): 339–41, 344.

Hooper, Beverley. "The Australia-China Student Exchange Scheme: Could It Be More Effective?" *Australian Journal of Chinese Affairs* 1 (January 1979): 113–24.

Murray, Douglas P. "Exchanges with the People's Republic of China: Symbols and Substance" [Educational exchanges], *Annals of the American Academy of Political and Social Science* 424 (March 1976): 29–42.

Nanca, P., and Neches, C. "What Cannot Be Forgotten" [Selected experiences of foreign students in Romania], *Romanian Review*, no. 4 (1981), pp. 92–98.

Richter, Harald. "The Teaching of Chinese to Foreign Students at Nankai University," *Journal of the Chinese Language Teachers Association* 12, no. 3 (1977): 226–38.

Rosen, Vladimir. "They Study in the U.S.S.R." [Foreign students], *New Times* (Moscow), no. 12 (1978), pp. 22–24.

Stepanidyn, G. "I Bow My Head in Gratitude—How Foreign Students Are Trained at VGIK" [The All Union State Cinematography Institute], *Soviet Film*, no. 1 (1981), pp. 37–38.

"Understanding on the Exchange of Students and Scholars between the United States of America and the People's Republic of China," *International Legal Materials* 18 (March 1979): 356–60.

Wang, L. L. "Peiping Program for Sending Students Abroad," *Issues and Studies* 15, no. 7 (1979): 10–12.

Zolotukh, S. I., and Borisova, E. O. "Our Experience with Teaching Pharmacology to Foreign Students" (in Russian), *Farmakologiya i toksikologiya* 42, no. 5 (1979): 557–59.

b) Monographs

Central Intelligence Agency. *Communist Aid Activities in Non-communist Less Developed Countries.* American Statistical Index accessions no. 244-7. Washington, D.C.: Library of Congress, Photoduplication Service. (Published annually.)

Clough, Ralph N. *A Review of the U.S.-China Exchange Program.* Washington, D.C.: U.S. International Communication Agency, 1981.

Committee on Scholarly Communication with the People's Republic of China. *Survey Summary: Students and Scholars from the People's Republic of China Currently in the United States.* Washington, D.C.: U.S.-China Education Clearinghouse and National Association for Foreign Student Affairs, 1980.

Donovan, Katherine C. *Assisting Students and Scholars from the People's Republic of China: A Handbook for Community Groups.* Washington, D.C.: U.S.-China Education Clearinghouse and National Association for Foreign Student Affairs, 1981.

Fingar, Thomas, and Reed, Linda A. *Survey Summary: Students and Scholars from the People's Republic of China in the United States, August 1981.* Washington, D.C.: U.S.-China Education Clearinghouse and National Association for Foreign Student Affairs, 1981.

International Research and Exchanges Board. *A Balance Sheet for East-West Exchanges: Working Papers* [Conference on scholarly exchanges with the USSR and Eastern Europe: Two decades of American experience, Washington, D.C., 1979]. New York: International Research and Exchanges Board, 1980.

Kupforberg, Herbert. *The Raised Curtain: Report of the Twentieth Century Fund Task Force on Soviet-American Scholarly and Cultural Exchanges.* New York: Twentieth Century Fund, 1977.

29. International Students Studying in Third World Countries

a) Articles

Brelis, D., and Reader, J. "Students Immerse Selves in Foreign Living and Fun Too" [International students in Kenya], *Smithsonian* 8, no. 1 (1977): 49–55.

Farah, T. G. "Group Affiliations of University Students in the Arab Middle East" [Foreign Arab students in Kuwait], *Journal of Social Psychology* 106 (December 1978): 161–65.

Hafeez-Zaidi, S. M. "Adjustment Problems of Foreign Muslim Students in Pakistan." In *Cross-cultural Perspectives on Learning,* edited by Richard W. Brislin, Stephen Bochner, and Walter J. Lonner, pp. 117–30. New York: John Wiley, 1975.

Jacobel, R. W. "Resources and Technology in Developing Nations: A Semester Study Abroad," *Journal of College Science Teaching* 9 (March 1980): 193–96.

Kureshi, Afzal; Ali-Khan, Rahat; and Singh, C. Jayanta. "Fear of Failure among Indian and Non-Indian Students at Aligarh: A Cross-cultural Study," *Psychological Studies* 25, no. 2 (1980): 86–89.

McCormack, W. "Problems of American Scholars in India," *Asian Survey* 16, no. 4 (1976): 1064–80.

Osorio, Migen L. "Are Foreign Medical Students Displacing Filipinos in RP [Republic of the Philippines] Schools," *Sunburst* 5, no. 7 (1977): 26–30, 66–67.

Profeta, Lydia, and Davie, Robert S. "Regional Approaches to the Development of Human and Economic Resources: Asia," *Journal of Cooperative Education* 17, no. 3 (1981): 62–69.

Starr, P. D. "October War and Arab Students' Self-Conceptions," *Middle East Journal* 32 (August 1978): 444–56.

b) Monographs

Bernardo, F. A., and Saladaga, Fe. S., eds. *Facilitating Academic Interchange among Graduate Schools of Agriculture in Asia: Proceedings of the Seminar-Workshop of Graduate School Deans in Asia, Jointly Sponsored by A.A.A.C.U. and S.E.A.R.C.A., Bangkok, Thailand, June 25–27, 1975.* Cebu City, Philippines: Asian Association of Agricultural Colleges and Universities, 1976.

Ganguli, H. C. *Foreign Students: The Indian Experience.* New Delhi: Sterling, 1975.

Hanna, Willard Anderson. *Semester in Southeast Asia: Sixth Session* [With student paper by Beth Goldstein]. Hanover, N.H.: American Universities Field Staff, 1976.

30. Foreign Aid for Study Abroad

a) Articles

Browning, K. R., et al. "Evaluating Agency-sponsored Study Abroad Programs," *College and University* 51 (Summer 1976): 457–62.

Dubbeldam, L. F. B. "Policies of the Netherlands International Education: Origins and Trends." In Maliyamkono, ed. (Sec. 5*b* above), pp. 131–52.

Dulst, A. J. "New Developments in International Educational Co-operation in the Netherlands," *Higher Education and Research in the Netherlands* 20, no. 2 (1976): 24–32.

Gee, T. W. "Policy on Overseas Students in the Post-colonial Period." In Maliyamkono, ed. (Sec. 5*b* above), pp. 229–89.

Glimm, H. "Training Foreign Students in the Federal Republic of Germany." In Maliyamkono, ed. (Sec. 5*b* above), pp. 302–37.

Hauch, C., et al. "Agency Services for International Students," *College and University* 53 (Summer 1978): 524–33.

Hayden, Rose Lee. "U.S. Government Exchanges: The Quest for Coordination" [Educational exchanges], *Annals of the American Academy of Political and Social Science* 449 (May 1980): 114–28.

Hetland, A. "Policy regarding Training Programmes for Students from Developing Countries." In Maliyamkono, ed. (Sec. 5*b* above), pp. 290–301.

Kann, U. "Policy and Training Programmes for Students from Developing Countries." In Maliyamkono, ed. (Sec. 5*b* above), pp. 153–94.

Keresztesi, Michael. "Diffusion of Modern Library Thought and Practice by Means of UNESCO Fellowships for Travel and Study Abroad," *Libri: International Library Review* 29 (October 1979): 193–206.

"Offres de bourses pour l'étranger," *Information universiteures et professionelles internationales* (May/June 1978), pp. 19–44.

Wells, S., and Boogaard, P. "Policy Issues in Overseas Training." In Maliyamkono, ed. (Sec. 5*b* above), pp. 195–228.

b) Monographs

Atelsek, Frank J., and Gomberg, Irene L. *Scientific and Technical Cooperation with Developing Countries, 1977–78.* Washington, D.C.: American Council on Education and Higher Education Panel, National Science Foundation, 1978.

Collin, A. E. *Education for National Development: Effects of U.S. Technical Training Programs.* New York: Praeger, 1979.

Ingram, J. C. *New Approaches to Training in the Overseas Aid Program* [Training centers for foreign students]. Canberra: Australian Development Assistance Bureau, 1980.

Inter-university Council. *British Universities and Polytechnics and Overseas Development: Report of a Working Group Chaired by Sir Michael Swann, FRS.* London: Inter-university Council, 1977.

Uhlig, S. J.; Crofton, H. E. M.; and Thompson, J. H. *Industrial Training for Kenya: An Evaluation of ODM's Technical Co-operation Programme.* London: Ministry of Overseas Development, 1978.

United Kingdom. Foreign and Commonwealth Office. *Overseas Student Fees: Aid and Development Implications. Government Observations on the Report of the Sub-committee on Overseas Development of the Select Committee on Foreign Affairs* [Of the House of Commons]. Command Paper 8010. London: Her Majesty's Stationery Office, 1980.

United Kingdom. House of Commons. Foreign Affairs Committee. Overseas Development Sub-committee. *Enquiry into the Implications for Aid and Development of the Government's Decision to Increase Overseas Students Fees—Council for Education in the Commonwealth, et al.* [Minutes of evidence, February 26, 1980], pp. 1–37. London: Her Majesty's Stationery Office, 1980.

United Kingdom. House of Commons. Foreign Affairs Committee. Overseas Development Sub-committee. *Enquiry into the Implications for Aid and Development of the Government's Decision to Increase Overseas Students Fees- -Institute of Science and Technology (University of Manchester, et al.)* [Minutes of evidence, February 19, 1980], pp. 50–76. H.C. 407-iii. London: Her Majesty's Stationery Office, 1980.

United Kingdom. House of Commons. Foreign Affairs Committee. Overseas Development Sub-committee. *Enquiry into the Implications for Aid and Development of the Government's Decision to Increase Overseas Students Fees (3/79–80/OM) British Council, et al.* [Minutes of evidence, February 12, 1980], pp. 1–28. H.C. 407-ii. London: Her Majesty's Stationery Office, 1980.

United Kingdom. House of Commons. Foreign Affairs Committee. Overseas Development Sub-committee. *Minutes of Evidence Taken before the Overseas Development Sub-committee and Appendices. Overseas Student Fees: Aid and Development Implications.* House of Commons Papers, Session 1979–80; Reports 1979-80. London: Her Majesty's Stationery Office, 1980.

United Kingdom. House of Commons. Foreign Affairs Committee. Overseas Development Sub-committee. *Overseas Student Fees—Department of Education and Science, et al.* [Minutes of evidence, March 11, 1980], pp. 1–28. H.C. 407-v, erroneous parliamentary no. on document, 407-vi. London: Her Majesty's Stationery Office, 1980.

United Kingdom. House of Commons. Foreign Affairs Committee. Overseas Development Sub-committee. *Overseas Student Fees: Monitoring of Effects on Aid and Development— Derby College of Further Education* [Minutes of evidence, July 21, 1981], pp. 21–51. London: Her Majesty's Stationery Office, 1981.

United Kingdom. House of Commons. Foreign Affairs Committee. Overseas Development Sub-committee. *Overseas Students Fees: Monitoring of Effects on Aid and Development— National Union of Students* [Minutes of evidence, July 14, 1981], pp. 1–20. London: Her Majesty's Stationery Office, 1981.

United Kingdom. House of Commons. Foreign Affairs Committee. Overseas Development Sub-committee. *Supply Estimates, 1983–84: Support for Overseas Students—Frank Hodley (Chairman)* [Minutes of evidence, April 19, 1983], pp. 1–26. H.C. 324-i. London: Her Majesty's Stationery Office, 1983.

United Kingdom. House of Commons. Foreign Affairs Committee. Overseas Development Sub-committee. *Supply Estimates, 1983–84: Support for Overseas Students—Frank Hodley (Chairman)* [Minutes of evidence, April 26, 1983], pp. 27–47. London: Her Majesty's Stationery Office, 1983.

United Kingdom. Ministry of Overseas Development. *O.D.M.'s Training Co-operation with Tanzania.* London: Ministry of Overseas Development, 1979.

United States. General Accounting Office. *Coordination on International Exchange and Training Programs—Opportunities and Limitations: Report to the Congress.* Washington, D.C.: General Accounting Office and Government Printing Office, 1978.

United States. General Accounting Office. *Defense Action to Reduce Charges for Foreign Military Training Will Result in the Loss of Millions of Dollars.* Government Printing

Office monthly catalog no. 78-1728. Washington, D.C.: General Accounting Office and Government Printing Office, 1977.

United States. General Accounting Office. *Millions of Dollars of Costs Incurred in Training Foreign Military Students Have Not Been Recovered.* Government Printing Office monthly catalog no. 78-1723. Washington, D.C.: Government Printing Office, 1978.

31. Overseas Training and National Development

a) Articles

Chiang, Shing Ho, and Klinzing, G. E. "How Would That Work Back Home?" *Technos* 5 (October/December 1976): 26–31.

Hara, Y. "From Westernization to Japanization: Replacement of Foreign Teachers by Japanese Who Studied Abroad," *Developing Economies* 15, no. 4 (1977): 440–61.

Lambo, T. A. "International Exchange and National Development," *International Educational and Cultural Exchange* 12 (Winter 1977): 25–33.

Okoh, Nduka. "Education, Attitudes and Development" [Foreign students], *Education for Development* 5, no. 1 (1978): 53–70.

Oxenham, John. "Study Abroad and Development Policy—an Enquiry." In Williams, ed. (Sec 6*b* above), pp. 150–64.

Wang, Lawrence K., and Rawls, James R. "The Transfer of Training Obtained Abroad to Taiwan," *Industry of Free China* 43 (February 1975): 11–25.

b) Monographs

Jenkins, Hugh M., ed. *The Role of the Foreign Student in the Process of Development.* Washington, D.C.: National Association for Foreign Student Affairs, 1983.

Maliyamkono, T. L., ed. *Overseas Training: Its Impact on Development.* Arusha: Eastern Africa Publications, 1979.

Maliyamkono, T. L., et al. *Training and Productivity in East Africa: A Report of the Eastern African Universities Research Project on the Impact of Overseas Training and Development.* London: Heinemann, 1982.

32. Poststudy Matters (Practical Training, Returning Home, etc.)

a) Articles

Bochner, Stephen; Lin, A.; and McLeod, B. M. "Anticipated Role Conflict of Returning Overseas Students," *Journal of Social Psychology* 110 (April 1980): 265–72.

Card, Josefina J. "The Correspondence between Migration Behaviour: Data from the 1970 Cohort of Filipino Graduate Students in the United States," *Population and Environment: Behavioural and Social Issues* 5, no. 1 (1982): 3–25.

Carey, Philip, and Mariam, Alemaheyu. "Socialization and the Process of Migration: Case of the International Student in the United States." In *Sourcebook on the New Immigration*, edited by R. S. Brycelaporte, pp. 361–72. New Brunswick, N.J.: Transaction Books, 1980.

Gama, Elizabeth M. P., and Pedersen, Paul. "Readjustment Problems of Brazilian Returnees from Graduate Studies in the United States," *International Journal of Intercultural Relations* 1, no. 4 (1977): 46–59.

Gaviria, Moises, and Wintrob, Ronald. "Foreign Medical Graduates Who Return Home after U.S. Residency Training—Peruvian Case," *Journal of Medical Education* 50, no. 2 (1975): 167–75.

Gaviria, Moises, and Wintrob, Ronald. "Latin American Medical Graduates. II. The Re-adaption Process for Those Who Return Home," *Hispanic Journal of Behavioural Sciences* 4, no. 3 (1982): 367–79.

LaBerge, Bernard E. "Practical Training and Cooperative Education Programs for International Students—Are They a Good Idea?" In *The Courier,* by the National Association for Foreign Student Affairs. Washington, D.C.: National Association for Foreign Student Affairs, 1980.

LaBerge, Bernard E., and Leavy, Bernadette. "Can Placement Serve Foreign Students?" *Journal of College Placement* 36, no. 4 (1976): 51–54.

Lee, Motoko Y. "An Unmet Need of Students from Developing Nations: The Need for Practical Training." In National Association for Foreign Student Affairs (Sec. 32*b* below), pp. 5–6.

Levitov, Peter, and Prenger, Suzanne. "An Abridged Report of the Practical Training Feasibility Study." In National Association for Foreign Student Affairs (Sec. 32*b* below), pp. 7–14.

Nelson, Donald N. "Foreign Students Do Return Home," *Journal of the National Association for Women Deans, Administrators and Counselors* 42 (Spring 1979): 19–21.

Smith, B. L. R. "The Brain Drain Re-emergent: Foreign Medical Graduates in American Medical Schools," *Minerva* 17, no. 4 (1979): 483–503.

b) Monographs

Gama, Elizabeth M. P., and Pedersen, Paul. *Readjustment Problems of Brazilian Returnees from Graduate Studies in the United States.* Cambridge, Mass.: Latin American Scholarship Program of American Universities, 1976.

Glaser, William A., with Habers, Christopher G. *The Brain Drain: Emigration and Return.* New York: Pergamon, 1978.

Government of Israel. Ministry of Immigrant Absorption. Central Bureau of Statistics. *Survey of Absorption of Students from Abroad: Final Results of a Follow-Up Study of Students Who Began Studies in 1969/70.* Jerusalem: Ministry of Immigrant Absorption, Central Bureau of Statistics, 1980.

Government of Israel. Ministry of Immigrant Absorption. Central Bureau of Statistics. *Survey on Absorption of Students from Abroad: 1972/73 Students Who Began Studies in 1969/70 (Fourth Interview) and in 1970/71 (Third Interview).* Jerusalem: Ministry of Immigrant Absorption, Central Bureau of Statistics, 1975.

Marsh, H. *Re-entry/Transition Seminars: Report on the Wingspread Colloquium.* Washington, D.C.: National Association for Foreign Student Affairs, 1975.

National Association for Foreign Student Affairs. *Resources for Practical Training* [Of foreign students]. Washington, D.C.: National Association for Foreign Student Affairs, 1983.

Oh, Tai K. *The Asian Brain Drain: A Factual and Causal Analysis* [Based on a study of Asian students enrolled at two U.S. universities]. San Francisco: R & E Research Associates, 1977.

Rao, G. Lakshmana. *Brain Drain and Foreign Students.* New York: St. Martin's, 1979.

United States. Agency for International Development. Office of International Training. *Principles for Practical Training Experiences for Foreign Students.* Washington, D.C.: National Association for Foreign Student Affairs, 1982.

33. Alumni Issues

a) Articles

Dolibois, J. E. "Alive and Well: International Alumni Program," *International Educational and Cultural Exchange* 11 (Winter 1976): 32–34.

Dudden, A. P. "Fulbright Alumni Association," *International Educational and Cultural Exchange* 13 (Spring 1978): 17–19.

b) Monograph

National Association for Foreign Student Affairs. *Foreign Alumni: Overseas Links for U.S. Institutions.* Washington, D.C.: National Association for Foreign Student Affairs, 1980.

English as a Second Language: An Overview of the Literature

ROBERT B. KAPLAN*

This overview of the literature on English as a second language is intended mainly to serve those concerned with foreign students. But it is impossible narrowly to circumscribe this literature survey since the linguistic problems of foreign students cannot be separated from those of other non-English speakers resident in the United States. Language skills differ, and I seek here to provide a list of publications in the field of English as a second language (ESL) that will be most relevant to those concerned with the application of the field to students and others. This overview does not take the place of a classic volume such as Spaulding and Flack,[1] and it is intended to complement Y. G-M. Lulat, "International Students and Study-Abroad Programs: A Select Bibliography," in this volume.

The language problems of foreign students, undocumented aliens, legal immigrants from non–English-speaking countries, and some U.S. citizens from Puerto Rico, Guam, and elsewhere are similar. Furthermore, the teaching of English is a major industry in many non–English-speaking countries around the world, and to a large extent the linguistic issues (though probably not the pedagogical issues) are similar for this population of genuinely "foreign" students as they are for technically designated foreign students in U.S. academic institutions. Given the impossibility of limiting this review to language matters affecting only classically defined foreign students, I have chosen to try to look at the field in other dimensions.

The obvious solution to the problem, of course, would be simply to eliminate any discussion of the teaching of English as a second (or foreign) language. Such a vacuum would be unfortunate for at least two reasons. First, the teaching of English to non–English-speaking students in U.S academic institutions (and even to those students still abroad who hope to enter U.S. academic institutions) is the key to the whole issue of international educational exchange. The fact is that most of the individuals who wish to study in the United States have had neither the leisure nor the financial resources to acquire high-level proficiency in English prior to the point of application. To impose an indiscriminate requirement, as a condition of admission to U.S. educational institutions, for such high-level language proficiency would tend to discriminate against exactly those

---

* Professor of applied linguistics, University of Southern California, and past president of the National Association for Foreign Student Affairs.
[1] S. Spaulding and M. J. Flack, *The World's Students in the United States: A Review and Evaluation of Research on Foreign Students* (New York: Praeger, 1976).

populations that are most eager to come and those populations that we appear to be most eager to serve. Second, no discussion of the foreign student in the United States would be complete without at least an awareness of the language problem inherent in that population; the language problem extends into any discussion of academic quality, information transfer, curricular relevance, and services to foreign students. Students who do not understand the educational language cannot benefit from instruction, counseling, or any of the other services offered to them. The simple solution of not admitting students who do not understand the educational language would reduce the population by 60–75 percent and would significantly alter the thrust of international educational exchange. On the other hand, offering instruction in something like a hundred other languages would strain the system beyond its capacity and would give new meaning to the unacceptable concept "separate but equal."

This review is intended not for the language professional but rather for persons interested in the several areas directly relating to the presence of foreign students in U.S. academic institutions. It gives an overview of some of the major concerns of language teachers. It assumes the population served by language teachers to consist of individuals whose native language is not English, regardless of their legal status.

In the past 40 years, the field known as English as a second language has expanded enormously. When interest in the field was first expressed in the United States, in the period immediately following the end of World War II, it was presumed that there was an absolute identity between the study of English as a second language and the study of applied linguistics; indeed, the term "applied linguistics" grew out of the concern for the teaching of English as a second language and out of a need to differentiate practitioners (language teachers) from "theorists" (e.g., teacher trainers, trainers of teacher trainers, and various hyphenated linguists who had a theoretical concern with the content of language instruction and with its sequencing). Only in relatively recent times has there been a recognition that applied linguistics was a field in its own right larger than the immediate concerns underlying the teaching of English as a second language.[2]

The teaching of English as a second language came into being in the mid-1940s as an outgrowth of the U.S. wartime evolution of behaviorist psychology, structuralist linguistics, and so-called audiolingual methodology related to the need to train foreign language specialists rapidly. The successes of the military language institutes are well known. When the

[2] Robert B. Kaplan, ed., *On the Scope of Applied Linguistics* (Rowley, Mass.: Newbury, 1980). See also Henry G. Widdowson, *Explorations in Applied Linguistics* (Oxford: Oxford University Press, 1979); Peter Strevens, *New Orientations in the Teaching of English* (Oxford: Oxford University Press, 1977); J. P. B. Allen and S. Pit Corder, eds., *Readings for Applied Linguistics* (London: Oxford University Press, 1973); S. Pit Corder, *Introducing Applied Linguistics* (Harmondsworth: Penguin, 1973); William F. Mackey, *Language Teaching Analysis* (London: Longman, 1965).

war ended, the United States was virtually the only large industrialized nation that had its industrial and educational structure intact; as a consequence of the drawing power of both the industrial and the educational capabilities of the United States, large numbers of students began to flow into the U.S. educational establishment. Initially, this flow came substantially from Europe, but gradually the sources changed to include most of what has come to be called the Third World.[3] The ever-increasing tide of students necessitated the development of mechanisms to teach the language of instruction (English) to large numbers of speakers of a wide variety of other languages in more or less intensive programs. Initially, there were perhaps half a dozen programs at major institutions engaged in teaching ESL; now there are hundreds of programs.[4]

Initially, the teaching of English as a second language was largely derived from techniques, methodologies, and materials developed during the war in the structuralist/behaviorist tradition. That tradition came under serious attack in 1959 when Chomsky published his review of B. F. Skinner's *Verbal Behavior,*[5] and since that time a number of new methodologies have evolved (some closely tied to linguistic theory, some to pedagogical theory, some to Rogerian notions of pscyhology, and others to psycho- or sociolinguistic ideas) to deal with the problems central to language teaching. Thus, publication had differentiated into a number of strands: descriptions of methodologies (e.g., community language learning,[6] silent way,[7] suggestology,[8] notion/functional approaches,[9] the natural approach,[10] and communicative approaches[11]), approaches to the various skills believed to underlie competence in a language (i.e., listening,[12] speaking,[13] reading,[14] and writing[15]), more theoretical concerns relating to which linguistic model

[3] Hugh M. Jenkins, ed., *Educating Students from Other Nations* (San Francisco, Calif.: Jossey-Bass, 1983).

[4] Joan Kertis, ed., *English Language and Orientation Programs in the United States* (New York: Institute of International Education, 1982).

[5] Noam Chomsky, "Review of B. F. Skinner's *Verbal Behavior,*" *Language* 35 (1959): 26–58.

[6] Charles A. C. Curran, *Counseling-Learning in Second Languages* (Apple River, Ill.: Apple River Press, 1976).

[7] Caleb Gattegno, *Teaching Foreign Languages in Schools: The Silent Way,* 2d ed. (New York: Educational Solutions, 1972).

[8] Georgi Lozanov, *Suggestology and Outlines of Suggestopedy* (New York: Gordon & Breach, 1978).

[9] David A. Wilkins, *Notional Syllabuses* (Oxford: Oxford University Press, 1976).

[10] Stephen D. Krashen, *Principles and Practice of Second Language Acquisition* (New York: Pergamon, 1982).

[11] John Munby, *Communicative Syllabus Design: A Scoiolinguistic Model for Defining the Content of Purpose-Specific Language Programmes* (Cambridge: Cambridge University Press, 1978).

[12] I. M. Schlesinger, *Production and Comprehension of Utterances* (Hillsdale, N.J.: Erlbaum, 1977).

[13] Julia M. Dobson, *Effective Techniques for English Conversation Groups* (Rowley, Mass.: Newbury, 1974).

[14] Frank Smith, *Understanding Reading* (New York: Holt, Rinehart & Winston, 1971).

[15] Donn Byrne, *Teaching Writing Skills* (London: Longman, 1979).

should underlie language instruction,[16] and studies differentiating acquisition from learning.[17]

The situation was complicated by a serious effort on the part of some governments (e.g., those of Australia, Britain, Canada, France, Germany, and the United States) to underwrite the teaching of languages in foreign environments, that is, to provide initial language instruction in settings in which the target language was not supported by a native-speaking environment—in the countries from which potential students were likely to come (e.g., English in Taiwan, French and German in the United States, etc.). This situation further subdivided the classification of publications in the field to differentiate between the teaching of a language as a second language (e.g., English to speakers of other languages in the United States or Britain) and the teaching of a language as a foreign language (e.g., the teaching of English to speakers of Arabic in Saudi Arabia or to speakers of Japanese in Japan).[18]

Clearly, concern for language teaching inevitably gave rise to a concern for the training of teachers.[19] In the United States and Britain, a number of graduate programs have been developed to train teachers of English as a second/foreign language.[20] This interest has expanded to include a concern for the preparation of trainers of teachers. A number of publishers began to issue books and monographs to serve this expanding market.[21]

During the 1960s and 1970s the situation was additionally complicated by virtue of the recognition that the United States is itself a multilingual nation, not—as had so long been believed—essentially a monolingual nation with a few small groups of nonnative speakers of English striving to accommodate themselves to the English mainstream.[22] This recognition has in turn given rise to the realization that there are a number of nonstandard varieties of English spoken in the United States (e.g., Black English,[23] Mexican-American nonstandard English,[24] Native-American

---

[16] Robert J. DiPietro, *Language Structures in Contrast* (Rowley, Mass.: Newbury, 1971).

[17] Evelyn Hatch, ed., *Second Language Acquisition: A Book of Readings* (Rowley, Mass.: Newbury, 1978).

[18] Ikuo Koike et al., eds., *The Teaching of English in Japan* (Tokyo: Eichosha, 1978).

[19] James E. Alatis, H. H. Stern, and Peter Strevens, eds., *Applied Linguistics and the Preparation of Second Language Teachers: Towards a Rationale*, Georgetown University Roundtable on Languages and Linguistics (Washington, D.C.: Georgetown University Press, 1983).

[20] For training programs in the United States, see Charles H. Blatchford, ed., *Directory of Teacher Preparation Programs in TESOL and Bilingual Education: 1981–1984*, 6th ed. (Washington, D.C.: Teachers of English to Speakers of Other Languages [TESOL], 1984).

[21] For a list of publishers, together with addresses and phone numbers, see Christine Aronis, ed., *Annotated Bibliography of ESL Materials* (Washington, D.C.: TESOL, 1983), pp. 235–43.

[22] Margaret A. Lourie and Nancy Faires, eds., *A Pluralistic Nation: The Language Issue in the United States* (Rowley, Mass.: Newbury, 1978).

[23] Joseph L. Dillard, *Black English: Its History and Usage in the United States* (New York: Vintage, 1972).

[24] Charles A. Ferguson and Shirley Brice Heath, eds., *Language in the U.S.A.* (New York: Cambridge University Press, 1981).

English[25]) and that the pedagogical approach to these nonstandard varieties must of necessity be somewhat different from either second-language or foreign-language approaches; thus was born the teaching of English as a standard dialect.[26] (In other English-speaking nations, depending on the indigenous language situation and political climate, other modifications have arisen, such as English as an auxiliary language in Canada.) The broad recognition of the real language situation—that is, of the presence of large populations in the United States that are not native speakers of English—has also given rise to a concern for multilingual or bilingual education.[27] In general, the term "bilingual" has come into general use because, although the population is multilingual, one of the components of such educational programs is always English, while the other component may be any one of the hundred or more other languages widely spoken in the United States (e.g., Arabic, Chinese, French, German, Hebrew, Japanese, Korean, Lao, Portuguese, Russian, Spanish, Thai, Vietnamese, Yiddish, etc.).

In the midst of this rather frenetic activity, the teaching of English as a standard language (i.e., the teaching of English in elementary, secondary, and postsecondary formal schooling situations to persons who are monolingual native speakers of mainstream dialects of English) continues unabated. The "back to basics" movement has had some impact on the teaching of English as a standard language, and that interest has brought applied linguists into greater contact with teachers in this specialization, but to a large extent this is not a category in the literature (extensive though it is) that is normally subsumed under ESL, largely because it deals with what has always been considered the mainstream population rather than with any of the "minority" groups in the United States whose native language is not English.[28]

This rather lengthy explanation of the various strands that constitute the interests of such groups as the Association of Teachers of English as a Second Language (ATESL of the National Association for Foreign Student Affairs [NAFSA]) and the organization known as Teachers of English to Speakers of Other Languages (TESOL) is provided here to demonstrate that the field is vast, to suggest that it would be impossible to cover it in any depth in a volume such as the present one, and to rationalize that sort of broad but shallow coverage that is provided here on the grounds that it is impossible to leave out ESL but equally impossible to cover it.

[25] P. Turner, ed., *Bilingualism in the Southwest* (Tucson: University of Arizona Press, 1982).

[26] James E. Alatis, ed., *Linguistics or the Teaching of Standard English to Speakers of Other Languages and Dialects*, Georgetown University Roundtable on Languages and Linguistics (Washington, D.C.: Georgetown University Press, 1970).

[27] A. Bruce Gaarder, *Bilingual Schooling and the Survival of Spanish in the United States* (Rowley, Mass.: Newbury, 1977).

[28] "The New Ellis Island," *Time* (June 13, 1983), pp. 18–22, 24, 25.

There are a number of regularly appearing bibliographies that are of value to scholars engaged in research in various subdisciplines of applied linguistics, and it would be inappropriate to attempt to duplicate those bibliographies here. A short list of generally useful bibliographies would include at least those items listed in Appendix A. In addition to these, most of the journals in the field publish annual or biennial indices of materials printed in those journals. The most commonly read journals in the field would include at least those listed in Appendix B. At the same time, it is important to note that much of what is reported in the general applied linguistic literature is not directly applicable to the teaching of English as a second/foreign language. Much of what might be included in a survey of material pertinent to the teaching of English as a second/ foreign language would consist of a long list of textbooks. Obviously, that would be inappropriate, but aside from its inappropriateness, the task would be monumental because of the very large numbers of textbooks available and because of the complex taxonomy through which they are classified. First, such textbooks would be classified according to the educational level at which they are appropriate (e.g., elementary school, intermediate school, high school, college and university, adult education, etc.).[29] Regrettably, the same terms—"elementary," "intermediate," and "advanced"—are also used to identify proficiency levels without reference to age; thus, a college-level program (one presumably serving largely students in the 18- to 22-year-old group) might be subdivided into levels defined in terms of the entering proficiency of the learners. Each of these levels might be further dissected according to the underlying skills (i.e., listening, speaking, reading, and writing—already discussed briefly above). Additionally, other curricular areas might be included (e.g., culture,[30] grammar, phonology,[31] vocabulary,[32] study skills[33]). More recently, a new orientation designed to prepare students for study in particular academic disciplines has evolved under the title "English for special purposes,"[34] and that designation has been additionally atomized into "English for

[29] Mildred R. Donoghue and John F. Kunkle, *Second Languages in Primary Education* (Rowley, Mass.: Newbury, 1979); cf. Seymour L. Flaxman, ed., *Modern Language Teaching in School and College* (New York: Northeast Conference on the Teaching of Foreign Languages, 1961); René Richterich and Jean-Louis Chancerel, *Identifying the Needs of Adults Learning a Foreign Language* (Strasbourg: Council of Europe, 1978).

[30] Howard Altman and Victor Hanzeli, eds., *Essays on the Teaching of Culture* (Detroit: Advancement Press, 1974); cf. H. Ned Seelye, *Teaching Culture: Strategies for Foreign Language Educators* (Skokie, Ill.: National Textbook Co., 1974).

[31] J. Donald Bowen, *Patterns of English Pronunciation* (Rowley, Mass.: Newbury, 1975).

[32] Anne-Marie Cornu, "The First Step in Vocabulary Teaching," *Modern Language Journal* 63 (1979): 262–72.

[33] Ann V. Martin et al., eds., *Guide to Language and Study Skills for College Students of English as a Second Language* (Englewood Cliffs, N.J.: Prentice-Hall, 1977) (a college-level example has been supplied on the grounds that most foreign students are pursuing work at that level).

[34] Mary Todd Trimble, Louis Trimble, and Karl Drobnic, eds., *English for Specific Purposes: Science and Technology* (Corvallis: English Language Institute of Oregon State University, 1978).

science and technology," "English for business and economics," "English for academic purposes," et cetera.

What has been described as a taxonomy of the textbook material pertains largely to the second-language teaching environment; there would be a slightly different but equally dense taxonomy to serve the needs of teachers in the foreign-language teaching environment. Such a taxonomy might include, in addition to the classifications already suggested, a number of items that are likely to be used only in the foreign-language teaching environment; for example, literature,[35] a variety of specialized word lists (i.e., idiom lists, phrasal verb lists, prepositions, etc.), and more general materials that have been adjusted to the culture in which they are intended to be taught (materials made nominally and geographically specific to the Brazilian environment, e.g.). A good deal of the material intended for the foreign-language teaching situation is produced by the group of publishers referred to in note 21 above; however, a fair amount of material specific to the local situation is produced in the local environment.

Although it is impossible to discuss English for foreign students as a distinct and separate area, there have been several important studies of the perceived language needs of foreign students as distinct from the other potential audience. Lee shows a strong correlation between English language proficiency and various categories of need among foreign students.[36] The Economics Institute at the University of Colorado has also undertaken a number of studies of the relationship of language proficiency and disciplinary knowledge. These studies have shown that proficiency in such basic skills as statistics and mathematics is as crucial to economics graduate students as is language proficiency.[37]

The fact is that most foreign students intend to study at the college or university level, and it is, therefore, probably fair to generalize that they need an essentially academic English. It is not clear to what extent the various skills (i.e., listening, speaking, reading, and writing) are critical to achievement in the academic environment; certainly, students need to be able to listen to lectures, to participate in discussions, to ask questions and comprehend the answers to their questions, to read extensive amounts of difficult material, and to write essay examinations, term papers, theses,

---

[35] H. L. B. Moody, *The Teaching of Literature with Special Reference to Developing Countries* (London: Longman, 1971).

[36] Motoko Y. Lee, Mokhtar Abd-Ella, and Linda A. Burks, *Needs of Foreign Students from Developing Nations at U.S. Colleges and Universities*, ed. Stephen C. Dunnett (Washington, D.C.: National Association for Foreign Student Affairs, 1981), pp. 60–62, 80–81.

[37] Wyn F. Owen, "Foreign Graduate Students in Economics and Related Fields" (University of Colorado, Economics Institute, 1983, typescript); see also Wyn F. Owen, "Expanding Opportunities for Higher Education Abroad for Foreign Students from Developing Countries" (University of Colorado, Economics Institute, 1983, typescript); and Wyn F. Owen and Larry R. Cross, "Foreign Graduate Students from the Perspective of the Economics Institute" (University of Colorado, Economics Institute, 1983, typescript).

and dissertations. The extent to which they need these various skills will vary somewhat by discipline and by level (e.g., graduate students may be asked to read more than undergraduate students and performing arts majors may write less than journalism majors). It is probably necessary to conduct needs analyses to determine where in an ESL program the emphasis ought to lie, given a particular kind of population and a particular kind of institution.

Finally, there is a vast literature on language testing. The subject is far too complex to summarize here, though there are one or two key studies that speak to the theoretical[38] and practical[39] issues. In general, tests are used as criteria for admission, placement, evaluation during instruction, and release from instruction. It is unlikely that a test used to measure broad proficiency as a criterion for admission (i.e., the Test of English as a Foreign Language [TOEFL] is the most widely used test of that sort; it is administered by the Educational Testing Service [ETS], Princeton, N.J.) would also be used for placement, and it is unlikely that a single test may be used for placement in vastly different populations (e.g., preliterate children, illiterate adults, and literate college graduate students).

There are whole vast areas omitted from this cursory review. Applied linguistics scholars will find the review totally inadequate. As noted earlier, it is intended for individuals unfamiliar with the field who wish to acquire some sense of the scope of work pertaining to language instruction and who wish to dip into the literature in order to have an acquaintance with the theoretical paradigms, the practical issues, and the pedagogical solutions available to language teachers at the present time. The *Annual Review of Applied Linguistics* typically cites approximately 1,000 items per year;[40] my review includes only about 100 items. Further, my review has been limited largely to full monographs and has consciously tried to avoid articles in journals or collections; it has done so in order to try to achieve currency over a longer period of time and to cite works easily accessible in most major libraries. Given these limitations, clearly, my review cannot be considered more than a general overview. In addition to providing a broad overview, it is also intended to suggest the importance of ESL in the educational exchange arena. Those who claim to know the educational exchange field must have some awareness of the language aspects (see Appendix C).

[38] John W. Oller, Jr., and Kyle Perkins, eds., *Research in Language Testing* (Rowley, Mass.: Newbury, 1980); see also John W. Oller, "Language Testing Research (1979–1980)," in *Annual Review of Applied Linguistics*, ed. Robert B. Kaplan, Randall L. Jones, and G. Richard Tucker (Rowley, Mass.: Newbury, 1982).

[39] Rebecca M. Valette, *Modern Language Testing*, 2d ed. (New York: Harcourt Brace Jovanovich, 1977).

[40] Robert B. Kaplan et al., eds., *Annual Review of Applied Linguistics* (Rowley, Mass.: Newbury, 1982–84).

Appendix A

Aronis, Christine. *Annotated Bibliography of ESL Materials*. Washington, D.C.: Teachers of English to Speakers of Other Languages (TESOL), 1983.

Cooper, Stephen, comp. and ed. *Graduate Theses and Dissertations in English as a Second Language, 1975–76*. Washington, D.C.: TESOL, 1977.

Croft, Kenneth, ed. *A Composite Bibliography for ESOL Teacher-Training*. Washington, D.C.: TESOL, 1974.

Croft, Kenneth, ed. *TESOL 1967–68: A Survey*. Washington, D.C.: TESOL, 1970.

Garcia-Zamor, Marie, and Birdsong, David, eds. *Testing in English as a Second Language: A Selected, Annotated Bibliography*. Washington, D.C.: TESOL, 1979.

Jungo, M. E., ed. *International Bibliography for a Didactics of Early Bilingualism in the Education of Underprivileged Children, Especially Children of Migrant Workers*. Quebec: Presses de l'Université Laval, 1982.

Kaplan, Robert B.; d'Anglejan, Alison; Cowan, J. Ronayne; Kachru, Braj B.; and Tucker, G. Richard, eds. *Annual Review of Applied Linguistics*. Rowley, Mass.: Newbury, 1982–84.

Kaplan, Robert B.; Jones, Randall; and Tucker, G. Richard, eds. *Annual Review of Applied Linguistics*. Rowley, Mass.: Newbury, 1981.

Lange, Dale L., and Clifford, Ray T., comps. *Testing in Foreign Languages, ESL, and Bilingual Education, 1966–1979: A Select, Annotated ERIC Bibliography*. Washington, D.C.: Center for Applied Linguistics, 1980.

Malkoc, Anna Maria, comp. *A TESOL Bibliography: Abstracts of ERIC Publications and Recent Research Reports, 1969–70*. Washington, D.C.: TESOL, 1971.

Tannacito, Dan J., comp. *Discourse Studies: A Multidisciplinary Bibliography of Research on Text, Discourse, and Prose Writing*. Indiana: Indiana University of Pennsylvania, 1981.

Appendix B

Applied Linguistics. Oxford University Press.

Canadian Modern Language Review. Ontario Modern Language Teachers Association.

ELT Journal. Oxford University Press.

English Teaching Forum. U.S. Information Agency.

Etudes de linguistique appliquée. Didier.

Foreign Language Annals. American Council on the Teaching of Foreign Languages.

International Review of Applied Linguistics in Language Teaching. Julius Gross.

Journal of Verbal Learning and Verbal Behavior. Academic Press.

Language Learning. Experiment in International Living.

Language Teaching and Linguistics Abstracts. Cambridge University Press.

Modern Language Journal. National Federation of Modern Language Teachers Association.

TESOL Quarterly. Teachers of English to Speakers of Other Languages (TESOL).

Appendix C

Alatis, James E., ed. *Contrastive Linguistics and Its Pedagogical Implications*. Georgetown University Round Table on Languages and Linguistics. Washington, D.C.: Georgetown University Press, 1968.

Alatis, James E., ed. *Linguistics or the Teaching of Standard English to Speakers of Other Languages and Dialects*. Georgetown University Round Table on Languages and Linguistics. Washington, D.C.: Georgetown University Press, 1970.

Alatis, James E.; Altman, Howard B.; and Alatis, Penelope M., eds. *The Second Language*

Classroom: Directions for the 1980's. New York: Oxford University Press, 1981.

Alatis, James E.; Stern, H. H.; and Strevens, P., eds. *Applied Linguistics and the Preparation of Second Language Teachers: Toward a Rationale*. Georgetown University Round Table on Languages and Linguistics. Washington, D.C.: Georgetown University Press, 1983.

Alatis, James E., and Twaddell, Kristie, eds. *English as a Second Language in Bilingual Education: Selected TESOL Papers*. Washington, D.C.: TESOL, 1976.

Allen, Edward D., and Valette, Rebecca M. *Classroom Techniques: Foreign Languages and English as a Second Language*. New York: Harcourt Brace Jovanovich, 1977.

Allen, Harold B., and Campbell, Russell N., eds. *Teaching English as a Second Language: A Book of Readings*. 2d ed. New York: McGraw-Hill, 1972.

Allen, J. P. B., and Corder, S. Pit, eds. *Readings for Applied Linguistics*. London: Oxford University Press, 1973.

Altman, Howard B., and Hanzeli, Victor E., eds. *Essays on the Teaching of Culture*. Detroit: Advancement Press, 1974.

Andersson, Theodore. *Foreign Languages in the Elementary Schools: A Struggle against Mediocrity*. Austin: University of Texas Press, 1969.

Blatchford, Charles H., comp. and ed. *Directory of Teacher Preparation Programs in TESOL and Bilingual Education: 1981–1984*. 6th ed. Washington, D.C.: TESOL, 1984.

Brown, H. Douglas, ed. *Papers in Second Language Acquisition*. Language Learning Special Issue 4. Ann Arbor, Mich.: Research Club in Language Learning, 1976.

Brumfit, C. J., and Johnson, K., eds. *The Communicative Approach to Language Teaching*. Oxford: Oxford University Press, 1979.

Byrne, Donn. *Teaching Writing Skills*. London: Longman, 1979.

Celce-Murcia, Marianne, and McIntosh, Lois, eds. *Teaching English as a Second or Foreign Language*. Rowley, Mass.: Newbury, 1979.

Corder, S. Pit. *Introducing Applied Linguistics*. Harmondsworth: Penguin, 1973.

Cornu, Anne-Marie. "The First Step in Vocabulary Teaching." *Modern Language Journal*. 63 (1979): 262–72.

Croft, Kenneth, ed. *Readings on English as a Second Language: For Teachers and Teacher Trainees*. 2d ed. Cambridge, Mass.: Winthrop, 1980.

Curran, Charles A. C. *Counseling-Learning in Second Languages*. Apple River, Ill.: Apple River Press, 1976.

DiPietro, Robert J. *Language Structures in Contrast*. Rowley, Mass.: Newbury, 1971.

Dobson, Julia M. *Effective Techniques for English Conversation Groups*. Rowley, Mass.: Newbury, 1974.

Dunnett, S. C. *A Study of the Effects of an English Language Training and Orientation Program on Foreign Student Adaptation at the State University of New York at Buffalo*. Special Studies, no. 93. Buffalo: State University of New York, Council on International Studies, 1977.

Fanselow, John F., and Crymes, Ruth H., eds. *On TESOL '76*. Washington, D.C.: TESOL, 1976.

Farb, Peter. *Word Play: What Happens When People Talk*. New York: Bantam, 1975.

Ferguson, Charles A., and Slobin, D. I., eds. *Studies in Child Language Development*. New York: Holt, Rinehart & Winston, 1973.

Finocchiaro, Mary. *English as a Second Language: From Theory to Practice*. New York: Regents, 1974.

Gardner, R. C., and Lambert, W. E. *Attitudes and Motivation in Second-Language Learning*. Rowley, Mass.: Newbury, 1972.

Gattegno, Caleb. *Teaching Foreign Languages in Schools: The Silent Way*. 2d ed. New York: Educational Solutions, 1972.

Giglioli, Pier P., ed. *Language and Social Context*. Harmondsworth: Penguin, 1972.

Grittner, Frank M., ed. *Student Motivation and the Foreign Language Teacher: A Guide for Building the Modern Curriculum*. Skokie, Ill.: National Textbook Co., 1974.

Grittner, Frank W., and LaLeike, Fred H. *Individualized Foreign Language Instruction*. Skokie, Ill.: National Textbook Company, 1973.

Gunderson, Doris V., ed. *Language and Reading: An Interdisciplinary Approach*. Washington, D.C.: Center for Applied Linguistics, 1970.

Halliday, Michael A. K.; McIntosh, Angus; and Strevens, Peter. *The Linguistic Sciences and Language Teaching*. London: Longman, 1964.

Harris, David P. *Testing English as a Second Language*. New York: McGraw-Hill, 1969.

Hatch, Evelyn. *Second Language Acquisition: A Book of Readings*. Rowley, Mass.: Newbury, 1978.

Jarvis, Gilbert A., ed. *An Integrative Approach to Foreign Language Teaching: Choosing among the Options*. Skokie, Ill.: National Textbook Co., 1976.

Jenkins, Hugh M., ed. *Educating Students from Other Nations*. San Francisco: Jossey-Bass, 1983.

Kaplan, Robert B., ed. *On the Scope of Applied Linguistics*. Rowley, Mass.: Newbury, 1980.

Kaplan, Robert B.; d'Anglejan, Alison; Cowan, J. Ronayne; Kachru, Braj B.; and Tucker, G. Richard, eds. *Annual Review of Applied Linguistics*. Rowley, Mass.: Newbury, 1982–84.

Kaplan, Robert B.; Jones, Randall; and Tucker, G. Richard. eds. *Annual Review of Applied Linguistics*. Rowley, Mass.: Newbury, 1981.

Kelly, Louis G. *25 Centuries of Language Teaching*. Rowley, Mass.: Newbury, 1969.

Kertis, Joan., ed. *English Language and Orientation Programs in the United States*. New York: Institute of International Education, 1982.

Kinsella, Valerie., ed. *Language Teaching and Linguistics: Surveys*. Cambridge: Cambridge University Press, 1978.

Koike, Ikuo; Matsuyama, Masao; Igarashi, Yasuo, and Suzuki, Koji, eds. *The Teaching of English in Japan*. Tokyo: Eichosha, 1978.

Krashen, S. D. *Principles and Practice of Second Language Acquisition*. New York: Pergamon Press, 1982.

Lee, William R. *Language Teaching Games and Contests*. London: Oxford University Press, 1974.

Lourie, Margaret A., and Conklin, Nancy Faires, eds. *A Pluralistic Nation: The Language Issue in the United States*. Rowley, Mass.: Newbury, 1978.

Lozanov, Georgi. *Suggestology and Outlines of Suggestopedy*. New York: Gordon & Breach, 1978.

Mackay, Ronald; Barkman, Bruce; and Jordan, R. R., eds. *Reading in a Second Language: Hypotheses, Organization and Practice*. Rowley, Mass.: Newbury, 1979.

Mackey, William F. *Language Teaching Analysis*. London: Longman, 1965.

Martin, Ann V.; McChesney, Beverly; Whalley, Elizabeth; and Devlin, Edward. *Guide to Language and Study Skills for College Students of English as a Second Language*. Englewood Cliffs, N.J.: Prentice-Hall, 1977.

Moskowitz, Gertrude. *Caring and Sharing in the Foreign Language Class: A Sourcebook on Humanistic Techniques*. Rowley, Mass.: Newbury, 1978.

Munby, John. *Communicative Syllabus Design: A Sociolinguistic Model for Defining the Content of Purpose-Specific Language Programmes*. Cambridge: Cambridge University Press, 1978.

Oller, John W., Jr., and Perkins, Kyle, eds. *Research in Language Testing*. Rowley, Mass.: Newbury, 1980.

Paulston, Christina B., and Bruder, Mary N. *Teaching English as a Second Language: Techniques and Procedures*. Cambridge, Mass.: Winthrop, 1976.

Politzer, Robert L. *Linguistics and Applied Linguistics: Aims and Methods*. Philadelphia: Center for Curriculum Development, 1972.

Politzer, Robert L., and Politzer, Frieda N. *Teaching English as a Second Language*. Lexington, Mass.: Xerox, 1972.

Richards, Jack C., ed. *Understanding Second and Foreign Language Learning: Issues and Approaches*. Rowley, Mass.: Newbury, 1978.

Richterich, René, and Chancerel, Jean-Louis. *Identifying the Needs of Adults Learning a Foreign Language*. Strasbourg: Council of Europe, 1978.

Ritchie, William C., ed. *Second Language Acquisition Research: Issues and Implications*. New York: Academic Press, 1978.

Rivers, Wilga M. *Speaking in Many Tongues*. Expanded 2d ed. Rowley, Mass.: Newbury, 1976.

Rivers, Wilga M. *Teaching Foreign-Language Skills*. Chicago: University of Chicago Press, 1981.

Rivers, Wilga M., and Temperley, Mary S. *A Practical Guide to the Teaching of English as a Second or Foreign Language*. New York: Oxford University Press, 1978.

Robinett, Betty Wallace. *Teaching English to Speakers of Other Languages: Substance and Technique*. Minneapolis: University of Minnesota Press, 1978.

Saville-Troike, Muriel. *Foundations for Teaching English as a Second Language: Theory and Method for Multicultural Education*. Englewood Cliffs, N.J.: Prentice-Hall, 1976.

Schlesinger, I. M. *Production and Comprehension of Utterances*. Hillsdale, N.J.: Erlbaum, 1977.

Schumann, John H. *The Pidginization Process: A Model for Second Language Acquisition*. Rowley, Mass.: Newbury, 1978.

Seelye, H. Ned. *Teaching Culture: Strategies for Foreign Language Educators*. Skokie, Ill.: National Textbook Co., 1974.

Spolsky, Bernard, ed. *The Language Education of Minority Children*. Rowley, Mass.: Newbury, 1972.

Spolsky, Bernard, and Cooper, Robert L., eds. *Frontiers of Bilingual Education*. Rowley, Mass.: Newbury, 1977.

Stevick, Earl W. *Memory, Meaning and Method: Some Psychological Perspectives on Language Learning*. Rowley, Mass.: Newbury, 1976.

Stevick, Earl W. *Teaching Languages: A Way and Ways*. Rowley, Mass.: Newbury, 1980.

Strevens, Peter. *New Orientations in the Teaching of English*. Oxford: Oxford University Press, 1977.

Thonis, Eleanor W. *Teaching Reading to Non-English Speakers*. New York: Collier-Macmillan, 1970.

Trimble, Mary Todd; Trimble, Louis; and Drobnic, Karl, eds. *English for Specific Purposes: Science and Technology*. Corvallis: Oregon State University, English Language Institution, 1978.

Valette, Rebecca M. *Modern Language Testing*. 2d ed. New York: Harcourt Brace Jovanovich, 1977.

Wardhaugh, Ronald. *Topics in Applied Linguistics*. Rowley, Mass.: Newbury, 1974.

Wardhaugh, Ronald, and Brown, H. Douglas, eds. *A Survey of Applied Linguistics*. Ann Arbor: University of Michigan Press, 1976.

Widdowson, Henry G. *Explorations in Applied Linguistics*. Oxford: Oxford University Press, 1979.

Widdowson, Henry G. *Teaching Language as Communication*. Oxford: Oxford University Press, 1978.

Wilkins, D. A. *Notional Syllabuses*. Oxford: Oxford University Press, 1979.